Lockheed F-104
Starfighter: A History

Martin W. Bowman

Pen & Sword
AVIATION

First published in Great Britain in 2019 by
Pen & Sword Aviation

An imprint of
Pen & Sword Books Ltd
47 Church Street
Barnsley
South Yorkshire
S70 2AS

ISBN: 978 1 47386 3262

A CIP catalogue record for this book is
available from the British Library.

Printed and bound by Replika Press Pvt. Ltd.

Pen & Sword Books Ltd incorporates the Imprints of Pen & Sword Aviation, Pen &
Sword Family History, Pen & Sword Maritime, Pen & Sword Military, Pen & Sword
Discovery. Wharncliffe Local History, Wharncliffe True Crime, Wharncliffe Transport,
Pen & Sword Select, Pen & Sword Military Classics, Leo Cooper, The Practorian
Press, Remember When, Seaforth Publishing and Frontline Publishing.

Design by Mad-i-Creative

For a complete list of Pen & Sword titles please contact
PEN & SWORD BOOKS LIMITED
47 Church Street, Barnsley, South Yorkshire, S70 2AS, England
E-mail: enquiries@pen-and-sword.co.uk
Website: www.pen-and-sword.co.uk

Contents

Acknowledgements

AFMC History Office; Brian Allchin; Ames Research Centre/Hugh L. Dryden, Flight Research Facility, Edwards AFB, California; Captain Argeri, 23° Gruppo, Aeronautica Militare Italiana (AMI); Press and Information Branch, HQ Defence Command, Norway; Lieutenant Colonel David Bashow RCAF (Retd); Ministere de la Defence National, Belgium; Alan Brothers, Lockheed Martin Corporation; Cactus Starfighter Staffel; Denis Calvert; The Canadian Starfighter Association; the late Robert F. Dorr; Jack Farstad, Royal Norwegian Air Force Museum, Bodø; Stephen M. Fochuk; Jan Govaerts; Andy Graham; Captain Luca Guadagno, Aeronautica Militare Italiana (AMI); Group Captain Sultan M. Hali PAF; Colonel Laurie Hawn RCAF (Retd); John Heathcott, Aerospace Publishing; Heritage and History, Winnipeg, Canada; Martin-Baker Aircraft Co.; Jorg Knodel; Frau Holger Krohn; Ben Jones; Richard Kleebaur, Dornier Luftfahrt GmBH; Denny Lombard, Lockheed-Martin Skunk Works; Peter Loncke; NASA; Duncan McTeer; Nigel McTeer; Mike Machat; Peter B. Mersky; Joe Mizrahi, Sentry Books Inc.; Mick Oakey; the late General Gordon Ockendon RCAF; Bert Oostmeijer; Hubert Peitzmeier web site; Harry 'Choco' Prins, International F-104 Society, Kolganas 7, 7827 SL Emmen, The Netherlands; Hans Redemann; Mike Rondot; Eric Schulzinger, Lockheed-Martin Corporation. Kelvin Sloper; Peter C. Smith; Roger 'Kicker' Seroo; Carl Stef RCAF (Retd); Ton 'Rabo' van der Zeeuw; 'Zipper' Magazine; Cecchetto Vito; Hans-Ulrich Willbold, WM/MK, DaimlerChrysler Aerospace; and the US 2nd Ait Division Memorial Library in Norwich.

F-104G 63-13243 from Luke AFB, Arizona. The F-104G had been originally licence-built by Fokker in the Netherlands for the Luftwaffe, but operated at Luke AFB in USAF colours to train German F-104 pilots. Early in 1960 German pilot training began with Lockheed's 'Conversion flight F-104F' course at Palmdale and American instructors trained German F-104 personnel at Luke AFB, Arizona using thirty F-104F trainers. They were all withdrawn from use in December 1971. Starfighters served the German Air Force training facility at Luke AFB in the 4510th CCTW from the early 1960s until operations ended in 1983 and the unit was nicknamed the `Cactus Starfighter Staffel` or the 'Lukewaffe'.

Introduction

In the early 1900s, Malcolm and Allan Haines Loughead, two young aviation-minded brothers in San Francisco, California, with the help of their half brother, Victor, started out on the road that was to lead two of them to form one of the biggest aviation corporations in the world. Allan Loughead, a fine engineer, aircraft designer and pilot and newly married, returned to San Francisco early in 1912 where he resumed work as a mechanic. He managed to convince Malcolm, who for the past eight years had worked as an automobile mechanic (designing the famous hydraulic brake in the process), that they should build their own aircraft, the Model G. In 1912 they set up the Alco Hydro-Aeroplane Company from a garage at Pacific and Polk Streets in San Francisco. At the same time they continued to work as automobile mechanics to help finance the construction of the Model G.

During the summer of 1913 the Model G made four flights before it was damaged in an accident at San Mateo. Allan and Malcolm bought out the interests of their fellow investors and acquired the Model G outright. In 1913 they were forced to seek their fortune by prospecting, followed by several exciting adventures at home and abroad, Malcolm and Allan moved to Santa Barbara in 1916 and together with other investors, they created the Loughead Aircraft Manufacturing Company. With the help of an architectural draughtsman by the name of John K. 'Jack' Northrop, the Lougheads built an F.1 flying boat and produced two Curtiss HS-2L single-engined flying boats. Unfortunately, both the Curtiss boats were built at a loss, a small S-1 sport biplane failed to penetrate a market dominated by war-surplus Jennies and a Navy contract for fifty scouts was cancelled before the first aircraft was completed. In 1921, the company went into liquidation and Jack Northrop went to work for Douglas.

On 13 December 1926 the Loughead brothers and other investors formed the Lockheed Aircraft Company. Fred E. Keeler, a wealthy brick manufacturer, acquired 51 per cent of the common stock and took the title of president.

Allan Loughead was vice-president. With the help of Jack Northrop, now Chief Engineer, Lockheed designed and built the trend-setting Vega cantilever monoplane, which was sold (at a loss) to George Hearst Jr., the wealthy San Francisco newspaper magnate. The company though, is best remembered for building what were arguably the fastest, finest and most sought-after monoplanes of the period from 1927 to 1934. Their unique single-shell wooden monocoque construction put their Vega and Orion cabin planes well ahead of their competitors' fabric-covered biplane designs. The speedy high-winged Vegas in the hands of accomplished trail-blazers like Amelia Earhart, Ruth Nichols and Wiley Post, completed many long-distance flights and set new speed records, while the most famous owner of a Lockheed 8 Sirius was Charles Lindbergh, who completed a number of survey flights around the world for Pan American Airways in 1930 and 1933. A Lockheed 3 Air Express won the 1929 National Air Race and a year later the same aircraft, in the hands of Roscoe Turner, set a number of new speed records.

In March 1928 meanwhile, the Lockheed Company had moved its offices to the Mission Glass Works in Burbank, where four Vegas, an Air Express and an Explorer were built. (The Explorer, which was designed for long-distance record attempts, was the least successful of the early Lockheed aeroplanes. Just four were built and three crashed. The fourth was damaged and parts from this aircraft were mated to an Orion fuselage to produce the Orion-Explorer in which Wiley Post and Will Rogers were killed in Alaska on 15 August 1935.) Jack Northrop left the company three months later. He was replaced by Gerald F. 'Jerry' Vultee as chief engineer. By mid-1929, well over seventy Vegas, seven Air Expresses and the Explorer, had either been built or were under construction. Keeler realized that this was the time to make a large profit and against Allan Loughead's wishes, in July 1929, a deal was made with the Detroit Aircraft Corporation which snapped up 87 per cent of Lockheed's assets. Just three months later the Wall Street crash plunged

The F-84 Thunderjet was greatly underpowered, even the 'interim' F-84G which was designed to deliver nuclear weapons, with just 5,600lb thrust. However, in the early 50's, the old 'Lead Sled' was expected to deliver nuclear devastation on a tactical level to any part of Europe or the world and be tough enough to bring her pilot home again. Like many other European air forces as well as the USAF the Netherlands AF practiced this mission almost for real in all weathers at low level and no doubt the accident rate reflects this. The same could be said for the later German F-84F Thunderstreaks.

the US into the Great Depression and many companies went into liquidation!

The Lockheed Aircraft Company was a Division of the Detroit Aircraft Corporation for two years until it too went into receivership. During this sojourn, Lockheed carried on producing Vegas, Air Expresses and Explorers, as well as building new designs, the most famous of which was the Sirius, the first being completed for Charles Lindbergh in 1929. In addition, a number of Altair and Orion aircraft were built. On 21 June 1932 at a bankruptcy court a group of investors led by Robert E. Gross, a San Francisco investment broker, bid $40,000 for the assets of the defunct company. There being no other bids, Judge Harry Holzer accepted their offer, adding, 'I sure hope you fellows know what you're doing!' Gross became chairman and treasurer of the new Lockheed Aircraft Corporation, while Lloyd C. Stearman was elected president and general manager.

The new regime saw Lockheed move away from single-engined to twin-engined designs, the first of which was the successful Model 10 Electra transport, followed in due course, by the Model 12 Electra Junior fast executive transport. In 1936 Lockheed delivered its first military aircraft, to the US Navy, Coast Guard and AAC and plant facilities were increased to build the Model 14 Super Electra, which would fly on 24 July 1937. Also conceived at about this time was the XP-38 (Model 22) twin-engined interceptor, which was submitted to meet AAC requirement X-608, in February 1937. Destined to become famous as the

Lightning, its designers where 34-year old Hall Livingstone Hibbard and 27-year old Clarence L. 'Kelly' Johnson. Johnson had advised the company about potential instability and control problems on the Model 10 and had joined the company as a tool designer in 1933. Model 22 development was protracted with the revolutionary turbo-superchargers causing the most delays and the XP-38 did not fly until 27 January 1939. In the meantime, Lockheed tried hard to carve a niche in the highly competitive transport market with the Model 10, 12, 14 and later Model 18, transports. There then came a breakthrough on 23 June 1938, when Britain placed an order for 200-250 Hudson aircraft.

The Second World War saw Lockheed grow enormously. On 31 March 1940 the workforce stood at 7,000 employees and in 1941 it had risen to 16,898 personnel. Between 1 July 1940 and 31 August 1945, Lockheed turned out 19,077 aircraft to become the fifth largest US aircraft producer. By far the largest proportion of Lockheed-built aircraft were P-38 Lightnings, Hudsons and Lodestars, although 500 B-17F and 2,250 B-17G Fortresses and B-34/37 and PV-1/-2s were produced at Burbank by the Vega Corporation (formerly AiRover Company), which was absorbed on 30 November 1943. Just over 94,300 personnel, thousands of them women engaged in building aircraft on the production lines, were working at Lockheed at this time.

Post-war, Lockheed sought other markets, notably in the field of civil and military propellerturbine and jet transports. In 1955 the Model 188 Electra turbine-powered airliner entered the design stage after American Airlines had shown their dissatisfaction with Douglas and the pricing of their DC-7 airliner by announcing that it was ready to receive bids for alternative aircraft for its hitherto Douglas-equipped fleet. On 8 June 1955 American Airlines ordered 35 Electras and on 27 September, Eastern Airlines ordered forty.

By the end of 1955 Lockheed had received orders for another sixty-one Electras. The Model 188 was completed in 26 months and flew, eight weeks ahead of schedule, on 6 December 1957. At this time the Electra was the sacred cow at Lockheed. The company in 1957 had suffered heavily from the cutbacks in defence spending in American which lost them $150 million in cancelled contracts in five months.' Deliveries of the Electra to airlines began early in 1959 to American but three Electras were lost in fatal accidents in fourteen months, from 3 February 1959 and Lockheed was forced to ground all 165 remaining Electras for a whole year while an expensive modification programme was carried out. Weakness of the engine mountings, which in turn caused nacelle vibration and then wing flexing and final failure at the root, was deemed to be the cause of at least two of the accidents. Although the problem was finally overcome public confidence in the Electra signalled its demise. The Electra was a financial disaster. Its repercussions prevented Lockheed from re-entering the commercial airliner market for ten years although a military development, the P-3 (P3V) Orion long-range patrol aircraft, went on to achieve great success.

In January 1951 Lockheed had reopened a government-built plant at Marietta, Georgia and the complex was used to build 394 Boeing B-47 Stratojets, C-130 Hercules and JetStar aircraft. The YC-130 prototype, which was to become famous as the Hercules, first flew on 23 August 1954. The type was to become hugely successful, with an eventual profit to Lockheed conservatively estimated to be roughly in the region of $300 million, while the Jetstar would continue in production until 1980. Other successes included the Constellation family of turbo-prop transports, 856 of which were turned out and a further 1,051 P2V Neptunes. (In 1961 the Lockheed-Georgia Division was reorganized as the Lockheed Georgia Company.)

Work on jet propulsion had started at the outbreak of war and Lockheed's first jet fighter, the XP-80, was contracted by the USAF in June 1943. At the

Clarence Leonard 'Kelly' Johnson (27 February 1910 – 21 December 1990), architect of the F-104 Starfighter pictured with his creation, one of over forty aircraft he played a leading role in the design of as a member and first team leader of the Lockheed Skunk Works. This American aeronautical and systems engineer worked for more than four decades and is said to have been an 'organizing genius'. (Lockheed).

beginning of the programme, Kelly Johnson, named chief engineer at Burbank in 1952, organized his famous Advanced Development Projects Section, which was housed in temporary accommodation next to a plastics factory. Its location earned the nickname 'Skunk Works' after the foul-smelling factory in Al Capp's 'Lil Abner' comic strip. The name stuck. (The Advanced Development Projects Section later became the Lockheed Advanced Development Company or LADC and in the 1990s was responsible for building the F-117A Stealth fighter.) Completed in just 143 days, the XP-80 project exemplified Johnson's credo - 'be quick; be quiet; be on time'. The P-80 became America's first production jet fighter and by 1958 no less than 8,507 related models had been produced.

Johnson and his design group then turned their thoughts to other military jets. Among the designs considered was the U-2 spy plane and the Model 83, created November 1952 and which finally emerged as the F-104 Starfighter. Unfortunately for Lockheed, as will become evident, although it promised much, the F-104 Starfighter was built in only limited numbers for the USAF. The first of the two XF-104 prototypes flew for the time on 4 March 1954. Seventeen YF-104As followed but service deliveries of the F-104A were not finally begun until January 1958. Then they were grounded for three months while problems with the engine were rectified. By December 1958 the USAF had cut back its F-104 orders from 722 to only 296.

Air Defense Command (later Aerospace Defense Command) accepted only 179 F-104A/-B Starfighters and fairly quickly phased out the

aircraft to make way for the more heavily armed
McDonnell F-10lb Voodoo and Convair F-106A
Delta Dart all-weather fighters. The only other
Starfighter versions to serve in the USAF were
seventy-seven F-104Cs and twenty-one two-seat
F-104D Starfighters, which were accepted by
Tactical Air Command during 1958-59.

A spate of losses in US service did not help
the Starfighter's cause. By the time the F-104 had
logged its 100,000th flight hour in April 1961, 49
out of 296 Starfighters operated by the USAF had
been lost and eighteen pilots killed - none of them
in combat. In Viêtnam, 1965-67, eight F-104C
Starfighters were lost in action and another six were
destroyed in operational accidents. The F-104C too
was soon dispensed with.

The Starfighter's failure to enter wide-scale
production was tantamount to another disaster for
Lockheed, certainly one on the same scale as that
of the failure of the Electra. Lockheed needed to
sell between 2,500 and 3,000 F-104s to maintain
profitability and unlike the P-3 Orion spin-off,
there seemed little likelihood of a spin-off this
time, for the F-104. Yet, unlike the situation with
the Electra, where Lockheed had borne not only the
enormous costs of the research and development
programme, but had also funded the expensive
LEAP (Lockheed Electra Action Programme), the
US government had funded the greater part of the
multi-million dollar F-104 programme. However,
previous attempts by Lockheed to develop a

successful commercial aircraft (Starliner) to rival
the Douglas DC-7 and a pure-jet airliner to rival the
Boeing 707 and Douglas DC-8 had both ended in
failure, so the company urgently needed a fighter
market if its 15,000 workers were not to be laid off.
Almost as importantly, an alternative market had
to be found if the company was to remain part of
the 'Big Three' with rivals Boeing and Douglas. All
hopes therefore rested on marketing and selling the
Lockheed military design to customers overseas.

Salvation for both Lockheed and the Starfighter
was provided by the German Federal Republic
where re-equipment of the Luftwaffe was needed to
help counter the growing Communist threat in the
east. Equally importantly, West Germany wanted
to become a fully paid-up member of the 'nuclear
club'. The Defence Committee had, since late 1958
been evaluating designs for a primary all-weather
fighter-interceptor, fighter-bomber and photographic
reconnaissance aircraft. With no aircraft industry of
its own, Germany looked to France, Britain and
the USA for possible fighter designs to replace the
Republic F-84F Thunderstreak in the strike role,
the North American F-86 Sabre in the air defence
role and the Republic RF-84F Thunderflash in
photo-reconnaissance. All of these aircraft were
obsolescent when they were first purchased and the
Luftwaffe had looked to replace them even before
the last of the American-equipped geschwaders had
been activated.

On 18 March 1959 Herr Franz Josef Strauss,
who since 1956 had been Federal German defence
minister, announced that 'after evaluating nearly
two dozen of the world's top fighter aircraft' he
had signed a contract for 96 Starfighters [32 two-

seat F-104F trainers and 66 single-seat F-104Gs]. His decision to buy the F-104G - at that time an unproven multi-mission aircraft -provided the momentum for what was to become known as the 'sale of the century'. The Starfighter would not only replace the F-84F Thunderstreak, F-86 Sabre and RF-84F Thunderflash in Luftwaffe service, it would also replace the Hawker Sea Hawk in the Marineflieger, even though the German Navy had preferred the British Hawker Siddeley Buccaneer, which was considered a superior aircraft in this role, especially for low-level offshore sorties. It was tantamount to a double body blow for the British, who earlier had lost any chance of success when the government, in its wisdom, decided to relegate the superlative English Electric Lightning Mach 2+ interceptor to the background and instead tried to promote the Saunders Roe SR.177.

At first West Germany showed a very keen interest in the SR.177 (an operational development of the SR.53 research aircraft powered by a Gyron turbojet and a Spectre rocket motor for high-altitude boost), but it was cancelled in Britain's infamous 1957 Defence White Paper. The English Electric Lightning was a more capable aircraft and did not have the very severe operational limitations of the Lockheed machine. The Lightning's ability to manoeuvre with the best and out-climb all of them gave its pilots an advantage which set them apart from others. The F-104 Starfighter had, eventually, the same straight line top speeds but it could never match the Lightning's rate of turn at any speed. It

Messerschmitt built F-104G KE-405 (7105) of JG 71 'Richthofen' in formation with Fiat-built F-86K Sabre JA-310. In 1963 JG 71 transferred from Alhorn to Wittmundhafen Air Base. May 1963 saw the introduction of the first F-104 Starfighters into German Air Force service.

was not until the F-15 years later that the Lightning had any real competitor. In a case of what might have been, the only Lightnings ever to operate from German soil were two RAF Lightning interceptor squadrons.

Apart from the lucrative sale of the aircraft a complete re-design involving an almost indeterminate number of costly ECPs (equipment change proposals) would have to be carried out if the Starfighter was come anywhere near to achieving its multi-mission role. Better still, these would be carried out by Lockheed or its licensees and paid for by the customer(s). Lockheed were also well aware that where West Germany led, the other European nations - The Netherlands, Belgium and Italy - would follow. First of these to put pen to paper was Holland, which badly needed a replacement for its ageing 'Kaasjagers' (cheese fighters) as their F-84 Republic Thunderstreaks were known.

After rejecting the Northrop N-156 (F-5 Tiger), Convair F-106 and Republic F-105 Thunderchief in September 1959 (because they were considered too heavy and expensive) and after the elimination of the Dassault Mirage III, on 20 April 1960 the Netherlands placed an initial order for 100 Starfighters, twenty-five of which would come free from the US Military Assistance Program (MAP) budget. The Netherlands had hoped to receive 100 aircraft as part of MAP, to which they proposed to buy a further 100 aircraft by direct purchase.

However, when the US government refused to improve the number of MAP-funded aircraft and then decreed that the offer was conditional on Italy being co-opted into the F-104 consortium, the Netherlands reduced their purchase from 100 to 95 Starfighters. Belgium followed on 20 June 1960. In February 1961 the US Air Force signed the order for MAP F-104Gs. (In June 1962 the US Air Force ordered additional MAP F-104Gs.) In a move which committed virtually all the resources

of the Italian aviation industry, on 2 March 1961 Italy signed a licence production contract to build the F-104G. Some 916 Starfighters were eventually acquired for the Luftwaffe and Marineflieger, 652 of them licence-built in Europe. Altogether, the Netherlands ordered 144 Starfighters, Italy, 155 and Belgium, 100.

Meanwhile, on 17 September 1959 Lockheed concluded a contract with Canadair for the Canadian company to build 200 CF-104 Starfighters to equip its eight RCAF squadrons in NATO (in 1962 another 140 F-104Gs were for re-export under the US Military- Assistance Programme).

In 1959 it looked as if Japan would buy American too, but its service chiefs were known to favour the Grumman F-11A Super Tiger. However, before the National Defence council formally approved the choice, Lockheed and some influential Japanese politicians who favoured the Starfighter, made much of the aircraft's 1958 and 1959 world altitude and speed records and lobbied hard for F-104 acceptance. Ironically, one of the Lockheed Starfighter's greatest supporters was General Minoru Genda, who in July 1959 became the new chief of air staff. Genda was the man who eighteen years earlier had planned and executed the surprise attack on Pearl Harbor in Hawaii, on 7 December 1941! Genda visited Lockheed in California and, at this own request, flew a Starfighter. He declared it to be the best fighter the world had ever seen. It was now clear to Lockheed that the Japanese would buy the F-104 and not the F-11A Super Tiger. A few months later Genda was awarded the Legion of Merit by the USAF. On 29 January 1960 Japan signed a licensed production contract. In November Japan announced plans to equip its new Japan Air Self-Defence Force with 230 F-104Js in the air-superiority role.

All told, Starfighters were produced by manufacturers in seven countries. In Europe

Line up of new production models at Palmdale.

a multinational programme carried out the manufacture of 996 F-104G/RF-104G Starfighters, led by Messerschmitt, who were to be the major corporate partner for Lockheed until the F-104 was phased out in both the Luftwaffe and Marineflieger. The Starfighter licence production was the first major order for the German aircraft industry since the Second World War. The European consortium employed up to 100,000 staff who worked in Starfighter production.

ARGE (Arbeitsgemeinschaft)-Sud (Work Group South) near Munich, which was made up of Messerschmitt at Augsburg; Heinkel at Speyer; Dornier at Munich; and Siebel at Donauwurth, built 210 F-104Gs for the Luftwaffe and Marineflieger. (Later, to replace losses, MBB (Messerschmitt-Bolkow-Blohm), built a further fifty F-104Gs for the German forces). Starfighter production commenced at the German plants on 1 December 1960. Messerschmitt was responsible for production flight testing and final assembly (carried out at Manching), painting, construction of the pilot seat, the fuselage, empennage and the installation of the powerplant. Siebel initially manufactured the canopy, the electronics bay hatch cover, the escape hatch, the nose landing gear doors, the fuel tank cover and the hydraulic access door and were responsible for the fuselage nose, the radome nose assembly, air scoops and the rear fuselage. Dornier constructed the mid-fuselage panels, upper panel assemblies for the fuselage, the mid-fuselage side

Altogether, Starfighters were produced by manufacturers in seven countries and on 1 December 1960 Starfighter production commenced at German plants. These F-104Gs are being produced by Messerschmitt AG at Augsburg, the major corporate partner for Lockheed. (Messerschmitt AG)

panels and the nose landing gear. Heinkel were initially responsible for the main landing gear and the droppable fuel tanks and manufactured the main landing gear doors, dive brakes, wings, fins, rudders, horizontal stabilizers and other minor equipment. As production intensified other manufacturers in Belgium, Germany and The Netherlands assumed the manufacture of some of these items. The intense preparation for production - organizing trained staff and importing materials, tools and manuals - was supported by Lockheed.

ARGE Nord (Work Group North) at Schiphol, Amsterdam, which consisted of Fokker and Aviolanda, at Dordrecht, in the Netherlands and the German manufacturers, Hamburger Flugzeugbau (HFB), at Hamburg, Weserflugzeugbau and Focke-Wulf at Bremen, built 254 F-104Gs and RF-104Gs for Germany's Luftwaffe and Marineflieger and 96 F/RF-104Gs for the KLu (Royal Netherlands Air Force). Fokker was responsible for production flight testing, installation of the powerplant, painting, the installation of 'loose' equipment, construction of the pilot seat and final assembly. Fokker also manufactured the electronics bay hatch cover,

escape hatch, after fuselage, wing, empennage, horizontal stabilizer, fin and rudder and, for all three European programmes, the droppable fuel tanks.

Aviolanda built the F-104G's fuselage nose, radome, fuselage, canopy, nose and main landing gear doors, canopies and fuel tank covers for all three programmes. Hamburger manufactured the windshields for all three programmes and the majority of fuselage panels for the Dutch programme. Wesser made mid-fuselage panels for the Dutch programme. Focke-Wulf built the hydraulic access doors, scoops and ducts for the same programme.

West Group (actually a geographical misnomer) at Gosselies, Belgium, which comprised Avions Fairey S.A. and S.A.B.C.A (Société Anonyme Belge de Constructions Aéronautiques) built 187 F-104Gs (100 for the Belgian Air Force and 87 for the Luftwaffe/Marineflieger) using fuselage nose radomes. Air scoops, ducts and aft fuselage sections built by Siebel and dive brakes, main landing gear doors, horizontal stabilizers, fins and rudders, manufactured by Heinkel and nose landing gears made by Dornier.

The Italian Group at Turin-Caselle, made up of Fiat, Aerter, Macchi, SIAI-Marchetti, Piaggio and SACA, built 329 F/RF-104G and F-104S Starfighters (124 F-104Gs and 205 F-104S aircraft for the AMI (Italian Air Force); fifteen F-104Gs and thirty-five RF-104Gs for Germany; twenty-five F-104Gs for the KLu (Royal Netherlands Air Force); and forty F-104S aircraft for the Türk Hava Kubbrylrti (THK, Turkish Air Force).

To co-ordinate the entire multinational production programme the NATO Starfighter management office (NASMO) was established in Koblenz, West Germany. It was here that the Bavarian Motor Works (with Fabrique National in Brussels), manufactured the General Electric J79-GE engine under licence for the Starfighter programme. In 1952 Gerhard Neumann, a German-born US-citizen, began development of what became one of the most successful military jet engines to enter production. The J79 was the first US single-shaft high performance axial flow turbojet, with adjustable guide vanes, a 17-stage compressor, three-stage turbine and ten can-type burners. The first flight of the engine was on 20 May 1955 where the engine was placed in the bomb bay of a J47-powered B-45C. The J79 was lowered from the bomb bay and the four J47s were shut down leaving the B-45 flying on the single J79. The J79 was developed as an outgrowth of the General Electric J73 engine programme and was known at first as the J73-GE-X24A. The X24A was designed for reliable Mach 2 performance with minimal required maintenance. Its innovative variable stator vanes increased compressor air pressure and helped eliminate compressor stall. Variable-incidence stators allowed the single-shaft turbojet to develop high pressures similar to those of dual-shaft engines, but at significantly lighter weight. The introduction of the variable stator vane turned out to be one of the most important developments in the history of jet aircraft engines. More than 17,000 examples of

TF-104G-LO D-5804 of the Koninklijke Luchtmacht (KLu, Royal Netherlands Air Force) was issued to CAV (Conversie All-Weather Vlucht) and is now on display at Bad Oeyenhausen. (Author)

F-104G aircraft being produced at Avions Fairey SA, Belgium, which, with SABCA.
(Avions Fairey SA)

the J79 were built in its thirty-year production run. In its long and successful career the dependable J79 accumulated well over 30 million flying hours and probably clocked more supersonic flying time than any other Western military aircraft engine produced during the Cold War. It was widely used on several types of aircraft, including the McDonnell Douglas F-4 Phantom II, Convair B-58 Hustler, Lockheed F-104 Starfighter, Israeli Aircraft Industries Kfir and North American Rockwell A-5 Vigilante. It was just over seventeen feet long, slightly more than three feet in diameter, weighed around 3,500lbs and produced around 9,000lbs of dry thrust. In full afterburner the YJ79 generated around 15,000 pounds of thrust with a fuel flow rate of ten gallons per second. Later versions of the J79 weighed anywhere from 3,500 to 3,800lbs and produced up to 17,900lbs of thrust in full afterburner. This engine was chosen by Kelly Johnson to power his design of F-104 Starfighter.

The Starfighter went on to equip no less than fifteen air forces. Starfighter production (less the two XF-104, 17 YF-104A pre-production models) eventually reached 2,559. Lockheed-California built 741 of these; the most widely used Mach 2 fighter aircraft ever built. The jet's career though, was marred by a very high loss rate. Forty-nine out of 296 Starfighters operated by the USAF were lost and eighteen pilots killed and in 1960 the type was withdrawn from Air Defense Command. In SE Asia, eight F-104s were lost in action and another six were destroyed in operational accidents before the type was phased out of theatre.

The F-104 suffered an even higher accident rate in NATO service. In 1961, when the Luftwaffe first put the Starfighter into service, the loss rate was eighty per 100,000 hours flown. By 1962 it had risen to 139. In 1963, though the loss rate per hour dropped because many more hours were flown, the number of accidents actually increased. By 1965 there had been a Starfighter write-off every ten days. Most alarming of all was the number of pilots killed flying Starfighters.

In 1965 the German Air Ministry asked Martin-Baker Aircraft Co. Ltd, the world famous English ejection seat company, if they could supply a rocket seat which could cope with zero/zero conditions, on the level and at an angle of 30 degrees. The Germans had already acquired some F-104s fitted with rockets with sufficient power to lift them into the air and keep them there until they reached flying speed. Martin-Baker completed some successful tests in England using an F-104 fuselage and these

were followed by demonstrations in Germany. The series of tests completed later successfully demonstrate the superiority of the Martin-Baker seat and the Germans specified the Mk.7 seat for retrofit in their F-104s. This marked the culmination of a protracted and often acrimonious debate, much of it conducted publicly, about the respective merits of the Martin-Baker seat and the Lockheed C-2 seat already installed in German F-104s.

In the summer of 1959, the German Ministry of Defence had stated their preference for a Martin-Baker seat for their F-104s rather than the Lockheed seat and James Martin had agreed to develop a version of the Mk.5 seat, which the German had already accepted for retrofit in the F-84F, RF-84F, T-33, Sabre 6 and F-86K, for the F-104. Lockheed were understandably hostile to this suggestion and made great efforts to have their C-2 seat accepted and to promote the problems, which they maintained were insurmountable, of installing a Martin-Baker seat into an aircraft which had not been designed to take it. Lockheed, however, were forced to place a development order with Martin-Baker and the prototype seat was successfully tested by Lockheed up to a speed of 700 knots on their sled test facility.

An order for production seats was placed but, during the flight trials of the aircraft, the Lockheed pilots made complaints about the Martin-Baker seat in relation to the sitting position, proximity to the instrument panel and the accessibility of certain instruments. Martin-Baker presented proposals to overcome these problems which Lockheed confirmed in February 1961 would remedy the complaints, but at a further meeting in March of that year to discuss the Martin-Baker proposals and the alternative Lockheed proposal to reinstall the Lockheed seat which they had originally offered for this aircraft, the committee expressed no interest in seeing the modified Martin-Baker seat. The C-2

A pair of TF-104Gs peeling away over Arizona during Luftwaffe pilot training. With almost 300 days of sunshine a year, Luke Air Force Base (AFB) in Phoenix, Arizona, was an excellent place to train and, given that German pilots could avoid the European bad weather, the airfield was chosen by the country to train its future F-104 drivers. Even so, 42 F-104s were lost during 20 years of training (+ 1 MAP aircraft loss) and 22 pilots were killed. By mid-1966 in Europe, 61 German F-104s had crashed, with a loss of 35 pilots.

F-104G-LO 63-13274, the pattern aircraft for Belgium.

was installed instead and the order with Martin-Baker was cancelled even though delivery of seats had already commenced.

A very public debate about this decision took place over the ensuing years, fuelled by inaccurate and derogatory comments about the Martin-Baker seat which outraged James Martin and which he insisted should be corrected and by the number of fatalities arising from the use of the C-2 seat. With the introduction of rocket motors, the Mk.5 seat could now be upgraded. By that time the performance of the Martin-Baker rocket seats had been verified by their extensive test programme and by the first emergency ejections using them and the decision to retrofit the German F-104s was announced in March 1967. (By 1967 the Luftwaffe had lost 66 F-104s and 37 pilots killed.)

By the time of the 1966 German Federal election the Starfighter played a role in the fall of the Chancellor, Ludwig Erhard. That summer Lieutenant General Werner Panitzki, commander of the Luftwaffe, gave a newspaper interview in which he claimed that the selection of the Starfighter had been a political decision and that the entire procurement programme had been flawed. Panitzki then offered his resignation, but he was suspended and sacked. His successor was the Second World War fighter ace (with 176 victories - six with the Me 262 jet) Lieutenant General Johannes 'Macky' Steinhoff, who immediately set to work restoring the shattered morale problem in the Luftwaffe. (As Kommodore of Jagdverband 7 in the Second World War, the first-ever jet fighter Geschwader, he was charged with evolving tactics suitable for the new Me 262 jet and was arguably the Experte who had the greatest influence on its subsequent operations). An erstwhile critic of the quantity and speed of introduction of the F-104 into service, Steinhoff had complained about the Bonn Defence Ministry's failure to implement the recommendations of his 1964 report on F-104G survival measures. He once said 'the Starfighter was forever jealous of the pilot's full attention. It rewarded discipline with deeds of airmanship; it could punish the dilatory or those who gave themselves to distractions. It was a marvel in capable hands and merciless to the careless.'

One of Steinhoff's first moves was to review the F-104G's ejection system to enhance the probability of a successful escape by a pilot at low level. Steinhoff grounded all the German Starfighters while the ejection seat system was thoroughly checked. The Lockheed C-2 ejection seat initially fitted to the F-104G had been fitted with a more powerful Talley Corporation 10100 rocket booster by November 1966 to give it true zero-zero capability. However, it was found that the Talley rockets had a destabilizing effect after ejection and had to be removed. After the German Starfighter had to be grounded once again for fixes to the C-2 seats in December of 1966, it was decided to switch over to Martin-Baker Mk.7A zero-zero ejection seats. The seat design was dictated by the narrow confines of the F-104 cockpit. The need to keep the original seat rails led to the Martin-Baker seat being somewhat forward of the normal seat position so the thickness of the seat was a major concern. This was addressed by the design of a new parachute container box which was designed to wrap around the main beam assembly to provide a thinner profile. The headrest design was changed as well to flatten it somewhat, which dictated changes to the shape and size of the drogue parachute container. Most of the rest of the mechanisms were retained with little modification.

One exception was the emergency oxygen systems. The oxygen bottle is mounted on the side of the seat bucket and connected to the European style Personal Equipment Connector (PEC) system. The GQ-7A came with more than one version of this, one of which included dual oxygen bottles for higher altitude use. A contract was signed on 8 March 1967 to re-equip the entire German F-104G force with the Martin-Baker seats. This took about a year to complete. The first successful use of a GQ7 seat to escape from a German F-104G took place during a ground-level overshoot at Ramstein on 24 September 1968. Another part of the programme to reduce the Starfighter accident rate was the revision of the training techniques and procedures. Steinhoff introduced a new training and retraining syllabus until losses and in particular fatalities were reduced to a 'more acceptable' level. In 1968 the Starfighter accident rate dropped by about half but this was only temporary and between fifteen and twenty Starfighters crashed very year between 1968 and 1972. Crashes continued at a rate of nine to eleven aircraft per year until the early 1980s, when all German F-104Gs began to be replaced by Tornadoes.

During its period of service with the German armed forces, about 270 German Starfighters were lost in accidents, just under 30 percent of the total force. About 110 pilots were killed. However, the attrition rate in German service was not all that much greater than that of the F-104 in service with several other air forces, including the United States Air Force. Canada had the unenviable record of losing over 50 percent of its 200 single-seat CF-104s in flying accidents. The loss rate of Luftwaffe Starfighters was not all that extraordinary, since the Luftwaffe had suffered a 36 percent attrition rate with the Republic F-84F Thunderstreak, the Starfighter's immediate predecessor. There was nothing intrinsically dangerous about the Starfighter, since the Royal Norwegian Air Force operating identical F-104Gs suffered only six losses in 56,000 flying hours and the Spanish Air Force lost not a single one of its Starfighters to accidents. Nevertheless, some of the Luftwaffe crashes could indeed be traced to technical problems with the F-104G itself. Engine problems, including difficulties with the J79's variable afterburner nozzle and contamination of the Starfighter's liquid oxygen system causing loss of consciousness of the pilot were listed as contributing factors in some of the accidents. There were also problems with the automatic pitch-up limiter during high-speed low-altitude flying and in tight turns, resulting in its temporary removal, with accompanying restrictions on the manoeuvrability.

In 1971 a report by the West German Government auditor general strongly criticized the original purchase of the F-104 Starfighter which had 'weakened materially and psychologically

Lieutenant General Johannes Steinhoff, the Luftwaffe chief, who was instrumental in getting the Lockheed C-2 ejection seat replaced on all Germany's Starfighters and in March 1967 Germany switched over completely to Martin-Baker Mk GQ7A zero-zero ejection seats.

the defensive power of the air force and entailed additional costs running into hundreds of millions of marks. He blamed Franz Josef Strauss, saying that when the order was placed he had given insufficient and in some cases, false, information, about the Starfighter to the Budget and Defence committees of the Bundestag (West German parliament). Later, the auditor announced that he had found enough spare parts for the F-104G stockpiled in depots to keep the Starfighter supplied for 100 years and that most would never be used.

By the end of 1975 the Luftwaffe and Marineflieger combined had suffered no fewer than 174 crashes. By late 1982 the Luftwaffe had lost or

Martin-Baker originally designed the Mk.GQ5 (90 knot) seat for the RDAF and West German aircraft in limited numbers, but it was soon replaced by the Mk.GQ7/7A for the Italian and Greek Air Forces, together with modifying the Mk.5 seats all having a zero zero (rocket-assisted seat) performance which restored confidence in NATO. (Martin Baker)

written off 252 F-104s. All told, Germany lost or wrote off 315 Starfighters, 248 of them F-104Gs, 33 TF-104Gs and 34 F-104Fs. Altogether, the Force Aérienne Belge (FAe)/Belgische Luchtmacht (BLu), (Belgian Air Force) lost or wrote off thirty-nine Starfighters and the Koninklijke Luchtmacht (KLu, Royal Netherlands Air Force), forty-four. The RCAF/Canadian Armed Forces lost thirty-seven CF-104 pilots. By 1975 Japan had lost or written off fifty-four of its 230 Starfighters. The sale of the Starfighter took place against a background of stiff competition in the US aircraft industry where winning is everything.

In 1969 Lockheed-Georgia won the VSX competition with the resulting S-3A Viking for the US Navy but while the Viking would remain in production until 1978, a 1965 contract to build 115 C-5 Galaxy jet transports was reduced to eighty-one aircraft in November 1969. Lockheed also had to come to terms with problems with AH-56A Cheyenne helicopter production for the US Army, a project which was finally terminated in August 1972, ultimately forcing Lockheed out of the helicopter business forever. The Lockheed Propulsion Company meanwhile, encountered insurmountable problems with a solid-fuel engine for the Boeing Short Range Attack Missile and the company was finally inactivated. Another highly expensive enterprise was the proposed L-2000 supersonic transport, which lost out to the Boeing 2707. At first there seemed no future for the three-engined (Rolls-Royce RB.211) L-1011 TriStar airliner, which lost out to the McDonnell Douglas DC-10. However, Lockheed landed orders for 172 TriStars from four major US airlines but in 1971 Rolls-Royce Aero Engines were placed in the hands of the receivers and production of TriStars ceased immediately. Without Government funded

help Lockheed Aircraft Corporation would have followed the British engine manufacturer into bankruptcy, but Lockheed faced many more financial and political setbacks until it entered profitability again in 1973.

Two years later, the Lockheed Bribes scandal broke when the publication of a Lockheed company report revealed that $22 million in 'sales commissions' had been paid to foreign officials, including at least $1 million to Prince Bernhard of the Netherlands. At the end of 1975 Lockheed Corporation's insurance companies finally agreed to distribute $1.2 million among thirty-one widows of German Starfighter pilots. In the summer of 1976 it was discovered that the entire set of files covering the German purchase of the F-104G had gone missing from defence ministry headquarters in Bonn. The bribes scandal rocked Lockheed Aircraft Corporation to its very foundations and the chairman of the Board and the vice-chairman and president were forced to resign. On 1 September 1977 the Lockheed Aircraft Corporation became simply, Lockheed Corporation.

The very last Starfighter, the 245th and final Italy-produced F-104S, was rolled out in March 1979. World-wide Starfighter production had therefore reached 2,577, 1,241 of them having been produced in Europe.

In his book *The Arms Bazaar*, Anthony Sampson sums up the role played by the Starfighter when he says:

As for the effectiveness of the Starfighter in the defence of Europe, no one will ever know. It was never proved in battle, whether in Europe, Viêtnam or the Middle East. By the mid-seventies it was already being replaced and its place in history rests less on its performance than its scandals.

■ **F-104G 4-46 of 4° Stormo 'Amendo d'Aosta' of the Aeronautica Militare Italiana (AMI).**

Missile with the Man in It

Rumour has it that Kelly Johnson gave birth to the F-104 on a restaurant napkin. Apocryphal or not, it must have been a small napkin because he obviously didn't have room for the wings. What emerged was a timeless design that looked like it was going Mach 2, just sitting on the ramp. Although the radical wing design produced very little drag at high speeds, its smallness resulted in high aerodynamic wing-loading (around 95lb/feet). Unfortunately, this doomed the aircraft to relatively poor manoeuvrability, since wing-loading is such an essential ingredient in turning performance. In all fairness to Johnson and the design team, however, the 104's initial role was envisaged as a high-speed point defence interceptor against the relatively poor manoeuvring manned bomber threat.

Royal Canadian Air Force fighter pilot, Lieutenant Colonel David L. Bashow

The Korean War 1950-53 shook the military might of America and it led to far-reaching changes in the equipment that it would need to fight any similar war anywhere in the world. Propeller-driven combat aircraft could no longer survive in the front line of any new conflict that flared up in the 1960s and in the aftermath of the Korean War, American and Soviet designers sat down with their design teams to think up powerful new replacements for the USAF, US Navy and US Marine Corps. Although the XF-90 Penetration Fighter had lost out to the McDonnell XF-88A Voodoo on 11 September 1950, the experimental Lockheed fighter had proved to be a valuable learning tool for the Advanced Development Projects at Palmdale. Following a Request for Proposal issued by the US Air Force in September 1950, Lockheed progressed onto an all-weather fighter interceptor studied under the Temporary Design Designation L-205. Powered by a 15,000lb thrust afterburning General Electric XJ53-GE-X10 turbojet, the L-205 won the design competition and two prototypes were ordered. Armament was to consist of six MX-904 air-to-air guided missiles carried in a fuselage bay beneath and aft of the dorsal intake and twenty 2.75 inch FFAR rockets on the sides of the armament bay. The L-205, now known as the Basic Model Number 99, was almost built in prototype form when concern over anticipated weight increases and resultant downgrading of performance led to the US Air Force cancelling the development contract in January 1951.

In May 1952 Lockheed was offered a new contract for the construction of prototypes of a Wright J67-powered, 16-ton interceptor, but the company declined to bid for the fighter when the USAF insisted on a clause forfeiting all patent features and allowing the US government to assign production of the new fighter to other manufactures. Another reason for Lockheed's reluctance to bid was because its Advanced Design Group was already working in secret on a much simpler and considerably lighter proposal designated the CL-246. After all, the Soviets had shown the way to the stars and in Britain W. E. W. Petter at Folland and in the USA, Ed Heinemann at Douglas had followed. Petter evolved the Midge and Gnat lightweight fighter designs while Heinemann's lightweight fighter, which unfortunately failed to interest the US Navy, would successfully be developed as the A-4 light attack aircraft. In France too several new L'Intercepteur léger (light interceptor) projects such as the SFECMAS 1402 Gerfaut, SE.212 Durandal, SO.9000 Trident and Marcel Dassault's MD.550 (forerunner of the Mirage) were under development.

At Lockheed, Hall Hibbard, chief engineer and Clarence L. 'Kelly' Johnson, assistant chief engineer and chief designer, were determined to make the Skunk Works facility number one when it came to jet-fighter design. And it would be a lean lightweight rather than a heavyweight, at least initially. Johnson had gone to South Korea in 1951 to see how his F-80 performed.

While there he visited fifteen air bases in a search for information from the USAF pilots themselves as to their requirements for an ideal fighter aircraft. USAF fighter pilots were

'Kelly' Johnson and Hall Livingstone
Hibbard, vice-president of construction at
Lockheed. Hibberd served on the board of
the newly revived Lockheed Corporation and
led the design departments as chief engineer.
Engineers such as 'Kelly' Johnson (left) and
Willis Hawkins worked under him.

unanimous in their wish list. They wanted a pure daylight air-superiority fighter that not only could surpass the Communist jets, but totally outclass them, both now and in the foreseeable future. What they did not want was an ejection seat, parking brakes, duplicated flying control systems, armour and radar equipment. Colonel Francis S. 'Gabby' Gabreski, the top scoring Second World War fighter ace and an ace in Korea, even went as far as to tell Johnson that radar was a waste of time: 'I'd rather sight with a piece of chewing gum stuck on the windscreen', he said. (As it turned out, Gabreski's ideas on radar would certainly hit the mark as far as the Starfighter was concerned). Using their hard-won experience against the MiG-15s, American fighter pilots knew that any new fighter had to be a lightweight, uncomplicated design so that greater speed could be achieved and it must be capable of greater performance and able to reach higher altitudes than the Communist-built MiG series.

The dedicated team of Advanced Development Projects engineers were of the same opinion. At this time the key personnel involved on the air superiority fighter programme included men with several years of jet design experience behind them. Johnson's Project Engineer was William P. 'Bill' Ralston. He had assisted Kelly Johnson on the XP-80 Shooting Star project and was one of the two Project Engineers on the XF-90 Penetration Fighter programme. As chief of engineering for Lockheed's experimental department, Arthur M. 'Art' Vierick supervised the shop group. Vierick, like Kelly Johnson and Dick Boehme, another key engineer on the air superiority fighter programme, were in the first group of twenty-eight original Skunk Works engineers who had worked on the XP-80 Shooting Star. Philip A. 'Phil' Colman was a key aerodynamicist on the Temporary Design Number L-133 project. Rus Daniell was an aerodynamicist who had been entrusted by Kelly Johnson to develop the YF-94 Starfire (Model 780) project.

Eugene C. 'Gene' Frost had, with Kelly Johnson, Phil Colman and Willis M. Hawkins (another member involved on the air superiority fighter programme), designed the L-133 airframe. R. Richard 'Dick' Heppe had joined Lockheed in 1947 and had been involved in the design of the XF-90. (In 1974 he became a vice-president of Lockheed Corporation and ten years later he became Vice-President and General Manager of the Skunk Works.) Benjamin R. 'Ben' Rich, who had joined Lockheed in 1950 as an aeronautical engineer after abandoning plans to become a medical doctor, moved to the Skunk Works in 1954 and instead worked on cures for thermodynamics and propulsion problems in the design of advanced aircraft. Later, he would work on the preliminary design aspects of the A-12, YF-12 and SR-71 aircraft and the D-21 Drone. It was his suggestion that led to the A-12, YF-12 and SR-71 aircraft being painted black to reduce the extremely high temperatures on these airframes at triple sonic speed. In 1975 Rich succeeded Kelly Johnson as a company vice-president and general manager of the Skunk Works, a position he retained until 1990. Rich (and Phil Colman and Gene Frost), were later involved in Kelly Johnson's Secret Project 'Aquatone' design, better known as the U-2. The remaining members of the key personnel involved on the air superiority fighter programme were John Stroud, Ed Baldwin, Henry Combs and James 'Jim' Hong.

After returning from Korea, in November 1952 Johnson began to design a dedicated air superiority fighter, even though at this time, the USAF had no requirement for such an aircraft. Johnson and his team could draw upon classified supersonic flight data produced both by the US Air Force and the US Navy. During the development of the F-104, Lockheed drew heavily upon information gleaned during NACA wind tunnel tests of the proposed Douglas X-3 Stiletto project, built to investigate the design features of an aircraft suitable for sustained supersonic speeds and which flew on 20 October 1952. Because of adverse drag divergence and pressure shifts at transonic speeds, the Douglas team designed the low aspect ratio wing for the X-3 with a thickness chord ratio of only 4.5 per cent. The F-104 wing would embody much the same characteristics as the X-3 wing. Johnson and his design team studied Lockheed's own programme of flight trials up to Mach 4 at over 150,000 feet using unmanned rockets. This programme clearly showed that at speeds in excess of Mach 2 a short, stubby, unswept very thin wing, was the most suitable. Thus far, only difficulties in building such a thin wing without a consequent loss of strength in the structure had prevented its manufacture. Being short and thin the F-104 wing (which would extend only 7½ feet from the fuselage) encountered little drag. It was said that the leading edge was so thin it was sharp enough to cut meat with. It eliminated such Mach effects as buffeting and tucking but the wing construction involved considerable design problems. Deflection of ailerons at high speed could cause a thin wing to twist with aeroelastic effects, perhaps causing structural failure, unless the wing had a sufficiently strong and rigid structure. Accordingly, the design team decided to build the wing around an aluminium alloy core having its longitudinal and transverse members machined from a single slab. Stretch-levelled aluminium alloy plate ½ inch thick at the wing root and ¼ in thick at the tip would cover the core.

A RAND Corporation study of F-104 development concluded with the following comment: 'The F-104 history illustrates that research and development in one programme can have a great carry-over value to another. [Apart from the low-aspect stubby wings, other features used on the X-3, such as smoothly-faired engine intakes mounted on the sides of the fuselage, an all-moving horizontal stabilizer and a downward-firing ejection seat were evidenced later in the Starfighter design]. Lockheed's success in building and flying a prototype less than a year after go-ahead would very probably not have been possible without the knowledge derived from the Douglas X-3 programme. Although the value of this experimental effort in the F-104 effort would hardly have been anticipated when the Air Force money was advanced to finance the programme, nevertheless the value to the Air Force of the X-3 programme extended far beyond the immediate results achieved with it. Regrettably, the X-3 never had the opportunity to approach its maximum design performance. The failure of the proposed Westinghouse J46 engine was judged by one RAND Corporation study as 'a classic case of engine-airframe commitments being made in the face of great uncertainty about all engine magnitudes'. As predicted, J46 development (which promised a maximum thrust of 4,200lb static thrust without afterburning and 6,600lb with afterburning), proved long and complicated. In the event, the X-3 was powered by the lower rated J34-WE-17. (The X-3 was powered by two J34s, each capable of developing 3,370lb static thrust and 4,850lb st with afterburner). If the Starfighter was to succeed, then the same hurdles of wing design and engine performance had to be overcome by Johnson and his team.

At least fourteen completely different designs were considered in 1952 before Lockheed decided finally on the F-104 configuration. The designs that were studied, tested and abandoned included, sliding intake centre body, flush cockpit, rocket propulsion, wingtip-mounted tail booms, nacelle-retracting landing gear, V-shaped windshield, low mounted stabilizer and delta and swept-wing. Swept-back airfoils require thick chord and long span (with attendant high drag) to give performance comparable to the short, straight wing. Extreme sweep also affects handling characteristics. Every square foot of delta wing has less drag in a certain Mach number region (somewhere between 1 and 2) than a corresponding square foot of straight-thin wing. Every square foot of straight wing, however, lifts roughly twice that of a delta. By the time there is enough delta wing area for a given load, total drag is considerably higher than a straight wing presents. The delta has lower transonic drag than straight wing (the reason why many subsonic aircraft use this configuration). So in the transonic regime, from Mach 0.85 to 1.3, a delta will accelerate faster through Mach 1, but above Mach 1.4 the F-104, with its trapeze wing planform would out-accelerate delta-winged aircraft such as the F-102 and F-106. While many aircraft can attain Mach 2 in 'dash-speed', the F-104 was designed to *cruise* at Mach 2.

Johnson's Model 83 design, considered to be years ahead of its time, was so radical, so revolutionary, that even the American fighter pilots would surely have been surprised by the Skunk Works' ingenuity. Apart from the extremely small, very thin straight wings that were angled downward 10 degrees and a long, tapered nose, the new aircraft was also characterized by a unique high T-tail configuration with all-moveable stabilators (stabilizers and elevators) which moved as one unit. Kelly Johnson, Phil Coleman, Dick Heppe and James Hong designed the F-104's unique empennage.

Wind tunnel tests proved that a high tail position was necessary for optimum stability and control about the pitch axis throughout the F-104's wide Mach range. The location of the horizontal stabilizer on top of the vertical tail raised the centre of pressure on the tail thereby increasing induced roll effect during sideslip. To compensate for the increased roll that resulted from the vertical tail, negative dihedral! (or anhedral) was put in the wing

(anhedral angle is approximately 10 degrees). The stabilizer, which was only 3½ inches thick at the inboard edge and slimming to a mere inches at the tip, was located only 11 inches from the top of the swept-back vertical fin. (It was later constructed with a single spar covered with skin panels and the hinge movement was along the spar line. Hinge and operating controls were both enclosed by the empennage contour. This avoided using external fairings that were normally used to cover such items. Built on two steel fuselage forgings supporting two fin forged spars, the fin contained boost servo units for empennage control surfaces.) The F-104's high 'T-tail' layout was also designed to counter pitch-up, a problem common to all aircraft but more so for small, high-speed aircraft. As it turned out, the configuration did not counter pitch-up enough and the tail had to be repeatedly modified later. Ultimately, the only solution to the problem was to install complex electronic systems to provide automatic pitch control.

The fuselage contained five bladder-type fuel cells and the retractable undercarriage and the other equipment was contained in the electronics' compartment or 'E Bay' located beneath the aft section of the cockpit canopy, about five feet along the aircraft axis. The semi-monocoque airframe was of steel, aluminium and titanium and the turbojet and the afterburner exhaust ejector nozzle were housed in the streamlined fuselage. To save weight, Johnson had dispensed with heavy pressurization equipment, but this meant that the pilot would most likely have to wear a bulky and highly uncomfortable spacesuit to protect him from the rapid decompression following flame-out at high altitudes. Stainless steel and titanium skins covered the aft fuselage section that housed the engine and carried tail loads into the mid-fuselage.

Kelly Johnson was firm in his resolve for the radical design of the Starfighter, as he was to recall: 'The large airplane exponents claimed that equal speed, range and fighting power could not he obtained in a smaller airplane because such fixed items as the pilot size, canopy size, engine thrust per square foot of frontal area and fixed equipment item weights, were a smaller percentage of the large airplane weight than of the smaller one. Likewise, the fuselage cross-section and size, in general, would be unfavourable for the smaller airplane, resulting in lower ratios of lift to drag and thrust to drag, even if the same percentage fuel weight could be carried. There was not in existence a small engine which had as good thrust-weight ratios or specific fuel consumption as the larger engines then available. These factors were all true at the time; so it was necessary to make some rather major advances on practically all of these fronts before a successful lightweight fighter could be developed.'

Johnson's design team had fashioned an extremely lean and lightweight fighter aircraft with a high thrust-to-weight ratio to give it an advantage in the supersonic speed regime in which it would fly and fight. At an all-up weight of just 11,500lb the XF-104 was half the weight of the competitors' proposed Weapon System 303A aircraft: the Northrop Model N-102 Fang, North American Model NA-212 F-100B(I) Ultra Sabre and the Republic Model AP-55 Thunderwarrior.

Johnson showed his radical design proposal to Colonel Bruce Holloway at the Pentagon, who was immediately enthusiastic. He even went as far as to say that, 'Well if there isn't a requirement, I'm going to make one. Stick around Kelly. Come back in a couple of hours!' The colonel produced a list of requirements under Weapon System 303A, calling for a pure air-superiority day fighter with exceptional climb rate, speed, ceiling, agility and manoeuvrability; in other words - a pedigree dogfighter. If successful, the new and advanced lightweight fighter would supplement and later replace, the North American F-100 Super Sabre. After obtaining authorization from General Donald L. 'Don' Putt (commander US Air Force Systems Command 30 June 1953-14 April 1954) and General Don Yates, a month later Holloway gave Johnson a General Operational Requirement calling for a lightweight air-superiority fighter. The colonel handed over the list of requirements and said, 'Kelly, go see what you can do with this.'

One of the biggest problems confronting the Skunk Works propulsion engineers was in deciding which turbojet would be the most suitable to power the XF-104. Foremost in the frame were the Allison J71, which was projected to produce up to 14,000lb thrust with afterburning, the Pratt & Whitney J75, which was projected to produce up to 21,000lb thrust with afterburning and the General Electric J79, which was projected to produce up to 15,000lb thrust with afterburning. In 1941 General Electric had produced the first American-built turbojet power-plant designated I-A. It weighed 780lb

and had a thrust - or pushing power - measured at 1,300lb. Pursuing its pioneering advantage, General Electric during the Second World War developed a new style engine built around an axial flow compressor. Earlier models, such as the J33 which powered Lockheed's F-80 Shooting Star, used a centrifugal compressor that propelled air outward from the centre of rotation. Axial flow means that the air flows straight through, 'packed' ever tighter by a series of spinning fan-like blades before fuel is added and ignited (the annular-design combustion chamber had a split casing that could be disassembled quickly and contained ten combustion chambers). The one big goal of engine manufacturers was an engine combining light weight with high thrust, mechanical simplicity and reasonable fuel economy. The J79 offered better specific fuel consumption and lighter dry weight than either the Allison J71 or Pratt & Whitney J75 competing engines. The J79 engine's thrust-to-weight ratio - 3,500lb weight and 15,000lb plus thrust - was unprecedented (pressure ratio was 12:1). Developed in cooperation with the USAF under the government's weapon system management concept, the J79 was the first US production engine capable of powering aircraft at twice the speed of sound. However, the face to achieve this was no quick dash, rather an extended endurance test. The prize would only be forthcoming after the difficulties and setbacks which one associates with any such complex new powerplant were overcome.

Design had to permit rapid acceleration from idle to full power without compressor stall. Variable-pitch stator blades therefore had to adjust automatically to reduce stall problems at low engine speeds and give maximum compressor efficiency under all flight conditions to match engine and airframe induction system for good stall margin at high aircraft speeds. The axial flow compressor had seventeen stages and a single rotor, with the first six stator stages and inlet guide vanes variable. (The rotors were made of thin webbed discs and spacer rings bolted together. Blades were attached to the rim sections by conventional dovetails.) The engine's separate fuel systems - main and afterburner - were flow-controlling units, hydro-mechanically operated. An integral part of the basic engine, controls had electrical trim, with both hydraulic and electric power. Overall,

the system served main fuel, afterburner fuel, nozzle area and variable stator controls (integrated with main fuel controls). Afterburner features included fully modulated, variable area, with a converging-diverging exhaust nozzle that worked automatically. Hydraulic power was assured by two independent systems working from engine driven variable displacement pumps which could operate in varying temperatures. An emergency ram air turbine lowered from the right-hand side of the fuselage was to provide hydraulic power in the event of engine seizure that left the primary system intact. (A flamed-out but rotating engine would give adequate hydraulic flow and pressure for surface control.) The ram air turbine permitted safe flight and moderate manoeuvres and supplied emergency electrical power.

Not unsurprisingly perfecting the J79 engine was anything but straightforward. Of course engine development problems were not restricted to General Electric alone - equally they had to be faced by the leading jet engine manufacturers in the USA and in Europe. Although the J75 turbojet (designated X24A under secret project MX-2118) was expected to be available sooner However, the J79 was not scheduled to be available until early 1956 (it would need more than 12,000 hours of factory, simulated altitude and flight testing time) and this would not be soon enough, because contractor Phase I flight-test requirements were due to start early in 1954. Therefore, the powerplant used initially to power the first XF-104, originated in Great Britain.

Lockheed finally selected the non-afterburning Wright Aeronautical XJ65-W-6, an Americanized version of the Armstrong-Siddeley Sapphire axial-

A General Electric J79 axial-flow turbojet engine built for use in a variety of fighter and bomber aircraft and a supersonic cruise missile, with a Woodward type 1307 main engine fuel control. The J79 was used on the F-104 Starfighter, B-58 Hustler, F-4 Phantom II, A-5 Vigilante, IAI Kfir and SSM-N-9 Regulus II supersonic cruise missile. It was produced for more than 30 years.

flow turbojet. This engine, which was built by the Buick Motor Division of the General Motors Corporation, was capable of 7,800lb dry thrust (later versions developed 10,300lb thrust with afterburning). Using two different engines meant that Lockheed was forced to design two different airframes because the J65 and J79 each required different engine air inlets and exhaust outlets. During the first eleven months of the flight test programme, the XF-104 prototypes averaged three flights per week and reached a maximum Mach number of 1.74 at 41,000 feet which represented a True airspeed of 964 knots or 1,110 mph. The XF-104s were limited in Mach by the inlet temperature of the J65 and this would be true of the J79.

The design targets for the Starfighter included lightweight, conventional structure and aerodynamic sleekness, as well as simpler maintenance (the F-104 had 165 interchangeable parts). These goals could only be achieved using some new fabrication methods such as cadmium plating, chemically milling, compression forming and zero draft forgings. Parts fabrication with tolerances as low as 0.010 inch were possible with contour forming, in which sheet metal was first shaped broadly, heat-treated, then precision formed in the cavity of a compression die. A high-pressure ram forced the metal to flow on both surfaces and edges of the part against the die face. Because of sharper flange bend radii, rivets could be seated almost in line with the web of wing stiffeners. This increased the connection's strength and cut down 'working' of the area under stress. Accuracy of compression forming eliminated waviness in wing panels that disturb airflow and promote unwanted friction and drag at high speeds. The same method was used with sheet metal for making wing spars and ribs that did not carry big loads. The ailerons were made with a steel beam that had been heat-treated to an ultimate tensile strength of 180,000psi. Actuated by ten rods, the ailerons were hung on steel piano hinges. Both the nose landing gear and the main landing gear retracted into the fuselage because of the thin wing design. The wings were attached to the fuselage with five heavy forged fittings that were attached to wing skins and intermediate channels. Upper and lower skins were formed from single, machine-tapered plates, 0.25 inch thick at the root and 0.125 inches thick outboard. Shaped exactly like the Starfighter's nose was a cone-like steel tool that wound fibre-glass threads into distortion-free radomes. Spinning at a controlled speed, it pulled fibreglass strands through a resin bath and, under regulated tension, wove layers of glass thread into the radome. When threading and cutting were completed, the radome was machined to exact dimensions by delicate cuts on the first and final layers. The electronically transparent nose was then checked for radar transmission characteristics with an intervelometer and boresighted on the Lockheed radar range.

During January 1953 the Model 83 design was selected by the Pentagon under Weapon System WS-303A and on 12 March 1953 Letter Contract AF 33(600)-23362 for two XF-104 prototypes was submitted to Lockheed. The mock-up was studied and led to the substitution of a rotary six-barrelled 20mm General Electric M61 30mm Vulcan cannon mounted in the forward fuselage in place of the two 30mm cannon originally suggested. The mock-up was approved on 30 April 1953 and two production XF-104-00-LO prototypes (Model 083-92-01) were given the go-ahead. But when the Korean War ended on 27 July the US Air Force requirement for a high-performance air superiority fighter was no longer a priority. However, a new

career unexpectedly opened up for the Starfighter. Air Defense Command had planned to replace the Convair F-102 Delta Dagger fighter-interceptor with the F-106 Delta Dart by 1954 but slippage had put these plans on hold. Lockheed now changed the main mission for the XF-104 from that of an air superiority fighter to an air defence fighter-interceptor. This volte face made the F-104 appear a very attractive proposition, especially since it could fulfil a multi-role function with its ability to operate in the air superiority role when required.

The first XF-104 example (53-7786), was built in strict secrecy in January 1954 with no official roll-out party. It was physically different from the eventual production models in several respects. The XF-104 was shorter, at 49 feet 2 inches, as opposed to the 54 feet 8 inches of the later Starfighters. The XF-104s neither had the inlet spikes (or cones) sported by their successors, nor the ventral fin. One of the distinguishing features of the prototype was the negative 10 degree dihedral angle of the wings. Maximum take-off weight of the X model was 18,530lb. The XF-104 was transported by road to the Top Secret North Base Area at Edwards Air Force base in the Mojave Desert where Lockheed Chief Test Pilot, Tony LeVier and test pilot Herm 'Fish' Salmon were to put both prototypes through the essential test evaluation programme. LeVier began his career

Tony Levier (left) and Herman 'Fish' Salmon, the two Lockheed test pilots most associated with the XF-104 Starfighter test programme. (Lockheed)

Tony LeVier with the XF-104 armament test prototype, 53-7787 at Edwards AFB, 1954. The air intakes of the two XF-104s were of fixed geometry without presence of half-cones, since the J-65-powered aircraft was incapable of Mach-2 performance. (USAF)

with Lockheed in 1941, became a test pilot in the P-38 Lightning programme and was promoted to Chief Test Pilot in 1945. He made the first flights of the XP-80, T-33, F-94, T2V, F-104 and the U-2. Salmon, a well-known air racing pilot, had been involved with flight testing Lockheed's tail-sitting turboprop VTOL fighter concepts, the XFV-1 and America's first turboprop airliner, the Electra.

53-7786 (Company 1001) was to be used as the aerodynamic test bed while the second XF-104,

53-7787 (Company 1002), was to be used as the armament test bed. Challenges on this programme involved investigation of supersonic performance, flutter, stability, controllability, very little data on which existed at this time. Both XF-104 prototypes were originally equipped with roll and yaw axis stability augmentation systems (SAS). The roll SAS was flown in two different configurations, one in which a single aileron was used, the other involving both ailerons. The two-aileron configuration was adopted for use in later models. Early problems with lateral directional stability resulted in the addition of a ventral fin and longitudinal stability problems resulted in the addition of a pitch axis stability augmentation system. All subsequent F-104 models were equipped with three axis SAS systems. The first XF-104 was to be used to investigate static and dynamic stability in all three axes, stick force per G, stall characteristics, airspeed calibrations and power plant thrust testing. Also, it would be used to evaluate all systems including air conditioning/pressurization, hydraulics, landing gear, brakes, fuel, flight controls and communications. Structural loads too would be measured. Instrumentation on the prototypes was crude by today's standards, but state-of-the-art for that time. Miller Model J oscillographs, Brown temperature recorders and photo panels were the primary recording devices used. Because Lockheed engineers perceived a danger during upward ejection posed by the high

Above: XF-104-LO prototype 53-7786, which was used as the aerodynamic test bed, flying for the first time on 4 March 1954 and 53-7787 (below) were years ahead of their time. These new aircraft had an extremely small, thin wing area and long, tapered nose (they also had a downward-ejecting seats) and they were powered by a Wright 11,500lb thrust XJS5-W-5 (Sapphire) with afterburner giving a maximum speed of Mach 1.79. On 27 April 1955 Major Howard C. Johnson powered the XF-104A to Mach 2 for the first time. (Lockheed)

T-tail, both XF-104s were fitted with a Lockheed-built downward-firing rocket-propulsion ejection seat system, the first fully automatic system used on any production fighter aircraft. Lockheed engineers also surmised that essentially, all ejections would be accomplished at altitudes high enough for successful completion of the downward ejection manoeuvre. The seat was designed so that after the pilot pulled the ejection ring the cockpit would depressurize and explosive bolts would blow the escape hatch off the bottom of the aircraft before the seat ejected downward and out. Obviously, the ejection sequence could not safely be used on the ground it was also only suitable for medium- to high-altitude emergencies. If the pilot needed to eject at low altitude therefore, he would have to roll the aircraft inverted (upside down) and then eject upward from the underside of the fighter!

Eventually, it was proved that the engineers' worst fears concerning the XF-104's tail proved groundless and all Starfighters were fitted with an upward-firing ejection seat. First to be used was the rocket-powered Lockheed C-2 seat (which although it was quoted as 'zero-zero'-capable (zero speed and altitude), a forward speed of at least 98 knots was required for successful ground level ejection). Lockheed promoted the C-2 seat thus: 'Capable of providing full recoveries at airspeeds from approximately 100-550 knots and altitudes from ground level to 50,000 feet the C-2 leaves the Super Starfighter via a rocket-catapult device. At or near ground level the timing mechanism is set to separate pilot from seat one second after ejection - and parachute deployment one second later.

To eject, the pilot pulls a D-shaped ring located between his feet on the seat bucket structure. The ring fires two initiators. One ejects the canopy. The other starts pre-ejection functions. In three-tenths of a second, this happens: Metal stirrups pull feet close to the body and hold them until time of man-seat separation. Knee guards rotate into position to present the leg spreading and to counteract effects of airloads. Arm support webbing flips up and prevents outward movement of arms. Moving up the rails, the seat hits a striker and - one second later - the lap belt is released, foot retention cables are cut and the pilot-seat reel operates. (Pulling the D-ring also operates a backup system that fires a delay initiator into the catapult unit and a second one into foot cutters.)

XF-104-LOs 53-7786 and 53-7787 in flight. 53-7787 (Company 1002), was used as the armament test bed and was armed with a single M-61 20mm multi-barrel gun. It could also mount a GAR-8 Sidewinder infrared air-to-air missile (or 110 gallon tip tank) at each wingtip. XF-104 53-7787 was lost on 14 April 1955 after accumulating over 1,000 flying hours when test pilot Herman Salmon was forced to eject during gun firing trials at 50,000 feet because the ejection seat hatch on the floor blew out. The two XF-104s amassed an approximate total of 2,500 flight hours. (Lockheed)

The XM-10 rocket-catapult, a pyrotechnic propulsion unit, fits on the seat back upper cross-beam members and moves up and down with seat adjustment. Forcible separation is actuated pyrotechnically by a windup reel behind the head rest. Nylon webbing is routed from the reel down the forward face of the seat back, under the survival kit and secured to the forward seat bucket lip. Sequenced with the lap belt release, the webbing is drawn taut between the head rest and the lip in two-tenths of a second, 'pushing' the pilot out and away from the seat one second after ejection.

To assure proper foot retention and retraction, the pilot wears foot spurs equipped with ball sockets at the back. The ball lock end, engaged by spurs, is attached to cables that pull feet rearward and secure them in foot shelf units. Two initiators, fired one second apart, cur cables free at the proper time.

Carried on the aluminium alloy seat is an automatic survival kit that includes disconnect hardware, automatic life raft inflation, high pressure emergency oxygen bottles with fifteen minutes' duration and a regulator suitable for partial pressure suits above 42,000 feet.

On 30 June 1959 Norvin C. Evans had need of the Lockheed ejection seat when 56-0768, an AFFTC support aircraft, crashed at Edwards Air Force Base after a broken oil-line caused a fire: 'Those of us in flight test at California's Edwards Air Force Base in 1959 accused the Lockheed F-104 Starfighter production engineers of turning the designer's drawings upside down. The wings of most aircraft employed dihedral - they were set at a slightly upward angle - but the F-104's wings angled in the opposite direction; the horizontal stabilizer and elevator sat atop the vertical stabilizer instead of below it; and the ejection seat fired down instead of up. We could recover from the spin that resulted from the aircraft pitching up uncontrollably when it stalled, which was due to the T-tail configuration, but most pilots who used the Stanley C-1 downward seat ejection system didn't live to complain about it. Twenty-one had died in downward ejection seat accidents, including in 1958, X-2 and X-15 test pilot Ivan Kincheloe.

'The seat required the pilot to wear metal 'spurs' on the heels of his flight boots, thus earning an F-104 pilot the nickname 'Cowboy.' The spurs

On 2 November 1959 YF-104A 55-2964 of ARDC was written off after an accident at Wright Patterson, Ohio. Approximately 90 seconds after takeoff, Major James William Bradbury heard and felt a moderate explosion. Over relatively open country and losing altitude (keeping in mind the downward ejection seat), the pilot ejected. His chute opened at 500 feet and Bradbury landed without injury and went to a nearby home to report the accident. The aircraft struck the ground and hit an automobile on a road and then a house approximately 8 miles from Patterson Field. Two girls aged 2 and 12 were trapped in the wreckage and were killed. Their 34-year old mother ran burning from the house and died six days later from her burns.

had slotted receptacles that the pilot slipped over steel balls at the base of the seat's foot rest. The balls were anchored to cables on the seat that automatically pulled the pilot's boots against the base of the seat so that when he ejected, he could safely clear the aircraft in one piece.

'I conducted my own investigation of these design decisions in late June 1959. I had just returned to the Mojave Desert from a couple of weeks leave on the East Coast and stopped by Test Operations to check on the status of the Republic F-105 that I was flying in a stability and control test programme. My boss, Lieutenant Colonel C. E. 'Bud' Anderson, asked if I would stand by for a safety chase flight he was scheduled to fly - it had been delayed all day and probably wouldn't go. It was already 5:30 pm and the colonel had to meet visiting Royal Air Force test pilots at the golf club. As soon as he left, Flight Lieutenant Jack Woodman called: The flight was on. He was evaluating a Grumman F11F-1F as a fighter for the Royal Canadian Air Force.

'In an attempt to give the F11F enough power to reach Mach 2, engineers had installed a General Electric J79 engine - the same engine used in the F-104. I was flying safety chase in an F-104A, even though the aircraft were still in test status. The -104s were the only aircraft we had that would reach twice the speed of sound.

'At 35,000 feet, 65 miles west of Edwards, Woodman and I had reached 1.87 Mach when my engine developed excessive vibration. A glance at the instrument panel showed I was losing oil pressure - a recurring problem with the early J79s.

'I immediately reduced power and turned back toward the base. I thought: This really can't be happening to me! Knowing the procedure for placing the minimum balanced load on the engine compressor bearings, I had throttled back to 88 percent power. I was fifteen miles from Edwards and at 15,000 feet and 450 mph when the pressure reached zero. I was too high to touch down safely on the 15,000-foot main runway, but the dry lake bed provided miles of overrun. Changing the throttle position would surely cause trouble, so I tapped the speed brake switch. Big mistake. The aircraft shuddered, the fire warning light came on, the engine ground to a stop and the cockpit filled with smoke. In just a few seconds, I was able to see my altimeter as it unwound through 7,500 feet - ground elevation was 3,000 feet - and my airspeed drop to 275mph.

'I had to eject. Immediately.

'I reached down and pulled the D-ring on the front of the seat, which would fire the ejection cartridge. Nothing happened. I pulled again - still nothing. Looking down to make certain I had gripped it properly, I pulled a gain with all my might. I felt a tremendous blast of wind as I was fired toward the ground.

'I had been told that if you had time to think about the parachute deploying that meant the

F-104A 56-0816 of the 83rd Fighter Interceptor Squadron at Hamilton AFB, California 1959 with nose art *Dads Special* for Lieutenant Colonel 'Bud' Evans. This Starfighter went to Taiwan on 4 August 1970 coded as '4250'. It was withdrawn from use in 1988.

lanyard that connected the seat to the parachute D-ring hadn't worked. I looked at my lap to see if my seat belt had opened - it had. At the same time, I reached for my parachute D-ring and found it still in place on my chest strap. To manually activate deployment, I grabbed the D-ring and threw it far from my chest. The pilot chute streamed between the seat and my body, pulling the parachute out. The parachute canopy began to unfurl from my left side. Next came a tremendous shock on my shoulders as the chute deployed, snapping me around like a rag doll. Now I was plummeting head-first toward the desert. The next shock was in my groin as the chute fully deployed. The canopy was above my head - the most beautiful sight I've ever seen - even if the horizon was running directly through the middle of it, indicating that I was horizontal to the ground, which was fast approaching.

'Using all my remaining strength, I pulled the parachute's top shroud lines and stopped my pendulum swing almost directly under the canopy. The ground was racing toward me and before I could get turned around to face downwind, I hit the ground rotating. I landed in what had been 'Pancho' Barnes' 'Happy Bottom Riding Club' dump and was dragged for forty yards on my back through broken glass and tin cans until my chute got hung up on a yucca tree.

'The aircraft went in five miles short of the runway at Edwards. I was one happy aviator, even though my flight suit was torn and covered with

XF-104-L0 prototype (53-7786) being preflighted at Edwards AFB adjacent to Runway 22 (the first YF-104A service test model is just visible behind the power carts). On 27 April 1955 Major Howard C. Johnson powered the XF-104A to Mach 2 for the first time. (Lockheed)

blood and sand, I had cracked several vertebrae in my lower back, an air police pickup truck almost ran over me and a doctor on his first day at the base hospital and a pediatrician on his first rescue helicopter ride dropped me from the stretcher a couple of times.

'Mine was the last downward ejection from an F-104. The aircraft got a Lockheed C-2 upward ejection seat, an oil pressure warning light and a 'butt kicker' system that throws an ejecting pilot out of the seat after the C-2 clears the aircraft.

'The investigation revealed the oil pressure loss was caused by a rupture in an expandable oil line. The loss of cooling oil melted the compressor bearings, which caused the compressor blades, rotating at 18,000 rpm, to shift, impacting the fixed stator blades and destroying the engine. A later examination showed that the cable, which was attached to the firing initiator, was wound in three loops and encased under a plate that was bolted to the seat front. The last time the seat was inspected, the last loop had gotten wedged between the seat and the plate when the cover plate was bolted to the seat. The investigators estimated that to stretch the inside strands of that trapped loop one-sixteenth of an inch, just enough to fire the seat ejection cartridge, I had to have pulled hard enough to create a force of 450 lbs.

'Someone up there must like me.'

The C-2 was used in all F-104s except for those built in Belgium, Germany and the Netherlands. The C-2 was later replaced by the Lockheed S/R-2, which offered true zero-speed, zero-altitude capability and after 1966, the Martin-Baker Mk.7(F) upward-firing ejection seat, was fitted to F-104s built in Belgium, Germany and the Netherlands.

On 28 February 1954 XF-104 53-7786 made an unscheduled short and straight hop before LeVier flew the number one aircraft for the first time on 4 March. (53-7786 was lost in a crash on 11 July 1957). On 25 March 1955 XF-104-2 53-7787, now powered by an afterburning Wright J65-W-7 and flown by Lockheed test pilot Ray Goudey, reached a top speed of Mach 1.79 (1,324 mph). On 14 April 1955 this Starfighter was lost during a gunnery test flight when Herman 'Fish' Salmon was forced to eject because the ejection seat hatch on the floor blew out. With sudden decompression, Salmon's pressure suit inflated and he could not see what had happened but he believed that he had experienced a gun-firing mishap, as LeVier had earlier. (On LeVier's one of the bolts had blown out of the gun, penetrating a bulkhead and fuel cell aft of the gun bay. The gun bay door also partially opened, allowing fuel from the punctured cell to enter the engine inlet. LeVier had made a flame-out landing on the lakebed at Edwards AFB. Subsequent investigation of the airframe and gun indicated that high temperatures in the gun bay allowed a round to swell up such that it jammed in the barrel, causing the bolt to blow out when it fired). Salmon ejected and landed safely. (Salmon retired from Lockheed in 1968. He lost his life in the crash of a Lockheed L1049H Constellation while on a ferry flight from Columbus, Indiana in 1980. LeVier retired from Lockheed in 1974 with over 10,000 hours in more than 250 different aircraft).

The XF-104 trials revealed that even with the afterburning version of the J65 turbojet, the production aircraft would not be able to reach design maximum speed. (On 8 June 1954

Captain Walter W. Irwin taking off at Edwards AFB on 16 May 1958 in YF-104A-1-LO 55-2969 when Irwin set a Fédération Aéronautique Internationale (FAI) World Record for Speed Over a 15/25 Kilometre Straight Course at 1,404.012 mph. On the same day, Irwin set two time-to-altitude records by flying -969 to 3,000 metres in 41.8 seconds, and to 25,000 metres in 4 minutes, 26.03 seconds. It reached an altitude of 91,246 feet. This was the first time, from this day, that one aircraft (YF-104A) held at the same time the world altitude and the world speed record. (USAF)

the XJ79-GE-1 was test-fired for the first time in a special test cell within General Electric's Evendale, Ohio facility and without afterburning, produced 9,290lb thrust). In addition, directional stability problems manifested themselves and the need to carry more internal fuel load meant that the nose would have to be lengthened on the next batch of YF-104A service trial aircraft. On 30 March 1955 the US Air Force placed an order for seventeen YF-104As against contract AF-27378. The YF-104s (and pre-production F-104As) had the fuselage lengthened from 49 feet 2 inches to 54 feet 8 inches and the tail surfaces moved aft. On the face of it, everything now seemed well starred for the future F-104. On 27 April 1955 Major Howard C. Johnson powered the XF-104A to Mach 2 for the first time. By the end of 1955 Lockheed had an order for 155 F-104s for Air Defense Command. The first YF-104 was rolled out from Shop B-1 at Burbank on 23 December 1955 but the appearance of the Starfighter was not made widely known until its first public roll-out, at Burbank on 16 February 1956. The next day the first YF-104A made its maiden flight, with Herm Salmon at the controls. On 28 February the YF-

Line up of F-104Cs of AFFTC (ARPS), Tactical Air Command. 56-0922 nearest the camera was lost on 22 November 1968. Major Kermit L. Haderlie died in the crash: 56-0911 was lost on 20 September 1965 at Đà Nẵng, when it had a mid-air collision with 56-921 after dark with navigation lights off, while looking for the missing F-104C 56-883. Captain Harvey Quackenbush ejected safely. Next in line are 56-0933 and 56-0909, which was lost on 21 June 1960 at Morón de la Fontera after suffering an engine failure. Captain William Langhorne Leitch attempted to relight the engine with negative results and ejected safely. On 28 August 1961 56-0913 failed to get airborne during the takeoff run at Morón AB, Spain; it ran off end of runway and exploded killing the pilot.

104A, flown by Joe Ozier exceeded Mach 2 for the first time. On 2 March Lockheed received contract AF-30756 for seven pre-production F-104As. The contract also authorized the procurement of 146 F-104As and six tandem-seat F-104Bs for Air Defense Command and fifty-six single-seat F-104C Starfighters for Tactical Air Command. (TAC needed a supersonic tactical strike fighter (fighter-bomber) to fill the gap between the North American F-100C Super Sabre and the Republic F-105B Thunderchief.) On 26 December 1956 Lockheed received a second order from Tactical Air Command, for a further twenty-one F-104Cs.

F-104C 56-0925 of 479th TFW in a 32-ship formation over Arizona in 1960. This Starfighter crashed on 3 October 1960 when it suffered an engine failure over Morón AB. 1st Lieutenant Richard E. Strickland ejected safely.

The YF-104As were to flight-test and evaluate the three early versions of the 14,800lb General Electric YJ79-GE-3, -3A and -3B turbojet series. (Unfortunately, the J79 made no provision for modulated afterburning and pilots soon found that bringing in the afterburner took them straight from Mach 1 to Mach 2.2 with no ability to stabilize at any speed in between! In addition, once they reached Mach 2.2, the engines began overheating and they had to return to Mach 1 again). Apart from exploring the entire performance envelope and testing the new canon armament, from April 1956 the YF-104As also would have to test the relatively new AIM9 (formerly GAR-8) Sidewinder air-to-air heat-seeking missile. Without such armament the Starfighter would be no use in an air defence role. Further refinements included the fitting of variable shock-control semitone, or ramp, in the fuselage-side air intakes to channel the huge amount of secondary airflow at supersonic speed.

F-104A/G 56-0801 A-12 (SR-71) chase plane with a SR-71 'Blackbird'. Delivered on 28 January 1958 to AF Proving Ground Center (Air Research and Development Command), Eglin AFB, Florida, it was leased by Lockheed and modified in May 1959 to F-104G configuration (1st prototype F-104G) with a bigger rudder for system tests (flight controls) and for nuclear weapon shape trials. It was leased to Lockheed for the A-12/M-12 programme (April 1962-December 1964) as the safety chase plane at AREA 51.

A forward-retracting undercarriage was installed in place of the rearward-retracting arrangement. (XF-104 53-7786 had experienced undercarriage retraction problems on its first flight on 5 March). Also, a brake-chute and an arrester hook were introduced and a ventral fin positioned on a level with the afterburner was added to improve stability.

While these improvements were successful, lingering problems in perfecting the afterburner for the J79 and other setbacks would only serve to delay the Starfighter's introduction to operational service. On 24 April 1956 Flight Test Center commander Brigadier General J. Stanley Holtoner advised Air Force Systems Command commander Lieutenant General Thomas A. Power that there had been a slippage in the flight-test programme of the YF-104A because of compressor problems with the J79 turbojet. There were also other problems to contend with, ones which would produce serious question marks over the Starfighter's ability to operate as an interceptor. By early June 1956 Holtoner had concluded that with internal fuel only, limited endurance and radius of action 'posed serious problems for use in any proposed tactical role' and that the F-104, using internal fuel only, had 'an intercept radius of 150 miles against a B-52 type target at 45,000 feet'. This would mean that intercepts at 70,000 feet would 'have to be made over the base'.

While this situation was very disquieting news for Air Defense Command, which was scheduled to receive operational F-104As before Tactical Air Command, the latter had a requirement for its F-104Cs to carry the two types of US nuclear payloads. One type was the 2,013lb B28 (formerly T28), which measured 170 inches long and 20 inches in diameter and was designed to be dropped from high altitude at subsonic or supersonic speeds. The other was the 2,195lb B28-1 (formerly T28-1), a parachute-drop bomb, which was 175 inches long, 20 inches in diameter and which was designed to be delivered at low altitude under high-g conditions (using the low-altitude bomb system of LABS). The Starfighter would be required to carry a nuclear store externally as well as wingtip and/or underwing auxiliary fuel tanks. Since single-seat F-104C aircraft were not yet available - by December 1956 - for the Special Weapon Configuration testing, F-104A 56-0801 was used for the performance phase and F-104A 56-0790 for the stability phase. Both F-104As were modified to carry ventral bomb racks to carry the nuclear device. Additional fuel would be carried externally also, in two 165-gallon wingtip tanks and in two 200-gallon underwing pylon mounted tanks. Internal fuel added another 908 gallons.

Not unsurprisingly, the Special Weapon Configuration programme, which was carried out over 37 flights totalling 37½ hours at Palmdale and at Edwards, revealed serious fuel limitations and a dramatic fall off in the Starfighter's overall speed and distance performance. The tests involving a Starfighter carrying a total of 1,638 gallons of fuel (i.e. with four external fuel tanks in addition to the internal fuel) and a 'special store', reduced the afterburning sea level rate of climb to 23,400 feet/minute compared to 36,400 feet/minute for the clean aircraft. Also, supersonic capability was

F-104A-15-LOs of Air Defense Command. On 26 July 1958 Captain Iven C. Kincheloe was killed in a flying accident at Edwards AFB while piloting 56-0772. 56-0737 became a QF-104A drone in the 3205th Drone Squadron in overall Day-Glo color scheme in 1962. It was shot down on July 3 1972 by AIM-9J sidewinder missile at 10,000 feet at 0.95 Mach after 21 drone flights. That was the last day that a QF-104 was lost during the QF-104 programme. ADC (later Aerospace Defense Command) accepted only 179 F-104A/-B Starfighters and soon phased out the aircraft to make way for all-weather fighters. The last F-104A was withdrawn from ADC in 1960. (Lockheed)

YF-104A 55-2971 nicknamed 'Slosher', which was severely damaged on its fourteenth barrier run test at Edwards AFB on 1 October 1958. Lockheed test pilot Jim Wood escaped. The aircraft was converted later to a QF-104A target drone for use by the 3205th Drone Squadron. (USAF via Robert F. Dorr)

no longer possible with the carrying of the five external stores, although about Mach 1.2 could be achieved if the underwing fuel tanks were removed. If the F-104 dropped its external fuel tanks as they became empty in a typical subsonic strike mission, the nuclear bomb could be delivered onto a target 828 miles from the home base and the aircraft returned safely. It might have been prudent to drop the tanks on any such mission anyway as it was found that the aircraft fish-tailed at speeds above 675mph IAS (indicated air speed) when any of the external tanks and the nuclear store were carried. Hence, the F-104 pilot would not be able to rely on supersonic performance on any nuclear strike mission. The best he could hope for while carrying the store would be a maximum flight speed using military power of about Mach 0.965 at 20,000 feet and Mach 0.945 at 35,000 feet. Clearly, the Starfighter would have severe limitations to say the least, if it were used in the nuclear strike role!

Other problems manifested themselves during the flight-test programme. (YF-104A-6 55-2960) was destroyed in a crash on 3 November 1956 and YF-104A-4 (55-2958) was lost on 15 February 1957.) Altitude errors noted in the transonic speed area during trimmability tests led to such novel test procedures as flying alongside another aircraft's level contrail to maintain a constant altitude! By 5 December 1956, when seventeen YF-104As and seven F-104As had been delivered to the Flight Test Center, it was evident to the flight-test personnel that although the Starfighter promised spectacular speed and climb performance, problems of pitch-up and delays generally caused by the need to develop and fit wingtip and underwing tanks and produce an adequate armament system would 'relegate the early production aircraft to little more than a training role'. Furthermore, flight-testing of ten early production F-104As for Phase VI functional development and Phase IV performance and stability tests, were still to take place, in 1957.

Pitch-up at high angles of attack was not the least of the Starfighter's problems. On 1 May 1957 the eighth YF-104A (55-2962) became the fourth test Starfighter lost. Lockheed experimental pilot Jack J. 'Suitcase' Simpson was just forty seconds into the test, at 30,000 feet the first test point on airspeed, angle of attack and yaw input, when the *Eight Ball*, as it was named, snapped into a pitch-up and inverted nose down roll. Simpson was born in Philadelphia and raised in Pittsburgh. After high school he served in the US Army Air Corps during WWII. After receiving a BS in Aeronautics from St. Louis University in 1951, he won his wings as a fighter pilot in the USAF, flying the F-86 Sabre in the Korean War. After the war he was a test pilot in Southern Japan. Upon returning to the USA Jack served the office of the USAF Plant Representative at North American Aviation as a project test pilot in the development of the F-100, the world's first supersonic fighter. Upon discharge he was hired by Lockheed as an experimental test pilot in the development of the F-104.

'I radioed the flight-test engineer in the control room at the Lockheed Flight Test Center and said, with more than a little trepidation, 'Larry, I'm sure I followed the flight-test procedures you detailed me on the mission profile card, but as I reached the first test point on airspeed, angle-of- attack and yaw input, the plane went crazy; it snapped into an inverted nose-down roll. It really surprised me; it took me over 9,000 feet to recover. Remember yesterday; it didn't act like this at all.'

'Lockheed Aircraft Company hired me because of my experience as an Air Force test pilot at North American Aviation, flying out of Los Angeles International Airport, on the development of the F-100 Super Sabre. The F-100 was the first supersonic fighter to move into mass production.

'As a Lockheed experimental pilot, I felt I was part of the legacy of famous aircraft and intrepid men. Lockheed designed and built the P-38 Lightning for WWII. It became famous in the Pacific theatre of operations. Lockheed also designed, in its renowned 'Skunk Works,' the

F-80 - the first operational jet fighter. I flew the Shooting Star, as it was named, both in gunnery training at Nellis AFB and in Korea in preparation for my first combat mission.

'The F-104 was born in Kelly Johnson's famous 'Skunk Works'. The design aim was to produce a supersonic fighter that would have a performance capability in excess of Mach 2 and combat altitude of over 60,000 feet. So, although I was a lone in the cockpit, that day trying to figure out what went wrong at 30,000 feet, I was in the company of esteemed designers, builders and widely known experimental flight test pilots.

'Not like yesterday at all,' as I stated earlier to Larry, meant that I had flown this specific stability and control test the day before and everything had gone according to the flight test plan. But the electronic mechanism designed to send signals from the test aircraft to the control room had malfunctioned; none of the data collected was usable for studying past performance before planning the next experimental flight. When you hear about aircraft accidents today, the familiar word is the importance of recovering the 'flight data recorder.' Well, 40 years ago, it wasn't as sophisticated; therefore, I was asked to do the experimental test over again. I agreed to do so.

'I took off, climbed to 30,000 feet and started my experimental flight. I controlled the aircraft as precisely as called for on the flight test card. I was less than forty seconds into the test, when wham, the plane snapped into a pitch-up and inverted

Below: F-104A-5-LO 56-0737 with two wingtip-mounted AIM-9 Sidewinders. The missiles provided a degree of lateral stability, with no reduction in G limits and also created lift. 56-0737 was delivered on 24 May 1957 and after supersonic Sidewinder missile tests and TTF (Target Towing Flight) duties at McClellan AB, California in 1959 became a QF-104A QFG-737 on 31 October 1961 in the 3205th DS. On 25 June 1971 it was hit by an AIM-9, but recovered. It was shot down on 3 July 1972 by AIM-9J sidewinder missile at 10,000 feet at 0.95 Mach after 21 drone flights. (Lockheed)

On 9 February 1961 F-104A 56-0761 ARDC from the ARDC took off from Edwards AFB on a chase mission for an F-4H test flight crashed at the Buckhorn Dry Lake, 4 miles west of Edwards. The 31-year old pilot, Captain Albert 'Al' Hanlin Crews Jr. ejected safely.

angle of attack coming-coming-there it is-holding angle-of-attack-airspeed OK, here comes the rudder-more-more-WOW! Why so much rudder? Damn it Larry! Here I go again!' I yelled. 'I have a vicious pitch-up! I have a huge roll input! Going crazy - I'm upside-down - the plane's going crazy!'

'The nose had yawed right with horrific violence. Everything became a blur as the plane tumbled out of control toward the ground. I said to myself, 'This is crazy; this isn't me, this is terrifying!' For a nanosecond, my first combat mission flashed before my eyes, with the terror I experienced in seeing flak and tracers and realizing for the first time that the enemy was trying to shoot me down with the intention of killing me!

'Now this @#%*?&# plane was trying to do the same thing!

'I couldn't talk anymore. I had to get control; the airplane had stalled out. I was about 60 degrees upside-down and yawing. I didn't even know which way, I was so disoriented, but I knew I was heading down-fast I didn't move the stick or push either rudder pedal. I didn't advance the throttle; I quickly checked the exhaust gas temperature and the rpm gauge; the engine had not flamed out.

'Take it easy,' I said to myself. 'Take it easy-don't fight the controls. You have altitude-let it go-let it go. OK now, roll it upright-little roll input-easy-easy-little rudder-whoops! The other way-easy on the stick-check the tuck-little more roll-little bit at

roll. It was then that I radioed Larry, after I got control of the plane and myself!

'OK,' I said to Larry, 'maybe I did something wrong. I'm going to try the test once again, but if it reacts the same, I'm coming home. I'll climb back to designated altitude and I'll talk my way through. That way, we'll both be able to try to determine the unusual behaviour of this lady with, it seems to me, an agitated composure.'

'That's a good idea,' said Larry, 'but everything seemed to go so well yesterday. Hope nothing is wrong.'

'How soon we were to find out!

'Roger,' I remarked, as I levelled off at the proper altitude. 'I'm ready! I'll talk through each step! OK! Here goes! I'm at altitude, attaining-there I am-at the indicated airspeed as called for,

YF-104A-11-55-2965 which on 1 March 1967 was shot down as drone by an AIM-4D missile from another aircraft on its 5th drone mission.

a time-just a touch of rudder-just a touch damn it! Don't know what's wrong - little bit - little bit.

'Slowly, ever so slowly, I started to lead and the lady was following me; we started our majestic waltz-gliding on thin air. I had talked her out of her determination to fatally test the law of gravity. I finally had number 55-2962, the eighth YF-104A manufactured, flying level. She had an 'eight ball' tattooed to her right side. I had lost 16,000 feet. Yes, I had literally been 'behind the eight ball.'

'I called Larry, gave him the particulars and told him something was definitely wrong. I didn't know what it was, but I knew something was amiss; so much so that I instinctively started to climb and head for the dry lake at Edwards AFB. The dry lake had saved me many times during past test flights when things were not functioning properly, particularly with the new YJ79-GE-3 (General Electric) engine; a beautifully designed, but, what turned out to be, an extremely vexatious-and deadly-engine.

'In experimental flight tests, we were stretching the state of the art for an innovative fighter. Everything was new: new design of aircraft, new engine, new variable guide inlet guide vanes, new main fuel regulator, new type of afterburner, new altitudes never explored and speeds never researched. It was the first time in any aircraft that the engine was combined with a fully variable duct system that could adapt itself to all contrasting conditions from takeoff to Mach 2.2; at least it was supposed to. The F-104's wings were also unique, tailored purely to the supersonic regime - extraordinarily small span and area-without sweep. The next time you take a look at the new generation of fighters - the F-14, the F-15; the F-16 - look at the leading edges of the wings. They look like Mount Rushmore to the F-104's 15/100 inch thick leading edges.

'The Starfighter had new radar and a new gun. A new pilot's handbook had to be written, meaning new operational and emergency procedures had to be written and tested.

'Front line, air-to-air combat pilots convinced Kelly Johnson to go for performance at all costs. The result was one of the most startling airplanes ever built; the 'missile with a man in it,' as it was called. A far as moving at high speed in a straight line, it had few rivals.

'But nothing worked as designed. More than a dozen times, I would be in the throes of an experimental test flight and the engine would flame out- just flat quit-for no apparent reason. I would get the engine started and gingerly head for home. Sometimes, no, many times, I couldn't get the engine started again, so I hurriedly took the option of the dry lake bed at Edwards (the same dry lake bed where the space shuttle first landed 25 years later) and landed the aircraft 'dead stick.' That five miles of lake bed gave us both lots of room.

'Was the lake bed going to save me one more time? I headed toward Edwards for a couple of reasons. I was too far away from Palmdale in case of an emergency; experimental pilots aren't paid to eject out of every test vehicle that presents a sudden, unknown problem. Also, Edwards (named after an experimental test pilot who died in the crash of a flying wing) is a wide-open lake bed that would give me options for direction of landing and a high indicated airspeed on final approach. I planned to avoid any pitch-up, yaw and roll situations. One Lockheed test pilot had recently been killed in a 104 during a flare-out at

F-104C-10-LOs 57-0926; 57-0923; 57-0927 and 57-0915 of the
479th TFW, Tactical Air Command at George AFB with 170
gallon wingtip and 225-gallon fuselage tanks. 57-0926 crashed on
17 June 1965 on landing at George AFB. The aircraft of Major
W. Ward; touched down 900 feet short of the runway, the MN-1A
weapon dispenser ripped off and the aircraft went through seven
rows of approach lights at the end. Ward was injured but he
survived. 57-0923 *Hello Dolly* operated from Udorn RTAFB in
1966-67. It crashed on 5 August 1968 on take-off from Savannah,
Georgia during summer training camp while trying to avoid
an F-104C already in the barrier after an aborted take-off and
caught fire when the tanks burst. The pilot escaped with first
and second degree burns. 57-0927 was among the first aircraft
to carry fuselage-mounted missile rails for a pair of AIM-9
Sidewinder air-to-air missiles and was involved in the early
trials. Named *Debbie Sue* it crashed on 19 June 1969 flying from
Savannah, after a flame-out at pattern altitude on the Poinsett
gunnery range near Shaw AFB. The pilot, who possibly activated
the fuel shut-off valve inadvertently, ejected safely. 57-0915 is now
on display at Heritage Air Park (Plant 42), Palmdale, California.

U.S. AIR FORCE

U.S. AIR FORCE

FG-927

U.S. AIR FORGE

FG-915

U.S. AIR FORCE

landing - the 'eating an ice cream cone' manoeuvre used to decrease sink rate just prior to touchdown. It had pitched-up and catapulted while rolling to the right, spewing pieces of airplane and fire that tumbled and reacted explosively along the edge of the runway and into the adjacent field. I was there and saw the results to both pilot and plane. We still hadn't been able to confirm why it happened. We think the plane stalled and pitched up, yawed and then rolled uncontrollably to the right. If I could help it, I wasn't going to let that happen to me.

'I reached what I thought was a safe altitude, called Larry and told him my plans. He told me to switch frequencies so Lockheed could monitor my approach to Edwards. I gave him a 'Roger' on that and radioed Edwards.

'Edwards tower, this is Lockheed test 2962 - over.'

'Roger 2962; go ahead,' came the instant reply.

'Edwards, 2962 is declaring an emergency although it is not a mayday. Request landing on the lake bed at speeds above normal; not sure of my direction as yet; don't want to make too many turns; not sure when I'll drop my gear; would appreciate, however, fire truck following, over.'

'Roger 2962. Wind is light, varying north to northwest at 5 knots, altimeter 30.01.'

'OK Edwards. I'll have to make a 90 toward the north-will call about three miles out on final-straight in toward north.' 'Wind's not that bad and I don't want to move this thing around too much,' I said to myself. 'I feel like I'm encased in an eggshell.'

'Edwards,' I radioed, 'I'm presently at three one thousand feet west of Barstow; parallel to 58 [highway 58]; have Harper Dry Lake at one o'clock. I'm on the letdown.'

'Roger 2962' replied Edwards. 'Keep us informed. I understand Lockheed is monitoring this frequency. The fire trucks are rolling.' Fire trucks! That sent a chill though my spine.

'I gingerly started to lose altitude; pulled the throttle back to about half quadrant and cracked open the speed brakes. I had descended about 2000 feet when I ran into a rumble of clear air turbulence. I inched back on the throttle and instinctively closed the speed brakes to reduce buffet. I told the tower I was in CAT; I knew Larry was listening. I then said to myself, 'OK eight ball; take it easy, we've been through a lot of things together. We'll get through this. Take it easy.'

'But just as I looked down to check the airspeed indicator, the nose violently pitched almost straight down and continued to move through 90 degrees. I was starting to tumble. I called 'Larry!' as I was pulling hard, real hard, back on the stick, 'I've lost control! I have zero pitch input! I've got to get the hell out! Now!'

'At that instant, I reached for the ejection ring between my legs with both hands and pulled as the aircraft continued to tumble. Boom! I was out, ejected upward, upside-down at 27,000 feet.

'I might explain. The F-104 was at first designed with a 'downward' ejection seat because it flew extremely fast at low altitude where, of course, the air is dense. Any ejection, up or down, at high speed would be like hitting a brick wall-a thick brick wall-at 700mph. No question: that's Excedrin headache number 1! The seat ejection systems at that time were not powerful enough to eject the pilot 'upward' for fear of jamming him, due to high pressure, into the horizontal and vertical tails, each having a leading edge with a .01-inch radius. I wasn't ready for sliced 'Suitcase'! Thus we ejected 'downward.'

'It's a funny thing about life; or fate. Three of my test-pilot friends were killed in the F-104 when they were forced to eject close to the ground. The ejection system didn't function for them at low altitude or they were too close to the ground when they made their decision to eject.

'I can still remember the powerful, full force of rushing air-pinning me to my seat-like going downhill in the front seat of a mile high roller coaster. Only this blast was instantaneous; it hit me at about 450mph. One second after I ejected, the lap belt separation system worked; it blew the belt in half and freed me from the seat. For a few seconds, the seat and I were inches apart floating to a stop as we reached the apex of our arc. A lanyard, one end attached to half of my seat belt and the other end attached to a pin in my chute, seemed to be hanging around, slithering like an eel in water. Then the seat drifted, or fell, away. The eel became a frozen rope and pulled the pin that armed my parachute to open at 15,000 feet.

'I started to roll and tumble and corkscrew for about 10,000 feet, like an oak leaf being blown from a tall oak tree in a vicious windstorm-sway and tumble, no control, no power over anything, no stability, just another body simply subjected, nakedly to the divine agency to which the order of things is prescribed. Would I be a favourite son, or a fatality? Would I be vicariously and rudely shoved back in time to Greek mythology and become Icarus and fall to my death by flying too close to the sun; or would I become the winged horse Pegasus carrying the thunderbolt of Zeus and be allowed to live and, like he, be captured by my Bellerophon (Lockheed) and continue to ride through many adventures?

'Speaking of thunderbolts: what the hell happened? This isn't me, falling through space hoping my chute will open. Where's the ring for manual opening? Where are my hands? What happened to my airplane? Was 'eight ball' angry with me? Did I step on the lady's toes too often?

'My thinking was interrupted with an abrupt, cruel and intense punch to my crotch and chest. My chute opened with a vicious snap, a whoosh, a big shaking, followed by a smaller one: it was extremely violent. I was a rag doll in the mouth of a giant killer lion and then he dropped me-plop! And there I was! Hanging by two leg straps and a

F-104C-5-LO 56-0922 over the battle zone during Exercise 'Desert Strike', a joint US Army/USAF Strike Command exercise carried out during 5-29 May 1964 on and over 9,600 miles of the Mojave Desert, California. 56-0922 crashed on 22 November 1968 after suffering explosive decompression at more than 69,000 feet during a 'zoom climb', a rehearsal maneouvre for possible future spaceflight. At 6,000 feet the aircraft broke up impacting the desert floor killing the 34-year old pilot, Major Kermit L. Haderlie (left). This was his first zoom flight alone. (USAF via Robert F. Dorr)

F-104A-LOs 56-0793; 56-0782; 56-0779 and 56-0791 of the South Carolina ANG in formation. Assigned to the 86th Air Defence Division of the Seventeenth Air Force at Ramstein AB, West Germany, during the Berlin Crisis, these Starfighters took part in the largest aerial deployment in the ANG's history. 56-0793, 56-0782 and 56-0791 later went to the Royal Jordanian Air Force. 56-0779 is now stored at the Yankee Air Museum at Chino, California.

chest belts -15,000 feet in the air. I was stunned- this wasn't me - I'm having a nightmare!

'I'm dreaming - Clark Gable and Spencer Tracy and a snazzy blonde in *Test Pilot*. But then, a sudden reality; the wind came, wheezing through the shrouds rocking me back and forth, back and forth. I was in a backyard swing; only I couldn't put my feet down to stop it. I was afraid to look down, but when I did, it was most frightening - oh my God! Would those straps hold me? Will I fall out? I still had about 12,000 feet to go: My first experience in a parachute. I will never forget it!

'I looked around. I could see San Bernardino, Barstow, Edwards, Lancaster, Palmdale and the Valley-all those places and hundreds of thousands of people; yet I was all alone. I looked at my legs and arms and hands. I moved them. My hands were holding on to the rigging with a tighter grip than snap-on pliers. I wasn't about to let go. Somewhere along the line I had lost my left glove and my watch; my flight suit looked like the remains of a flag flown at full mast during a hurricane. It was in shreds. But my helmet and oxygen mask stayed with me; I was sucking, rather readily I might add, emergency oxygen. My laced up boots were still on my feet. I looked down and moved my head around. I didn't dare make a body turn; didn't want to disturb anything. The wind still had that eerie sound as it continued to pick its way through the shroud lines. It reminded me of 'intersanctum,' but that was a squeaky door. I really felt depressed. How could this happen to me? And I started to think, 'You're in the

big leagues now, Suitcase. This is serious stuff, ejecting out of an experimental aircraft. You're not a 'flyboy' anymore. You are dealing with a very profound, abstruse, difficult subject matter- this test-flying stuff. It's beyond the ordinary knowledge or understanding of almost everyone. Most people think of you in a leather jacket and a white scarf in the company of glamorous women. No glamour here. You better pray it wasn't your fault because of a dumb mistake.'

'I was looking for smoke from my crash- nothing!! I remember thinking that I hoped a United Airlines DC-6 wouldn't run into me. Why United? Why a DC-6? I have no idea.

'I looked down. 'Wow!' I said to myself, 'I'm coming down pretty darn fast, I better get ready for a sudden stop.'

'I don't know at what rate of descent I hit the ground; I went from so many feet per second to stop! Just like that! I do remember, as I neared the ground, seeing a small ranch house, or cabin, with clothes hanging on a wash line. A blessing! The clothes gave me an indication of which way the wind was blowing so, when I hit the ground, I would be prepared to get up and run in the direction of my chute and grab the lower shroud lines and collapse it. Sounds good! That's what they do in movies. But everyday life is serious play and you're never given any time to practice. This was my first ejection and parachute ride and I was never given any in-depth lectures or practices in landing-in a harness, say, by jumping from a tower as you see in the training movies.

'The clothes line was strung from the roofline of the cabin to a pole about thirty yards away. It was high enough to help me in my depth perception. When my eyes were even with the clothesline I closed them, tucked in my legs a bit, went limp and waited. *Whomp*! I hit the ground-hard. The chute did not collapse; the wind was stronger than I anticipated. And let me tell you, there was none of this get-up-and-run stuff; I was being dragged. I managed to roll over onto my stomach, used my elbows for speed brakes - I still have the scar tissue - and slowly crawled forward to shorten the distance to the bottom of the chute. I finally managed to get it to collapse-then I did too!

'In a few long minutes, I sat up and looked around. Nobody came from the cabin, but I was more concerned about what had happened to the aircraft. I kept thinking! My God! What if I was responsible?! This really isn't happening! I'm going to lose my job! Is my experimental career over already?

'I also was looking for smoke from the wreckage, but there was nothing except a lot of dust and haze on the 360-degree horizon. The wind was getting stronger-blowing from the west. I pulled in more of the chute. I was alone in the middle of nowhere, sitting in a dusty, dried-up, brown, grass-like field and my back was killing me. I decided not to move, Lockheed would be looking for me by now anyhow. I unhitched one side of the parachute risers and let the chute flare out.

'I heard a motor. It wasn't the sound of an airplane. I struggled to stand up and saw a truck driving toward me. It continued until it came right up beside me and stopped. It was driven by a farmer with eyes the size of an 'on-deck' batter's circle. I had taken off my helmet, so at least he knew I wasn't from another planet - I think!

'I seen ya come down from way off,' he said. 'Took me a time to git here. What happened? Is you busted up? You one of them paratroopers from out yonder at Bicycle Lake? Wher'd yawl come from?'

'I said, 'I don't know what happened. I just got here myself.' My try at dry humour went directly over his head. 'I'm OK, but I would appreciate a ride to the nearest town. I'd like to make a phone call.'

'Boy, ain't no towns 'round here. Yawl in the middle of nowhere. This yous'd to be Alfalfa-ain't nothin' now. No water. As I says ain't no towns, but I kin take you to a country-like store. They got a phone outside. C'mon git in.'

'He,' his name was 'Gus,' helped me gather my chute and helmet and off we went. I made the mistake of telling Gus my back hurt a little. From that time on, until Lockheed picked me up at the edge of a dry lake bed, Gus told me about his back troubles, his wife's lumbago troubles, his kids' troubles and money troubles. On the way to the 'country-like' he asked, 'How much do you trouble shooters make?'

'Not enough,' I answered.

'You married?'

'No thanks.'

'Hey, hey, hey! Yeah marriage is like jumping int'a a hole in the ice in the midd'l winter; you do it once and you remember it the rest of your days! Yer Smart! Got girl friends?'

'Not enough! Although I am dating a blonde right now.'

'What's 'er name? She pretty?'

'Her name is Jane and, yes, she is very pretty; she could make a bishop kick a hole in a stained glass window just to see her pass by.'

'Heh, heh, heh! Probably wanted to see mor'n that. Heh, heh! That's a good'n.'

'How long have you been married Gus?'

'Heck man, I've been in love with the same woman for thirty-eight years. If my wife ever finds out, she'll kill me. Heh, heh, heh! Naw! Just kiddin',' Gus said, 'I'm married to mah third one. Nice lady. Took on two of her kids and I guess she liked that. We ain't got much money, but we git along. You seem I drive a tractor for a big rancher near'n Ridgecrest and, when I work, pay's pretty good. Long hours though.'

'We were now bouncing along a dirt trail in Gus's pickup truck headed toward the edge of Harper Dry Lake. I had called Lockheed, collect. Ellie Hawks, the chief of all flight tests accepted the call. The conversation was surreal.

'Hi, Suitcase. Where are you calling from?'

'I'm out here at a crossroads gas station.'

'Oh? Where?'

'I dunno, somewhere south of Harper Dry Lake, so I'm told.' I was beginning to realize that, for some reason or other, Ellie didn't know I had lost an airplane. I found out later that the guys upstairs in engineering were in a panic and Ellie had just returned from the bank or something; no one had had the chance to call him.

'Did you have a breakdown or something?'

'Yeah, Ellie, Your number eight airplane is broken way down-into a thousand pieces, is my

On 26 June 1961 F-104C 56-0923 piloted by 30-year old Captain Richard E. Derrick of Salt Lake City and F-104C 57-0917 flown by 29-year old Captain Daniel R. Klix of Detroit in the 436th TFS, 479th TFW at George AFB, California were involved in a mid-air collision at 38,000 feet while in a five-ship navigation and training mission from Richards-Gebaur AFB to Andrews AFB, Maryland. Derrick's aircraft was seen to disintegrate and fall inverted; the pilot did not eject and went down with the plane. Newspaper accounts state that Derrick was found in the cockpit section of the F-104 approximately 1½ miles from where most of his Starfighter fell. He was identified by his name tag. His aircraft came down 20 miles southeast of Lexington, Virginia. Klix stayed with the F-104 as long as possible to avoid populated areas before ejecting and the aircraft impacted on the farm of Daniel Van Clief at Old Woodville, near Keene, Virginia, 15 miles southwest of Charlottesville, in the Blue Ridge Mountains area.

■ 52

'Suitcase' Simpson with his Lockheed JF-104A 55-2955 'Appleknocker' circa 1957. This aircraft was written off in a successful dead stick landing. (Jack Simpson)

'Hey! Wait! Wait! What's the number there? I'll call you right back.'

'So in a few minutes the phone rang and, after discussing what happened in more detail and Ellie reaching his zenith of excitement and then calming down-plus knowing I was OK - Ellie told me my boss, famous test pilot Tony LeVier, was on his way by plane to pick me up. I suggested to Ellie to have Larry accompany Tony so he could brief him on the way.

'My conversations with Gus were vapid, passing the time as we drove, but he turned out to be a very nice man. And it helped me through my anxiety of being in the middle of nowhere, having lost an experimental airplane worth tens of millions of dollars and not knowing the reason why; that's what was haunting me.

'Tony landed the twin Beech on Harper Dry Lake and taxied to a stop, bringing a cloud of thick red dust with him. Larry, my flight test engineer, was in the co-pilot seat. I introduced the two men to Gus and while Larry was helping with the chute and helmet, Tony took me aside and said, 'Don't worry, Suitcase, we think we know what went wrong. Larry and I could see the wreckage from the air. We saw the hole the airplane made, then the ripped off tail section and a finally the mangled tip tank. It looks like the tip tank was torn loose due to the clear air turbulence you reported. It probably wasn't installed correctly. It then, somehow, jammed into the tail and cut through it like butter. It reminds me of the fatal accident we had at Big Spring in a T-33; the tip tank came off and tore into the tail. Only the instructor was at low altitude. Do you remember that?'

'How could I forget? The pilot was one of my instructors.'

'Anyhow, we think that's what caused your tumble; thank God the ejection seat worked perfectly. We have some experts on the way to the sites now; I radioed the coordinates.'

'I was relieved, but depressed. How could something like this have happened? I asked Tony if he had a few bucks. He went over to Gus and thanked him and then we said our goodbyes. When Tony shook Gus's hand, his palm had a 100-dollar bill in it. Tony LeVier was that kind of man. When it was my turn I didn't say much, just shook Gus's

guess. For God's sake Ellie, I just ejected from number eight.'

'Dead silence for a long, long second!

'Wha! What! Ya, ya, ya, mean ya, bailed out? Wha-wha-where?? What happened? Are you OK? Where are you calling from?? Are you OK? Can we come get you? Ca-ca-can you walk?'

'Yeah, yeah, Ellie; I'm OK. I don't know what happened. I lost all pitch control. The airplane just pitched down and started to tumble on me, so I had to get the hell out. I had a nice guy pick me up; took me to this 'Grapes of Wrath' junction.'

'Gosh, I can't believe it. Wait a second! Larry just walked into my office. Just a minute.' Mumble, mumble. ' OK! Can you get to Harper Dry Lake?'

'Yes, I'm sure this man will take me. But I want to give him a tip: I didn't bring any cash with me.'

'Heck, don't worry about that. We'll pick you up in the Bonanza-within the hour.'

'OK! Great! Have Larry review the voice tapes with you. That's all we have left anyhow. See you in about an hour. And Ellie, I'm OK. Relax.'

Jack 'Suitcase' Simpson (pictured in May 1953 as a 26-year old and superimposed aged 76 in Los Angeles in May 2005) was born in Philadelphia and raised in Pittsburght. After high school he served in the USAAC during WWII. After receiving a BS in Aeronautics from St Louis University in 1951, he won his wings as a fighter pilot in the USAF, flying the F-86 Sabre in the Korean War. After the war he was a test pilot in Southern Japan. Upon returning to the USA, Jack served the office of the USAF Plant Representative at North American Aviation as a project test pilot in the development of the F-100. Upon discharge he was hired by Lockheed as an experimental test pilot in the development of the F-104.

hand, gave him a hug, turned and climbed into the airplane.

'When we arrived at Palmdale, I was given a big welcome, reported to the flight surgeon (my back was just a bruise and I was given a prescription for pain if it got worse), filed a tape recorded detailed report and visited with Ellie, Tony and Larry. Things were getting serious; we were losing too many aircraft. I didn't know it then, but my time would come again.

'Tony flew me to Burbank. On the way Tony told me my aircraft, the number 1 YF-104A Simpson's Appleknocker (my crew chief had painted a flying suitcase on the right side), which I had been test flying was still down for maintenance and would not be ready for another week. The Appleknocker was the first YF-104A off the assembly line as a test aircraft. He said 'I don't want to even hear from you until a week from tomorrow.'

'I went to my apartment a few miles from Burbank. I did go to the plant a few days later though. It took me a few days to recover any semblance of walking correctly because I had never hurt so much in my life: my neck, shoulders,

chest, elbows, inner thighs and even my rear end. I played tennis or worked out religiously every other day and I thought I was in good shape. Tarzan probably could not have taken the abrupt tugs, pulls and shakes on his body without hurting in the same way and he had a Jane who worried about him, too!

'Anyway, I had our flight-test secretary type a letter for me thanking Gus. I wanted it on Lockheed stationary. I also packed a model of the F-104 and sent it to him - with the tail on!

'Tony talked to me while I was there. His first premise turned out to be true. The tip tank had been installed improperly. The rest is history. He didn't offer to show me the pieces.'

A few weeks later, on 17 May, YF-104A-16 (55-2970) was lost in a crash and a year later on 6 May 1958 the fourteenth YF-104A (55-2968) was damaged and converted to a QF-104A drone. Another sad loss, on 26 July 1958 was Captain Iven C. 'Kinch' Kincheloe, born on 2 July 1928, who during the Korean War flew F-80s on thirty combat missions and F-86s on 101 combat missions, downing five MiG-15s, was killed in

a flying accident at Edwards AFB while piloting F-104A-15 56-0772. In the mid-1950s Kincheloe joined the Bell X-2 programme and on 7 September 1956, flew at more than 2,000 mph and to a height of 126,200 feet (some sources list 126,500), the first flight ever above 100,000 feet. For this he was nicknamed 'America's No. 1 Spaceman' and he received the 1956 Mackay Trophy for setting the record. The X-2 programme was halted just three weeks later after a fatal crash resulted in the death of Mel Apt in a flight in which Apt became the first person to exceed Mach 3. Three years later, Kincheloe was selected as one of the first three pilots in the next rocket-powered aircraft programme, the X-15 and would have been part of the 'Man In Space Soonest' project. He was buried with full military honours at Arlington National Cemetery. He was only thirty years old. Altogether, eight service test air vehicles, including the two XF-104s, were destroyed during the period of Starfighter testing, 1955-November 1959.

On 2 November 1959 YF-104A/JF-104A 55-2964 piloted by 34-year old Major James

William Bradbury of the Directorate of Flight and All Weather Test section at Wright Patterson AFB, Ohio was lost approximately ninety seconds after takeoff. Bradbury taxied out to the active runway and at 0942 (Eastern Standard Time) the tower cleared the JF-104A for take-off on runway 23-Right with a left turn out of traffic'. Bradbury was given a wind direction of 310 degrees. He pointed the needle-like nose straight down the long airstrip. Upon brake release he switched on the photo-panel camera and advanced the throttle slowly into the afterburner/reheat range according to the instructions received in the pre-flight briefing. Takeoff was normal. With a trail of flame produced by the afterburner 55-2964 rapidly accelerated to take-off speed. Bradbury rotated and entered the ascent phase of flight but when he retarded the throttle to disengage the afterburner he heard and felt a moderate explosion. Bradbury radioed the tower and declared an emergency, reported engine problems and gave the aircraft's position as east of Wright Field. The tower operator answered immediately and stated that he had seen a flash out of the tailpipe'. Bradbury 'decided that he could not make the field and to attempt it would only place him over a populated area for bail out. He informed

YF-104 55-2964. This Starfighter was lost on 2 November 1959. The pilot, Major James W. Bradbury, ejected but the Starfighter hit a house killing two small children whose mother also died, six days later.

F-104D 57-1329 in the 479th TFW at Tinker AFB, Ohio, which crashed on 22 May 1961. The pilot, Captain Robert Gerald Ashcraft evacuated the aircraft safely after it crossed over the taxi way where the left main and nose gear sheared and slid to a stop. The aircraft was soon repaired.

the tower of his intention to proceed southeast to an open area and bail out and squawked emergency on the IFF frequency. By then the crippled F-104 was losing altitude and Bradbury knew that with the Stanley Aviation Corporation C-1 downward ejection seat he could not delay his ejection much longer. This feature made low-altitude ejections dangerous and 21 American pilots died after activating the units.

Bradbury was over relatively open countryside and could see no appreciable change in topography ahead so at approximately 0947 and about two minutes from brake release at an estimated altitude of 1,000 feet he reported he was bailing out. As Bradbury reached for the O-Ring to activate the ejection seat the Starfighter suddenly pitched downward so he reached back to the stick, pulled the nose up slightly and again reached for the O-Ring and ejected. The seat separation and chute deployment took place automatically with the chute opening at an estimated 500 feet. Hanging beneath the parachute canopy Major Bradbury observed the JF-104A make a slight turn to the left. Tragically, the Starfighter struck the ground in a very shallow

angle just to the rear of a frame out-building and careened into the northwest corner of a brick house. Two young sisters, one age twelve and the other two years of age inside the structure were undoubtedly killed immediately. The girls' 34-year-old mother dashed from the inferno that erupted around and in what had been the house, a converted brick school building, with her clothing afire. Simultaneously a man was driving past the house when the plane hit and slid across a road which was more than fifty feet away. Fire completely enveloped his vehicle. He lost control and hit a ditch about fifty yards down the road. When the driver saw the house he realized that the structure was a complete wreck and he spotted the mother running cross the yard with her clothing alight. Neighbours extinguished the flames by beating the burning fabric and then rushed the screaming woman to a hospital where she died six days later.

Major Bradbury extricated himself from the tree and walked, unhurt, a few metres to an adjacent home and telephoned WPAFB to report the accident. The following day a *Dayton Daily News* account noted the pilot's survival: 'Major

In 1959 the US Navy at NWTC China Lake were loaned three YF-104A/F-104As (55-2956 and 56-0740 and 56-0757 and crewed by USAF personnel from the 83rd FIS) to test the effectiveness of the AIM-9 Sidewinder AAM at supersonic speeds. The majority of the test firings took place during 1960-61. The YF-104 later became a QF-104A drone. On 22 September 1960 F-104A 56-0740 (pictured) crashed into the southern face of Josephine Peak at an elevation of 4,500 feet; the cause of the crash was thought to be oxygen depletion at altitude. Captain Howard O. Casada Jr. USMC was killed.

F-104A-15-LOs 56-0777 and three F-104A-20-LO Starfighters, 56-0805, 0808 and 0810 of the 83rd Fighter Interceptor Squadron from Hamilton AFB, San Francisco, passing the Golden Gate Bridge in 1958. The 83rd FIS became operational on 20 February 1958. On 14 September 1972 56-0777 crashed in Royal Jordanian Air Force service. 56-0805 was sent to Pakistan on 21 June 1961. 56-0808 was written off in RoCAF service on 16 April 1984. 56-0810 was lost at Homestead AFB, Florida on 17 November 1966 after an engine flame out due to fuel starvation during the landing pattern. (Lockheed)

Bradbury is one of the few men to survive ejection from a Starfighter one Air Force source said.'

In 1959 the Navy Weapons Training Center (NWTC) at China Lake were loaned three YF-104A/F-104As to test the effectiveness of the AIM-9 Sidewinder air-to-air missile at supersonic speeds. (At this time the Navy was still awaiting delivery of its own high-performance jets such as the Chance Vought F9U Crusader). Testing using YF-104A-2 (55-2956) and two F-104As (56-0740 and 56-0757), all of which were crewed by US Air Force personnel from the 83rd Fighter Interceptor Squadron, began in 1959 although the majority of the Sidewinder missile test firings took place during 1960 and 1961. The YF-104 completed the AIM-9 test programme safely and later became a QF-104A drone, but F-104A 56-0740 crashed at China Lake on 22 September 1960 and 56-0757 was also lost when it crashed on 7 April 1961.

On 7 April 1961 F-104A 56-0757 stationed at NAS China Lake crashed just off the north end of the runway on takeoff from George AFB on the return flight to China Lake following the failure of the afterburner. Captain David Lanstaff Hess USMC evacuated the aircraft but he suffered 52% burns to his body and was flown to Brooke General Hospital in Fort Sam Houston, Texas where he died on 28 April.

Originally, the F-104A was intended to equip Tactical Air Command where it was to replace its F-100 Super Sabres beginning in 1958, but delays in Starfighter delivery and a more urgent requirement by Air Defense Command for a fighter-interceptor changed all this. The first batch of F-104As was delivered (as an interim measure pending delivery of the F-106 Delta Dart), to ADC on 26 January 1958 and the 83rd Fighter Interceptor Squadron at Hamilton AFB near San Francisco became operational on 20 February. The

F-104A-20-LOs 56-0769 and 56-0781 of the 83rd Fighter Interceptor Squadron from Hamilton AFB, San Francisco, California in formation near the Golden Gate bridge. (Lockheed)

83rd FIS also became the first unit to receive the F-104B two-seat trainer version of the Starfighter, in early 1958. However, just three months after going into service the squadron's F-104As were grounded after a succession of accidents caused by compressor stall and flame-out of the J79 turbojet engine. When this happened not only did the F-104 lose power, extremely critical in an aircraft with such high wing loading, but it also lost engine-driven flap-blowing. At low altitudes this was usually fatal. (Blown flaps for both leading and trailing edges had to be adopted for the F-104A. This provided a thin sheet of very high energy air, preventing breakaway and separation, increasing lift and reducing crucial stalling speed by fifteen knots. Landing speed of the F-104 was high for its time, nearly 150 knots and its sink rate on the approach was considerable.)

The first operational loss of an F-104 occurred on 3 March 1958 when F-104A 56-776 in the 83rd FIS crashed on final approach two miles short on final into the San Pablo Bay when the engine quit, killing the pilot, Lieutenant Colonel Raymond E. Evans (36) the Squadron commander. Colonel Evans had flown 154 combat missions in WWII and 48 F-86 combat missions in the Korean War. He was also a test pilot. Colonel Evans was recovered from the cockpit in about ten feet of water. Hamilton's F-104s were grounded

for approximately seven weeks following this accident. Hamilton had received the F-104s just eleven days prior. The Starfighters remained grounded for three months while a new General Electric-3B engine was fitted.

During 1958 three other ADC units were equipped with F-104As and F-104Bs. In April the 337th FIS at Westover AFB, Massachusetts received its Starfighters and in June the 538th FIS

Lieutenant Colonel James 'Jabby' Jabara, the first USAF jet ace who in early 1957 helped test the F-104s in the 3243rd Test Group at Eglin AFB, Florida.

Lieutenant Colonel John W. Bennett, CO, 83rd FIS at Hamilton AFB at the time of the Quemoy Crisis in August 1958 beside his Starfighter, *Vociferous Viking*.

at Larson AFB, Washington was also so equipped. In July the 56th FIS at Wright-Patterson AFB, Ohio commanded by Lieutenant Colonel John E. Gaffney became the fourth and final Starfighter squadron in Air Defence Command. By January 1957 Lieutenant Colonel James 'Jabby' Jabara, the first USAF jet ace, was at Eglin Air Force Base, Florida to join the 3243rd Test Group to test F-104 Starfighters before assuming command of the 337th FIS at Westover. Late on the afternoon of 15 July 1953, Jabara shot down his 15th MiG-15, making him a triple ace and the second-highest-scoring jet ace in Korea, next to Captain Joseph McConnell, who scored sixteen MiG kills. In August 1958 during the Quemoy and Matsu crisis with Red China, Jabara and the 337th went to Taiwan, where they flew their F-104s near the coast of mainland China for three months. 'We used to fly up and down the Straits of Formosa at…twice the speed of sound,' Jabara recalled 'and had the Chinese Communists take a look at us on their radar…I'm sure it shook them up a little.' Jabara flew with the 337th until July 1960.

On 23 August 1958 China began massive artillery shelling of Quemoy, a tiny group of islands off the China coast but was still held by General Chiang Kai-shek's Nationalist China Government in Taiwan. The US was committed to defend Taiwan. In response to the shelling of

Quemoy the 7th fleet was ordered into the Taiwan Straits and provided naval escort of Nationalist re-supply ships to Quemoy up to the three miles limit. In Operation 'Jonah Able', twelve F-104As of the 83rd FIS at Hamilton AFB now commanded by Lieutenant Colonel John W. Bennett were disassembled, crated and airlifted by USAF Douglas C-124 Globemasters on temporary deployment to Tao Yuan Air Base, near Taipei in Taiwan. (Although a few F-104As had been fitted with an experimental air refuelling probe none of the production batch was fitted with the device).

F-104A 83rd FIS at Taoyuan AFB Taiwan on 15 September 1958 during Operation 'Jonah Able', the US response to the Quemoy Crisis.

The first cargo aircraft of the movement departed Hamilton AFB on 8 September, less than 48 hours after the official notification. The first F-104A arrived in Taiwan on 11 September. Within thirty hours, at 1600 hours on 12 September the first F-104A flown by the Squadron Commander was airborne to defend the Republic of China. In December the control of the twelve F-104As was transferred to the 337th FIS. The shelling of Quemoy was reduced on 13 September and was suspended on 6 October. The F-104As were all transferred back to McClellan AFB in Sacramento, California for depot maintenance work in March 1959. They were later transferred to other units within the Air Defense Command.

Deliveries of the Starfighter to ADC (later Aerospace Defense Command) continued until December 1958 when the final eight F-104As of the 153 built were delivered. The Pentagon had provided the bulk of the $30 million cost of the four-year F-104 flight test programme so they might have been expected to persevere with the F-104. However, they decided otherwise and to cut their losses. By December 1958 the USAF reduced its Starfighter procurement from a total of 722, to just 296.

The F-104A had the speed and the altitude to deter an aggressor, but the anticipated early availability of more flexible supersonic fighters and the lack of an all-weather radar capability led to a review of the entire F-104 programme. (Lockheed had tried, unsuccessfully, to install the radar sight system in the needle nose and it had proved totally inadequate in range and power - on

Top left: AIM Sidewinder AAMs ready for loading during Operation 'Jonah Able' when twelve F-104As in the 83rd FIS at Hamilton AFB were deployed to Taiwan. Main picture: F-104A-20-LO 56-0791 in the 83rd FIS at its revetment at Tao Yuan AB near Taipei in Taiwan

Top right: Ordnancemen loading AIM Sidewinder AAMs on the wingtip of an F-104A during Operation 'Jonah Able', the US response to the Quemoy Crisis.

NF-104A models. Boosted by a 6,000lb Rocketdyne AR-2 auxiliary rocket engine, they zoomed astronauts aloft in a training programme conducted at Edwards AFB, California (see Chapter 11).

YF-104-LO 55-02959 with a Regulus II which was designed as the supersonic follow-on to the Navy's Regulus I ship-launched cruise missile. Airframe GM-2001 made the first test flight of a Regulus II vehicle at Edwards AFB on Tuesday, 29 May 1956. The USN would go on to conduct 47 more Regulus II flight tests through November 1958 but the emergence of the UGM-27 Polaris Submarine-Launched Ballistic Missile (SLBM) rendered the Regulus II missile obsolete amd the Navy cancelled the programme in December 1958.

a good day it had a radar sight range of between five to ten miles. The type of radar required for a supersonic interceptor capable of Mach 2+, if it was to be effective, was too big and heavy for the F-104.)

Disastrously for Lockheed only 153 F-104As were built and just twenty-six F-104B trainer versions, the first flying on 7 February 1957. (Lockheed ultimately produced just 277 F-104A/B/C/Ds for the USAF). F-104As and -Bs equipped the 83rd, 56th and 337th Interceptor Squadrons for less than a year before they were handed over to the 151st, 157th and 197th Squadrons of the Air National Guard, although later some F-104As, fitted with the GE-19 engine, returned to first-line service. Twenty-four F-104As were converted to QF-104 target drones, while three were modified to

Below: The Starfighters was released in 1964 but it did not go into wide release and was labeled one of Paste magazine's '10 most unwatchable films'.

THE BLAZING ADVENTURE of the men and planes who rocket to the very edge of OUTER SPACE!

THE STARFIGHTERS

TECHNICOLOR®

Starring
ROBERT · RICHARD · SHIRLEY · RICHARD
DORNAN · JORDAHL · OLMSTED · MASTERS
Written, Produced and Directed by WILL ZENS
A ROBERT PATRICK Presentation · Distributed thru PARADE PICTURES

F-104C-5-LO 56-0894 of the 476th TFS, 479th TFW, which crashed on 2 August 1961 after the loss of the main gear door caused structural damage to the flap and stabilizer which caused a loss of control 44 miles SE of Morón AB, Spain. The pilot was killed.

They Flew The 'Zipper'

Even when I was a kid, the Starfighter was my favourite airplane and it was the first plastic model that I built in the '50s. Then twenty years later, I actually got to fly it after stints in the F-4 Phantom and then the AT-38 'Lead-In Fighter' (training new fighter pilots with gun, rockets, bombs and air combat flying). After flying the 'Zipper' in Europe for three years, I finished off my Air Force career in the F-111 and the EF-111.

The Starfighter was difficult to learn to fly and it did 'bite' many pilots, but that just increased the mystique and the pride of mastering it. Besides 'Widowmaker', the F-104 had all kinds of nicknames including 'Missile with a Man in It' and of course - 'ZIPPER'. The movie 'The Right Stuff' had the F-104 sequences filmed at Luke Air Force Base in Arizona, but I had transferred to Germany to fly with NATO pilots. In the early '80's many NATO nations still flew the 'Starfighter' and I gave Tactical Evaluations around Europe with weeklong war games at their bases. It was a great adventure that I'll never forget. I flew over 1000 hours in the F-104G, the Italian 'S' and the Turkish 'MAP' Starfighters from 1979 to 1985.

The 'Zipper' carried only 5,800lbs of fuel internal plus two tip tanks with 1,100lbs each. For nuclear strike missions it carried an additional two tanks with 1,200lbs each. On most missions, we were expected to be in the landing pattern with 1,200 remaining to give us a twenty minute reserve. At the 450 to 510 knots speeds flown, that still only gave about a two hour or so mission carrying a B61 nuclear bomb. We did fly with that configuration, but of course, with a 'shape' instead of the actual B61. Normal training or tactical check ride missions were with two tip tanks, 4 x 25lb blue BDU33 smoke bombs for 'iron sight' dive bombing (no computers) and two orange Mk106s for 'skip' bomb simulation of Napalm. These were also used to simulate drogue chute nuclear deliveries. We also carried 2.75 inch folding fin rockets plus 100 20mm rounds for the internal M61 cannon. Although I always stayed qualified in dive bombing and did fairly well in the monthly 'Turkey Shoots', my best events were skip bomb, rockets and gun which got me 'Top Gun' occasionally. Just as a comparison, using equivalent distances releasing the bomb (High Altitude 4,500 feet pull-off for small arms fire) and the qualification bombing circle diameter, getting the bomb in the circle is equivalent to sinking a 40 foot putt every time! A clean F-104 without the tip tanks had 23 feet wingspan and what a climb & roll rate!

A magnificent engineering marvel, the F-104 'Century Series' Starfighter was a real joy to fly and was the first production fighter to exceed MACH 2 in level flight! ... and I flew it!

Yes, the F-104 'Zipper' is still my favourite fighter - single seat, single engine, deadly and FAST! - A Fighter Pilot's pride!

Mach II in the 'Zipper' over Arizona by 'Ike' Sweesy

In November 1956 Mike Vivian, formerly an aviation mechanic and crew chief in the Arizona Air National Guard entered USAF pilot training as an Aviation Cadet. During the course of training, he was assigned to Graham Air Base, Marianna Florida, where he flew the T-34 and T-28 and Greenville AFB, Mississippi, where he flew the T-33. Upon graduation and subsequent completion of F-86D training at Perrin AFB, Texas, he was re-assigned to the Arizona ANG at Phoenix. In March 1958 he was assigned to the 197th Fighter Interceptor Squadron which flew the F-86L. As

a guard pilot he was regularly scheduled for alert duty and was frequently 'scrambled' as a part of the Air Defense Command. 'About that time we heard a noise that we had never heard before. With its distinctive howl, except maybe for a hunter who had experienced a lonely wolf in the White Mountains, the J79 equipped F-104 was coming to Phoenix. Well, we began training in earnest. Ground school started in Phoenix but also temporary duty at George AFB California for systems training was part of the programme. And then back to Phoenix as the aircraft began to arrive. Not all was smooth as one of the first to arrive blew two tyres. Another, a B model with one of USAF pilots aboard, came in too low over the overrun and caught the cable of the chain link fence with one leg of the main landing gear. As he started a go-around the cable just pulled the right main landing gear leg out of the bottom of the airplane. The subsequent two gear landing at nearby Luke AFB was not uneventful as the airplane departed the hard surface of the runway and skidded out into the gravel. Although repairable, it was a long time before that B was flyable again.

'And then it was my turn. I was to fly a B ride for checkout with Lieutenant Colonel Phillip Rand, our USAF advisor. We briefed, pre-flighted, strapped in and I signalled for the ground turbine compressor to start. With the GPU up to speed, I raised one of the ignition switches and the air hose inflated. As engine RPM came up, I opened the throttle to idle at 10-12% and signalled one finger to the crew chief. As RPM continued to increase, the now familiar rumble of combustion occurred and EGT began to rise.

Twenty percent, two fingers, thirty percent, three fingers and at forty percent four fingers. I watched the GPU air hose deflate. As the engine continued to accelerate to idle, it seemed the whole machine had come to life. It was not a vibration but more like a tone. A low frequency pulse was felt through the downward ejection seat as the generators came on line and radios began to work. After all the checks, taxi to the runway, canopy closed and ejection seat pins removed, we took Runway 8 for departure. Engine checks all normal, brake release, then afterburner. Acceleration was fantastic! After being accustomed to the acceleration rate of the heavy F-86L, this was a ride on a rocket! Our departure was to the east and Colonel Rand had suggested we make an afterburner climb to 35,000 feet. Well it was a ride to never forget! A clean B model, in AB, nose up but still unable to keep the airspeed at 400. Rand said it was OK for the speed to go to 450 for an AB climb. I really tried and as best as I could but airspeed was only in the vicinity. But it

General Curtis E. LeMay, commanding SAC, suiting up for a flight in F-104B 56-3720 in 1958. This Starfighter was lost on 8 January 1963 at the Eglin AFB ranges in Florida during a remote control training flight when the crew were scheduled as chase aircraft on a QF-104 drone.

didn't make any difference 'cause all of a sudden here was point nine Mach. I just held onto that as all of a sudden here was Flight level 350. It couldn't have been much over two minutes and here we were already! So now it was time to solve the pitch trim as our acceleration was already pushing us above Mach one. I tried so hard to keep us level and probably never did completely stop the altimeter when Colonel Rand suggested a bit of nose down trim. It seemed to work as the machine seemed to begin to groan as the Mach meter just raced around the instrument.

'At 1.7 or maybe 1.8 Mach, T-2 reset started and the engine RPM increased to 104%. Actually, even more acceleration was easily felt. Here came Mach two and immediately Colonel Rand said now let's start a slow climbing turn and slowly come out of afterburner. I started the turn and as I retarded the throttle, the entire cockpit filled with FOG! I thought explosive decompression and it was, but it was caused by a Flame-out! We had flamed out! First ride in the airplane and I had broken it! Colonel Rand said, 'Keep the turn going! Back towards Phoenix'! Well, I tried but as I felt him shake the stick, I knew he wanted control. So I just sat back and let him fly. It seems the fog was beginning to go away and I was able to see the instruments again. I certainly could now see the RPM going down to 40%. I do not recall if we had interphone during all of this but I do recall the RPM just did not want to come back up, no matter how often I hit the starter switches. As a matter of fact, the EGT was also on the bottom of the gage. I do not recall our descent back to Sky Harbour save for the part when the engine finally started and the RPM again began to follow the throttle. Colonel Rand gave me back the airplane and I flew a straight in approach to the runway. It was a takeoff flap approach since we had had engine problems. Yep, I landed the machine, used the drag chute to help stop, taxied back and shut down. Guess what, as maintenance lowered the electric access panel, all four boost pump switches were OFF! We had taken off, climbed, gone to altitude, reached Mach two and as long as I never moved the throttle, the J79 just kept running fine! As soon as the throttle was retarded, with no boost pressure, it just ran out of fuel. Well, since I only got one landing that day, I was scheduled for another B model ride before I could solo.

'Solo came soon as we were already hearing rumours of having to go on active duty soon. We didn't know where, but as Guardsmen, we were always subject to being called up if the Active folks needed us. As it turned out, we started making plans for Germany. At first we thought we would just fly to Ramstein AB and we started making a lot of four tank rides around the Arizona desert just to see how far we could go and how many hops it would take to get us there. But it was not to be. Caution said there were too many possible problems hopping across the Atlantic. So we were not surprised to see the C-124 Globemasters begin to arrive. Lots of activity was apparent as wings were removed, tails taken apart and fighters being pushed into the giant swinging doors of the transport. Proficiency flying suffered a bit as we were all trying to stay current with the T-33, hardly a craft to keep one sharp enough for the F-104. But as the summer days became fall we finished all the going away parties and got on board. My ride to Germany was in a C-54. Actually I was happy 'cause just the day before I had seen a C-124 Globemaster make three attempts to take-off. He had aborted each time for some reason. Finally, with his departure, I knew it was serious.

'Arrival in Germany was filled with reassembly of fighters, running over perfectly good horizontal stabilizers with fork lift trucks and getting bedded down in ancient quarters equipped with steam heat. As aircraft became ready, the German weather would not give us our minimums we needed for our first rides. So we sat. It was probably good for our maintenance guys as they had extra time to fine tune the machines for the day the weather would permit flying. And fly we did, only to be met one morning by a picture of our first bird, on its first flight, on final approach, gear and flaps down right there in the gunsight of a Canadian Sabre. The photo, taken from gun camera film, was posted on our Squadron's front door. And so we were welcomed to Germany. But we were not prepared for the lower temperatures, icy taxi ways, (engage nose wheel steering, turn right to park and watch as the aircraft continued straight ahead). But we learned to take it easy. Engines had other problems as compressor corrosion, or other problems made engine stalls and subsequent high speed landings all too frequent. And then there were other problems with tire failures and the lack of a tail hook on the A model to catch a barrier cable to help get stopped.

'One takeoff turned into a disaster when Jim Floor decided to stop, after a right main gear tire burst. His early braking attempts only got the wheel ground down to a flat spot and when he crossed the Barrier cable, it caused the fighter to turn right and go up the high speed taxi way into the F-102 alert facility. Of course he got it stopped, but the pylon tank had been dragging on the ground for long enough to cause a fuel leak. This caused fuel to run into the hot wheel and brake assembly and fire was immediate. As he opened the canopy he was immediately met with flames coming in from the right side. So he closed the canopy, jettisoned it and then was able to exit the airplane to the left side. Naturally, he came to an abrupt stop when, at the end of the dingy lanyard, he was jerked backwards. But he finally unhooked the lanyard and got away only to see the arrival of the fire trucks. That was good, he thought, but it was not so. As the F-104 burned, the fire truck could not produce any foam to put out the blaze. Scratch one beautiful fighter which melted right there on the taxiway. But I've mentioned only the rough spots. That's not totally fair and may give an inaccurate picture of the absolute magnificence of the performance; not only of the Arizona ANG but also of the F-104 we began to love. Yes, its radar was not as good as what we had in the old F-86. The gunsight was pegged as we had no computing sight since we had no gun. A five inch ballast weight was installed. But we were high and we were fast and Tom Delashaw and Ray Holt were showing the Soviets we were capable of 90,000 feet! It was a good show. Yep we learned to shoot the Sidewinder, the AIM 9, but it was also only the beginning model so it too had problems. My first shot was at a 5 inch rocket fired from the left wingtip. As it accelerated away, one of the flares

on its fin broke off. My Sidewinder, looking for the first heat source, found the flare instead of the five inch rocket and detonated almost directly in front of my aircraft! I flew directly through the debris. As it turned out, no damage was apparent and the landing back at Wheelus AFB, Libya was uneventful. I'll never forget the return trip through Pisa, Italy where my flight leader, (then) Captain Don Owens and I stopped for fuel. Of course we had to visit the leaning tower.

'Back in Germany, we flew, had many successes, made a few errors and as soon as it had begun, were on our way back to Phoenix. Well, I did not want to leave the F-104. I asked for and received what was called extended active duty. This meant, if selected, I could remain in the active Air Force and be re-assigned based on the needs of the USAF. As it turned out, I was re-assigned to George AFB California, home of the 479th Tactical Fighter Wing. I was assigned to the 476th Tactical Fighter Squadron (TFS) which flew the F-104C.

'To me this was all new. Not only was a cannon installed, we had a real gunsight and a centreline bomb rack that was nuclear capable. With 30 inch lugs, as opposed to the 14 inch lugs necessary for conventional weapons, I was suddenly in the bombing business. I had never dropped a bomb before. I had never fired a six barrel Gatling gun before and I had never refuelled in flight before. Talk about suddenly being thrown into the first team, I was ecstatic! We were briefed, taught,

F-104C Starfighters in the 434th TFS, 476th TFS. (Jim Flemming)

cajoled, convinced, watched and written about. One of my first Officer Effectiveness reports reads, *Lt. Vivian was one of my most improved pilots this reporting period*. Talk about being non committal. But it was progress. We learned and we became ready for the next task which was South East Asia and Viêtnam. Because The US was committed to the South East Asia Treaty Organization, our unit was placed on standby status in preparation for that deployment. We sat, flew refuelling missions, fired at and hit the Dart! It was clear were to be in an air defence posture if we went to Asia. I chose to leave. Volunteer assignments were coming in regularly for duty with the South Viêtnamese Air Force. We would fly with the VNAF in single seat Skyraiders, the A-1HI went to Naval Air Station Corpus Christi, Texas for checkout. In no time I found myself leaving family, wife and children at George while getting ready to use this huge single engined eighteen cylinder fighter bomber equipped with fourteen bomb stations and eight hundred rounds of 20 millimetres to engage our opponent. No it was not meant to be agile, or accelerate, or even be fast. All of that was left behind. Now it was a manual bombsight, visual slant range, Kentucky windage and a pickle button. But it was amazing. Rewarding in its accuracy, when a worthy target was found and reliable in that for every takeoff I made, I got at least one landing. We lost no aircraft save for a comedy of errors at Biên Hòa Air Base one day when incoming rockets and a bad parking

plan, together with revetments made of tritonal filled bomb cases caused numerous Skyraiders and B-57 Bombers to be lost. A real fiasco. The report at the Command Center in Sàigòn was 'Numerous aircraft going up in ripple'. The problem was not our allies and their outdated Skyraider aircraft, or our fighter bomber efforts made up of F-100 and, at that time A-37 aircraft. It was totally our command decision to run the war from Washington. I cannot think of a single target that was struck that was not first provided approval from the Washington Military Command Center. Local commanders, who knew the people, knew the defences, knew their area of responsibility and knew what weapons would work!, were repeatedly overruled by the Washington idea, although dismal, of graduated increase in pressure placed upon the military efforts of the north by the Johnson administration and his Secretary of Defense Robert S. McNamara. I retch each time I think of the closeness of success and the singular reason for failure.'

'Ike' Sweesy's best mission was a January flight taking off from Luke AFB early in the morning when it was nice and cool. 'From a standing start, the J79 afterburner had a hard light that really gave a clean 104 a real kick. Acceleration was awesome with liftoff at about 170 knots as I recall

F-104C-5-LOs 56-60903, 56-0908, 56-0906 and 56-0907 of the 479th TFW, Tactical Air Command on a training mission from George AFB. 56-0907, which was the aircraft of the Commander of the 434th TFS, Lieutenant Colonel John Rosenbaum, was flown by the 434th Ops Officer, Captain Ed Skelton who was leading a four ship formation on 29 January 1959 when it crashed 5 miles SW of George AFB. Ed was taking off on the long runway at George AFB. As he rotated and the gear started to come up he had a compressor stall and a complete loss of power. The 104 nosed over and hit the ground dead flat about 600 metres from the runway end. Skelton was unhurt apart from minor abrasions after ejecting and was flying again within a week. It was the first F-104C lost due to a crash. F-104C 56-0906 was lost on 19 July 1960 during a live firing exercise when it made an emergency landing on a dry lake bed near China Lake following nozzle problems. Captain John Houston was killed. He radioed that he was going to land on Cuddeback Dry Lake. 56-908, which is fitted with a removable in-flight refuelling probe, was lost at Chu Lai, South Việtnam on 22 July 1965 while assigned to the 436th TFS when it swerved off the runway into a sand dune after a gear up landing. 56-0903 was lost on 27 July 1966 after the aircraft control stick kicker activated 16 miles SW of George AFB. (Lockheed)

The Bundes Luftwaffe flew officially for the first time on 24 September 1956, the biggest problem being the recruitment of pilot trainees and technical ground staff, but although there were many candidates, it was soon found that relatively few of them were fit for training on jets. Training began under the auspices of the USAF at Fürstenfeldbruck, a station already housing a NATO flying training school (T-33 conversion). In January 1956 a small batch of pilots reported for initial flying training at Landsberg where they were checked out on Piper L-18Cs. All had been flying on operations in World War II on such aircraft as Bf 109s and Stukas. After completing their basic flying on the T-6G Texan, they reported to 'Fursty' for training on the Lockheed T-33 at the end of May and on 24 September 1956 ten pilots received their wings during a big parade and hand-over ceremony of the first three aircraft bearing the insignia of the new Luftwaffe. The youngest of these pilots was Oberleutnant Werner Forster, aged 29, who had entered the Luftwaffe at the age of 16, had been flying Bf 109s and Fw 190s and finally, the Heinkel He 162 Volksjäger at the end of the war. The two oldest pilots were Major Fritz Schröter who had joined the former Luftwaffe in 1936 and Hauptmann Heinz Dudeck, both 40 years old. They were not the first Germans to get their wings as some staff officers – Hauptmanns Steinhoff, Kurt Kuhlmey and Dietrich 'Dieter' Hrabak and Majors Gerhard 'Gerd' Barkhom, Krupinsky and Herbert Wehnelt (the last three, pictured, with Colonel Ray Toliver USAF at 3FTS for a flying refresher course at RAF Feltwell in 1956) - had already been trained in the USA and in Britain. The other pilots were Hauptmanns' Werner Siebert (36), Gerhard Limberg (36), Gunter Ludigkeit (37), Axel Stuth (34), Hans Klaffenbach (32) and Oberleutnant Horst Bauer (31) and Klaus Neumann (33).

(fully loaded with bombs the liftoff was up to 227 knots with those small wings!) At 400 knots, I pulled up to about 45 degrees and rocketed up to 40,000 gradually reducing the climb angle as the air got thinner. I turned south towards Gila Bend Gunnery Range and pushed it up to Mach 2. The only indication of this 20th Century speed was the round gage with '2' in the little window! That calculated out to over 1,300 mph! The Arizona of one hundred years earlier was traversed at 'burro speed'. As I entered the unrestricted gunnery range, I gently pulled the nose up bleeding off airspeed to a mere 600 knots, but topping out at 60,000 feet. The sky was black that high up and I could see the curvature of the earth. Black above, the bright blue sky ahead and the brown Arizona dirt below! In full afterburner the whole time, it was a short 20 minute flight and I was at Bingo Fuel already. Easing the throttle out of AB and back to Idle, I pulled the nose around to the northeast and aimed slightly left of Phoenix. LUF TACAN on the nose. I got below FL450 before leaving the gunnery range and continued gliding the sixty or so miles back to 'homeplate'. I actually had to use a little speed brake to get down to 1,500 feet AGL [Above Ground Level] for the 325 knot pitchout and 135 knot touchdown. Adding the standard five minutes for 'taxi time', I logged a seven hour flight for the day and jumped out of my jet with a real smile of satisfaction. It was 7:45 am and most 'ground pounders' were just driving to work.'

Norvin 'Bud' Evans, USAF flight test pilot of all F-104 models at Edwards AFB, California from 1956, recalls: 'Most pilots know what the 'Fire Warning' light on the instrument panel signifies when it illuminates! Most Pilot Manuals just say: 'EJECT'! Well that's well and good but if all pilots followed those instructions when a Fire Light came 'On', the military would be a lot shorter on aircraft than it is. When the light comes 'On' it gets your full attention! Fortunately most of us have checked for more definite signs of actual fire before panicking. What I am about to relate to you happened to me me in 1960. I had been selected to be the USAF's test pilot on the Northrop N-156F (Later to be designated the F-5A). The aircraft was built on Northrop funds but someone in the USAF decided at the last minute that they should put some money into the project and put money into Northrop's programme. (I'm not sure but believe the amount was $33 million). Regardless, it was enough to have the USAF Flight Test Center

furnish a test pilot and flight test engineer to work right along with the Northrop test crew.

'The arrangement was for me to fly from the very beginning of the testing as though I was a company test pilot. This was something the military never did and it is to Tom Jones (President of Northrop) credit that he went along with the agreement. Lew Nelson was the Chief Test Pilot for the company and was scheduled for the first flight. In order to get his 'Bonus' he had to take the aircraft supersonic but the landing gear unsafe light remained 'On' so he had to return and land. I was chasing him in an F-100F with a Northrop photographer in the back seat and although we could not see any problem with the landing gear from the outside, the prudent thing to do was to cut the flight short. After the ground crew adjusted the micro-switches on the landing gear, Lew made the second flight. It was supposed to have been my flight but with bonus money on the line for Northrop's pilot, I couldn't argue. From that point on in the programme, I rotated flights with Lew and later some other Northrop Test Pilots. I chased all of the Northrop flights and the incident that I am about to relate happened on one of those flights.

'One of the big problems with it not being a USAF test aircraft was that the J85 engines (which

Norvin 'Bud' Evans, USAF flight test pilot with F-104G DA+113 of the Luftwaffe.

it had been designed to use) were available only for the three T-38s that were being used in the USAF funded test programme. The N-156F had two early J85 engines that had no afterburners and fewer compressor stages than the T-38's engines. They were designed for a missile and the total thrust of the two engines was less than one of the T-38's engines in afterburner. Our testing began on 31 July 1959 and we were operating under the handicap of short funding and it was nearly one year after the first flight when the following event took place. It was July 1960 and we were flying in extremely hot weather from a runway that was nearly 3,000 feet above sea level. The good news was that the runway was 15,000 feet long with a seven mile lakebed overrun.

'We reached the stage in our test programme where we were to see if the aircraft could fly with a 2,200+lb bomb under the centreline station. This put the centre of gravity right at the design forward limit. The engineers predicted that the airspeed would have to be considerably above normal to have enough elevator power to lift the nose-wheel from the runway. It was Lew's turn to fly the first take-off and my flight would be to drop the bomb. I was flying the chase flight in an F-104D with a Northrop photographer in the back seat. We had to wait until Lew was a couple of thousand feet down the runway before I released the brakes on the F-104. It was noon on a 105-degree day and having the very heavy weight with low thrust engines we had predicted it would take 8 to 10,000 feet of roll to get the N-156 airborne. I was judging my timing so as to be airborne with my gear up and in a closing position when he lifted off the runway (if the aircraft was really going to fly with that heavy load).

'The Starfighter accelerated rapidly and as soon as I was airborne I retracted the gear and left my flaps in the 'Take-Off' position. The J79 engine's afterburner had four segments which allowed the pilot to make power adjustments. But because of the tremendous power of the engine the pilot had to use care in the amount of throttle movements he made while operating through those four segments, to prevent the engine from suffering a compressor stall (which was not a desired situation at low altitude). A 'Chase Pilot's' job is to lock his eyes on the aircraft on which he is flying safety chase and cannot take time to check his own instruments This can be serious business if something goes wrong with your aircraft such

as having a fire warning light come on, as you will probably not see it until it is too late to do anything about it. Had I not had the Northrop man in the back seat I would probably not be here to write my account of this adventure!

'I was gaining on the N-156 and we were close to 10,000 feet down the runway when it literally leaped into the air. The photographer called over the hot mike about fire coming from the back of the aircraft. This puzzled me as we were about 50 feet behind the N-156 and about 20 feet above him and I had my eyeballs locked on to it. My first thought was: What's he talking about? I answered that I didn't see any fire coming from the back of Lew's aircraft. His anxious reply peaked my immediate attention! 'Not his aircraft. OURS!' We were now about 300 knots and accelerating when I glanced at my left rear view mirror that was mounted on my windscreen frame. I will never forget nor have I ever been able to adequately describe the sight. All I could see was an extremely bright large orange fireball with a shower of orange sparks blazing from the outer portion of the ball of fire. It was a bright desert noon and even so the fireball was almost blinding. It appeared as though the whole aircraft just behind the rear seat was merrily blazing away. If the fire warning light was 'ON' I will never know. Instinct made me retard the throttle rapidly being conscious that too quick of a movement from afterburner towards 'Idle' would cause me to lose the engine. We were approaching the end of the 15,000 foot runway; the altitude was about 100 feet as I guess I pulled back a little the stick while reducing the power as fast as practical. I needed to slow the aircraft quickly and set it down on the lakebed. Ejecting seemed not to be an option at that low altitude. I had full tip tanks and was afraid that if they didn't jettison evenly, we would roll right into the ground. I vaguely remember the tower calling me advising that my aircraft was on fire. It was a little late as I was already well aware of the fact!

'Speed brakes were already extended while adjusting my overtake speed of the N-156F. I put the landing gear handle to the 'Down' position, although I knew I was still above the gear down speed limit. I also was aware that I had to get the aircraft on the ground immediately. The landing gear lights indicated that they were down and locked. There were many things racing through my mind in those long seconds: First I knew that my best method of getting on the ground was to make a gentle turn so as to help judge my height above the flat steaming lakebed surface which produced a severe 'Mirage' effect. As soon as I reached 225 knots I lowered full flaps, rolled wings level and put the aircraft on the ground above 200 knots. I knew that the lakebed had very large holes on the surface, which was not marked by runway lines, but I had no choice. (When it rained every few years the lakebed would flood. In the following weeks the wind would blow the water back and forth over the surface smoothing it to a hard smooth surface. The water also had to find its way down to the underground river that was 1,600 feet below the lake, thus these large holes were created in various parts of the large lake surface).

'My flight controls had become noticeably stiff and I was thinking that the aft section of the F-104 might be burning off of the rest of the aircraft. Once on the ground I began to realize there was no way of avoiding one of these holes, even if I saw it front of me. The 'Mirage effect' made everything in front appear as though there was a lake that I was running into. When I was solidly on the ground I shut down the engine, I pulled the drag chute handle. I felt a slight tug on the aircraft and then it felt as though we accelerated as the chute obviously departed from the aircraft. Shutting down the engine caused me to lose my power brakes, nose wheel steering and radio. All that I could do was pray we would miss the lakebed holes (which would have ended this adventure and the two of us permanently). The Starfighter rolled and rolled and rolled. It seemed as though it would never come to a stop. My next sudden concern was a big yellow fuel truck looming directly in front of me. There was a North Base airfield on the Northwest corner of Rogers Dry Lake and the truck was sitting there on the ramp. I pushed on the manual brakes but with very little effect. I can't adequately describe the feeling of helplessness while waiting for the aircraft to gradually slow to a stop. The photographer was out of the back seat on the hot lakebed before we were fully stopped. I wasn't far behind him!

'Quickly moving to the rear of the aircraft I expected to see that the aft portion of the fuselage would be severely scorched. It wasn't until I walked behind the tail and looked back at the tailpipe that I could see what had been happening. One of the afterburner nozzle guides support arm had failed allowing the section to drop down directly into the full flow of afterburning fuel and

directed it straight up into the horizontal stabilizer. The fire burned through the titanium upper engine housing and then burned the rudder and inside of the vertical stabilizer. This housed the actuators for the rudder and stabilator. Both actuators were melted, as were the hydraulic lines to them. It was unbelievable that the aircraft was controllable until touchdown although it was assumed that the controls were frozen in the landing attitude before we landed. It took 10 minutes for the crash trucks to reach us and by then we were both relaxed and ready for the cold drink of water they handed us. It turned out that the 'Fire Warning Harness' did not reach the area where the fire occurred and therefore it was believed that the light never illuminated. You couldn't prove it by me but it wouldn't have changed the way I responded to the situation once I was made aware that we were on FIRE! Yes the Northrop photographer did fly with me again. In fact we flew together on a number of subsequent flights. I was always happy to have him with me.'

During 1960 the F-104As and F-104Bs were phased out of Air Defense Command to make way for the more heavily armed McDonnell F-104A and -B. Starfighters were transferred to three Air National Guard squadrons, beginning in February 1960 with the 157th FIS, South Carolina ANG, which activated at Congaree Air Base ANGB, Eastover in South Carolina. It was renamed McEntire ANGB on 10 November 1961 in honour of Brigadier General Barnie B. McEntire, the late commander of the South Carolina ANG who was killed on 25 May 1961 when he crashed into the Susquehanna River after staying in his crippled F-104A to avoid crashing in a populated area at Harrisburg, Pennsylvania. Barnie McEntire's love of aviation began as a teenager when he washed Piper Cubs at Columbia's Owens Field. After graduating from the University of South Carolina, he entered pilot training in 1939, earned his pilot's wings in 1940 in the Army Air Corps and began a 22-year military career. He served in World War II as chief pilot for Air Transport Command's North Atlantic Division flying B-24 bombers. In 1946 he organized the first South Carolina Guard units. On 18 February 1959 he earned rank of Brigadier General and became the first ANG pilot to be proficient in flying a F-104 Starfighter in 1960. The 151st Fighter Interceptor Squadron, Tennessee ANG was activated at McGhee Tyson Airport, Knoxville, in June and the 197th FIS,

Below: F-104A-25-LO 56-0834 of the 151st Fighter Interceptor Squadron, Tennessee Air National Guard, in front of the 151st hangar at Ramstein Air Base, West Germany in 1961 during the Berlin Crisis. The inscription 'TENN AIR GUARD' was later replaced replaced by 'US AIR FORCE'.

Arizona ANG was activated at Skyharbor Airport, Phoenix in July.

The Berlin Crisis broke out on 13 August 1961 and preparation for the mobilization of ANG flying squadrons was still underway when East German and Soviet troops closed all the crossing points between East and West Berlin by erecting the Berlin Wall. On 30 August President Kennedy ordered the National Guardsmen and Reservists to active duty and he mobilized 28 Guard squadrons, of which eleven were sent to Europe to reinforce USAFE. In late October-early November eight of the tactical fighter units flew to Europe with their 216 aircraft in Operation 'Stair Step,' the largest jet deployment in the Air Guard's history. Because of their short range, sixty Air Guard F-104As of the 917th FIS Arizona ANG at Skyharbor Airport, Phoenix, 157th FIS South Carolina ANG and the 151st FIS Tennessee ANG at McGhee-Tyson ANGV at Knoxville were airlifted in C-124 Globemasters of

the Military Air Transport Service (MATS) during Operation 'Brass Ring'. (Unlike the F-104C the F-104A could not be fitted with a refuelling probe to take on fuel from a KB-50 tanker). Fortunately, the Starfighter was easy to disassemble. The entire tail assembly, including the aft fuselage behind the wing came off as a unit to allow removal of the engine. The forward fuselage was winched aboard a C-124 through the big cargo door in front and stowed according to the predetermined loading plan, surrounded by the tail, wings and nose. The 157th FIS remained at its home base at McEntie for the first three weeks of November before relocating to Morón Air Base in Spain on the 24th. The 151st and 197th Fighter Interceptor Squadrons

Below: F-104A-25-LO 56-0844 of the South Carolina ANG. This Starfighter later served in the RoCAF as '4243' until on 8 February 1988 it crashed due to a compressor stall after taking off near Tai Zhong Port.

were based at Ramstein Air Base, West Germany. The 151st assumed alert duty at Ramstein on 19 December. In addition to the F-104As, each ANG squadron also sent two F-104Bs along for proficiency training while stationed in Europe. The tension ended in the summer of 1962 and the three F-104 squadrons were officially demobilized on 15 August. When these three ANG squadrons returned to the USA they once again came under the control of their respective states, although the 197th FIS F-104A/Bs were retained by the US Air Force (in September 1962 the 197th FIS re-equipped with the Boeing C-97G and it was re-designated the 197th ATS and became MATS-gained).

south Florida because Cuba lacked a bomber force. The Air Force withdrew F-104s from the 159th Fighter-Interceptor Squadron at McEntire ANG base to equip the Homestead squadron.

The 435th TFS deployed to Naval Air Station Key West, Florida to carry out air strikes against targets in Cuba in case an invasion proved to be necessary. Fortunately, the crisis was peacefully resolved. Following the crisis, Air Defense Command (ADC) organized a squadron of F-104As at Homestead AFB to defend against possible intrusions by Cuban fighters. However, the F-104A was armed only with AIM-9 Sidewinder missiles and ADC began retrofitting its F-104As

F-104s 56-0793, 56-0782, 56-0779 and 56-0791 of the South Carolina ANG

When the Cuban Missile Crisis erupted on 22 October 1962 the ANG F-104s were returned to duty with Aerospace Defense Command where they equipped the 319th FIS at Homestead AFB, Florida. On 22 October 1962, before President Kennedy told the nation that missiles were in place in Cuba, the squadron dispersed one third of its force, equipped with nuclear tipped missiles to Hulman Field at the start of the crisis. The F-104s returned to Bunker Hill after the crisis. However, ADC continued to maintain deployed fighters from other squadrons on alert in Florida. ADC decided to make its deployed fighter unit at Homestead AFB permanent and equip it with Starfighters because of the F-104A's superior fighter on fighter performance. ADC had released all its F-104s to the Air National Guard in 1960 because its fire control system was not sophisticated enough to make it an all weather interceptor. However, the lack of all weather capability was not a factor in

with Vulcan cannons. During the first half of 1964, while these planes were being modified, the 479th deployed F-104Cs to Homestead to augment ADC's alert forces there. The 151st FIS ANG gave up its Starfighters in March 1963 when it converted to the Convair F/TF-102A and the 157th FIS ANG relinquished its Starfighters in June 1963 when it re-equipped with the F-102. Also in 1963 the 331st FIS at Webb AFB, Texas received Starfighters that had been assigned to the Air National Guard. Although the F-104A had been withdrawn from active service in 1960 because its fire control system was not compatible with the SAGE (Semi Automatic Ground Environment system) this did not affect the squadron while it operated from Webb, because the 4752nd Air Defence Wing operated a manual NORAD Sector Combat Center.

Walter Elliot Bjorneby, an F-104 pilot in the 319th FIS at Homestead AFB from 1964 to 1967

had amassed 600 hours in the F-86 and 1,500 in the F-102. Born in Alaska, he was always interested in flying, enlisted in the USAF in August 1951, went through airborne radio school, applied for Aviation Cadets, made corporal working on aircraft radios and was finally accepted, starting class in January 53. 'Walt BJ' flew in nine fighter squadrons, which is rather rare, spurning three higher headquarters assignments to stay in the cockpit. He valued flying fighters more than promotion. He flew no less than 150 combat missions in the F-4D/E Phantom in the 366th Tactical Fighter Wing (TFW) at Đà Nẵng, of which fifteen were flown into North Viêtnamese airspace. Bjorneby is credited with kills against five North Viêtnamese S-75/SA-2 'Guideline' Surface to Air missile sites during this period. His last tour had been at Thule in the Deuce and at 40 below it was a sprightly performer.

'Like a takeoff roll of 1,300 feet! But my first ride in the F-104 - hey, I'd been on test hop orders since 1960 and was used to checking gauges on the roll! But after releasing the brakes on the F-104B I'd managed to check three of the five gauges one checks after the burner light and my IP said quietly 'Rotate!' We were nearing 180 KIAS (Knots Indicated Air Speed)! If you don't get the gear handle up as the aircraft breaks ground at 186 you could trap the main gear doors open. No big deal; just nose up to slow below 250 knots and cycle the gear. No blow except to one's pride.

'SAGE was a giant dinosaur of a dual computer that could calculate 600 intercepts simultaneously. Each SAGE system covered roughly a 600 mile square. Many ground radars transmitted data to it - it integrated the inputs and solved each intercept every two seconds. The commands were transmitted to the interceptors by data link. There were two dials, one target altitude, the other commanded altitude and a data-link command steering dot on the scope. A small circle was positioned on the scope where the computer thought the target would be. It was accurate enough even for the 104A's 'spinscan' radar. I liked SAGE and data link after the bugs were gone - it was nice and quiet; the only voice communications were for safety. It even worked pretty good! Never as good, though, as an expert GCI controller who knew the ropes of fighter v fighter combat. For example: 'BJ, Dave here - he's

20 port 15, turning hard into you... hard port 140; he'll be 12 o'clock for 10, 10,000 high...' But to compare SAGE with what we have now - well, the core RAM was 100 kilobytes! It was vacuum tube design, using a lot of twin triode tubes and used ferrite core memory. The beast required 15 tons of air conditioning to keep it from overheating. The SAGE building was five stories high and almost a perfect cube of grey cement. It looked like Stalinist architecture minus windows.'

In addition to single-seat F-104As, 331st FIS at Webb AFB received the two-seat F-104B. The 331st FIS deployed to Puerto Rico during the Dominican Republic Crisis of May 1965 and served as the ADC combat crew training squadron for the F-104, continuing to fly F-104s until it was inactivated in 1967 when its personnel and F-104s transferred to the 4760th Combat Crew Training Squadron, which assumed the F-104 training mission for Royal Jordanian Air Force F-104 pilots. The 4760th was discontinued on 1 October 1967 when the Jordanian pilots were recalled because of the war with Israel. The F-104s were finally phased out when the 319th FIS was deactivated in December 1969. After this, serviceable F-104As and F-104Bs went to Taiwan and Jordan and all non-serviceable aircraft went into storage at the Aerospace Maintenance and Regeneration Center (AMARC) at Davis-Monthan AFB, Arizona.

Walt BJ recalled: 'The 319th was the only combat flying outfit I've ever been in where we had payday afternoon off. The availability rate was limited only by parts. The airplane was extremely reliable. The radar could be changed in twenty minutes; the engine in two hours. Every comm/ electronic box could be changed at the end of the runway in the quick check area in matter of a few minutes - and was. Our QC crew had spare boxes in their van and saved many a sortie.

'ADC had an exercise where they put up targets in a racetrack and tested the unit on how many sorties it could crank out. One afternoon we put sixty sorties up in three hours. The pilots were RTB'ing in AB and the ground crews were giving us fifteen minute turnarounds!

'The F-104 is the only airplane I ever heard of where the squadron dog would exceed all the Flight Manual red line limits - 750 knots, M2.0 and 100C engine inlet temp and the SLOW light which came on at 121C in the generator cooling air duct. The bird originally had the GE-J79-3B engine and by the time I got to fly it that engine was getting worn out. The engine frames were so warped now that hot air leaks would set off the aft overheat light if one got too slow at altitude (generally under 315 knots or so). Finally a fine officer and gentleman Colonel (now Brigadier General Retd) Dave Rippetoe got us the J79-19 engine. This is the same engine that is in the F-104S and a variant of the F-4E engine. The replacement was simple enough so that the majority were installed in the squadron.

'The -3B gave us 9,600lbs in military and 14,000 in AB - when it was new, that is. The -19 gave us 12,850 in military and 18,900 in afterburner, later reduced for peacetime longevity to 11,870/17,500. Suffice to say the increase in performance was outstanding. The old bird would take about 4 minutes to get to Mach 2 from .9, covering about 100 miles and using about all the fuel one could spare. The new bird took 1 minute 45 seconds, 27 miles and 1,000 lbs of fuel! We normally flew 1:20 sorties clean (no external tanks); now we could fly 1:30. The bird now cruised at 35000 at 315 knots at 2,700 PPH. Two reasons for greater efficiency, a new nozzle and a higher compression ratio in the compressor. With 2 x 165 gallon tip tanks we could now go HST - Big Spring, Texas, BGS to Palmdale, 2 hop XC from Florida to California.

'We intercepted U-2 fairly often on their training flights, usually above 60,000. Of course we had to wear p-suits. Fuel was our limitation on the old bird; we couldn't afford to wait more than about five minutes if he was behind on his ETA.

Colonel (now Brigadier General Retd) Dave Rippetoe. ▮

But with the new bird! I was fortunate enough to fly the first U-2 mission and during pre-brief the controller at MOADS and I talked it over. Of course he had nothing in his computer about the bird's new performance. I asked to be rolled out 35 miles behind the U-2 at .9 Mach at 35,000. He did just that. I selected full afterburner and started accelerating. As the bird pass 1.4 I started a gentle climb. At something like eighteen miles (on a 20 nm scope) I saw his blip on our 'spinscan' ASG14 radar. I glanced at the gauges and saw we were 1.8 Mach passing 58,000! I don't recall what the fuel gauge read but it was nothing to worry about. Completed the intercept and peeled off for home with about 2,400lbs of fuel left! In the old bird if we had 1,200 left then we were in fat city! Gs. Yeah, just about everybody could out turn a -104 in the usual subsonic dogfight area. But the only birds that gave us a hard time - with the old engine! - were the -106 and the F-8. The secret was never slowing down and using the vertical to the max. We had a good gun and sight combo and practiced (some

of us) deflection shooting out to 3,500-4,000 feet. We got to where we could hit the dart (5 x 12 feet) about 85% of the time at ranges exceeding 2,500 feet using the radar ranging gunsight. The plan was to force the bogey into a turn and then phase our attacks so one bird was always threatening the bogey. This is the TAC lead wingman switch concept. We thought of it and flew it as 'fluid four' without the wingmen, covering each other and the responsibilities switching according to the fight. Our unit sent people up to Tyndall to fight the F-106s when they were trying to sell the 106 as a deployable air superiority team. The J79-19 F-104 waxed the 6. Later some of the guys (not me, sob - I was going to the F-4 now) went out to Edwards to fly against some of the 'oppo birds'. Later while working for Air Florida I talked to their 737 chief pilot. He was flying a very capable 'oppo bird' against the USAF planes as was curving in behind what he thought was a lone F-4 at about 25,000. All of a sudden he saw a -104 pull up vertical off the F4s wing - and knew he was in trouble!

'The -19 -104 would go supersonic - M1.05 - in true level flight at 25000 in military power. It could maintain .97 on the deck in mil. The fastest

I've had one on the deck was 750; the red line. I do know one pilot who let it run out to 825. He was at that time a bachelor and immortal. Its maximum was far beyond 2.0 at altitude. The most I've heard of is 2.4 (same bachelor) which is above the aluminium one-time limit. (2.2 for five minutes) I have personally flown the aircraft in a zoom climb high enough so the altimeter stopped turning at around 87,000. We were still going up in a 50 degree climb. I suppose the pressure differential was too low to overcome the friction in the gears driving the needles. I know the bird will cruise at 73000 at Mach 2.0; Paul Da San Martineo and I RTB'd from Tyndall to Homestead that way. It certainly impressed Miami Center; I remember the controller's answer when we called 'Level Flight Level 730'. 'Roger and you weren't lying about your true airspeed either!' (We'd filed a TAS of 1,150 knots)

'The bird could, on an 85°F day from sea level, at combat weight and configuration, go through 45,000 in ninety seconds after brake release. This was a bird right off the line with no tweaking.

'What always struck me about the aircraft was the way it could accelerate in a zero-G bunt. It seemed like it could jump from 250 to 550 in about twenty seconds. It was certainly fast enough so one had to hold the pitch trim button forward and yet still apply pressure to maintain zero-G for the unloaded accel.

'Fighting the bird entailed two tactics; the deep six zoom attack with the AIM-9B and the gun pass followed by a vertical zoom and re-attack at 600+. Get a radar lock-on and try for a high angle deflection shot on the planform of the bogey. The instant the gunsight was saturated - could no longer track - quarter roll wings level and zoom vertical again.

'It was not uncommon to belly up through 50,000 on the re-attack. NO ONE could follow us in these manoeuvres. Certainly not an F-4. An F-15 could but they weren't around yet. After the second pass the F-4 was all out of airspeed. The 6 was in the same boat; it lost speed fast when it started pulling G. We could spiral climb away from them and when they paid off split-ess back onto their tail.

'I just wish USAF hadn't got into a hissy fit with Kelly Johnson. The CL1200 Lancer was an F-104 updated and improved. He solved so many complicated problems so simply on the -104 when I got to the F-4 I was disappointed in the crudity of the solutions to the same problems. There was some real engineering done on the 'Zipper'; it seemed to me the F-4 team just grabbed an answer book off the shelf and leafed to the right page.

'The F-104 was sort of like owning the sharpest knife in the world. It was an honest airplane; you knew what was going on all the time but like using a sharp knife, you better not make any mistakes. It did not suffer fools at all. The engine-out landing pattern was wild; 15,000 and 260 over the runway and one turn, 240 knots over the threshold. Drop the gear by the emergency release during the flare! Rate of descent stabilized with gear down, engine off, at 240 knots was about 11,000 feet per minute.

F-104A-20-LO 56-0821 of the 331st FIS in flight from Webb AFB, TX in 1964. This Starfighter crashed in a swamp 3 miles from the end of the runway at Homestead AFB, Florida on 21 September 1965 after the pilot failed to lock the canopy, which opened on lift-off and loose gear on top of the glare shield went down the scoops. The pilot tried to clear the stall, but he failed to eject and was killed. (USA)

No slack there. The bird got a bad reputation during its infancy - in the USAF about a third of them were lost to engine failure before GE got the bugs out of it. In the Luftwaffe a lot of accidents were due to a combination of green pilots, poor maintenance and lousy (normal) European weather. With four tanks - fairly common LW configuration - the liftoff speed is around 215 knots. On an 8,000 foot runway there is NO slack at all.

'Range. Carrying one bomb (guess what kind) with four tanks an F-104 will go about half again as far as an F-4 on a low-low-low sortie. And it will do it faster, too.

'Bomb load. The TAC version can carry four but why would one want to mess up an air superiority fighter with bombs?

'Deployability. The 'Zipper' was designed before the perceived need for IFR. Because of the way it's built it can be disassembled and loaded on a C-141 and flown to wherever you want it. Wings off and it sits on its gear. Tail off, elevator off rudder, load it board. Unload it at destination and reassemble it. Four bolts hold the after section on, five bolts for each wing. The Lancer could have incorporated a retractable probe and with its afterburning turbofan would have deployed nicely.

'Summary. I amassed 2,000 hours in the F-4D/E and grew to like it for what it could do. But love it? No way. My love was first the Sabre and then the 'Zipper'. Both were true pilot's aircraft. The Sabre handled like it was part of you; the 'Zipper' only came alive above 450 knots. But at 600 it started to hum and at 700... oh, baby!

'Hope you enjoyed this - my paean to the Lockheed F-104A and to Kelly Johnson and his team!

'F-104 - you got that right. I spent a year in Greenland and the knowledge my first two choices for a follow-on assignment were the two 104 squadrons kept my spirits up through that tour. 3rd choice was the 106. I got my first one!

'I feel like sounding off about the 'Zipper', so hang on.

'So few people really know what that bird could do and how easy it was to keep in commission. We always had payday afternoon off and very seldom ever flew Saturdays to get the time in. Engine change done in about 2 hours. All the electronics including the radar T/R (Transmit/Receive)

Walter Elliott Bjorneby of the 319th FIS at Homestead AFB from 1964 to 1967. (Bjorneby)

package could be changed in minutes. The radar itself was a simple set: range-only, limited to 20 miles by design. It worked about 99.95% of the time. The gunsight was very accurate. Parts were the only thing that could ground a bird for more than a day. It had VOR, TACAN and ILS and was a very good instrument aircraft. Also very good in formation flying. Note: overlapping the wings got you very close - the wing panel from fuselage fillet to missile rail was just about 75'. Wing loading was about 145lb/square feet but nevertheless with the boundary layer control bleed air in Land Flaps she could be brought in at 150 and touched down about 140. (No-crosswind; about 135) but the ailerons were pretty weak that slow. Doing that and using the drag chute, you could easily stop in 3,000 feet after touchdown without punishing the brakes.

'I spoke of old and new engines. The F-104A was the first aircraft in service with the GE-J79-3B engine. The 'Zipper' had a pretty poor record until GE cured two serious bugs. One was an oil leak would let the engine exhaust nozzle go wide open. Then at full power you didn't have enough thrust to maintain level flight. When you got too low you had to get out and walk. The other was the engine inlet vanes which would crank wide open if its control failed. Now if you reduced power below say 90% she'd start stalling. No more thrust. They got that fixed after a year or so. Meanwhile about fifty or so 104s were lost. The -3B engine had 15,000 and 9,800lbs of thrust in afterburner or in military (max without afterburner). The -19 engine had 18,900/12,500lbs, same conditions. It also had a more efficient nozzle and a higher compression ratio. Since a 104 weighed about 14,000lbs empty and just over 20,000lbs sitting on alert (pilot, about 5,500lbs fuel, two missiles, 750 rounds of ammo) you can see that new engine gave it sparkling performance.

'The Lockheed C-2 ejection seat was capable of a safe ejection once over 200 knots on takeoff (which was pretty dang quick - 3,000 feet give or take a couple hundred.) By the way that seat also protected you if you had to eject at high IAS. Cables pulled your feet in and deployed webbing restrained your elbows and arms. A couple seconds later the 'butt snapper' kicked you out of the seat and if your zero-delay lanyard was hooked to the D-ring it deployed the chute for you right then.

'Brake release to .97 Mach was 43 seconds at Sea Level and 85 Fahrenheit in our re-engined birds. 45,000 feet in 90 seconds after brake release - I did it once. .97 Mach in military power on the deck, about 1.25 in burner, again on the deck. Would accelerate past 1.0 Mach at 25,000 in military - no afterburner needed. Did that, too. Cruised at 2.0 Mach (310 knots) at 73,000 feet burning 100lbs per minute. 'BT, DT' 'BT, DT' ('Been there, done that'). Using T/O flap setting would out-corner the F-4. Plus that flap setting limit was 550 knots/1.8 Mach (whichever you hit first). We used T/O flaps for tight turns; then on relaxing stick to zero-G A/B on and flaps back up to regain energy back - quickly!

'Red Lines - 710 knots, 2.0 Mach. 100 degrees Centigrade CIT and a SLOW light that comes on when the generator cooling air reaches 120° Celsius. All, repeat ALL are artificial and serve as the manufacturer's statement that if you go faster and something bad happens don't complain to them. 710 knots was for compressor case strength, 2.0 Mach was for the directional stability damping coefficient dropping below 0.003, the USAF limits; 100° Celsius for aluminium skin. Every single one of our aircraft, single and two-seaters, would far exceed every one of those limits. The old J79-3B engine (15,000lbs in burner) when new would take the bird out to 2.36 Mach; the newer -19 engine (18,900lbs in afterburner) to the far side of 2.5 Mach. Both are too fast for an all-aluminium airplane. I was somewhat handicapped by being a husband to a fine woman and father of two great daughters and also the custodian of a damn fine dog. I only saw about 750 on the deck and 2.2 up high. Two guys in my flight saw 2.5 Mach at 50,000, another good friend and ferocious fighter pilot was getting into some F-106s and saw 825 knots at 25,000 feet on his first pass.

'Beauty - in flight - wow! I was going through the transition phase and about ride 6 or so I had to take it out to 1.7 Mach. Well. I'd been out to 1.3 Mach in the Deuce but - the old -3B engine had a 'T2 reset' to cope with the temperature change as the CIT rose - it would suddenly push up the revs about 3%. That is about 10% more thrust and you can definitely feel it as a solid push. Also at that speed the directional stability is degrading and she begins to wag her tail slightly - a half second oscillation. Like she's telling you how fast she's going. Neat! Anyway there I was going a hell of a lot faster than I'd ever gone before, knowing there was even more speed on tap and - I was also flying as a target for 4 of the outfit. All of a sudden I hear them all calling

'MA' (Mission Accomplished - weenie-speak for 'Kill')) to the GCI controller and then 'ZIP' x 4 - those hightailed stub wing beauties, bunched up tight, blew right past me about a hundred feet out on each side.

'Later on I went out to Mach 2.0 as part of the check-out – as #4 while we all intercepted a 1.7 Mach target. We got him, went out a couple more miles and Lead said Zoom Now! Of course we were wearing P-suits but it was a thrill arcing up over 75,000 feet in spread formation!

'The F-104 had none of the newer control system kluges that compensated for airspeed changes, what you felt was what you got. Thus at slow speeds - 300 on down - she took a lot of stick motion to manoeuvre about. But at 450 she felt great and up at 700 she still felt great. She was not too sensitive, jumpy, even over 750 right down at 50 feet AGL. She was also a good strafing bird; at 450-550 you could move the pipper a half a mil' or so.

'With tip tanks we could go from Homestead direct Kelly (to refuel) then direct Palmdale, IFR. The 104s didn't have in-flight refuelling (except a weird stuck-on affair with the probe hanging out all the time) but you could take the wings off (5 bolts each, take off the aft section (four bolts) stuff the whole setup in a 141 cargo plane with a bunch of spare parts, pilot, crew chiefs and fly that anywhere in the world. Take about three hours to disassemble and then three more to reassemble.

'We regularly made hot scrambles in three minutes. My first two years at Homestead we were averaging two hot scrambles a day. (First man to the runway led - average pilot flying time was about 2,400 hours - we were screened for the job.)

'A word about the Gatling gun - the dispersion was 3 mils - all the bullets inside a 3 foot circle at 1,000 feet; that also means a 9 foot circle at 1,000 yards. 67 rounds a second, 4,000 rounds a minute. There were 750 rounds in the ammo cans. The gun was driven by a 15 horse electric motor, thus the 'slow' rate of fire. It had a radar-ranging gunsight and the system was very accurate. Some unfamiliar with the gun claim it is slow getting up to speed. My experiences on the firing-in butts say no. There was one bullet up and left - the first one out the spout. All the others were randomly spotted inside that 3 foot circle. (So was that first one, it was just outside the perimeter of the others. It was neat firing it on the ground. The bird was jacked level and chained down - recoil force was about 3,000lbs. Fifty rounds went out so fast it was all over before the first empty case dropped out the belly. *BRRRRMP!*

'We scheduled and flew 36 air to air gunnery sorties a week, so we got and stayed proficient. Our target was the 'Dart', towed by another 104 on a 1,500 feet cable. This thing was about twelve feet long, five feet wide at the tail and looked just like a pair of grade-school paper dart gliders glued belly to belly, giving a + cross section. You focused your eyes on it, flew the airplane to bring the sight pipper up onto the target, tracked the dart smoothly and shot a half-second burst. The key was keeping your eyes on the dart and never looking at the pipper itself; that led to chasing it by pumping the stick which about 95% of the time guaranteed a miss.

'The bloody F-4D/E took about 120 miles to get from .9 to 2.0 Mach; we did it every engine change. The old -3B engine was about the same, maybe twenty miles shorter, both taking about four minutes plus. The -19 engined bird took about 27 miles, about 1'45' and burned 1,000 pounds of fuel doing it. I zoomed an F-4D once starting at the end of that Mach 2.0 check run - 67,000 feet tops. Boo Hoo. The -19 bird went off the top of the altimeter still going up at a great rate. That 3-needle altimeter has a mechanical stop at 86,000. GCI height finders routinely read out 95,000 plus when zoomed without regard to minimum IAS. (I used between 125 and 175 and zero-G over the top, being a trifle cautious by nature.)

'People knocked the 'Zipper' for its short range. Very few people knew that with four external tanks the 104 could fly a low-low-low mission about half again as far as the F-4. That was the NATO F-104G's mission in Europe - and it carried one bomb along with the fuel tanks. We were intercept-only with no bomb or rocket capability. We scheduled 1:20 hour for the old engined-birds minus external tanks. That went up to 1:30 hour with the new and more efficient engine. That equates to 8½ miles a minute cruise giving about 700 miles for the old-engined birds; 800 for the -19 birds. Considering it was designed for a point-defence interceptor using lessons learned in the Korean War - well, it met that criterion just fine. Another point was that it was not an all-weather interceptor. True, but then the Earth is not all that cloudy; about 85% of time (so I heard) the weather would be adequate for a 104 intercept. Radar could lead you to the target; if you had at least half-mile visibility you could fire Sidewinders at him. Using radar plus the simple infra-red sight you could shoot at him once in gun range.

'What else? The only bird with a faster roll rate was I believe the T-38/F-5 at about 470/second. The 'Zipper' - 420 or so, for one roll. Too many rolls and you would get into roll-yaw coupling - not good. To use full aileron at 400 knots you had to grab the underside of the canopy rail with your left hand to keep yourself from being thrown to one side by inertia and probably taking out some aileron as you inadvertently dragged the stick towards neutral, To roll out on a point after full stick deflection you had to lead the rollout about 45 degrees.

'There was a slight but definite burble as you got close to a stall. Get too ham-handed here and she would pitch up - if you managed to ignore first the stick shaker and next the stick kicker which would push the stick forward to reduce the AOA. Note - if the auto pitch control (APC) system was inoperative, it was pretty easy to ignore that little burble in the heat of simulated combat. I did - once. Snap reaction of jamming the stick into the radar hood brought the nose back down smartly. Engine gyro force kicks the nose right as she goes up; back left when recovering smartly. Note two - there is zero warning supersonic - no burble whatever. Oh and it flames out as you pitch up - duct stall. But she lights up immediately once you get the angle of attack to zero and hit the dual ignition switches.

'Note 3; the APC system can be negated by trimming way nose high - the kicker is then reduced to tapping the stick. The shaker is shaking away but ineffectively. As the AOA increases you can feel the aero centre moving forward nearer the CG and pretty soon you are pushing the stick forward of neutral to keep the AOA under control. (I think the broad shoulders of the intakes are also generating lift at this high AOA. This is essentially a useless manoeuvre as almost every other airplane in the world save maybe the 101 can out-slow you.

'We flew in pairs, always. We practiced the USN Double-Attack tactics, otherwise known as Loose Deuce. Basically it is a system of alternate attacks as the tactical lead switches back and forth depending on what the opposition is doing. Looking at it historically, it's Fluid Four without the wingmen - you keep each other clear and as one attacks and forces the opponent to react the other guy is repositioning to become the attacker as the first guy repositions. We usually repositioned straight up, bellying up through 40-50,000 if needed as our attack speed was usually well over 550 knots - as high as 675-700 fighting F-106s and Crusaders. (The -19 engine afforded amazingly very quick zero-G acceleration.) We also practiced high angle off gunnery as our radar sight was accurate and a little mod I got the radar troops to kluge up gave us instant lock-ons. We could adjust the lock-on sensitivity in flight - up until it locked onto air, back it off until it wouldn't and then it'd give an instant lock-on as you got your nose on the bogey. It was almost impossible to set it correctly on the ground because of clutter.

'There were at that time about 125 MiG-21s down in Cuba. We never saw one. We never worried about them; we were confident our airplane, skills and training gave us the edge. We had a good clear ROE; never had to use it. Everything I intercepted was friendly. One funny thing - any intercept we made south of latitude 24 was head-on, supersonic. Lead (eyeball) would pass about 500 feet below the bogey; #2 would lag about four miles as the shooter if needed. If the bogey had been a bandit (hostile) Lead would have pitched straight up to reposition while two manoeuvred to engage the bandit.

'Well, I've become a genuine old coot talking about the good old days - damn, they were GOOD! It's all your fault, you got me thinking about my favourite airplane.'

It was in 1967 that Walter Bjorneby and Paul Da San Martino were sent up to Tyndall AFB in the Florida Panhandle to do some fighter affiliation with a U-2 to test its new self-protection device. 'We got to fly the missions' recalls Bjorneby, who was born in Alaska, 'because we both had full pressure suits, a USAF modified version of the Navy Mark IV. Very comfortable compared to the old partial pressure MC3 and MC4s, even comfortable enough to perform air combat wearing them, something that was not true of the MC3/4 suits. Anyway the U-2 was up at his operational altitude for the tests and we made numerous intercepts, playing the enemy for him. His device didn't particularly bother us and we deduced from what we could see on our radar scopes that our ASG14 radars were not sophisticated enough to be bothered. The ASG14 was a modern analogue to the RAF AI 10 used in WW2; basically, a spiral scan search radar with no angle track capability. Just find him on the scope, turn toward him to fly him to the centre and go get him. You know when he's dead ahead (on boresight) because then he paints as a circle around the centre of the scope - the circle's radius is his range. The set could, however lock on and track a target in range from ten miles on in. The pilot had to keep the target directly ahead since there was no angle track capability at all. It could, when locked on, feed range to the computing gunsight; effectively, too, I might add. Range showed up on the sight; miles when missiles were selected, feet when guns were selected.

'A side comment on intercepting U-2s. We had been doing this from some time in our F-104As with the original J79-3B engine. The mission was fuel-critical; a five minute delay meant everything had to go just right or we'd be low on fuel for the required IMC approach. The installation of the J79-19 engine (a slightly modified -17 engine) increased our excess thrust about 25%, so we expected an improvement, but were uncertain as to how much. We were pleasantly surprised.

'The first time we ran an intercept on a U-2 at his operational height in the Dash 19 bird, we had no data to plan from nor did the FSQ7 SAGE computer. To make things simple and sure, I had the controller roll me out 35 miles behind the U-2 at 38,000 (tropopause that day). Catching the U2 would be no problem since the overtake at attack speed would be in excess of M1.2. I went to max afterburner and followed the controller's steering. I was mostly looking out for him since often the U-2 emitted a wisp of a contrail. Then at eighteen miles I saw a contact at 12:00 on the radar. (20 miles was the only range selection in search) and glanced at the gauges. I was now doing M1.8 at 58,000 and I was most impressed since the old 3B would have still been way below that struggling to get to M2.0. I completed the intercept, getting a tallyho at about two miles and pulled off the target with about 1,000lbs more fuel than I'd ever had left with that old engine.

'At Tyndall when the U2 system test was over it was time to go home. I looked at Paul and suggested 'Let's wear our pressure suits and go home at high altitude.' He was all for it and so we filed for Homestead, doglegging south into Warning Area 168 to avoid civvie traffic and incidentally not boom anyone. I did a little dash-one research and fiddled with my E6B a bit and came to the conclusion FL730 was attainable at M2.0 and would give us an IAS we could comfortably fly at. I filed the IMC clearance for a TAS of 1150 TAS which certainly raised the eyebrows of a C119 aircraft commander standing next to me at the clearance desk. We suited up, got our clearance and took off. We climbed in military to the tropopause. There I called Miami Center and got clearance to accelerate for the M2.0 climb on up to FL730. We

went into afterburner, my throttle back a shade from full, to give Paul a little slack out there in loose wing. Arriving at 2.0 fairly quickly I started the climb, maintaining 2.0. We levelled at 73,000 on the altimeter and eased back to about 3/4 afterburner to maintain 315 IAS, on the good side of max L/D. I called 'Level Flight Level 730' to Miami Centre and he came right back with 'And you weren't lying about your true airspeed, either!' I chuckled to myself, envisioning the vector arrow simply jumping across his radar scope at 20 miles a minute. It was a standard Florida day, bright sun, some towering cumulonimbus scattered about, the tops well below us, lots of puffy white cumulus, even further below. The sky overhead was noticeably darker than down on the deck, yet not as dark as it got at the apex of a zoom climb. Our motion across the dark blue Gulf of Mexico was perceptible. We were burning about 100 pounds of fuel a minute and covering twenty miles a minute and the TACAN mile-meter was really counting down, a tenth of a mile (smallest division) clicking past every third of a second. Coming up on the coast, still about 275 miles from Homestead AFB (HST), I raised my fist, jerked it back to signal to Paul 'out of AB', nodded my head for execution and eased the throttle slowly back to idle. Paul was out in loose wing, staying right with me. (He was an ex-TAC F-100 type with lots of fighter time and a skilled and aggressive pilot). We held 315 knots all the way down the descent and hit the initial for runway 05 about ten miles out of Homestead. I think we burned less than 200 lbs or so of fuel all the way down to 1500 AGL. What a great flight and what a great view of the world from up there. Not as different as the view is up around 90,000 on a zoom climb but still visibly darker overhead with more white haze on the horizon than at 35-40,000. The curvature of the horizon was faint but discernible. It was odd to look way down and see contrails along the airways.

'The J79-19 engines made the U-2 intercepts and the XC really pieces of cake! To my present-day sorrow I threw away the clearance sheet and my navigation card and then compounded that error by turning in my full pressure suit when I transferred from ADC to TAC - it was on a hand receipt and I realized later I could have kept it and no one would have been the wiser. It was tailored personally to me and would fit no one else and would have made a damn fine souvenir of some awesome flights. But I will always remember the great times flying the 'Zipper' - and the rare flights like the ones I just described.'

Seventy-seven examples of the F-104C fighter-bomber variant, which first flew on 24 July 1958, were built for Tactical Air Command. The 'C' was powered by a J79-GE-7A whose turbine had a 2-inch increase in diameter, providing 15,800lb of thrust. It also introduced a probe for in-flight refuelling and was the first Starfighter to have operative flap blowing from the outset. It could carry two 170-gallon tanks or two 1,000lb bombs, a Mk 28 nuclear weapon, or four Sidewinder missiles. The 476th Tactical Fighter Squadron of the 479th Tactical Fighter Wing at George AFB, California, was the first to receive the F-104C, beginning in September 1958.

Australian Air Force pilot James Hilary Flemming was the first foreigner to fly the F-104C and the first RAAF pilot to get to Mach 2. Born 4 December 1926 at Randwick, NSW he joined the RAAF in 1943 and flew as a Sergeant pilot in 1944 in New Guinea and at Darwin. Post war he converted to Mustangs and flew on first the RAAF mission in Korean War in 1950. His exchange with the USAF began in 1958 and he flew the F-100 and F-104. As the 479th TFW Standardization Officer he flew with

Below: On 13 May 1961 F-104C 56-0884 in the 476th TFS crashed near Gondorf, Germany, while performing an air show at Bitburg AB. After takeoff the pilot, Captain William Laurent Mathews, performed an Immelman and made several rolls descending on a heading of approximately 060 degrees before experiencing problems with his g-suit. The aircraft then engaged a pitch-up situation for 5-8 seconds. From 500-1000 feet the aircraft rolled very abruptly into a steep nose down attitude. Just before impact the seat was seen to fire but Mathews was too low and he was killed.

the 434th TFS, completing about 700 odd hours in the 'Zipper'. 'In 1958, being the first TAC squadron to be re-equipped with the F-104C Starfighter, the 476th TFS had to perform operational testing of tactics, procedures and capabilities. These included Phase 2 nozzle tests and high altitude operations. There had been a spate of nozzle failures in the J79 engine fitted to the F-104C. It was found that the nozzles, being operated by the engine oil system, were failing to open or close due to sludge on the oil filters, The system was changed so that the nozzles were controlled by the engine fuel system and the problem was solved. The aircraft were being modified at the next major inspection so some squadron aircraft continued to operate with without the oil system control being modified.

'For the high altitude tests we were fitted with the early 'Moon suit' pressure suit which was based on the same principle as the 'G Suit' but with a full body fitting. Prior to donning the pressure suit you were required to be powdered all over with talcum powder and then don long underwear, inside out, so that the seams would not cause irritation points which could not be reached while wearing the 'Moon suit'. Sitting for an hour in the crew room pre-breathing oxygen was a most boring experience.

'I was scheduled for a high zoom flight to 65,000 feet and after the required pre-breathing I carried my portable oxygen unit out to my F-104C, 56-899, strapped in, converted to the aircraft oxygen system and departed for the high speed area 'Stovepipe' up over Death Valley.

'My scheduled profile was to climb to 36,000 feet; a level, run out to Mach 1.7 in full afterburner and a pull to 1.5 G. When the Mach meter showed Mach 2 or better, I was to then increase to 3G for the zoom. At 38,000 feet the Mach meter was indicating Mach 2.1 with about 35 degrees nose

Main picture: F-104A 56-0910 in the 434th TFS, 479th TFW USAF with Wing Commander marks (3 stripes) at Lajes Air Base in November 1959. This Starfighter was lost at Homestead AFB, Florida on 17 November 1966 after an engine flame out due to fuel starvation during the landing pattern. Inset: TF-104 63-8455 (27+57) at Luke AFB, Arizona. This Starfighter later operated with the RoCAF (coded 4183') until it crashed on 7 August 1986 at Pingtung AB after loss of control of the flight controls system during takeoff. (Keith Heywood).

up. The airplane was zooming like an angel and we rapidly passed 50,000 feet where all indications were normal.

'As the airplane neared 60,000 feet I had to throttle back to keep the EGT within limits. The afterburner blew out and when the throttle was near idle I heard slight 'thump' down the back end but all seemed normal. The Starfighter was still climbing but at a reduced angle of attack, about 20 degrees. As 65,000 feet was reached I stop-cocked the throttle to prevent an overspeed over temp and eased the stick forward to about level attitude. The cockpit de-pressurized and I felt the suit pressure come on. It was like being in an all-over G suit and it was difficult to move my arms or legs. The outside light was poor due to the blue/black sky and I had to pull out the instrument panel shades to help the cockpit lighting.

'I thought that the aircraft would start to descend but, to my amazement, we kept climbing in a level flight attitude. As we reached 70,000 feet I eased the stick forward to get a more nose down attitude. The airspeed was about 155 knots and the attitude changed but the Starfighter kept slowly climbing until it peaked at 72,300 feet when it started to pitch down and descend with wings level. As the speed increased I popped the speed brakes, slowly increased the dive angle and commenced a glorious high speed dive down to lower levels.

'At 40,000 feet I tried a relight without success. At 35,000 feet I tried another relight procedure

with same result. At 33,000 feet I managed to get a relight and was delighted to see the RPM and EGT started to rise. With everything appearing normal I turned towards George passing over the base at 30,000 feet prior to entering the pattern. At this stage I knew something was wrong, as an increased throttle movement produced the desired RPM but no apparent increase in thrust. Fortunately, I was aware of the nozzle failure problem where the nozzles remain open and you have a perfectly good engine but no thrust. This was my situation then. The book indicated that level flight could be maintained at 2,000 feet above sea level in this configuration. With the altitude at George at 1,800 feet I was not about to test this theory. At 25,000 feet and descending I declared an emergency and requested a straight-in to Muroc Lake, which was almost right in front of me. I turned so that the approach would be to the North East and at 15,000 feet commenced a high key-low key dead stick approach, which I had practiced many times, on to the world's longest runway marked out on the lake bed.

'On final approach the engine was developing a little thrust but I continued the dead stick approach, dropping the gear at 250 knots and touching down well into the lake bed at about 185 knots. When I came to a stop, Edwards Tower me to vacate the airplane and await pick-up. I shut down the engine and when I descended, by hanging over the side of the airplane, I saw that the nozzles were stuck wide open. On looking around I could have been on the Moon; nothing but desert to all horizons. After about fifteen minutes, I was pleased to see a chopper coming over the horizon from the West. The rescue crew took me back to civilization and

AVIATION WRITERS ASSOCIATION CONVENTION

MAY 26-27, 1958

HOUSTON, TEXAS

GENERAL ELECTRIC

LOCKHEED AIRCRAFT CORP.

I had a pleasant time in the Officers Club before being returned to George by car that evening.

'After the maintenance crew at the Test Pilot's School had completed the engine oil/fuel nozzle control modification 56-899 flew on for some years before being destroyed in an accident in Spain in the early sixties.'

Subsequently, the three other squadrons in the 479th - the 434th, 435th and 436th - were also equipped. (The 'C was joined on the Burbank production lines by twenty-one tandem-seat F-104D models, which, like the F-104C was powered by a 15,800lb J79-GE-7 and were fitted with blow flaps and in-flight probe-and-drogue refuelling equipment. They could also operate in the ground-attack role. The F-104D Starfighters were accepted by Tactical Air Command during 1958-59.)

In November 1959 the 479th TFW made an overseas deployment to Morón Air Base, Spain, where one squadron remained on a rotational basis until 1963. During the 1960 Berlin Crisis the Morón-based squadron of F-104Cs transferred to Bitburg air Base, West Germany, while the other three squadrons at George AFB, deployed to Hahn and Ramstein Air Bases in West Germany. By early 1962 all except the Morón-based squadron were

Cartoon marking the achievements of Major Howard 'Scrappy' Johnson.

back at George AFB and then, when the Cuban Missile Crisis broke out in October 1962, all of the F-104Cs at George were redeployed to Key West, Florida. In 1963 a number of F-104Cs of the 479th TFW were employed in operational testing and in November a detachment was sent to the Arctic as part of Project 'Diamond Lil'. (A second Arctic deployment was made by the 479th TFW in 1965).

Despite the cut backs in Starfighter orders and the disappointments in equipping Air Defense Command the Starfighter did achieve considerable fame, starting in 1958-59 with a series of outstanding record achievements. In 1958 the F-104 became the first aircraft to hold World Airspeed and Altitude records simultaneously. First, on 7 May 1958, Major Howard C. 'Scrappy' Johnson of the 83rd Fighter Interceptor Squadron reached 91,249 feet at Edwards AFB. Johnson served as a fighter pilot flying over 7,000 hours in fifteen different fighter planes during his career. In 1953, Major Johnson transferred to Hamilton AFB where he had the first opportunity to hear about the Air Force's newest, fastest airplane, the F-104A. In 1958, with only thirty hours of flight time in the Starfighter, he shattered the World's Altitude Record zooming to 91,243 feet. In recognition of the record, Vice President Richard Nixon presented him with the Robert J. Collier trophy for aeronautical achievement. Then, on 16 May 1958 Captain Walter W. Irwin set a world air speed record of 1,404.19 mph over a 15/25 kilometre course at Edwards AFB. On 18 December 1958 the Starfighter set more records. Flying from NAS Point Magu, California an F-104A set three time-to-climb records: 3,000 metres (9,842 feet) in 41.35 seconds; 15,000 metres (49,212 feet) in two minutes 11.1 seconds; and 25,000 metres (82,020 feet) in 4 minutes 26.03 seconds. On 14 December 1959 an F-104C piloted by Captain Joe Jordan, Edwards AFB test pilot beat the 1958 Starfighter height record, reaching 103,389 feet (31,513 metres), making the Starfighter the first aircraft taking off on its own power to exceed the 30,000 metres and 100,000 feet marks. Hitting a top speed of 1,400 mph, the F-104C also established a 30,000 metre time-to-climb mark of 5 minutes 4.92 seconds and even surpassed the existing balloon record of 101,516

Captain 'Scrappy' Johnson being congratulated by President Richard Nixon. ▮

feet (30,942 metres). For his design work on the aircraft, Johnson received the prestigious Collier Trophy in 1959 from the American Institute of Aeronautics and Astronautics.

▮ **Captain Joe B. Jordan USAF in the cockpit of F-104C-5-LO-56-0885 which he used on 14 February 1959 to set a World Altitude Record.**

In the Ascendancy

Captain Charles Ehnstrom Tofferi representing the 479th Tactical Fighter Wing at George AFB flew his F-104C (57-0914) to the September 1962 'William Tell Fighter Weapons Meet' title. Held biennially at Nellis AFB near Las Vegas, the single F-104C took on ten North American F-100 Super Sabres and three Republic F-105 Thunderchiefs. Lockheed's publicity machine proudly reported that: 'The loner generally was regarded as an interloper in the four-day competition, since the 479th was equipped and trained more for nuclear weapons delivery and the contest included several categories in conventional weapons. Captain Tofferi and his F-104C were unstoppable. At meet's end, he had outscored all other pilots - top marksmen from top TAC units around the world - to post a remarkable victory. He scored 19,018 points out of 24,000 possible. His nearest competitor had 17,304 points. Three of his close-support missions were scored as perfect 1,000s. Downing a towed dart target with his Vulcan 20mm cannon in just 63 seconds with 86 rounds he set a new record and picked up the maximum 3,000 points for that division. Among the Starfighter's features, he gave particular credit to its short turning radius (with manoeuvring flaps) and tremendous acceleration for his championship showing. He said also, 'Thank you, one and all, for the best airplane I've ever flown. The F-104 really shines. It is so simple to maintain, people with little experience can do it.'

'All of which' wrote Kevin V. Brown **'prompted *Popular Mechanics* to request the Air Force for a ride with the sharpshooter to see how he does it and to translate what he does into what he would do in case of a 'little war.' *I Flew With TAC's Top Gun* published in October 1963; essentially the story of all TAC fighter pilots, boils down to the man the plane and the tactics.'**

'Doc Holliday started out to be a dentist, John Wesley Hardin was the son of a preacher and Charles E. Tofferi of Fitchburg, Massachusetts entered teacher's school but all three ended up as gunmen. Holliday and Hardin, depending on which biography you read, were either heroes or bad men. Tofferi, who had no biographer until now, is definitely a hero and he's on our side. What's more, his accuracy with some of the deadliest weapons ever conceived by man would make all the gunfighters who ever lived blanch with fear.'

As a 19 year old boy Tofferi enlisted in the Air Force on 7 July 1952 and started pilot training. Two years later he graduated in Air Cadet Class 54-P at Reese AFB in Texas and started flying the twin-engine Convair T-29 at Harlingen AFB, Texas. After a few months he decided these aircraft were too slow and in 1955 requested fighter pilot training which he received at Perrin AFB, Sherman, Texas and Craig AFB, Selma, Alabama. Following fighter training he and wife Nancy (his childhood sweetheart, whom he married in December 1954 in the Harlingen AFB chapel) moved to Westover AFB, Chicopee, Massachusetts. As a member

of the 337th Fighter Interceptor Squadron (Air Defense Command) he flew the F-86D and L radar mounted Sabre aircraft which were soon replaced by the F-104A Starfighter in February 1958. Chuck flew the F-104 until the 337th disbanded in 1960 and the Starfighters were phased out at Westover. In August 1960, Chuck transferred from the ADC to TAC (Tactical Air Command) joining the 479th Tactical Fighter Wing, George AFB, Victorville, California to fly the F-104C Starfighter in a new role, as a fighter bomber aircraft.

'Captain Tofferi (it rhymes with BOFF-ery) is a fighter pilot in the United States Air Force - specifically, the Tactical Air Command. TAC, in time of war, fights the dirty battles, the unglamorous battles; the ditch-digging battles. In short, it would be on the front lines strafing tanks and dropping bombs on bunkers from altitudes as low as 50 feet while the boys at the missile bases were pushing buttons and sending warheads to targets 5,000 miles away. Not to make too fine a point, if a 'little war' broke out in Cuba, TAC would fight it. And Tofferi is the best man they've got. He proved it the hard way. TAC periodically holds a so-called 'fighter-

weapons meet,' which is really an old-fashioned Western shoot-out in which TAC units all over the world send their best men to compete against one another in strafing, dive bombing and air-to-air gunnery. Tofferi beat them all and he set a record doing it. Moreover, he did it in an F-104 Starfighter, a plane built originally as a high-altitude fighter. It was the only one in the meet. To add a vulgar note, the meet was held at Nellis Air Force Base in Nevada and the gamblers in nearby Las Vegas had Tofferi pegged at 14-1 in a 14-plane meet.

'Captain Charles Tofferi, at 29, is a nine-year veteran of the Air Force with more than 3,000 hours in jets. He and his pretty wife Nancy - pretty wives are traditional in the Air Force - live in a comfortable home at George Air Force Base, California with their two pre-school-age daughters, Susan and Seayn. I was invited to dinner while visiting the base and it was an amusing contrast to watch a man, who could easily be rated the deadliest gunman in the world, listen to his shy little girls as they told him the troubles they had that day with their teddy bear, or some such playmate.

On the flight line, Tofferi is a personable and articulate spokesman for the Air Force. My request was simple and his reaction even more so. I'd like to ride along with him while he went through all the manoeuvres a tactical fighter pilot might be called on to use in a 'little war.'

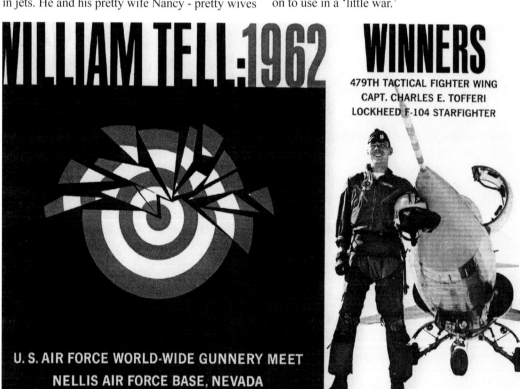

WILLIAM TELL:1962 WINNERS

479TH TACTICAL FIGHTER WING
CAPT. CHARLES E. TOFFERI
LOCKHEED F-104 STARFIGHTER

U. S. AIR FORCE WORLD-WIDE GUNNERY MEET
NELLIS AIR FORCE BASE, NEVADA

'Sure.' he said, 'Want some coffee?'

'So while we sipped coffee, the erstwhile school teacher took a pencil and paper, diagrammed the techniques and pointed out the small details that mean the difference between hitting a target and missing it by an embarrassing margin. At speeds up to 700 mph missing is easy.

'Tofferi and other Starfighter pilots are trained to drop 750lb high-explosive bombs and napalm bombs (jellied gasoline which bursts into sticky flames on impact) and fire a 20mm, six-barrel cannon, rockets or the heat-seeking Sidewinder missile. Plus - and this is a shocker - nuclear bombs starting from a level of 50 feet. (In training of course, they can only simulate nuclear runs. The use of atomic weapons is highly restricted.) They also learn low-level navigation, finding targets 500 miles or more away whole flying above the tree-tops to sneak in under the radar screen.

'The Sidewinders are air-to-air weapons,' Tofferi explained. 'The cannon is either air-to-air or air-to-ground and the others are all air-to-ground. For air-to-ground manoeuvres we have three basic passes. We come in at a 45-dregree angle for dive bombing, about 15 degrees for strafing and straight-and-level for napalm, skip-bombing and nuclear weapons.'

'He sipped his coffee and added casually, 'We do a little something extra on the nuclear pass though.'

'Let's hope so, I thought.

'Before going out to the plane, he helped me into a half-size G-suit. This differs from the full-size pressure suits worn by pilots who regularly fly high-altitude missions. The full-size suit protects the pilot in case cabin pressure fails in the thin air of high altitude. The half-size suit is strictly for G-forces encountered when racking the plane around in low-altitude manoeuvres,

'On the ramp Tofferi's attitude changes slightly. No longer the patient school teacher, he becomes part cold-eyed efficiency and part little boy with the best toy he's ever owned. His pre-flight inspection - which involves walking around the plane and 'kicking the tyres' - is an important ritual of Air Force pilots to make sure it is ready to fly. In Tofferi's case, he gives it a few extra pats that are more affection than inspection.

The Starfighter is an unusual airplane and there is an inordinate love affair going on between it and the pilots who fly it. Smallest of the Air Force fighters, its stubby wings and slim fuselage make it look more like a missile than a plane. But it's one of the most manoeuvrable and fastest (more than 1,500 mph) jets in the sky and probably the simplest to fly and easiest to maintain.

'It is also a stray of sorts. Originally a high-altitude air-superiority fighter (it set an altitude record of better than 100,000 feet), its low-attitude capabilities were developed to give it a role in TAC's plans and Tofferi's feat of beating out the best of the other planes, notably the F-100 and the F-105, now gives it prestige.

'I got strapped into the rear seat of the two-seat version, while Tofferi made a few appropriate and tasteless remarks about how to bail out in case the plane blew up. Soon we were taxiing out.

'Takeoff in an F-104 is like accelerating a dragster, only at the end of the roll you're off the ground and climbing at a weird angle. It's hard to believe, because the wings, stubby to begin with, are far behind the cockpit and almost impossible to see. But then altimeter told me we were heading up fast. Tofferi took it to 11,000 feet within a few seconds, levelled off and headed for the California desert where the boys from George practice gunnery.

'We'll try a dive-bomb run first' he said, as he launched into his lecture. 'We'd normally carry two 750lb bombs and use them against semi-fixed or fixed targets such as command posts, bridges or railroad yards. We pick up enough speed in the dive, so I'll idle back, put out the speed brakes and roll over into the 45-degree bombing run. See the targets?'

'He pointed out some fly specks on the ground that I assumed were bull's-eyes.

'How he lines up the target can't be seen from the rear cockpit. His gun sight, a round circle (reticule) with a dot (pipper) in the middle, is projected onto his front windshield. He gave me a running account.

'I'm rolling over now and when I straighten up I'll put the reticule over the target and then try to put the pipper dead centre and keep it there. When the altitude is right - bombs away! If we have to figure on wind drift, we make slight adjustments depending on wind direction.'

'It sounded easy, but I knew it wasn't. The plane dropped like a bullet and kept dropping for what seemed an interminable time. Finally, too close to the ground for me, he racked it back into a climbing turn and I felt like some gorilla was jamming me through the bottom of the cockpit. My jaw sagged; my eyesight went grey and that suit bit into my intestines.

Ignoring my slight indisposition, he went on amiably, 'We fire the rocket pods, either one at a time or both together, from the same kind of a run, except that we start lower - from about 3,000 feet. There are nineteen rockets in each pod and the individual rockets go off a millisecond apart, so we get a spray effect. The targets would be semi-fixed or moving - bunkers, tanks and the like. Here we go again!'

'He rolled into another dive and I achieved another mild black out when he racked it back. Going at better than 600 mph, even a slight nudge on the control stick jumps up the G-forces. Climbing turns are real back-breakers.

'It didn't bother the school teacher, however and he plunged into the next lesson.

'Strafing's next,' he said laconically.

'The cannon, which I had examined before the flight is the only armament built into the 104. Missiles are carried on the wingtips; bombs and rocket pods from beneath the wings. The cannon, which shoot's 20mm shells that explode on impact is therefore ready on all missions. The 104 could conceivably fire missiles from the wing tips, or drop bombs or fire rockets from beneath the wings and still come back and strafe with the cannon - all on the same deadly mission.

'The cannon has six barrels which revolve like an old-fashioned Gatling gun and fire at a rate of 6,000 rounds per minute. Each barrel is slightly offset from the others, so they spray the target with shells instead of all firing at the same point.

'Targets on a strafing run are usually smaller than for rockets - small vehicles, troops, parked aircraft,' Tofferi said.

'He pointed out another fly speck on the ground, dipped the nose toward it and started down at a slight angle from about 2,000 feet. Although the angle was much less, the ground was much closer than on bombing runs and I got the impression he was trying to ram the nose boom through the target. He swished over it at better than 500 mph at what he said was 100 feet of altitude but, looking back, I could see the cloud of dust stirred up by the jet.

'On strafing runs, he explained, he keeps the pipper right ion the target all the way in. But about this point I began to understand why the Air Force puts so much emphasis on depth perception for pilots. Flying down to treetop level at close to the speed of sound and keeping his eye on the target and his finger on the trigger - and in combat, worrying about anti-aircraft fire - a pilot must depend on instinct to tell him when to pull up. The best, like Tofferi, wait until the last split second. There are

plenty of tales about World War II pilots who came back with tree branches and telephone wires in the wings because they became too absorbed in their work.

'If I had thought 100 feet was low, the straight-and-level runs cut it in half.

'We come in at better than 500 mph on conventional runs,' he said 'and push it up to about 700 mph for nuclear runs.'

'Well, as we went skimming overt the desert floor at 50 cotton-pickin' feet - about the level of a theatre marquee - he pointed out some more fly specks to hell and gone across the arid valley. All I saw was the shimmering heat rising from the desert floor.

'For skip-bombing,' the school teacher continued, 'we'd use bombs with delayed-action fuses, perhaps fragmentation bombs depending on the target. We'd try to bounce them into a tunnel or up against a bunker on a hillside.

'Straight-and-level aiming is different than on an angled attack. I'll keep the reticule below the target and when its top hits the target I'll let go.' A pause, then 'Steady, now - voom!'

'I still hadn't seen the target - oops there it went! Swish!

'Tofferi racked around for another go and when I recovered from my umpteenth grey-out, I picked up his lecture.

'... with napalm, we'd drop the bomb short of the target - and the targets are usually something with motion involved, tanks or troops - and just let the goop hit and roll over them. It's really nasty stuff.

'I'll keep the reticule on a line with the target, but use the nose boom for reference. When the target hits the nose of the plane at the base of the boom, I let go. Ready, now - bombs away!'

'Again, a slight delay before the target swished past below us and this time I could imagine those sticky flames rolling over everything like high-speed lava.

'Last was the nuclear run.

'It came as something of a surprise when I first heard they were simulating atomic-bomb runs from 50 feet, but the techniques give it considerable accuracy.

'We come in pretty fast on these runs, about as fast as you can go without breaking the sound barrier,' Tofferi explained' 'but it isn't the blast we're worried about. It's radiation. We're well away from the blast by the time it hits.

'Now, the bomb is larger than a conventional bomb, but it includes a parachute. For each target - and we use these only on the biggest targets - perhaps an air base or a large railroad switching yard - we pick a geographical point some miles away. The boys in Intelligence figure these out for us. Knowing the distance, we come in at a predetermined speed and, when we hit that pre-picked point, we pull up at a specific angle. After a predetermined delay, we let the bomb go, roll over on our back, pull the nose back toward the deck, gun the engine, straighten up and get the hell out of there. The parachute slows the bomb down and, if we've done it right, it will arch over into the centre of the target and make a nice little mushroom cloud.'

'Again, it all sounded so simple and it even looked simple when Tofferi simulated one for me. You can't but admire the skill of a man who can handle an instrument like the Starfighter with such precision, especially when he hits the top of the lift up, rolls over and starts back for the deck - at 700 mph on his back.

'The F-104 is a supersonic aircraft, but the ground manoeuvres are performed subsonically, because there is more precision at these speeds and no real necessity for the extra 'go.' The supersonic speeds are primarily for interception and Tofferi offered to demonstrate one. He called ground control for the locations of aircraft, found two flying together and headed for them.

'We'd be using Sidewinder missiles here' he said. 'They have a heat-seeking device in the nose and we can monitor what it sees in the cockpit. We line up the target in the reticule and, when the missile picks up the scent, we wait for its signals to reach a peak and then send it on its way. This usually happens from about one to three miles from the target. If we've done it right, it will fly right up the tailpipe.

'He spotted the pair of planes we were tracking and, because they knew we were coming, turned

F-104C-5-LO 56-0883 of Tactical Air Command. On 2 March 1956 Lockheed received an order for 56 F-104C fighter-bomber variants for TAC. Altogether, 77 F-104C all weather, fighter-bombers were ordered for the Command. The first F-104C flew on 24 July 1958 and TAC accepted the first example on 15 October 1958 during the annual USAF Fighter Weapons Meet at Nellis AFB, Nevada. The last F-104C was delivered in June 1959. (Lockheed)

into us, cutting down the range. Since the 104 is one of the fastest and most manoeuvrable aircraft the best way to avoid it is straight ahead and hope it runs low on fuel before it catches up. Otherwise, a slower aircraft might try to outmanoeuvre the Starfighter and make it miss with its missiles, reducing the odds.

'He let me fly it awhile on the way back to George and then completed the flight with a nest pattern and smooth touchdown. When I climbed out, my flight suit was soaked with perspiration but Tofferi was still the cool gunman.

'I spent another day at George, soaking up the atmosphere of the flight line and was impressed with the computer like precision of the activities. Every mission gets off and running with a minimum of fuss. Aborts require a good explanation.

'TAC and Tofferi is its best example, is a lean outfit. And, with 'little wars' becoming more popular, the pilots seem real 'gung-ho' about their role. At the coffee bar I asked one of them whether, if a war should come, he'd want to get in on it.

'Hell man, I'd be sick if I didn't. That's what we're here for.'

'TAC is here and if Tofferi and the others are examples, it's ready.'

Two years after this article was written, in April 1965, twenty-five F-104Cs of the 436th Tactical Fighter Squadron (TFS), 479th Tactical Fighter Wing (TFW), were sent to Đà Nẵng Air Base in South Việtnam to fly MiG combat air patrol

(MiGCAP) missions. Detachments were also sent to Kung Kuan, Taiwan. To protect strike aircraft from the MiGs of the NVNAF, the F-104Cs were armed with their single M61A1 20mm Vulcan cannon and four AIM-9 Sidewinder air-to-air missiles. The F-104Cs (and Northrop F-5As) were too short-ranged and carried an insufficient weapons load for this kind of operation and consequently, the McDonnell F-4C Phantom II took over the MiGCAP mission. In November 1965 the remaining F-104Cs of the 436th TFS were rotated back to George AFB, California. In Việtnam the Starfighter had flown 506 combat sorties, totalling 1,706.9 combat hours, with the loss of four F-104Cs.

Beginning in May 1966 the first F-104Cs of the 479th TFW were sent to South East Asia, to be based at Udorn Royal Thai Air Force Base (RTAFB) in Thailand under the control of the 8th TFW. This time the F-104Cs, which by now were camouflaged, flew low-level, close-support strikes against North Việtnamese lines of communication. By June 1967 all four squadrons were in action but the Starfighter's short range, even with in-flight refuelling, was insufficient for the majority of missions in South East Asia and in July the 479th TFW was rotated back to George AFB for the last time, to be replaced by the McDonnell F-4D Phantom. In thirteen months the F-104Cs had flown a total of 2,269 combat sorties, totalling 8,820 combat hours. Losses now totalled eight Starfighters missing in action (two to Soviet-built SA-2 surface-to-air (SAM) missiles and six to AAA) and another six were destroyed in operational accidents. In the summer of 1967 the surviving F-104C/Ds in the USAF inventory were transferred to the 198th TFS of the Puerto Rico Air National Guard where they replaced the F-86H. This unit operated Starfighters until its conversion to the LTV A-7D Corsair in the summer of 1975 and the last Starfighter in USAF service was phased out of operational service in 1975, although they continued to be used in a training role until 1983.

F-104Cs served in South East Asia in 1965-66 and 1966-67 during two separate deployments. Over the course of these two deployments, seven F-104s were lost to enemy ground defences; one F-104 was shot down by an enemy aircraft and no enemy aircraft were engaged by F-104s while flying escort or CAP missions. It has been said that the F-104s 'never had a mission and never made a mark' in SE Asia. Misconceptions, myth and misinformation about the F-104 have led to this impression. The facts tell a different story. By 1964 the USAF's only primary air superiority aircraft, the F-104C, had been forward deployed on several occasions to project US power and assure control of the air during world crises. The F-104 was widely regarded as the world's foremost daylight air-to-air platform and the pilots of TAC's 479th TFW, the only operators of the F-104C had proven themselves to be masters of their trade in numerous mock air-to-air encounters. It was therefore understood that

F-104C 56-0892 of the 435th TFS/479th and 8th TFWs, Udorn RTAFB, Thailand, 1967. Major Floyd Totten flew this F-104C, nicknamed *MISS BEVIE J. VI* after his first girlfriend - his five previous aircraft had also been *MISS BEVIE J.s.* The Starfighter was renamed *My Darlin' Dorothy* when Totten married.

the F-104Cs of the 479th's 435th, 436th or 476th TFSs would rapidly deploy to any trouble-spot where air superiority must be quickly established. Such a spot was South-East Asia in 1965.

Soon after the Gulf of Tonkin incident in August 1964, TAC began deploying aircraft in Operation 'Two Buck', a TDY jet force build-up in South-East Asia. At the time of the initial 1964 build-up, PACAF advocated deployment of an F-104 contingent to protect US air traffic over the Gulf of Tonkin from harassment by PRC and North Việtnamese aircraft. However, in January 1965 when TAC proposed sending F-104s to relieve TDY pressure on its overtaxed F-100 units, PACAF reversed its initial stance, citing the logisttic complications of adding one more aircraft type to the South-East Asia mix. PACAF was convinced that the existing MiG threat in South-East Asia did not warrant a unit dedicated to the air superiority role. Events in the following months would change PACAF's opinion. With the beginning of 'Rolling Thunder' strikes in March 1965, the tempo of bombing over North Việtnam escalated substantially. Unfortunately, the tempo and aggressiveness of North Việtnamese and PRC MiG also increased. Initially the heightened aggressiveness was felt primarily by the USN as PRC harassment of aircraft over the Gulf of Tonkin stepped up. North Việtnamese aircraft then began to dog US bombing missions over North Việtnam.

On 3 April 1965 three North Việtnamese MiG-17s attacked a USN strike on the Dong Phuong Thong Bridge, damaged an F-8 Crusader and escaped unharmed. The following day, two North Việtnamese MiG-17s attacked a flight of four F-105s that were waiting their turn to bomb the Than Hóa Bridge. The MiGs approached without warning, shot down two of the F-105s, completely disrupted the strike and then evaded escorting F-100s to escape unscathed. Obviously, the existing

F-104C-5-LO 56-0902 Miss Judy of the 436th TFS, 479th TFW, assigned to the 8th TFW at Udorn heads for its target in South Việtnam armed with two 750lb M117 bombs. In the summer of 1967 this Starfighter and the other surviving F-104C/Ds in the USAF inventory were transferred to the 198th TFS, 156th TFG of the Puerto Rico Air National Guard (PRANG) replacing the F-86H. (via Robert F. Dorr)

early warning and fighter assets in South-East Asia were insufficient to guarantee US air superiority in the region. Accordingly, an EC-121D 'College Eye' unit was dispatched to extend radar warning coverage over North Việtnam and TAC was asked to deploy F-104s to escort the EC-121s over the Gulf of Tonkin and to provide a MiG screen for USAF strike aircraft over North Việtnam. On 7 April TAC issued the deployment order to the 479th TFW and the first F-104Cs of the 476th TFS landed at Kung Kuan Air Base, Taiwan on 11 April. Kung Kuan was renamed Ching Chuan Kang Air Base on 20 March 1966 in memory of ROC Army General Qiu Qingquan and was thereafter known throughout the theater by its initials, CCK. The base was to serve as the main operating base for the F-104s, with regular rotation of aircraft to the forward operating base at Đà Nẵng. Twenty-four F-104s were deployed to CCK and of these; fourteen would be maintained at Đà Nẵng by rotation every ten days. This deployment scheme would be utilized throughout the F-104's 'Two Buck' commitment. 'At CCK the military there was on a high state of alert, ready to go to war at any moment' recalled Alan Baker, a C-130 pilot. 'Before we reached the runway, the Chinese scrambled their F-104s and in a rush to take off, one taxied under our right wing!'

After a work-up period of seven days, fourteen F-104s arrived at Đà Nẵng on 19 April and flew their first escort mission the next day. EC-121 escort missions typically involved three flights of

F-104C's 56-0912 and 56-0928 of the 479th TFW at Udorn AB, Thailand from Đà Nẵng on MIGCAP over the Gulf of Tonkin in 1965. They are carrying GAR-8 Sidewinder missiles. 56-0928 was transferred from Puerto Rico ANG to museum status and stored at Muñiz Airport in June 1975. It was destroyed on 11 January 1981 during the attack by Puerto Rican separatists. 56-0912 was on display at Sheppard AFB, Texas. (USAF)

four F-104s and two KC-135s. The escort sorties typically lasted from two to five hours and the operating area was normally between 250 and 300 miles NNW of Đà Nẵng. MiGCAP missions over North Việtnam utilized one to three flights of four F-104s deployed at various altitudes between the strike area and the Hànôi-Hảiphòng area. CAP points were 225 to 275 miles NNW of Đà Nẵng and on-station times varied from forty to ninety minutes. Aerial refuelling was only required for the longer duration missions. The effect of F-104 deployment upon North Việtnam and PRC MiG operations was immediate and dramatic. North Việtnamese MiGs avoided contact with USAF strikes being covered by F-104s and PRC MiGs gave the EC-121s a wide berth despite the proximity to Hainan Island, from where PRC harassment flights had previously originated. Much to the frustration of the pilots of the F-104s, during the entire deployment of the 476th only two fleeting encounters between F-104s and enemy fighters occurred. As it became apparent

that the MiG threat had decreased, PACAF sought to find other uses for the F-104s to supplement their air superiority role. Toward the end of the 476th's deployment, the F-104s began to be tasked for weather recce and ground attack missions. Weather recce missions normally involved two F-104s,

Two F-104A-15-LO Starfighters (56-0769 and 56-0781) from the 83rd Fighter Interceptor Squadron at Hamilton AFB, California in flight with Lockheed RC-121D-LO Warning Star (55-0127) of the 552nd AEW&C Wing, McClellan AFB, California, in 1958. 56-0769 went to the RoCAF (4208) where on 18 December 1963 it crashed 3,000 feet off shore South of Hsinchu AB into a mud-bank where it exploded after an attempted emergency landing due to a fire-warning light indication. The pilot, Fan Huan-Ron, was killed. On 9 April 1961 56-0781, now with the 197th FIS USANG crashed near Phoenix Airport, Arizona when the engine failed after a compressor stall while trying to reach Phoenix Sky Harbor Airport. The pilot, Major Erich Hettlinger was killed after ejecting.

which flew near enough a North Viêtnamese strike target area to determine the pre-strike weather conditions without revealing the target's identity. Twenty-one strike and AAA-suppression sorties were flown against targets in North Viêtnam, but the great majority of the 476th's ground attack sorties were in-country CAS missions flown while under the control of airborne FACs. From these CAS missions, the F-104s quickly gained a reputation for accuracy with their cannon and bombs and were specifically requested by FACs on numerous occasions because of their fast reaction time. The F-104's high speed and simplicity of systems allowed it to reach targets 250 nautical miles from Đà Nẵng within forty minutes of alert - including the ten minutes required for the pilot to travel the quarter mile to his aircraft.

On 11 July 1965 the 476th TFS completed its 96th day of TDY deployment. In all, 476th aircraft had flown 1,182 combat sorties. 52% of these sorties were EC-121 escort; 24% were MiG screen; 5% were weather recce and 18% were ground attack missions. During this period, the 476th F-104s maintained an in-commission rate of 94.7%, a testimony both to the quality of 476th maintenance personnel and to the simplicity and maintainability of F-104 systems. Operation 'Cross Switch' saw the 436th TFS assuming the 476th commitment in Đà Nẵng on 11 July and the 436th began flying combat sorties the next day. From the outset however, the overall mission of the 436th was of a different flavour than the 476th's. Although a small number of MiGCAP and escort sorties were flown in July, the great majority of the sorties initially flown were of the CAS type.

Beginning in late July the 436th was fragged to maintain four F-104Cs on fifteen-minute alert to provide quick-reaction close support of friendly ground troops. This alert commitment was not dropped until the end of September when the escort missions again took precedence. Interdiction/strike and RESCAP (Rescue Combat Air Patrol) missions in North Viêtnam were also flown. By the end of their three-month deployment, 56% of the combat sorties flown by the 436th were of the ground attack type. Although the F-104C's high speed and small size made it a difficult target for AAA gunners, questionable missions such as strafing AAA sites inevitably had an impact. On 29 June F-104C 56-0937 piloted by Captain Richard Cole in the 436th TFS, 479th TFW was hit by ground fire, possibly caused by pitch-up while rolling in on the dive pass, during a close air support mission near Tri Đào, fifteen miles northwest of Kontum and 100 nautical miles SSW of Đà Nẵng. Cole was rescued by an Army helicopter although he had suffered minor injuries during the ejection. Aircraft began returning from CAS missions with battle damage.

On 22 July F-104C (56-0908) piloted by Captain Roy James Blakeley was hit by ground fire during close air support mission in Quang Tin province south of Đà Nẵng. The left leading edge flap departed on the pull-out from a dive bomb pass with two M117 750lb bombs and 750 rounds of 20mm. There was a large gash in the left fuselage above the left wing and Blakeley experienced oil pressure-failure and landing gear extension failure. He attempted to crash-land his battle-damaged at Chu Lai Marine Air Base. Blakeley successfully set his aircraft down gear-up, but died when his F-104 skidded off the runway into a sand dune. PACAF headquarters apparently took notice of Blakeley's death, because mission fragging took a more realistic turn soon thereafter. The 436th's

F-104Cs 56-0908, Captain James Roy Blakeley's Starfighter on 22 July 1965 which was hit by ground fire during CAS in Quang Tin Province; and 56-0892, which is now on display at Luke AFB, Arizona. Blakely was killed trying to land wheels up at Chu Lai, MCAS, South Vietnam.

19S) flown by Chinese Navy pilot Gao Xiang who downed the Starfighter with cannon fire. The official cause of the loss of Smith's aircraft was AAA fire received during roll-in for a dive bomb pass. Smith ejected safely but was captured and taken prisoner, the only F-104 pilot to hold this unenviable distinction in the war in South East Asia. Smith was held captive by the Chinese for over seven years until his release in March 1973. Subjected to near-total isolation, torture and brainwashing, Smith resorted to strict adherence of the PoW's Code of Conduct and to iron-willed self-discipline to keep his sanity and was able to survive without long-term psychological damage.

Two more F-104Cs of the 436th TFS, meanwhile, who were flying RESCAP returning from searching for Captain Smith's F-104 collided while penetrating weather on a night-time approach to Đà Nẵng. 56-0911 was piloted by Captain Harvey Quackenbush, 56-0921 by Captain Dale W. Carlson. Both pilots ejected and were recovered unharmed. The aircraft and pilots landed in Đà Nẵng Bay approximately six miles north of Đà Nẵng AB. Both aircraft had been launched on a RESCAP mission after Captain Phillip Smith had been shot down by a Chinese MiG-19 over Hainan Island. They took off at 1707 hours Local. The two aircraft remained in the search area for 45 minutes, refuelled from a C-130 tanker and then returned to the SAR area. The search was terminated at 1930 hours. Letdown to land at Đà Nẵng AB was made through overcast and both aircraft flew minimum AB with speed brakes to burn down heavy fuel loads. They had been flying around the area for a long time and it had become dark when returning to base. Their nav lights were not operational as they were day fighters and were inbound for landing when one lost track of the other. A right turn was made at approx 10,000 feet aligning with Runway 1 at Đà Nẵng. The other pilot was requested to light his afterburner so that he could find the other during the dark circumstances. When this was done it was found that the other was in very close in front and slightly above. The afterburner lightning was too late to avoid the collision. The aircraft became

■ **Captain James Roy Blakeley.**

bad luck did not end with Blakeley's death, nor with the return to escort missions.

On the night of 20 September 1965 30-year old Captain Philip Eldon Smith became lost while flying an EC-121 escort mission over the Gulf of Tonkin when he tried to relieve another F-104C pilot who had been flying MiGCAP on station in bad weather. After several equipment failures and numerous incorrect steering commands from Đà Nẵng and a tanker, Smith was forced to seek lower altitude in an effort to establish his position and his F-104 wandered over Hainan and was shot down over the centre of Hainan Island; the victory being credited to a People's Republic of China J-6 (MiG-

Philip Eldon Smith who on the night of 20 September 1965, flying F-104C 56-0883 and due to equipment failure and incorrect navigational commands strayed into Chinese airspace over Hainan. His aircraft was intercepted and shot down by two Shenyang J-6 fighters of the People's Liberation Army Naval Air Force. Captain Smith ejected successfully and was captured by PLA forces. He was first taken to Canton for interrogation and then later transferred to Peking. Most of his captivity was spent in solitary confinement. Captain Smith was released on 15 March 1973. He returned to USAF duty and retired with the rank of Colonel in December 1996. Captain Smith became the only F-104 pilot to be shot down and taken prisoner in the Việtnam War by the Chinese.

uncontrollable and both pilots safely ejected and they were rescued by naval patrol boat. The three Starfighters were the last to be lost by the 479th before the squadron re-deployed back to the States on 20 November.

The events of 20 September would have far-reaching effects on the employment and eventual removal of the F-104 from South-East Asia service. Following Smith's loss, there was official concern about the F-104's lack of advanced navigational gear. It was feared that F-104s would be susceptible to border violations because they did not have a Doppler, INS, or even a UHF/ADF system. Such equipment did not guarantee against wayward

F-104Cs of the 479th TFW on the ramp at Udorn in Thailand in 1967.

aircraft however, as was stressed when two USN A-6Es with INSs and navigators wandered over China and were shot down in 1967. F-104C pilots were very adept at navigation and beside Captain Smith's loss - which was due to equipment failure and bad luck - there were no instances of F-104s unknowingly violating buffer zones, bombing the wrong target, getting lost on the way to a target, etc.

Despite its five losses, the 436th's deployment was a success. People's Republic of China and North Việtnamese MiGs were never encountered during any of the escort or MiGCAP missions, a sign of the enemy's continued respect for the capabilities of the F-104. The 436th also expanded on the 476th's tradition of quick-response and accuracy while flying in-country CAS missions

Ben McAvoy the Tech Rep for Lockheed assigned to the 435th in Vietnam in the cockpit of an F-104C at Udorn. The rarity of the F-104C in the USAF and its proximity to a planned phase-out date, led to numerous parts shortages. Even equipment common to other aircraft in SE Asia was not available to the 435th and cannon spares were particularly scarce. The level of F-104 operations was only able to be maintained because of the quality of the 435th's maintenance personnel and the dedication of individuals such as Ben McAvoy (USAF)

and North Việtnamese strike missions. During their deployment, 436th F-104s flew 1382 combat sorties, for a total of 3116 hours, while maintaining an in-commission rate of 88%. The first seven F-104s of the 435th TFS arrived at Đà Nẵng on 14 October 1965 to assume the mission commitments of the 436th TFS. The arrival of the 435th also marked the practical end of F-104 fragging for CAS missions in 1965. Only twelve CAS sorties were flown by the 435th; the other 407 combat sorties were of the escort or MiGCAP type, including twelve ResCAP sorties. The primary mission of the 435th was the escort of EC-121D and C-130E-II 'Silver Dawn' aircraft over the Gulf of Tonkin. The aircraft were escorted separately, with flights of four F-104s rotating to cover the general area of the EC-121 and flights of two F-104s rotating to provide constant visual escort for the 'Silver Dawn' aircraft. Coverage was maintained ten hours per day. Captain Harold Alston of the 435th TFS was the first pilot to fly 101 combat missions in Việtnam flying the F-104C on 30 September 1966. The 435th's deployment was cut short when, on 21

November, its F-104s and personnel were recalled to Kung Kuan in preparation for re-deployment back to the US. TDY units were to be replaced by permanently based units and the F-4Cs of the 390th TFS assumed the 435th's escort mission at Đà Nẵng. The 435th deployed back to George AFB, with the final equipment-carrying cargo aircraft landing on 25 December, the start of the 1965 Christmas bombing halt. During the F-104 'Two Buck' deployments, North Việtnamese and PRC MiG activity had decreased to the point where MiGs were not considered a primary threat to USAF aircraft in South-East Asia. TAC and the State Department recognized the F-104's contribution to the decrease in MiG activity, but PACAF seemed only to dwell on the 'waste' of maintaining single-mission aircraft in South-East Asia. PACAF felt that the F-4C could effectively fill the F-104's MiGCAP and escort roles while also providing the capability of delivering larger tonnage (read: high bomb counts) in CAS missions.

In the early months of 1966 MiG operations in South-East Asia again began to increase. In addition, North Việtnamese MiG-21s began to be spotted in recon photos in March and were first seen flying over North Việtnam on 23 April. On 26 April, two MiG-21s attacked a pair of F-4Cs that were escorting an EB-66C over North Việtnam. One of the MiGs was shot down by one of the F-4s and the other MiG escaped, but the limitations of the F-4C and its missile-only armament soon became of great concern to 7th Air Force. Air superiority in South-East Asia was again in jeopardy. On 29 April 7th AF's request for more F-104s was met with approval by the Air Staff. PACAF then explained the need for an F-104 re-deployment to CINCPAC and received concurrence on 14 May. After granting of JCS approval, eight F-104Cs of the 435th TFS, 479th TFW landed at Udorn on 6 June 1966. (They were modified to carry four rather than two AIM-9 Sidewinders, as well as bombs and rockets for air-to-ground missions). At the time of the F-104's second deployment to South-East Asia, TAC was in the process of phasing-out the type. The 479th TFW was converting to F-4 aircraft and when the 435th's F-104s crossed the international dateline, they were attached to PACAF's 8th TFW. On 7 June, the eight F-104s began flying missions in concert with 8th TFW F-4C aircraft, escorting F-105 strikes over North Việtnam.

Special tactics were employed which exploited the unique capabilities of the F-104s and the F-4s.

Colonel Arthur Thomas Finney who was KIA on 1 August 1966.

Unfortunately, no MiGs were encountered. These missions also involved close coordination with the F-105 strike aircraft, the Thuds providing SAM warnings for the F-104s, which lacked RHAW gear. Soon after the F-104s arrived at Udorn, the 'Wild Weasel III' EF-105Fs deployed to Korat, Thailand. After some unsatisfactory attempts at using F-4s to escort the 'Wild Weasels', it was decided to give that mission to the F-104s. The F-104's range and speed was superior to the F-4s in the 'Weasel' escort mission. The Weasels appreciated the F-104's ability to stay with their Thuds, often tailoring missions to the availability of F-104s for escort. F-104 availability was enhanced on 22 July when an additional twelve F-104s deployed to Udorn and joined the 8th TFW.

1 August brought tragedy to the 435th FIS when two F-104Cs were lost to SAMs within one hour while flying with three other Starfighters as MiGCAP for 'Iron Hand' missions ('Wild Weasel' SAM suppression). 57-0925 nicknamed *Smoke II* piloted by Lieutenant Colonel Arthur Thomas Finney, born in Canmer, Kentucky on 26 June 1928 and 56-0928 flown by Captain John Charles

Members of the 435th Tactical Fighter Squadron. 479th TFW at Udorn in 1966-67 with F-104Cs 56-0936 *Lil' Poo II* (Tom Mahan, the pilot's nickname for his wife Shirley), 56-0891 *Snoopy Sniper/ Nancy J* and 56-0892 behind. 56-0891 was the first F-104C handed over to the 479th TFW, at Nellis AFB on 15 October 1958.

Kwortnik, call sign 'Dagger 02)', as number two in a flight of four were orbiting a SAM site thirty miles northwest of the iron and steel producing town of Thai Nguyen in North Việtnam when they were hit. Kwortnik was hit by a SAM and immediately burst into flames and broke up. It was reported that a good ejection and parachute had been seen, but intense ground fire prevented any further investigation and no beeper signals were heard. If Captain Kwortnik did eject safely, he did not survive as he never appeared in the North Việtnamese PoW

105

system, although a Hànôi newspaper reported the capture of a pilot on this date. Kwortnik's remains were returned to the USA on 14 August 1985. At the same time that Captain Kwortnik's flight was encountering intense ground fire, another flight of Starfighters was escorting F-105 'Wild Weasels' over Thai Nguyen when *Smoke II* suddenly turned into a ball of flame. This was assumed to be another SA-2 SAM hit and Lieutenant Colonel Finney, who was on his third mission in Viêtnam, was posted as missing. His wingman said that he saw him eject and that he had a good parachute. That was the last time he was seen. When the PoWs were released in 1973 Finney was not among them and no PoW recalled him. His wife Peggy had his status changed to KIA in 1974 and she and her two children moved to Las Vegas. She passed away in 1981 without knowledge of what happened to him. His remains were returned to the USA on 14 August 1985.

The loss of one-tenth of the USAF's remaining combat F-104C force in one day led to a re-assessment of the need to escort 'Wild Weasel' missions. It was reasoned that at the speeds and altitudes at which Weasel F-105s operated, the MiG threat was negligible. Furthermore, the Weasels were regularly exposed to intense target defences and it was judged a reckless utilization of very limited F-104 assets to place them in harm's way if a viable MiG threat could not be demonstrated. The F-104s were therefore withdrawn from strike escort missions over North Viêtnam until they could be fitted with ECM gear and until the MiG threat increased - because, once again North Viêtnamese MiG activity dropped perceptibly when F-104s entered the theatre. By late August 1966 F-104s had been shifted to a primary ground-attack role. Missions in the lower RPs, in Laos and South Viêtnam were deemed safe enough for F-104Cs. However, losses continued to mount. On 1 September another F-104C (57-0913) of the 435th TFS was hit by AAA as it pulled up from attacking a truck park near Tróc while conducting a road recce mission over northern Laos. The aircraft flew for a further ten miles before the pilot, 39-year old Major Norman Schmidt, who was from Ben Lomond, California was forced to eject. Despite an intense rescue effort, Major Schmidt was captured and held in captivity in the notorious Hŏa Lò prison, built in Hànôi by the French in 1896 and called the 'Hanoi Hilton' by the nearly 600 American airmen to be captured by the Communists during the Viêtnam War. In August 1967 Schmidt was taken

Major Norman Schmidt of the 435th TFS, 8th
TFW who was shot down and taken prisoner
on 1 September 1966. In August 1967 he was
probably beaten to death by his guards.

over North Việtnam in the F-104C from Udorn
Royal Thai Air Base on 30 September 1966. 'The
target was an ammo storage site. My ordinance was
finned napalm which allowed delivery from a 30
degree dive bomb profile. I led a flight of four and
we also had two A1-E aircraft that spotted the target
for us. I put both napalms directly on the target. My
accuracy even impressed me let alone the others. On
our return to Udorn RTAB I had my flight in combat
formation. The radar site, call sign 'Brigham' gave
us flight following back to base. At about fifty miles
I left their frequency for tower. I had briefed my
flight that I would bring them on to initial for a
three second break, I would 'go around' and they
would land. I flew a closed pattern for a high speed
pass with a victory roll at 100 feet. Unknown to
me was that the F-102s were scrambled to escort
us back. The 102s joined up with me as I turned
final for the high speed pass. At the approach end
of the runway, I pulled the nose up slightly and did
two aileron rolls, then a 3/4 roll to the right with
a left break to downwind and my landing. I was
met with a crowd of people, all the pilots, all the
maintenance people, the Squadron Commander
Lieutenant Colonel Ed Gaines, the *Stars and Stripes*
newspaper reporter and others. Mike Korte had
flown the squadron's 1,000th combat mission that

from his cell to the interrogation room and never
returned. Some of his fellow PoWs heard sounds
coming from the interrogation room and believe
that Major Schmidt was beaten to death by his
guards. In March 1974 Major Schmidt's remains
were returned to the USA, presumably having been
buried in the prison grounds since 1967.

Captain Harold Alston, 435th TFS 479th TFW
George AFB completed his 100th combat mission

F-104A 56-0902 *Miss Judy* at Udorn AB in
November 1966 which was piloted by Ace Rawlins
who named the Starfighter after his wife.

morning so he was there with Lieutenant Colonel Gaines. They all congratulated me and Lieutenant Colonel Gaines gave me a bottle of champagne. Since I am a non-drinker, I poured some over the head of the crew chief, Staff Sergeant Holiness and gave him the rest of the bottle. It was shared with the assistant crew chief, Airman Goodwin in a champagne glass. Airman Goodwin asked me to autograph the glass with a grease pencil. I wrote: *Harold Alston, 100, 30 Sep 1966.* There were a lot of pictures taken, interviews for the news media. This day made me the 'first pilot in the USAF to fly 100 combat missions over North Việtnam in the F-104'. 'Later Tony LeVier, Lockheed test pilot and the first to fly the F-104, presented me a plaque that acknowledged my accomplishment. Since we had just moved into a new officer's club at Udorn a few days before, I was the first to throw a '100 mission party' at the new club. It cost me over $100, but I felt it was worth it to have survived. I drank Coke. The next day I left about noon for Bangkok for a couple of nights and then was homeward bound to Los Angeles and a reunion with my family at George AFB. It was a good feeling.'

On 2 October 1966 another 435th TFS, F-104C (56-0904) went down over northern Laos when a flight of Starfighters was detailed to fly an armed reconnaissance mission to hit suspected truck park near 'Sam Nooie' as part of the 'Barrel Roll' campaign in northern Laos. Captain Norman R. Lockhard who was on his 83rd combat sortie, had given a 27 July 1965 interview for his hometown newspaper, *The San Bernardino County Sun* and also, a talk for a chamber of commerce luncheon, in which he had said: 'It's a strange war. A frontal attack on an area of dense jungle could cost half the troops in casualties. But that large building is full of ammunition. We have to burn everything that looks like it may be of military use. It's the first time I've dropped a bomb or fired a rocket in anger. You don't see the people you hit...it's the cost of war...Who's to say that man running across a field didn't harbour a Việt Công last night in his hut.' Many farm workers change clothes at night and become Việt Công fighters. The Việtnamese have the best air-sea rescue organization I've seen. I've seen a pilot rescued under fire as he taxied toward the beach.' The trim young officer of George Air Force Base said he expected to return to Việtnam in 'another three to six months.'

'The 436th TFS is now on three-month rotational duty there. There are 25 officers of the squadron. Captain Lockhard has 2,400 hours flying time; 800 of it in the Starfighter. He said that while flying his

F-104, he saw only one MiG which 'high-tailed' for safety. 'They're not fighting until they have every advantage,' he said. The 104 and MiG are similar in capabilities. Some other observations: 'Đà Nẵng, 'garden spot' of Việtnam, has 'the biggest mosquitoes I've seen. Air traffic at the base was nearly as heavy. The F-104 has about two hours flying time, fully loaded; thus, pilots flying 4-hour missions, one or two a day, rely on about two mid-air refuellings. He believed that the enemy would have to be hit in the 'sanctuary' of Hànôi to remove the 'real threat' of surface-to-air missiles being based there. 'We have to take the sites out. The only other choice is to exploit weaknesses of the missile. Mobile launch bases pose another threat, he admitted, but, added, 'We're definitely stopping them... Look out next spring when weather conditions are better. The tide is already turning.'

'Spring came and went and then on 2 October Lockhard's flight prepared to bomb a truck park when 904 was hit by an SA-2 missile. The pilot, Captain Norman R. Lockhard recalled: 'Briefed no flak - right? We rolled in high, dumped our nape. During the pull off we took 37 and 57mm fire. Charles 'Chuck' Tofferi broke left, I broke right. The flak was right on us during the dive and 'the golden BB got me'. As I pushed up the throttle-nothing happened. At 80% power the F-104 flew like a brick! I went through a quick stall clearing procedure-no luck. I called 'Chuck' telling him, 'I'm hit, ejecting; check east of the target'. I got out just above the stall at about 4,500 feet. The chute opened fast and about pulled off my right leg. I had hung on to the ejection ring too long. I also noted my helmet was gone or at least not on my head. I looked up - good chute - I looked down - lot of green! Best of all, no people, not even a road. I then deployed my survival kit which dropped 20' down-all's well so far. I tried to put my helmet back on-it had slipped off my head, rotating from back to front. I must have tumbled when I separated from the ejection seat. The trees were coming up fast so I dumped the helmet. I was drifting west into a bowl shaped area-solid jungle. I hit on the up-slope about 200 yards from the lip. I was in tall bamboo. My survival kit and life raft hit first and then me, then my chute which stopped my downward drop. I found myself 50 feet up, hanging parallel to the ground between the life raft and my chute. I tried to pull the life raft loose; no go, it was impaled or tangled up in the bamboo. I cut it loose and swung

vertically down under my chute. I stopped two feet from the ground! Talk about being lucky! I popped the quick release and dropped into Laos. I could hear 'Chuck' overhead, but couldn't see him due to the heavy canopy of trees. I turned off the chute pack beeper and came up on our two-way radio. I still have both of those units. I called 'In the blind'. Chuck, I'm down OK; any bad guys in the area?'

'He came up right, 'No one but you. The choppers on the way; hang in there!'

'Good old Chuck! He held up high while I checked out the area and got ready for 'Jolly'. Never did recover my survival kit nor chute. I could hardly see the chute! Humus on the jungle floor was knee deep. I noticed high ground to the West covered with Elephant grass. I called Chuck telling him I was heading for high ground, grass to the West to set up a better pick up site. Sure! Talk about thick, I hacked and bullied my way for thirty yards and gave up. Even the grass was five feet high! About this time 'Chuck' called to say he had to leave-choppers are ten minutes out! That was a long ten minutes. 'Chuck' Tofferi was lead that day. We flew many missions together. We lost him three weeks later about forty miles from the area in which I was shot down.

'Want to know the sweetest sound in the world-to a downed pilot? It's WAP-WAP-WAP! That means the chopper is coming in and did he come fast! As I later found out; they make a fast pass to see if any bad guys shoot at them. Good thinking by golly for a chopper in a hover is really a great target! He passed right over me and I called up 'You missed me!' Dumb! I should have said, 'Come back Shane'. He then banked right and pulled the nose up to slow down. I popped a can of red smoke and he rolled out right over my head. This guy was sharp! I looked up to see the biggest, baldest sergeant in the Air Force lowering the penetrator. Little did I know, but he couldn't see me! I pulled out my trump card, a 3 feet square piece of red parachute silk and draped it over a bush. He dropped the line two feet from the target and I dove for the cable because the penetrator was lost in the under growth. I pulled it back to me, strapped in and gave two pulls. The slack went out and I knew another sharp guy was on the ball- what a team, they made it easy! At this point I felt that winch couldn't move fast enough. I took my last look at that jungle and wondered how they ever got me out. When that big, bald sergeant put the bear hug on me I knew things were in good hands. I don't know which of us was

F-104C 57-0929 at Udorn in 1967. This Starfighter is displayed at the Southern Museum of Flight, Birmingham, Alabama.

grinning the most. He got me off the penetrator, laid me on a bunk and the youngest airman I ever saw gave me a quick physical - little did I know I was in the presence of a hero! He gave me a shot of water and handed me a chute! #1, that canteen didn't have bourbon in it-damn! #2, put a chute on? Any self respecting fighter jock who has just been shot down doesn't want to go for two jumps in the same day! 'The Kid' says, 'Regulations Sir.' The pilot laughed and called me up to 'The Office'. He pointed left and down- flak so thick the sky was a black and grey blanket. He grinned and says, 'I think we pissed them off!' What a guy- yes I kept the chute on! After clearing the local firing range, we headed for what was called a 'Lima' site. Our chopper sat alert at these forward positions and what a place they must have been, for they changed hands often. One day we had it, then the bad guys took it and we took it back again. Those defenders must have had their hands full! The trip to Lima was great! We enjoyed a birthday cake one of the crew had received. What a day!

'The same crew that picked me up went right back on alert when we sat down. That evening they returned to Udorn. I was his 1st or 2nd pickup. Quite a crew, one great bunch of guys.

'I was transferred to another chopper and flown to Udorn. The 'Doc' grounded me for two days to check my leg (A-OK). He said, 'Get drunk' and I did that night along with the chopper guys. What a party!

'One group I haven't mentioned we call, 'Sandys'. They flew A1 Skyraiders and provided fire support for the Jollies when needed. These guys carried more ordinances on one bird than five F-104s. This team, 'Sandys and Jollies' have saved many a downed pilot. They all did one heck of a professional job that day and I couldn't even repay what they did for me. I'm proud to say that I was

Below: F-104C-5-LOs of the 479th TFW assigned to the 8th TFW at Udorn armed with 750lb M117 bombs en route to their target in Việtnam, in November 1966. This second deployment to South East Asia was made in June 1966 and the mission was largely MiGCAP. 56-0910 (nearest the camera) was transferred to the Puerto Rican ANG after use in SE Asia and finally to Lowry AFB for display. (USAF)

fortunate enough to meet some of them and wish I could have thanked all of them for saving me that day. This guy will never forget what they did that day.'

Lockhard's F-104 was apparently the first time a US aircraft had been brought down by a SAM over Laos. He rotated after 100 missions and went home with 106. He stayed on the F-104 until 1973 and never had to jump again.

Losses continued. 57-910, which was delivered to the 435th TFW at Udorn on 18 November 1966, ran off the runway after a mission of eight hours in December. Joe Nevers was unhurt and aircraft had no real damage. However on 12 January 1967 it encountered a severe landing accident at Udorn resulting in damage beyond economical repair. The accident was caused by a so-called 'hard rudder' problem which results in a very bad control of the aircraft during landing. The aircraft was parked away on the Udorn flight line ramp and used as donor aircraft to service the other Starfighters. F-104C 57-922, one of the twelve additional Starfighters delivered to the 435th TFS at Udorn on 22 July 1966 was lost on 15 May 1967 when Major Karl H. Hofmann crashed into the Gulf of Tonkin due to an explosion following aerial refuelling. Hofmann was flying MiGCAP as number two in

flight of two escorting 'Commando Lance' and 'College Eye' (EC-121) missions over the Gulf of Tonkin. Shortly after refuelling there was a severe explosion below and behind the cockpit followed immediately by illumination of both fire warning lights and loss of engine thrust. Hofmann attempted to make an emergency radio transmission and to select T/O flaps but was unable to due to loss of electrical power. He attempted one air start without success. With both fire warning lights on and fuel fumes in the cockpit, Hofmann chose to eject at approximately 19,000 feet. He opened his chute manually at 14,000 feet and deployed his survival kit at approximately 6,000 feet. Hoffmann landed safely but his dinghy was only one-third inflated. He was unable to climb into the dinghy and chose to remain in the water supported by his underarm life preserver since rescue aircraft were in the area. He used an Mk.13 flare to attract the attention of a US Navy helicopter and was rescued safely by this helicopter suffering only minor cuts and bruises.

Although the Air Staff had repeatedly questioned F-104 use in the ground attack role, there was no mission change until Tofferi's death. In early December, the F-104s were assigned exclusively to escort missions. By late 1966, all F-104s in South-East Asia had received APR-25/26 RHAW gear

F-104Cs en-route Puerto Rico with a JC-135 aerial tanker (B.Preciado).

F-104A 56-0898 *Sex Machine* **at Udorn in March 1967. This Starfighter was one of the twelve aircraft which landed at Udorn on 22 July 1966 and was flown by Hugh Spencer.**

under Project 'Pronto'. So equipped, the F-104s once again began flying missions over North Việtnam. Sixteen F-104s took part in Operation 'Bolo' on 2 January 1967. Four more F-104Cs in the 435th TFS were lost in 1967. On 12 January F-104C 57-0910 crashed during landing at Udorn at the end of a CAP mission, the pilot survived. 16 January F-104C 57-0914 suffered an engine failure during a CAP mission and crashed in Thailand, the pilot survived. On 28 January F-104C 56-0921 also suffered an engine failure while on combat air patrol over Thailand. The pilot survived. On 14 May during an armed reconnaissance mission an engine on F-104C 57-0922 failed and the aircraft crashed in Thailand, the pilot survived. This was the fourteenth and final F-104 lost in Southeast Asia.

Notably however, the F-104s were not used to actively entice and engage MiGs, but were fragged instead to protect the egressing F-4 force. The F-104s of the 435th continued flying escort missions over the Gulf of Tonkin until 19 July 1967 when they were withdrawn from the theatre and replaced by F-4Ds of the 4th TFS. The official reasons for the withdrawal were the need to shepherd remaining F-104C assets in case the MiG threat increased in South-East Asia or elsewhere in the world, the imminent phase-out of the F-104 from active USAF service and the deficiency in air-to-ground load that could be carried by the F-104. During their second deployment to SE Asia, the F-104s of the 435th TFS had flown a total of 5,306 combat sorties, for a total of 14,393 combat flight hours. Due to increasing parts shortages and unrelenting sortie rates, aircraft in-commission rate dropped from a high of 85% to a low of 62%. Nevertheless, despite their tired birds, the 435th maintained the reputation of the F-104 among the warriors in South-East Asia. If the F-104C is judged against other US aircraft for its ability to sustain battle damage, to deliver large bomb loads or to conduct operations in bad weather, the 104 rates as an also-ran. If, however, the F-104C is judged for its ability to deter MiGs, to ensure the safety of the aircraft entrusted to its escort, or to out-perform any aircraft in existence at the time, the 'Zip 4' is unrivalled. The F-104 had a mission in South-East Asia: air superiority - a mission it performed brilliantly.

The Starfighter's short and uninspired career seemed to be over and in the USA it was, but Lockheed, desperate for success, pursued more lucrative markets in Europe and beyond.

Charles Ehnstrom Tofferi, in one of his statements made to Lockheed: 'Thank you, one and all, for the best airplane I've ever flown. The F-104 'really shines' in maintenance capability, so simple to maintain, people with little experience can do it.'

F-104C 57-0914, which crashed over Thailand on 16 January 1967. (Julio A. Fuentes)

USAF F-104C Việtnam Losses 1965-1967

Date	Tail No.	Service / Remarks
29 June 1965	56-0937	(476th TFS, 479th TFW attached to 6252nd TFW, Đà Nẵng). Hit by ground fire during close air support mission near Tri Đảo. Pilot Captain Richard Cole ejected and was rescued by Army helicopter.
22 July 1965	56-0908	(436th TFS, 479th TFW attached to 6252nd TFW, Đà Nẵng), hit by ground fire during close air support mission in Quang Tin province south of Đà Nẵng. Pilot Captain Roy James Blakeley killed.
20 September 1965	56-0883	(436th TFS, 479th TFW attached to 6252nd TFW, Đà Nẵng). Pilot Captain Phillip Eldon Smith ejected safely and was held captive by the Chinese until March of 1973. 56-0911 and 57-0921 collided at night. Both pilots killed.
1 August 1966	56-0928	(435th TFS, 8th TFW, Udorn Air Base, Thailand) hit by a SAM and immediately burst into flames and broke up. Captain John Charles Kwortnik killed. 57-0925 assumed to be another SA-2 SAM hit. Lieutenant Colonel Arthur Thomas Finney posted as MIA, later KIA.
1 September 1966	57-0913	(435th TFS, 8th TFW, Udorn Air Base, Thailand) hit by AAA. Major Norman Schmidt ejected, was captured and held in captivity in the 'Hanoi Hilton'. In August 1967 Major Schmidt was probably beaten to death by his guards.
2 October 1966	56-0904	(435th TFS, 8th TFW, Udorn Air Base, Thailand), Hit by an SA-2 missile. The pilot, Captain Norman R. Lockhard ejected immediately and was rescued by an Air Force helicopter.
20 October 1966	56-0918	(435th TFS, 8th TFW, Udorn Air Base, Thailand). Shot down by ground fire. Captain Charles Ehnstrom Tofferi KIA.
12 January 1967	57-0910	(435th TFS, 8th TFW, Udorn Air Base, Thailand) crashed during landing at Udorn at the end of a CAP mission. The pilot survived.
16 January 1967	57-0914	(435th TFS, 8th TFW, Udorn Air Base, Thailand), Suffered an engine failure during a CAP mission and crashed in Thailand. Pilot survived.
28 January 1967	56-0921	435th TFS, 8th TFW, Udorn Air Base, Thailand). Suffered an engine failure while on combat air patrol over Thailand. The pilot survived.
14 May 1967	57-0922	(435th TFS, 8th TFW, Udorn Air Base, Thailand). Engine failure. The aircraft crashed in Thailand. The pilot survived.

The 'Widowmaker'

The Widowmaker
is a real brain-shaker
the Widowmaker
is easy to fly
the Widowmaker
is a young life taker
the Widowmaker
is a pie in the sky.
The Widowmaker
is a good way to die.

Long and lean
a silver queen
have you ever seen
such a flying machine
hits the ground
as fast as sound
seven hundred thousand pounds
of little pieces lying around.

The *Starfighters*, an American movie released in 1964, written and directed by Will Zens and starring Bob Dornan. Some called the F-104 the 'Lawn Dart' or the 'Aluminum Death Tube' because of the high loss rate. After the Starfighter was introduced into the German Bundeswehr there was a humorous saying: *How do you get your own F-104? - Buy a piece of land and wait for one to drop on it!* Sick jokes abounded. Starfighters became known as the *Fliegender Sarg* ('Flying Coffin') or the *Witwenmacher* ('Widowmaker'). The Luftwaffe's definition of an optimist was 'a Starfighter pilot who gave up smoking because he was afraid of dying of lung cancer.'

In December 1957 Oberstleutnant Werner and Major Walter Krupinski were among the German representatives to arrive in the United States to test fly both the Grumman F11F-1F and the F-104 Starfighter. Krupinski, a mentor of Erich Hartmann, had ended the Second World War as a top scoring Luftwaffe fighter pilot with 197 victories, 177 of them in the east. Generally, he was known as 'Graf Pinski' owing to his propensity for living life to the full. Krupinski would have been an outstanding character in any air force. In the air he was a bar-room brawler type of flyer with a habit of getting himself into impossible situations which he somehow survived.

The fact that the Grumman design and the French contender, the Dassault Mirage, were still in the prototype stage while the F-104 was about to be introduced into USAF service, probably helped to speed up the German decision-making process when it came to selecting the winning fighter design. Although the Mirage was thought to be superior in dogfights, it could not outweigh the Starfighter's overall superior performance. Although both the F-104A and B, as demonstrated, did not deliver the all-weather capability nor the weapon load requirements West Germany expected, Lockheed suggested that an improved version - the F-104G 'Super Starfighter' - would have the necessary

structural improvements and radar and flight navigation systems installed that would make it suitable for *all* West Germany's needs.

As has already been explained, in 1959 Lockheed won the contract to supply West Germany with the Starfighter and the company would build the first F-104Gs and TF-104Gs for the Luftwaffe. Thereafter, F-104G production would be carried out in Europe. The export models represented a quantum leap in avionics over the A and C models. All of the avionics were packaged in containers referred to as 'gas cans' due to their appearance. All of these gas cans were in turn installed in the avionics bay in a 'tee tack' so-called because of its shape, an inverted 'T'. All avionics interface wiring, cooling air ducting and installation hard-ware were included in the tee rack. The entire installation was quite compact and efficient. Avionics systems packed in this manner included the MH-97 Autopilot, M-2 Bombing Computer, F15A North American Search and Ranging radar (NASARR), Multi-mode Radar System electronics, LN-3 Inertial Navigation

System, ARC-552 UHF Receiver/Transmitter, AN/ARN-52 TACAN Receiver/Transmitter and AN-APX-46 IFF Transponder. Also installed in the avionics bay were the Position Homing Indicator (PHI) System, the C-2G Directional Gyro/Compass System, various models of Emergency UHF radios and components of the Infra-red and Optical Sight Systems. None of these systems were installed in the F-104A and C models except for the sights.

Before the Starfighter export models were ready for operational use the Luftwaffe needed a cadre of instructors and later pilots and ground crews, so at the outset American instructors trained German F-104 personnel at Luke AFB, Arizona using thirty F-104F two-seat trainers (identical to the F-104D) for flight-training. Early in 1960 German pilot training began with Lockheed's 'Conversion flight F-104F' course at Palmdale. The German pilots on this first course were led by Oberstleutnant Günther Rall, the famous Second World War fighter pilot and third highest scorer with 275 victories, all but two of them on the Russian Front. Rall was shot down five times. On 12 May 1944 he was shot down by a

USAF F-104A-10-LO 56-0748, which later became a JF-104A for use in the North American X-15 test programme and F-104G XF-134 of the Luftwaffe in flight.

F-104F BB+375 which crashed on 29 March 1961 due to malfunction of the fuel control unit was the first Luftwaffe 104 lost. Hauptmann Hans-Ulrich Flade and his student, Oberleutnant Wolfgang Strenkert are all smiles having ejected safely.

USAAF P-47 Thunderbolt and he lost his left thumb in the process. Returning to postwar Germany, he was unable to find work. Rall started a small wood cutting business in the forest. He eventually joined Siemens as a representative, leaving in 1953. Rall rejoined the newly established West German military in 1956, after meeting a wartime friend and Luftwaffe pilot who encouraged him to return to flying. He joined the new Luftwaffe der Bundeswehr. The five other pilots on the course comprised Hauptmann Hans-Ulrich Flade, Oberleutnant Berthold Klemm, Edmund Schultz, Oberleutnant Wolfgang von Stürmer and Oberleutnant Bernd Kübart. The first F-104F two-seater was handed over to German military officials in October 1959.

F-104Gs of JaboG 31 in parade line up for the commissioning of the F-104 on 20 June 1962 at Nörvenich AB F-104G. On 26 April 1962 DA+122 with 27 flight hours was airlifted to Germany in a Canadair CL-44D of 'Flying Tiger Line'. This Starfighter last flew on 27 August 1987 at Manching AB and was struck off charge on 19 July 1988 before becoming an instructional airframe.

Three F-104Fs became available and these were flown by Lockheed test pilots Bob Faulkner, Glen L. 'Snake' Reaves[1] and Bill Weaver. After seven days of classroom training, on 22 February 1960, flight training commenced. Each trainee F-104 pilot had to make twenty-six flights and record thirty-two hours' stick time. Each trainee was expected to solo after only two flights with his instructor. Günther Rall was the first 'student' to solo, on 24 February 1960. Rall thus became the first of over 2,000 German Starfighter pilots.

In April 1960 it was Flade, Klemm, Schultz, von Stürmer and Kübart who established the OTU (Operational Training Unit) for 4 Staffel, Waffenschule der Luftwaffe (WaSLw 10) at Nörvenich. Oldenburg, the previous home of Waffenschule 10, was unsuitable for Starfighter training because the runway was not long enough and also because the city of Oldenburg nearby would have suffered substantially from the increase in jet-noise. Flade was appointed Kommandant of WaSLw 10, a unit which eventually numbered 350 staff. Flade, together with Major Walter Irwin, Captain 'Chuck' Lloyd and Captain Bruce D. Jones laid down the curriculum for the training schedule. On the technical side the flying team was supported by twenty staff from Lockheed, General Electric and Litton. After the first German ground crews had been trained in the United States, ground crew training was carried out in Germany at the Technische Schule der Luftwaffe (TSLW) 1 at Kaufbeuren.

Towards the end of May 1960 the F-104Fs arrived and on 14 July 1960 Bob Faulkner was the first to put one through its paces. In September 1960 the first regular training began and the first five German pilots - Oberleutnant Jürgen Schultess, Heinz Freye, Erhard Gödert, Dietrich Filsinger and Günther Rödel, were destined to fulfil the role of instructors. The first students - Major Klaus Neumann, Oberleutnant Siegfried Heltzel, Hans-Martin Mudrack, Peter Müller and Eckhardt Schilling - all came from jagdbombergeschwader (JaboG) 3l 'Böelcke' and they were put through twenty-five hours of flying training on their new aircraft. (Oberstabsfeldwebel

Franz-Josef Heltzel was killed flying a Starfighter on 26 October 1973.) In May 1961 4.Waffenschule 10 acquired another eight instructors - Oberleutnant Bodo Koppe, Joachim Liedtke, Mandred Menzelm Dietrich Schlichting, Hermann-Josef Sensen, Wolfgang Strenkert, Lutz Tyrkowski and Erwin Willing.

On 29 March 1961 the Luftwaffe lost its first Starfighter. Hauptmann Hans-Ulrich Flade and his student, Oberleutnant Wolfgang Strenkert were on a routine training flight when the fuel feed system occurred over Korbach forcing them to eject from F-104F BB+375. Six months later, on 6 September, Oberleutnant Erwin Willing and Oberleutnant Hermann Hammerstein had to eject from F-104F BB+378 at Neckarmuhlbach when they suffered total navigational instrument failure and had to use their ejection seats when the aircraft's tanks ran dry. On 25 January 1962 the Luftwaffe lost its first pilot killed while flying a Starfighter. Hauptmann Lutz Tyrkowski and his student pilot Oberleutnant Horst Völter had to eject from F-104F BB+366 when the afterburner failed during takeoff at Nörvenich. An attempt was made to get the machine into the air on 'dry power' alone but it ended up by hitting a building to the west of the field. Völter survived after ejecting at the last second but Ryrkowski was killed. Four months later, on 22 May, Oberleutnant Siegfried Heltzel of JaboG 31 'B' was forced to eject from F-104G DA+107 at Jülich.

In August 1961in the presence of Inspekteur de Luftwaffe General Josef Kammhuber the first F-104Gs built by Lockheed were handed over to

F-104Fs BB+377 and BB+ 376 (29+12) of Wafenschule 10 at Nörvenich in 1961. BB+377 (29+13) made a belly landing at Jever AB on 6 March 1970.

the Bundeswehr. Kammhuber, born in Tüßling, Bavaria on 19 August 1896, the son of a farmer was famous in the Second World War for establishing the night fighter division and the 'Kammhuber line'. Kammhuber developed an efficient ground-controlled interception (GCI) technique called 'Dunkelnachtjagd', later 'Himmelbett', which literally translated, is 'bed of heavenly bliss' or 'four-poster bed'). After the fall of the Reich in May 1945, Kammhuber was held by the United States, but he was released in April 1948 without charges being brought against him. He later spent time in Argentina helping to train the air force under Juan Perón. Josef Kammhuber returned to Germany and joined the German Air Force while it was being formed. He was promoted to Inspekteur der Bundesluftwaffe, serving in that role between 1956 and 1962. After the 1961 F-84 Thunderstreak incident, when two West German Republic F-84F Thunderstreaks strayed into East German airspace and flew to West Berlin, Kammhuber and his superior, the West German Minister of Defence, Franz-Josef Strauss, removed Oberstleutnant Siegfried Barth, commander of the pilots' unit, from his command. After protests, three official investigations and a formal complaint by Barth against Strauss, the former was reinstated in his position.

F-104Gs built in California were flight tested before they were disassembled and shipped to Manching, Germany. Four months later, in December 1961, the first F-104G built under licence by ARGE-Sud was completed in Manching and plant manager, Willi Langhammer handed the aircraft over to the Luftwaffe. Only a few F-104G models remained in the United States for pilot training by 1962. These aircraft were also used in the Multinational 'Joint Test Force' at Edwards AFB for evaluating sub-system (autopilot and navigation system and so on) before the F-104Gs were shipped to Germany. It was this test force that recommended modifications and additions such as the tail hook for the Starfighter, a second artificial horizon (Standby Attitude Indicator) and the Emergency Nozzle Closure System. These tests were carried out by pilots from all the companies in the countries that formed the European consortium, as well as those from Canada, the United States and later Japan. Major Heinz Birkenbeil and Oberleutnant Erhard

Gödert of the Luftwaffe were among the test force personnel. In December 1961, during these tests, Gödert was most probably the first German pilot to fly a F-104G faster than the speed of sound below sea level at Death Valley.

Since not enough F-104Fs were available to satisfy all the training needs, Belgian, Dutch and Italian Starfighter pilots were also trained by the Luftwaffe. Major Thomas Perfili and 29-year old Captain John G. Speer from the US Air Force Advisory team joined them in training pilots like Ton van Soest and Henk Vendrig from the Netherlands, Camille Goossens and Rene Janssens from Belgium and Vincenzo Paternico from Italy. Speer was killed on 19 June 1962, the worst day so far in WaSLw 10's short history, when near Steilkurve, he was one of four F-104F pilots lost during a formation fly-by to mark the complete conversion of the F-104G in JaboG 31 Böelcke at Nörvenich under Kommodore Gerhard 'Gerd' Barkhorn.[4] The highlight of the flying programme in front of a number of high ranking officers including a beaming General Josef Kammhuber, Generalleutnant Werner Panitzki the GOC Luftwaffengruppe Nord and the Defence Minister and other politicians would be a 4-ship F-104F formation demonstration by 4 Staffel WaSLw 10. There had even been talk of taking General Kammhuber up with them. Günther Rall had been thunderstruck. 'The Starfighter is the most exciting aircraft that I've ever flown' he wrote 'but it's about as suitable for an aerobatics programme as a Formula 1 racing car would be for the Monte Carlo Rally.'

Captain Speer the 'lead' pilot and 27-year old Oberleutnant Heinz Freye his number two, Oberleutnant Bernd Kübart number three and Oberleutnant Wolfgang von Stürmer number four had trained often, starting in a 'finger-tip-formation' although the runway of Nörvenich was not very wide. But without tip tanks it was no problem. The

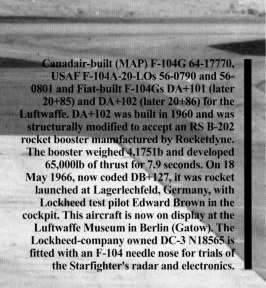

Canadair-built (MAP) F-104G 64-17770, USAF F-104A-20-LOs 56-0790 and 56-0801 and Fiat-built F-104Gs DA+101 (later 20+85) and DA+102 (later 20+86) for the Luftwaffe. DA+102 was built in 1960 and was structurally modified to accept an RS B-202 rocket booster manufactured by Rocketdyne. The booster weighed 4,175lb and developed 65,000lb of thrust for 7.9 seconds. On 18 May 1966, now coded DB+127, it was rocket launched at Lagerlechfeld, Germany, with Lockheed test pilot Edward Brown in the cockpit. This aircraft is now on display at the Luftwaffe Museum in Berlin (Gatow). The Lockheed-company owned DC-3 N18565 is fitted with an F-104 needle nose for trials of the Starfighter's radar and electronics.

F-104G JA+240 of JG 71 and USAF advisory pilot Major Thomas Perfili (centre) pictured on 19 April 1964. Perfili crashed after touching the ground on 2 May 1964 near Bremerhaven during slow flight demonstration at the 'Armed Forces Day' at Bremerhaven, Major Thomas Perfili ejected too late.

four-ship flew in from the west along the runway at low level and in diamond formation. All four had their afterburners going full blast and at the eastern end of the runway pulled up and away to the right in a ninety-two-seventy. This manoeuvre consists first of a 90 degree climbing turn in one direction, immediately followed by a 270 degree turn in the opposite direction up to a point where a moderate bank then develops into a steep diving turn. In plan-view the whole thing resembles a giant question mark and, if executed perfectly, it will end in the F-104s departing in exactly the opposite direction to their original route of approach. They changed neatly from the 90 into the 270. Now Speer went into a steep climbing turn and the German pilots held formation to the centimetre. In a programme such as this none of the three was flying independently. Each must keep his gaze firmly fixed on the leader, who alone initiates the figures, determines the tightness of the turns and knows the altitude. Each is constantly juggling the throttle with his left hand in order to maintain station, while stick and pedal movements demand the utmost sensitivity. Major Tom Perfili performed some solo manoeuvres during the moments the team was out of sight.

For a moment the onlookers lost sight of the formation behind a cloud. They must be at the apex of the turn. But the manoeuvre did not close with their barrelling back out along the runway at Nörvenich. It ended in a brown-coal quarry near Knapsack, only eight kilometres to the east of the airfield. Four explosions and four dirty, dark columns of smoke were seen rising into the sky to the east. Günther Rall, who was flown out in a helicopter saw three burning craters 'in eerie symmetry, as if shot into the ground by some Titan; a fourth crater not far away.'

F-104F BB+365 of WaSLw 10 at Nörvenich Air Base in 1960. This aircraft and the pilot, Oberleutnant Bernd Kubart were lost on 19 June 1962 near Knapsack, Nordrhein-Westfalen when four Starfighters crashed into the ground after disorientation of one of the (trainee) wingmen. All three German pilots (Oberleutnants' Heinz Frye (No.2 piloting BB+387); Bernt Kubart (pilot of No.3, BB+365) and Wolfgang von Stürmer (No.4, BB+385) and Captain John Speer USAF, leading in BB+370, were killed.

The wreckage of BB+365 following the formation disaster on 19 June 1962. All told, the Luftwaffe lost 246 F-104s and 97 pilots and crew killed. The Marineflieger (West German Navy) lost 46 Starfighters and 23 pilots and crew killed.

A subsequent enquiry determined that Speer had too little experience as a leader in formation aerobatics. He entered the cloud inadvertently which resulted in the loss of spatial orientation. The apex of the manoeuvre was too low, its radius of turn too tight, the pull-out too late. To return to the runway/demonstration area faster for the next display sequence, Speer had decided to make a 180 degree turn by cutting a small cumulus-cloud in a steep diamond formation. But he had probably lost spatial orientation and he overturned the aircraft. All three aircraft following flew vertically towards the ground out of the cloud. Wolfgang von Stürmer, flying in the aft-position 'slot' of the formation had the best view and tried to recover from the turn but he entered a high speed stall near the ground.

In all, eight USAF instructor pilots died flying Luftwaffe F-104s, 19 June 1962 to 1 July 1975. Tom Perfili died flying an F-104G at the Armed Forces Day at Bremerhaven on 2 May 1964. Touching the ground during a slow flight demonstration, Perfili ejected too late and was killed.

Oberleutnant Wolfgang von Stürmer (No.4) who was killed piloting BB+385 on 19 June 1962.

Kammhuber could not get over the catastrophe. 'Why didn't I fly with them?' he asked himself out loud and over again as the helicopter flew back. He was retired shortly afterwards. As a result of this tragic accident aerobatic team-performances at Landsberg and Fürstenfeldbruck were dissolved with immediate effect.

Oberleutnant Bernd Kubart, pilot of BB+365 (No.3) who was killed in the four-ship collision on 19 June 1962

F-104Gs DC+238 and DR+233 of JaboG 33 at Buchel in formation in 1963. DC+238 went to the Turkish Air Force (62-2087) on 27 June 1983 and was issued to 4.AJU at Mürted AB and later, with 8.AJU at Diyarbakir AB before being withdrawn from use on 26 August 1991. DR+233 went to the Turkish Air Force on 10 April 1986 and was issued to 193 Filo of 9.AJU at Balikesir AB in 1989, The aircraft was scrapped at Izmir in 1996.

At its peak, in the mid-1970s, the Starfighter equipped five Luftwaffe Jagdbombergeschwadern (Tactical Support units), each of two staffeln (squadrons), two Jagdgeschwadern (Interceptor units) - also of two Staffeln each - and two Aufklarungsgeschwadern (Tactical Photoreconnaissance units) with four Staffeln between them. The first of the five nuclear-armed Jagdbombergeschwadern to be equipped with the Starfighter was JaboG 31 'Boelcke' at Nörvenich. This unit, which had been the first Luftwaffe attack wing when it formed at Büchel on 1 September 1957 with F-84F Thunderstreaks, began receiving F-104Gs in June 1960 and 311 and 321 Staffeln of JaboG 31 were declared fully operational on 20 February 1962. JaboG 33, which formed out of Waffenschule 30 at Büchel on 2 July 1958, also with F-84F Thunderstreaks, received its first F-104Gs in August 1962. Both 331 and 332 Staffeln of JaboG 33 were declared operational by December 1964 - JaboG 31 'Boelcke' gave up its last F-104G on 30 April 1983 and on 1 August became the first wing in the Luftwaffe to re-form as a Tornado IDS (Interdiction and Strike) unit. JaboG 33 flew its last Starfighter sortie on 30 May 1985 and the wing received its first Tornado in September 1985.

If war ever came the F-104s were on a 'hairtrigger' alert that meant that they would all be airborne within seventeen minutes of the start of a war. Each staffel kept six aircraft on 'hair-trigger alert' at all times and these would be loaded with their B-34 nuclear bombs (during the Cold War's 'peacetime' periods, the weapons were held by the

USAF). The Luftwaffe's nuclear mission involved the low altitude penetration of the East Bloc at high speed. The aircraft would accelerate to its optimum speed of Mach 1.4. Passing through high threat areas, it could accelerate to over Mach 2.0, making it a very difficult target. Those who returned would rearm to begin 'round two' - if anything was left to bomb.

The three other jagdbombergeschwadern were JaboG 32 comprising 322 and 323 Staffeln at Lechfeld; JaboG 34, comprising 341 and 342 Staffeln at Memmingen; and JaboG 36, comprising 361 and 362 Staffeln at Rheine-Hopsten. JaboG 32, established on 22 July 1958 with F-84Fs, received its first F-104G on 31 December 1964 - JaboG 34, which had formed at Fassberg on 29 November 1958 with F-84Fs, began receiving Starfighters at Memmingen on 1 July 1964. JaboG 36, which was formed on 13 March 1961 at Nörvenich on F-84Fs, began receiving F-104Gs on 20 February 1965. JaboG 36 began converting to the F-4F Phantom in 1974 and conversion was completed by mid-1976. JaboG 32 began phasing out the F-104G in April 1984 and began receiving Tornado aircraft on 27 July. JaboG 34 had received additional Starfighters in 1983 to increase the strength of 341 and 342 Staffeln to around ninety F-104Gs. The wing - the last in the Luftwaffe to operate the Starfighter - began receiving the PANAVIA Tornado IDS (Interdiction and strike) in 1987.

The F-104G also equipped two Jagdgeschwadern (Interceptor units) - Jagdgeschwader (JG) 71

F-104G DC+324 of JaboG 33 at Buchel in 1967. ■

Lineup of F-104Gs of JG 74 ■
'Mölders' in June 1965.

'Richthofen' at Wittmundhafen and JG 74 'Mölders' at Neuburg. JG 71 has borne the name of Germany's most famous airman since April 1961 when this unit formed at Alhorn as the first day fighter wing of the new Luftwaffe in January 1958. JG 71, which comprised 711 and 712 Staffeln, received F-86 Sabre Mk.6s on 6 June 1959 and in May 1963 began conversion to the F-104G. After spending a decade in Soviet gulags, Germany's greatest ace of World War II, Erich Hartmann (352 confirmed victories), was released and repatriated to West Germany. He was a shell of his former athletic, trim self, but his spirit remained undimmed. At the end of WWII Hartmann was among those deported to Siberia, where he was sentenced to fifty years of hard labour. The Soviets pressured him to support a build-up of an East German air force and tried to turn him into an undercover agent against the West. Hartmann refused, even though the Soviets threatened to kidnap and kill his wife and daughter, living in West Germany. Hartmann did not return to Germany until 1955, when the last German PoWs were released along with the establishing of diplomatic relations between West Germany and the Soviet Union. In 1956 Hartmann joined the newly established West German Luftwaffe and contributed to the build-up of new fighter units. A fighter pilot above all else, he managed to pull

strings to reenter the Luftwaffe within just one year of his release in 1955. In 1959 he became the first commodore of Jagdgeschwader 71 'Richthofen' and was soon flying Canadair Sabres. By 1961 he was flying the F-104G Starfighter. His personal aircraft was painted with the black tulip nose art that he had carried on his Messerschmitt Me 109s while flying on the Eastern Front. He considered the F-104G a terrible dogfighter (with its small wing) and a dangerous plane with poor handling characteristics. Ultimately, his harsh criticism of the plane (and the Lockheed bribes scandal that was involved) resulted in him being forced into retirement in 1970. The final words of General Werner Panitzki, who helped orchestrate the retirement were, 'Erich is a good pilot, but not a good officer.'

JG 71 'Richthofen' flew the Starfighter until 7 March 1974 when the first F-4E Phantoms arrived to begin a further round of re-equipment. JG 74, which comprised 741 and 742 Staffeln and was formed on 16 July 1959, was the Luftwaffe's first all-weather F-86K Sabre fighter wing. Moving to Neuburg from Leipheim on 1 May 1961, JG 74 flew Sabres until 31 December 1965, although

F-104G KG+324 of Jagdbombergeschwader 32 (JaboG 32) in the south of Germany at Lechfeld in full 14,800lb afterburner thrust during a night engine run. (Lockheed)

Inset: F-104G DC+119 of JaboG 33. ∎

F-104Gs began arriving from 1 July 1964 - JG 74 operated the Starfighter in the air defence role until September 1974. The wing began receiving F-4E Phantoms in July that year.

Two Aufklarungsgeschwadern (Tactical Photoreconnaissance units) - AG 51 'Immelmann', comprising 511 and 512 Staffeln at Ingolstadt/ Manching and AG 52, made up of 521 and 522 Staffeln at Leck - also received the F-104G Starfighter. In addition, the Starfighter also equipped Luftwaffenversorgungsregiment 1 - Kommando F-104 at Erding and a second Staffel was added to

F-104G 26+07 of Jagdbombergeschwader 33 (JaboG 33) with 22+56 behind passing Hohenzollern Castle in 1982. Built by SABCA 26+07 first flew on 10 September 1964. It was withdrawn from use on 15 May 1985 and SOC that November. It was sold to the Turkish Air Force on 21 January 1986 and served as (64-9135) until 1 September 1993, being stored Diyarbakir in April 1994 and now preserved on pole at Erzurum AB as '8-135' with markings of 8.AJU. 22+56 was also sold to the Turkish Air Force (64-7137) but was used as spares before being scrapped.

Waffenschule 10 after it moved to its new home at Jever on the Upjever aerodrome. Initially, it lacked any F-104G/TF-104G models so between 1961 and 1962 Lockheed trained some fifteen German pilots on the F-104G. These pilots came mostly from JaboGs' 31 and 33. Training was further supported by additional American pilots who were sent to German units to train pilots on the G model.

Between 1962 and 1964 the 479th TFW also trained German Starfighter pilots on the F-104D

at George AFB, California. To instruct pilots on the F-104's radar, initially the NASARR C-47 of the Flugvermessungsstaffel in Lechfeld was used. In October 1962 the first TF-104G was flown. Altogether, 104 TF-104Gs were built for the Luftwaffe and the Marinefliegerdivision (Navy Flying Division) of the Bundesmarine (Federal Navy).

Beginning in spring 1963 two Marine fliegergeschwadern (MFG/wings) – MFG 1 at

RF-104Gs of Marinefliegergeschwader 2 (MFG 2) in 1983. Messerschmitt (MTT) built 23+16 crashed on 17 October 1984 near the island Aeroe, Denmark during a Navy support mission, simulating a hostile aircraft, the F-104 hit the mast of the German Navy speedboat (class 134A). The pilot was killed. (Peter Doll)

Schleswig and MFG 2 at Eggebek - began re-equipping with the F-104G. From 1964 onwards they replaced Hawker Sea Hawks in the anti-shipping role in the Baltic, where they successfully operated on strike/attack and reconnaissance until 1986. From 1977 their Starfighters were armed with a pair of MBB AS.34 Kormoran (cormorant) anti-shipping missiles in place of the French AS30 missiles. The Kormoran used an inertial guidance system for the midcourse phase, switching to active radar homing during the terminal attack phase. It carried a 363lb delay-fused warhead, designed for 90mm of penetration prior to detonation. The Kormoran gave the Starfighter the ability to fire at enemy shipping from a distance of 18.6 miles (30 kilometres). The Marineflieger received additional ex-Luftwaffe F-104Gs and RF-104Gs when the Aufklarungsgeschwadern reconnaissance units replaced the latter with the RF-4E Phantom from 1971 to replace those Starfighters lost in accidents.

F-104G (62-7002) YA+102 ErpSt 61 (test station 61) at Cazaux AB, France for 'Kormoran' anti-ship missile tests in 1966. This F-104G was built by Messerschmitt and manufactured by ARGE-Süd (South Group) with parts from Lockheed, with assembly at Messerschmitt-Manching starting 9 October 1961. The aircraft was SOC on 18 December 1984 and the Turkish Air Force took delivery on 23 April 1985 (as '6-002'). It was withdrawn from use on 1 August 1995 and was likely scrapped. (Frank Matthes collection)

In all the Marineflieger received 119 F-104Gs and 27 RF-104Gs. MFG 1 operated the F-104G between 1964 and 1 July 1982, while MFG 2 operated the Starfighter between 1965 and the summer of 1986; both wings converting to the PANAVIA Tornado IDS (Interdiction, strike, anti-ship).

In Luftwaffe and Marineflieger service the Starfighter soon got a poor reputation due to a large number of accidents. In 1961 just two crashes took place as the planes were only just entering

Marienflieger F-104G armed with Kormoran anti-shipping missiles, in April 1972. (MBB GmbH

25+17 & 22+57 of JaboG 34 in formation.
(Luftwaffe via JaboG 34).

service. Yet by 1962, flight operations were
expanding and the Luftwaffe was taking deliveries
of more aircraft - as a result, there were seven
crashes. Then, there were twelve more in 1964. In
1965, a total of 28 F-104 Starfighters crashed. In
the first half of 1966, the situation reached crisis
levels when another 61 crashed. More than half
of the pilots died. By 1965 all NATO Consortium
pilots were training in northern Germany, but F-104
accidents began to occur on an increasing scale.
They are recalled by Wolfgang 'Wolf' Czaia, born
in Andernach, Germany who even before reaching
school age, wanted to become a pilot and at 14, began
his aviation career flying gliders. He had graduated
in the USA in 1962 as 'Outstanding Student' and
'Top Gun' at the Fighter Weapons School at Luke
AFB and who flew Republic F-84F Thunderstreaks
assigned to JaboG 34 at Memmingen for two years.
In 1964 JaboG 34 transitioned to the F-104G and
Czaia checked out in November that year. He
recalls: 'Many problems with the 104 in the early
days were mainly due to the shallow learning curve
that maintenance was on. They had to get used to a
rather sophisticated technology and were not able to
provide the pilots with the flight hours necessary to
build efficiency.

'For pilots returning from the US, the 104 was
their first operational assignment. Most of these
guys had never been inside a cloud! They'd always
flown in beautiful weather in both Texas and
Arizona and faced radically different conditions
in the rather restricted and geographically small
airspace of Germany. Even though they went
through a 40-hour 'Europeanization' programme at
Luftwaffe Weapons School 10 at Jever they lacked
the experience of their Canadian, Italian, Belgian
and Dutch counterparts who needed to accumulate
at least 1,000 hours in operational jets before being
even eligible to check out in the F-104.'

F-104G 26+89 of MFG2.
(Axel Ostermann)

F-104G 20+37of JagdBomberGeschwader (JBG) 34 now preserved inside the Air Museum Hall in Berlin Gatow.

A crew chief directs TF-104G 66-13622 (28+03) on the ramp at El Paso Airport in 1979 during the training of Luftwaffe pilots by members of the 69th Tactical Fighter Training Squadron at Luke AFB, Arizona. Although German, the F-104s had USAF markings and it operated in USAF colours from 31 May 1967 until end of operation on 16 March 1983 and was acquired in the summer of 1983 by the USAF and sold to the RoCAF and coded '4195' it operated with the 41st TFS of 2 Wing. Withdrawn from use in 1996, it became an instructional airframe at the China Institute of Technology in Henshan Township, Hsinchu County. (US Defense Imagery photo)

Luke trained German fighter pilots from 1964 on the F-84 Thunderstreak to 1984 on the F-104 Starfighter. In *Those wonderful men in the Cactus Starfighter Squadron* Colonel Barney Oldfield USAF Ret. and Chief Master Sergeant Tom Rhone, USAF Ret wrote in glowing terms of the training the Germans received: 'We cry with one eye and laugh with the other when we leave our second home in Arizona!' So has departure from Luke AFB been described by German student pilots during their flying training period here during the years 1957-1983. As are the tourists from America's northernmost states they were captivated by the Arizona lifestyle, the good life in the almost continuous Arizona sunshine. The tug of leaving the desert eventually evolves into a pleasant keepsake memory they will retain for the rest of their lives. Many came back to Luke for a second course or full time duty. A few have married and settled in the Copper State and American girls have gone to Germany as fighter pilot brides. With so much living and playing in the sun they often wonder how they had time to do it all.

'Scottsdale still echoes from rousing and boisterous singing at Peter's Hofbräu. Tempe and Arizona State University are still places where the girls are. Steaks and fun can still be had at 'Pinnacle Peak' and 'Reata Pass'. Food that reminds of home at 'Vienna Kitchen' on McDowell Road. The Rodeo at 'Veterans Memorial Coliseum' or watching 'Roadrunners' hockey and the National Basketball Association 'Phoenix Suns'.

Jever-based F-104G 23+50 of JaboG 34 (2nd Staffel) at Memmingen in formation in 1976 with F.6 XR772/C of 11 Squadron from RAF Binbrook. F-104G 23+50 was later sold to Turkey (62-8029) and crashed on 24 May 1989. The Starfighter had, eventually, the same straight-line top speeds but could never match the Lightning's rate of turn at any speed. (Tony Paxton)

'Those who came to Arizona competent glider pilots soared over the mountains near Prescott and viewed the majestic vastness of the Grand Canyon. Some went on horseback into the Superstition Mountains, met and talked with real gold prospectors. Others sat in with gunslingers and Old West 'bad men' in the Scottsdale Wax Museum. Joe Hunt's famous Restaurant became a favourite waterhole. That necessary shopping spree for the western clothing to take back to Germany. The two pilots who lived out of saddlebags for two weeks between Roosevelt Lake and Williams AFB. Sunday afternoons with families and girlfriends gathered in Monterey Park or at some other soccer field. The time the Luftwaffe won both the Knockout Cup as well as a League Championship. The 'Go-Go' girls at Chick's lounge. That talented Abu, the Luftwaffe pianist, who sat in with the combos at Calhoun's.

'Luke's Officers Mess on Friday nights. The Instructor Pilot parties. The Wickenburg Kay El Bar guest ranch providing happy hours in saddle and swimming pool and the suntans on those attractive, leggy Frau's and Frauleins! Graduations and 'Auf Wiedersehens' to friends. That day when Instructor pilots shook their student's hand and said: 'Welcome to the Club, Fighter Pilot!' Learning the tools of fighter pilot trade at Luke, so important; the German-American friendships and mutual respect deep and warm enough to last forever, so enduring.

'The 'Arizona Life Style' means 'Gemütlichkeit' ('heart, mind, temper, feeling').'

But back home in West Germany, the life style changed radically and not for the better. 'By 1966' continues Wolfgang Czaia 'the accident rate was unusually high and a lot of it was weather-related. Quite often small technical problems would - due to the pilots' inexperience and lack of proficiency - he the trigger for chain reactions resulting in accidents. Once the wings began flying steadily and pilots were getting the required flight time the accident rate dropped to 'normal' (ten accidents per 100,000 flight hours) - but the public still perceived it as a dangerous machine, with names like the 'Witwenmacher' ('Widowmaker') or 'Flieglender Sarg' ('Flying Coffin'). Compounding the problem was that every subsequent ground or flight accident

25+32; 24+74: 26+05 and 26+15 of MFG 2 in formation.

F-104Gs 26+70 and 26+69 of MFG 2
in formation. (Stefan Petersen)

A well-attired Kapitän J. Imhof sporting a suitably painted bone dome in the cockpit of his Starfighter in 1975. (Herbert Mennen)

continued to make major headlines. We had just as many accidents in F-84s and F-86s, but these stories would he buried on page 5 or 4.'

By 7 December 1967 the Luftwaffe had lost 73 F-104s and 42 pilots and crew killed (including one MFG 2 pilot in a Canadian-built, USAF-owned F-104G). Between 4 April 1968 and 12 November 1970, a further twenty-six German pilots and crew (21 Luftwaffe personnel and five Marineflieger crew) lost their lives in fifty-two (45 Luftwaffe/seven Marineflieger) Starfighter accidents. By April 1989 the Luftwaffe and Marineflieger combined had lost or had written off, 292 Starfighters with 120 pilots and crew killed. Twenty-three Marineflieger pilots and crew were killed in the period 18 March

1965 to 17 October 1984. One of these, on 10 March 1979 was Oberleutnant zur see Joachim von Hassel of MFG 2, the only son of Herr Kaiuwe von Hassel, president of the Bonn parliament. It was von Hassel who had been Defence Minister at the height of the public outcry in West Germany at the rate of F-104 losses when they had reached one a week. At that time the minister had tried to reassure everyone, saying that he considered the Starfighter a safe aircraft and that he had no reservations about his son flying it.

Lieutenant Robert Hummel, a US Navy pilot on exchange duty with MFG 2 at Eggebek, had a narrow escape from a Starfighter on 10 July 1984 as he recalled later: 'The Starfighter - a beautiful and sleek machine twenty design years ahead of her time. She could seduce you with her speed, transitioning to hyperspace in a heartbeat. It was the opportunity of a lifetime: NATO exchange duty with a German F-104G squadron in Europe for two and a half years. As the only naval aviator in the country, I rapidly achieved the qualifications and experience to fly the F/RF-104G throughout the entire operational envelope and was designated 'full combat ready'. The tactical training opportunities in central Europe are unparalleled. The air below 9,000 feet belongs to the military, with relatively few operating restrictions. And then there were the Baltic Sea and North Sea operating areas in Ivan's backyard. It was some of the best flying I've ever experienced.

'Following final checks we taxied onto runway 01 in left echelon for a formation go. The tower gave take-off clearance, reporting the winds out

Pilots of MFG 2 pose with their steins of beer atop 21+37 in 1967.

F-104G 23+18 of MFG 2. On 10 July 1984 this Starfighter suffered a loss of control during a formation takeoff at Eggebek. The pilot ejected to safety.

of the west at 10 to 15 knots. Engine-run-ups and control wipe-outs were completed, followed by a thumbs-up from my wingman. I gave the signal to release brakes and light the burner. During this transition phase of engine operation, the nozzle opens up prior to the afterburner igniting and results in a notable loss of thrust for one to three seconds. On this section take-off, my wingman had a quick burner light; I had a slow one. As a result, he ended up acute and accelerating further in front of the lead. It seemed safer to pass him the lead and assume a wing position than have him attempt to re-establish himself in the wing position. I never thought of aborting. So, a positive lead change was executed in the first 1,000 feet to the take-off roll. If I had known then what I know now, I would have aborted and saved a beautiful expensive aircraft.

'Although I was established in an acceptable wing position at rotation, I was on the downwind side of the formation. The F-104 generates tremendous circulation about the wingtips during take-offs and landings and the vortices are often visible. Immediately after becoming airborne it became all too clear that things were not quite right. A high-speed abort now was out of the question since the aircraft was already rolling through 10 degrees angle of bank to the left and into my lead. While I held right stick and full right rudder, my Starfighter hesitated for a moment as if the worst was over. Then the left wing began to drop rapidly.

'It was time to jettison the reusable container and I pulled the lower handle of the Martin-Baker Mk.7-A ejection seat with my left hand. The aircraft continued to roll and drift as I waited for the eternity of 0.4 seconds to click off. In 30 to 40 degrees angle of bank, at an altitude of maybe six feet, the roll reversed violently to the right. The canopy was gone, but I was still in the aircraft. I think that the left wingtip had impacted the runway. A cartwheeling explosion had to follow in the very next instant as the wing was ripped off

'If only I had initiated ejection earlier! If only I had aborted when I first detected the lack of roll control after rotation! I heard the roar of the ejection seat rockets and felt the acceleration as I was catapulted clear of my lost craft. I was now an ejection statistic [the 5,338th life saved by a Martin-Baker seat]. The seat worked perfectly, giving me about half a swing before landing dead centre on the runway. From initial aircraft rotation to nylon landing was about ten seconds. The crosswind dragged me across the runway about fifty feet until I managed to release my chute. I just lay there on the runway for a moment waiting for it to start hurting somewhere, then initiated a functional check of the major body parts. They were all still attached: I was, in fact, uninjured. The same could not be said for Starfighter 23+18. She was a twisted mass of fire

Marienflieger pilots of MFG 2 with F-104G VB+231 behind, taking a break at Eggebek.

141

and metal about a quarter mile away; her flames were being suppressed by the quickly responding crash crew. She became the 191st Starfighter to crash and it wasn't her fault. In retrospect, the take-off should have been aborted when the non-notice lead change occurred. Speeds are slow and control of the aircraft is easily maintained. The effects of wingtip vortices cannot be underestimated. Whether during formation or flight leader separation take-offs, sufficient wingtip-to-wingtip separation must he maintained to ensure avoidance of the vortices, which can wrestle control of your aircraft out of your hands in the blink of an eye.

'Know the performance capabilities and characteristics of your aircraft. There are very few aircraft that don't give ample indications of impending departure from controlled flight. Know these indications and listen out for them when you are operating at or near the edge of the performance envelope. Know when it's time to jettison the reusable container. The best time to think about ejection situations is in the ready room or at mid-rats with some of your squadron mates.'

Mike Vivian, former USAF F-104A to F-104G pilot, Luke IP recalls: 'Having volunteered for duty in Việtnam, I received my choice of assignment coming home. It was a return to the F-104 and duty with the German Air Force Training Squadron at Luke AFB. I was assigned to the 4512th and 4518th Fighter Training Squadrons for Flight instructor duty and with the 4516th Tactical Training Squadron as academic instructor. I was to teach school. I was going to heaven. The choicest of the choice. Under the direction of, (then) Captain Dirk C. Prather, Mr. Bud Stoddard and (then) Colonel Charles Pope. I taught F-104 systems - engine, hydraulics and egress. There never could have been finer duty. Teach Academics in the AM and fly an air-to-air or Air-to-Ground sortie in the PM. Heaven! I worked closely with the German side of the house. After all, they were paying the bills. They bought the aircraft and allowed them to be painted with USAF colours. Oberstleutnant Richard Eibl was in charge and it was a pleasure to serve him and his country. As it turned out, the G was extremely capable, although heavier that either the A, or C. It had radar that neither the A, nor the C could compare with. It was equipped with a vastly superior flight control system with a REAL

Formation of F-104Gs of JBG 31 at Nörvenich en route to RAF Wittering in May 1965 for an exchange visit with 1 Squadron's Harrier GR.3s. The aircraft nearest the camera is 25+75 with 22+56 and below, 24+42. (Hauptmann Schmidt) ▮

autopilot. The ground mapping portion of the radar coupled with a terrain clearance mode of the radar that really worked, was a pleasure. Actually, one could see a train on the railroad and a reflector on the target pylon. Surprising radar bombing accuracy was possible. Lastly, the G model had real flaps! I mean real manoeuvering flaps! I mean flaps to takeoff at 296 in the A model and 450 in the G model is a vast improvement! G available because of flap availability caused the G, even though heavier, to outmanoeuvre any dash three or dash seven equipped 'A' model that ever existed. Dash 19 equipped models of the A are a horse of a different colour, I should say thoroughbred 'cause very few of us had the pleasure of that combination. I stand by the point though, if only the engine was changed, I'm sure it was exciting. But if the flaps were not, the added G available in the Gustav due to the 450 down - 520 up flaps of the G was amazing. Additionally, for strictly political reasons, I must mention the Inertial Navigation System platform available in the MAP and G versions, in spite of its various problems, was a giant step forward in the technological sharpening of the fighter pilots ability to reach targets. I know people have been killed but

without the necessity of revealing ones position thru Doppler radar (vertical measurement), the LN-3, although a first step, was huge in the improvement to visual methods of dead reckoning to targets in the eastern zone. From where I sat in the QRA of my unit in Southern Germany as I personally briefed Herr Dr. Schlesinger on my targets, much to my chagrin ('cause I felt he had no need to know), a giant step in the ability to reach one's target and return was most assuredly a part of my convincing him of my fighter bomber wing's capability.

'And then came the realization that it could not last forever. Even though, through the assistance of Jürgen Stehli, Peter Müller, Jörg Kuebart and Harry Liedke, I was able to go over two thousand hours in the F-104. These people all helped me in the realization of a goal that I had never dreamed ('cause one only dreams of such things). I could only stay in the F-104 as an exchange officer with the German Air Force or if I could get a follow on assignment to a headquarters assignment, perhaps Ramstein AB Germany. From there I could maybe get a return

assignment to South East Asia, (you do remember we still had a war, excuse me, conflict, going on over there). I served my time in Memmingen and departed (with both tears and a smile) to headquarters USAFE DOON, a division of USAFE charged with the responsibility to assure CINCUSAFE of NATO's ability to reach assigned targets. It was fun! Each week, Lieutenant Colonel David Clardy and I would visit one of the various Air Bases which had been assigned the strike mission. Under the guidance of Allied Command Europe Directives 75-5 and 75-6, we would look at weapons, their loading crews and their ability to deliver. WOW! That meant flying the machines of ALL the nations! From south to north. Sometimes I didn't know where the shelter was. Sometimes, I couldn't find the shelter after the sortie. Some of the 'craft were clean, some had discrepancies. In the main I have never met more interesting, dedicated loyal countrymen. Many had no, or insufficient budget! Some had no heat, but they had fuel. ALL had a common desire to accomplish the NATO assigned mission. But what a learning experience. I will be forever grateful to all with whom I have flown. The young Turk who asked if I liked acrobatics, (yes) to the young Italian who said we will do acrobatics, yes, but only after we have reached the assigned target and returned to base. That is because, if we fall, we can fall on Government property. But it was time to leave. I had to leave my beloved F-104.

'After a short year in Korea, it was time for a retirement assignment. I chose to return to Luke AFB. It was my home of record. I could go there, work with the continuing training programme for the German Air Force and retire. I asked for a return to the academic squadron, became chief of academics, chief of the Flight test section. Worked with one of the most personable German officers I have ever met, at that time, Oberstleutnant Heinrich Thüringer and, at that time, Hauptmann Horst Martin and Wolfgang Daberkow. These people and folks like them, made up the strength, indeed the backbone of the Luftwaffe, in spite of what others may say. It was not those assigned 'auf der Harthoehe', (Ministry of Defence level folks). As it has turned out, Heinrich Thüringer, Gary Vance, Colonel Bud Jones and I flew my last ride at Luke in September 1982. I briefed and lead a four ship to the range. We dropped bombs, fired rockets, strafed, all old stuff for you new guys, but for me it was the magnificent culmination of an Air Force career. My family met

me on the ramp at Luke. David Bashow poured ice water all over me and someone handed me an open bottle of champagne. While it may not be interesting to all, it sure was a pleasure for me.'

Lloyd M. Enochs was stationed with the USAFE 50th Ammunition Supply Squadron near Morbach from 1976-1980. 'Like all NATO (and French) air forces, the Luftwaffe used our bomb dump as a practice target - completely illegally, I hasten to add. All of these air arms would practice bombing and strafing runs; a worthwhile enterprise designed to deny enemy resupply of things that go 'BANG' during warfare. F-104s regularly passed over the outlaying portions of the dump at under 100 feet AGL. Quite noisy. Scared the living daylights out of you the first time one made a pass like that from behind you. No warning at all and then, suddenly, 'ROAR'. I thought a weapons storage shelter had blown up the first time I heard it.

'The Luftwaffe F-104s were used in conditions and with tactics incompatible with their design as a straight line interceptor. The flying weather in Central Europe, quite frankly, sucks rocks most of the time and when you turn a rocket sled into a dogfighter/bomber and force it to fly in the crud day after day, you get accidents. The German pilots worked very hard to make this airplane work in their conditions and had to push the envelope to do it. About 200 times or so, they pushed just a bit too hard. I always thought the F-104 to be the sharpest looking fighter around until I saw an F-16 for the first time!'

■ **TF-104G 27+34 getting airborne.**

Mike Schmitt a former OH-58 Scout helicopter pilot recalled: 'Considering that the other operators of the Starfighter did not suffer similar levels of attrition even with a worse mistreatment of this exigent aircraft, what is really the cause of these losses? Luftwaffe pilots flew the '104' like they drive their Mercedes on the autobahn - and I'm serious. I've been in enough manoeuvres where Luftwaffe F-104s were in support - I've been on hilltops looking 'down' into the cockpit - coming in so close I could tell if the pilot shaved or not - put that together with the tremendous 'wire-hazard' problem - wires and electric train wires meander through the valleys F-104 pilots like to fly 'low' very low through the valleys - they have no margin for error. I've been flying border traces in my OH-58 Scout helicopter and have F-104 pilots fly under me - I've seen them fly under high bridges - I've seen them pull up to come over a hill and almost take my antenna off my track. I'd venture to guess that the majority of accidents were pilot error. I have

F-104G 22+62 of JaboG 34 dramatically photographed from another Starfighter in the same formation.

no facts - just judgement - observation - and many officer club discussion with 20-year old, unmarried, dashing, gallant, daring, Porsche racing Luftwaffe 104 drivers. I'm sure glad we're supported by 20-year old, unmarried, dashing, gallant daring, Porsche racing USAF A-10 pilots! The difference is: You can't hear the A-10 coming at you!'

After long study and debate, Germany finally had to admit that the F-104G Starfighter was not entirely to blame for the accident rates being suffered. Indeed, other nations in NATO flying the F-104G had varying accident rates, which pointed to another cause. As the best examples, Norway's Starfighter fleet suffered just six losses, despite an extraordinarily high operational tempo (56,000 hours flown); and Spain's air force suffered no losses whatsoever. Both of these air forces featured excellent training programmes and highly experienced personnel. Further, on review, it was uncovered that the Luftwaffe's previous aircraft, the Republic F-84 Thunderstreak had suffered from an accident rate that was approximately the same. The causes were also identical - maintenance mistakes, pilot disorientation (particularly in weather), mid-air collisions, bird strikes and lightning strikes.

Starfighter phase-out began in 1971 when AKG 51 and AKG 52 received McDonnell RF-4Es, while two jagdgeschwarden re-equipped with F-4Fs in 1973-74 and JBG 36 obtained Phantom IIs in 1976. In other units, the scheduled replacement of Starfighters by Tornadoes got underway in 1982 and by the mid-1980s the F/TF-104Gs were fast

disappearing from German skies. Large numbers of Starfighters were then transferred to allies. Italy received six ex-Luftwaffe TF-104G Starfighters, Greece received 58 F-104Gs and 23 TF-104Gs and 39 F-104Gs and 27 TF-104Gs were handed back to the USAF for onward shipment to Taiwan (three ex-Luftwaffe F-104G/TF-104Gs were given to NASA), while Turkey received 165 F-104Gs and 36 TF-104Gs.

The West German Navy demonstration duo, the 'Vikings', were officially formed in 1983. Four years earlier, a previous Navy F-104 aerobatic duo had been formed with no name but, after a crash during a non-aerobatic flight, that team had been disbanded. The 'Vikings' performed their first public display on 14 August at Eggebek Airshow with two F-104 Starfighter aircraft painted in the standard German

▌ F-104G 20+37 in formation with a Luftwaffe Tornado.

▌ RF-104G 25+50 of JBG 34 at Memmingen with two F-4 Phantoms in specially painted red, yellow and black on 5 May 1984 to celebrate the 25th anniversary of JaboG 34 and the 50th anniversary of airbase (Fliegerhorst) Memmingerberg. This Starfighter had only a few airframe hours left before retirement and therefore retained its anniversary scheme once it was transferred to ground instruction duties at Memmingen. The aircraft is on display at Deutsch-Kanadisches Lw-Museum in special marks at Baden-Airpark (Baden-Söllingen).

Navy camouflage paint scheme - grey and light grey. The pilots were the same ones who had flown in the 1979 team. Both the pilots and planes were drawn from the Marinefliegergeschwader 2 based in Eggebek. Originally the team's display lasted just eight minutes in duration, but this was later increased to a twelve minute display. The following year, the Navy HQ formed a second F-104 duo also carrying the 'Viking' name so that displays could be performed in two places at the same time. A highlight of the team's history was a North American tour in August 1986, when they performed in both the USA and Canada. After the 'Vikings' returning from their North American tour, the team aircraft were given a special white, blue and red colour scheme, but after just five demonstrations with this new paint scheme, they performed for the last time on 27 September 1986 due to the retirement of the F-104 from West German Navy service.

In Germany the last operational flight of a Luftwaffe F-104 was with JaboG 34 at Memmingen on 23 October 1987. Other F/TF-104Gs were used by LwWersRgt 1 at Erding and Eprobungstelle 61, a test unit at Manching. WTD 61 had the honour of flying the last German Starfighter sortie, on 22 May 1991.

26+63 30+37 26+72 and 20+37 of the 'Vikings' of MFG 2 in formation.

F-104 Starfighter Losses 1961-1989
(Pilots/Crew killed in parentheses)

Luftwaffe			Marineflieger	
1961	2	(10)	-	-
1962	7	(6) +	-	-
1963	-	-	-	-
1964	10	(3) +	-	-
1965	*25	(15)°	2	(2)
1966	19	(10) +	3	(3)
1967	11	(3)	2	-
1968	15	(7)	4	(4)
1969	16	(9) +	-	-
1970	14	(5)	3	(1)
1971	14	(4)	5	(3)
1972	11	(5)	1	(1)
1973	15	(5) +	-	-
1974	7	-	3	(2)
1975	9	(6) +	2	(1)
1976	11	(2)	1	-
1977	8	(3)	2	(1)
1978	10	(2)	3	-
1979	5	-	5	(1)
1980	10	(5)	1	(1)
1981	8	(2)	1	-
1982	9	(2)	3	(2)
1983	2	-	-	-
1984	6	(1)	2	(1)
1985	1	-	3	-
1986	1	-	-	-
1987	-	-	-	-
1988	-	-	-	-
1989	1	-	-	-

+ inc. 1 USAF;   ° inc. 2 USAF;   * inc. 1 USAF

Total German F-104 losses	292
Total German pilots/crew killed	180
Total USAF pilots killed on German F-104s	8

Versions and Project Models 5

Chapter

F-104G ZELL on the launching ramp in California. The Zero-Length-Launch, or ZELL programme was conducted in great secrecy at Edwards AFB. The Luftwaffe had identified a need to launch their F-104s from no-runway areas in Europe and so the rocket-boosted concept was conceived. Altogether, twelve dummy and eight piloted launches were carried out in two phases. The first involved a Lockheed-built launcher while the second involved evaluation of a different launch platform manufactured by Vereinigte Flugtechnische Werke (VFW) in Germany. The first phase took place during 14 December 1962 to 28 August 1963 and the second phase took place during 18 March 1964 to 22 July 1964. (Lockheed)

■ XF-104-LO (Model 083-92-01)

Designation applied to two single-seat tactical fighter prototypes (53-7786/7787), ordered on 12 March 1953, with Wright XJ65-W-6 engines of 7,800lb static thrust and 10,200lb with afterburner. The first flight, with non-afterburning engine, took place on 4 March 1954. The maximum speed reached by the XF-104, with the afterburner working, was Mach 1.79. A downward-ejection seat was fitted and provision made for a 20mm six-barrel M-61 Vulcan cannon.

■ YF-104A-LO (Model 183-93-02)

Designation applied to 17 aircraft (55-2955/2971) of the pre-production series ordered in October

1954. The YF-104A differed from the XF-104 by its longer fuselage of 5 feet 6 inches, by modifications to the air intakes and by the new engine, General Electric YJ79-GE-3 with a maximum thrust rating of 9,300lb static thrust and 14,800lb with afterburner. Later, the equally powerful J79-GE-3A with improved afterburner was standardized. The first flight took place on 17 February 1956 and reached Mach 2 on 27 April 1956. The seventh YF-104A (55-2961) was transferred to NASA in August 1956.

■ F-104A-LO (Model 183-92-02)

First series production (fighter-bomber) of the F-104; very similar to the YF-104A. Some 153

149 ■

examples were ordered (F-104A-1; 56-730/736; F-104A-5; 56-737/737; F-104A-10; 56-748/763; F-104A-15; 56-764/788; F-104A-20; 56-789/825; F-104A-25; 56-826/877; F-104A-30; 56-878/882). The first F-104A flew in February 1956. Last deliveries to the US Air Force were in December 1958.

Power initially was provided by a General Electric J79-GE-3A of 9,600lb static thrust and 14,800lb with afterburner, but beginning in April 1958, F-104As were retrofitted with the more reliable J79-GE-3B engine. A further retrofit saw the J79-GE-19 of 17,900lb afterburning thrust on some USAF aircraft. Design armament consisted of a 20mm M-61 Vulcan cannon and two AIM-9B Sidewinder air-to-air missiles with AN/ASG-14T-1 fire control system. Unreliability of the early cannon in November 1957 resulted in its removal before delivery of F-104As to Air Defense Command and the improved M-61A1 cannon was reinstalled in 1964. During operational service use the Lockheed-designed downward-firing ejection seat was replaced by a Lockheed-designed upward-firing seat (C-2) and standard installation of the ventral fin and flap-blowing system. Ten F-104As were given to Pakistan and these were later retrofitted with the J79-GE-11A of 15,800lb maximum thrust. Forty-six went to the Republic of China Air Force (RoCAF) on Formosa (Taiwan) and 32 were given to Jordan. Three went to NASA (56-734 and 56-749 between October 1957 and December 1962 and, when 56-749 crashed, 56-790, acquired in December 1966) and one (F-104A-15-LO 56-770) went to Canada as a prototype to initiate the production in this country. In 1960 24 F-104As were modified to QF-104A target drones and three as NF-104s (56-756, 56-760 and 56-762).

■ NF-104A Aerospace/Astronaut Proficiency Trainer

Designation applied to three F-104As (56-756, 56-760 and 56-762) modified for use in training candidate astronauts at the USAF Aerospace Research Pilots School (ARPS) at Edwards AFB, California (see Chapter 11).

■ QF-104A-LO

Designation applied to four YF-104As (55-2956/57, 55-2969 and 55-2971) and twenty early production F-104 As modified in 1959-60 by Lockheed in conjunction with the Sperry-Phoenix

Company as remote-control target drones. These could be flown by onboard pilots, pilots with remote-control from other aircraft and pilots on the ground with radio-control equipment. Initially, six QF-104As were to be maintained for use at Eglin AFB Auxiliary Field Number 3, with the remaining drones to be maintained in storage at Sacramento ALC (the depot responsible or F-104 support) until they were required for use to replace expended drones (QF-104As were rarely destroyed - each cost $1.7 million - and were normally recovered and used later in testing the Boeing IM-99A and IM-99B Bomarc air defence missile). The QF-104A was designed to work in conjunction with a DT-33A airborne director aircraft, a mobile ground director station and four Eglin Test Range drone control sites.

Each QF-104A was produced by removing all combat and fire control systems and subsystems and the installation of radio receivers, transponder beacons, a telemetry transmitting system, an optical scoring system (consisting of five 16mm cameras), an electronic scoring system, a self-destruct system, a smoke generator, a field arrestor hook and additional fuel tanks in the gun bay area to provide a further l00 gallons of internal fuel capacity. Range was further extended by the continued use of the F-104's wingtip tanks and optional 195 gallon pylon tanks. To permit manned ferry flights by personnel of the 3205th Drone Squadron (DS) a minimum of communications equipment was retained and an upward-firing Lockheed C-2 ejection seat replaced the original downward-firing seat.

The first flight of a QF-104A drone occurred in late 1960. Operational use was marred by J79-GE-3A compressor stall problems, landing gear retraction problems and initially, severe tyre wear on landings. Operational support for the QF-104A drone programme was provided by the 3201st Maintenance Group (MG) and 3208th Test Group (TG). The final QF-104A drone operations were carried out in the early 1970s.

■ JQF-104A

Designation temporarily applied to the QF-104A.

■ RF-104A-LO (Model 383-93-04)

Designation applied to the unarmed photo-reconnaissance version of the single-seat F-104A which would have equipped four reconnaissance squadrons in Tactical Air Command had the design progressed to production. Design began in November 1954 and 19 RF-104A-LO models (56-939/956) were ordered by the US Air Force in 1955. However, in January 1957, before the start of production, all development work was cancelled and TAC decided instead to equip its reconnaissance squadrons with the McDonnell RF-101C Voodoo, which had a longer range and heavier load-carrying capability.

■ TF-104A-LO

Designation applied to the projected and un-built two-seat non-combat-capable (unarmed) trainer version of the single-seat F-104A, but which was not proceeded with as the US Air Force preferred the combat-capable two-seat F-104B.

■ F-104B-LQ (Model 283-93-03)

Two-seat, dual-control, combat trainer version of the F-104A. Although the USAF had ordered the Northrop T-38 Talon dedicated supersonic primary jet trainer in June 1956, this aircraft would not be available for some time so Lockheed's suggestion that its proposed tandem-sea derivative of the F-104 A be used in the interim was accepted. On 2 March 1956 the USAF placed an initial order for six F-104B-1s (56-3719/3724) and on 4 December a contract for twenty additional production F-104Bs (F-104B-5; 57-1294/1302; F-104B-10: 57-1303/1311; F-104B-15: 57-1312-1313) was received by Lockheed.

The first F-104B-1-LO was quite literally built by hand at Palmdale, California, using an F-104A airframe (c/n 283-5000/56-3719) built on the production line at Burbank. 56-3719 was transported by road to Edwards AFB for its first flight, on 16 January 1957. At first the F-104B was classified as a service test aircraft and was therefore unofficially designated YF-104B. Later, this aircraft, which was used subsequently to test the downward-ejection seat initially fitted to all USAF Starfighters, was brought up to F-104B production standard.

The first production F-104B was delivered to the USAF in September 1957, the last F-104B-15-LO in November 1958. To provide space for the second seat, mounted aft beneath an extended canopy, the 20mm Vulcan cannon of the single seater was removed, some of the electronics were relocated, internal fuel capacity was reduced from 897 US gallons to 752. The vertical stabilizer was increased in area by twenty-one per cent and it featured a power boost rudder. The nosewheel was repositioned to the front of the landing gear well and retracted rearward (as used on the two XF-104s) instead of forward as on the F-104A. Provision for two underwing and two wingtip-mounted drop tanks was retained. Power was provided by a General Electric J79-GE-3A/3B engine of 9,600lb static thrust and 14,800lb with afterburner. The fin area was increased by 35 per cent and a fully powered rudder was adopted. Armament consisted of just two AIM-9B Sidewinder missiles with AN/ASG-14T-1 fire control system.

Four F-104Bs were given to the Republic of China Air Force (RoCAF) on Formosa (Taiwan) and eight were received by Jordan. In December 1959 one F-104B (53-1303) was given to NASA.

■ F-104C-LO (Model 483-04-05)

A total of 77 F-104Cs (56 F-104C-5s 56-883/938 and 21 F-14C-10s, 57-910/930) all-weather, fighter-bomber variants was ordered by Tactical Air Command. The first F-104C flew on 24 July 1958 and the first example was accepted by Tactical Air Command on 15 October 1958 during the annual USAF Fighter Weapons Meet at Nellis AFB, Nevada. The last F-104C was delivered in June 1959.

The F-104C differed from previous versions in having the possibility to refuel in flight using a removable in-flight-refuelling probe fitted on the port side of the fuselage. The F-104C was also fitted with the all-up AN/ASG-14T-2 fire control system and had the ability to carry a single nuclear store (either a Mk-28 nuclear bomb or a Douglas AIR-2 Genie air-to-air rocket). Initially, power was provided by a new General Electric J79-GE-7 engine of 10,000lb static thrust and 15,800lb with afterburner. By early 1963 operational problems - not least caused by the troublesome J79-GE-7A engine - had led to forty serious incidents which resulted in the deaths of nine pilots and the loss of 24 aircraft; all in a period of less than five years. As a result, Project 'Seven Up', a General Electric modification programme on its 7A turbojet, began in May 1963 and ended in June 1964.

Early in 1963 the USAF initiated Project *Grindstone* whereby Lockheed were to modify all remaining F-104Cs so that in addition to the 20mm cannon and two wingtip-mounted AIM-9 Sidewinders, the aircraft could carry two more Sidewinders beneath the fuselage, or bombs and

The M61 Vulcan hydraulically or pneumatically driven, six-barrelled, air-cooled, electrically fired Gatling-style rotary cannon which fires 20 mm rounds at an extremely high rate. The first aircraft to carry the M61A1 was the F-104C, starting in 1959. The Vulcan is a Gatling gun (the first, used in the American Civil War is at left in the picture). Each of the cannon's six barrels fires once in turn during each revolution of the barrel cluster. The multiple barrels fire around 100 rounds per second.

unguided HE 2.75 inch diameter rockets in pods on underwing and fuselage stations. Tactical Air Command phased out the last of its F-104Cs in 1967.

■ F-104D-LO (Model 383-04-06)

Designation applied to 21 two-seat combat trainer versions (F-104D-5; 57-1314/1320; F-104D-10; 57-1321/1328; F-104D-15; 57-1329/1334) delivered to Tactical Air Command from November 1958 to September 1959. The F-104D combined the cockpit layout of the F-104B with the armament, engine and flight-refuelling capability of the F-104C. Like the B model, it incorporated the larger area vertical fin and its nose landing gear retracted rearward like the F-104Bs. The first F-104D example was flight tested on 31 October 1958.

■ F-104DJ (Model 583B-10-17)

Designation applied to 20 two-seat trainers almost identical to the F-104D (the F-104DJ had a Japanese-built engine and upward-firing ejection seat). The first F-104DJ was assembled by Lockheed-Burbank and the remaining 19 were reassembled in Japan by Mitsubishi (fuselage and final assembly) and Kawasaki (main wing, tail and nose section) between July 1962 and January 1964 for the Nihon Koku Jieitai (Japanese Air Self-Defence Force/JASDF). Electronics and other items were compatible with those of the F-104J

version. Power was provided by the J79-1H1-11A engine of 10,000lb static thrust and 15,800lb with afterburner which was built under licence by Ishikawaj ima-Harima.

■ F-104E

Designation not assigned.

■ F-104F-LO (Model 483-04-08)

Designation applied to thirty two-seat trainers identical to the F-104Ds produced by Lockheed for the Federal Republic of Germany. Deliveries began at the start of October 1959 when they were temporarily serialled 59-4994/5023 (later being assigned German codes BB360/BB389 and lastly, after 1 January 1968, 2901/2930). They were all withdrawn from use in December 1971.

■ F-104G-LO (Model 683-10-19)

A total of 1,127 multi-role, all-weather fighter versions for NATO, built by MBB, Fokker-Aviolandia, SABCA-Fairey, Fiat and Canadair. All were delivered from 1960 to 1973. The F-104G differed from the F-104C principally in having a reinforced structure, larger tail surface area with fully powered rudder as used on the two-seater Starfighter, combat manoeuvring flaps, vastly improved electronics centred around the Autonetics F15A NASARR and a larger capacity for weapons loads.

The Lockheed Model C-2 upward-firing ejection seat fitted at the time of delivery was, beginning in 1967, gradually phased out in favour of the Martin-Baker Mk.7(F) 'zero-zero' seat. While the F-104G retained the Vulcan cannon of the earlier versions, it had additional attachments to take up to four Sidewinder missiles, as well as the NASARR system to provide radar search, acquisition and automatic tracking for lead-collision or lead-pursuit attack with missiles. A director-type gun-sight was used for the cannon, giving optical indication of line of sight, with the lead angle furnished by the Autonetics F15A NASARR computer. The bombing computer was linked with the inertial navigator, the air-data computer and the NASARR fire control system.

The first F-104G, a Lockheed-built model (c/n 683-2001) was flown on 7 June 1960. The first Canadair-built 'G' flew in July 1963. The Canadian-built F-104G model differed from those manufactured in Europe, principally in having the F15AM-11 NASARR which was optimized for both the air-to-air and air-to-ground roles. Power was provided by a General Electric J79-GE-11 engine of 10,000lb static thrust and 15,800lb with afterburner. European-built aircraft were fitted with engines co-produced under licence by MAN-Turbo in Germany, the Fabrique National in Belgium and Fiat in Italy. Most Luftwaffe and Bundesmarine F-104Gs were later retrofitted with the updated, German-built J79-MTU-JIK engine. The 1,127th and last F-104G was delivered by MBB in 1973.

■ RF-104G-LQ (Model 683-04-10)

Designation applied to 189 tactical photo-reconnaissance versions almost identical to the F-104G except for the removal of guns and the adoption of photographic equipment. Lockheed built forty RF-104Gs (61-2624/2633; 62-12232/12261); the North Group (Fokker) 119 (67-14891-?) and the Italian Group (Fiat-Aeritalia) thirty. The aircraft for the KLu (Royal Netherlands Air Force) had an external ventral camera pack, while the majority of the others carried three KS-67A cameras in the forward fuselage. In both cases the M61 cannon and its 725-round magazine aft of the cockpit were removed to make room. Many RF-104Gs were subsequently modified to F-104G standard.

■ RF-104G SLAR (Sideways-looking Radar)

A Fokker-built RF-104G (8222) was modified to carry a Goodyear 102R nose-mounted sideways-looking radar (SLAR) system in a programme which entered the design stage in June 1966. It was actually a follow-on to an earlier programme involving a SLAR installed in an external centreline pod. The test aircraft carried the Luftwaffe number EF3+121. The most noticeable exterior changes were the long radome which was extended to house the 6 feet long SLAR antenna and the Data Link antenna mounted just forward of the nose landing gear doors. The flight test aircraft also contained an external centreline pod to accommodate flight test instrumentation. Internally, the Vulcan cannon and drum were removed and SLAR major electric components were installed in the vacated gun bay. These included an Amplifier/Modulator, a Frequency Converter/Transmitter and the system Junction Box unit. The system contained a large recorder with 9.5in film which replaced all space previously occupied by the ammunition for the Vulcan cannon. Additional

ancillary systems installed included a Kearfott Trackkeeper System for providing straight ground tracks and steering information to the SLAR, a Fairchild-Hiller Annotation Unit which encoded information concerning time and aircraft flight data for placement on the radar film and an additional refrigeration package for cooling new system components. The Trackkeeper Indicator replaced the fire control radar scope in the cockpit. All of these components took up the space flight test normally reserved for flight test instrumentation components, thus the centreline pod as added.

A major set of components of the system which were not installed in the aircraft were contained in the supporting mobile Ground Station. This consisted of two German Army five-ton truck chassis containing a receiving, dish antenna and pedestal for the data link system, data link

XF-104 Lockheed C-2 downward ejection seat. Lockheed had initially supplied the Luftwaffe F-104Gs with the C-2 ejection seat which used a powerful 10100 booster rocket manufactured by the Talley Corporation. The use of the Talley rocket was said to give the ejection seat a zero-zero capability however they caused a destabilizing effect following ejection from the aircraft. On 8 March 1967 the F-104 fleet was grounded again and all C-2 series ejection seats were replaced with improved Martin Baker Mk-GQ7A zero-zero ejection seats. Initial successes in the improvement of the Starfighter's safety record were soon overshadowed with F-104 crashes climbing to between 15 to 20 aircraft each year between 1968 and 1972. The attrition rate would continue at a 9:11 ratio each year until the type was phased out and replaced by the Panavia Tornado.

electronics, processing and signal conditioning equipment and a Correlator/Processor which processed the downlink data into a duplicate of the in flight recorded film, about 7-10 minutes behind real-time.

In order to evaluate this SLAR system, two ranges containing a variety of corner reflector arrangements were constructed, one in the Panamint Valley for cross-track target resolution and one in the Pahrump Valley for along-track target resolution. Rosamond dry lake was used for small target clusters and Moving Target Indication (MTI) evaluation. Fifty-three flights were flown during the test programme, which ended on 21 June 1968 after having met all goals.

■ TF-104G (Model 583-10-20)

Designation applied to the two-seat advanced combat trainer version of the F-104G. The TF-104Gs were combat-ready aircraft fitted with NASARR and under-wing racks for carrying stores. Including 48 TF-104G (583C/D/E/F/G & H) aircraft with components manufactured by the European consortiums, Lockheed built a total of 220 TF-104Gs in these six versions.

The Models 583C to 583H were respectively for MAP delivery to the Luftwaffe and the AMI (Italian Air Force) and for direct delivery to the KLu (Royal Netherlands Air Force), the Luftwaffe and the Force Aérienne Belge (FAe) Belgische Luchtmacht (BLu) and the AMI. Germany received 136 TF-104Gs from Lockheed, thirty of which were retained in the US where they were used at Luke AFB, Arizona, for training Luftwaffe pilots. The TF-104G had a similar basic airframe to the single-seat version and carried the full NASARR radar. The type was intended principally for pilot training in low-level navigation. Both the autopilot and the Vulcan cannon were deleted, as was the centreline rack for the nuclear store. Fuel tanks and avionics were relocated to make room for the additional cockpit. The TF-104G could carry missiles and additional fuel tanks, fuel capacity being reduced by 180 Imperial gallons.

■ RTF-104G1

Designation given to a projected all-weather, day and night photographic reconnaissance version of the TF-104G1 fitted with cameras, infrared and sideways-looking (SLAR) radar for use by the Luftwaffe. The RTF-104G1 never emerged from the proposal stage as the Luftwaffe instead chose the McDonnell RF-4E Phantom II for the reconnaissance mission.

■ F-104G ZELL

The Zero-Length-Launch, or ZELL programme was conducted in great secrecy at Edwards AFB on the second production F-104G, which at the time carried the German identification DA+102 (Company 2002). The Luftwaffe had identified a need to launch their F-104s from no-runway areas in Europe and so the rocket-boosted concept was conceived. DA+102 was structurally modified to accept an RS B-202 rocket booster manufactured by Rocketdyne. The booster was 29 inch in diameter, 13 feet 3 inches long, weighed 4,175lb and developed 65,000lb of thrust for 7.9 seconds.

The F-104 was mounted in a 20 degree nose-up attitude on a static launcher. Prior to ignition of the booster, the J79 was started and advanced to full afterburning thrust. Hold-back fittings kept the Starfighter in position on the launcher until the booster was ignited, causing them to shear and release the F-104.

F-104G ZELL configurations resulting in gross weights of 23,900lb to 28,600lb were launched by this combined thrust (engine and booster) of 80,800lb. At booster burnout, the ZELL was about 2,000 feet down-range at anything from 420 to 700 feet AGL and 250 to 350 knots depending on the weight. The Starfighter's landing gear retracted automatically following separation from the launcher. The booster and its cradle were then jettisoned and the F-104G ZELL proceeded with the scheduled test mission. In the heaviest launch configuration, the ZELL contained full wingtip fuel tanks, full pylon fuel tanks and a 200lb centreline mounted bomb.

Prior to launches of the actual aircraft, Lockheed constructed for launch several 'Iron Crosses' - concrete and steel beam replicas of the F-104 airframe with weight, centre of gravity and moment of inertia accurately duplicated for various external store configurations. The launch of the second such 'iron cross' resulted in separation of the booster rocket, which collided with the dummy aircraft and began burning out of both ends, which one Lockheed observer described as 'resembling a huge 4th of July pinwheel fireworks display'. Several flight test crew members were injured, not by the rocket, but by fleeing the scene and stepping in chuck holes or running into

F-104G DA+102 ZELL at Lakehurst,
New Jersey in 1964.

vehicles. The problem with the separation of the booster rocket was soon remedied and Lockheed went on to launch seven 'iron crosses' before the F-104G ZELL tests began. Subsequent to the first piloted launch, dummy and piloted launches were intermixed to clear new stores configurations.

Altogether, twelve dummy and eight piloted launches were carried out in two phases. The first involved a Lockheed-built launcher while the second involved evaluation of a different launch platform manufactured by Vereinigte Flugtechnische Werke (VFW) in Germany. The first phase took place during 14 December 1962 to 28 August 1963 and the second phase took place during 18 March 1964 to 22 July 1964. A few problems occurred prior to the initial aircraft launches. The access stand to the cockpit was rather high and made it difficult to reach switches from the platform. On a mission pre-flight, the crew chief reached into the cockpit to pull the drag chute handle, got the wrong one and jettisoned the canopy.

On the day of the first real launch, test pilot Ed Brown was obviously nervous - he overslept and was late for the scheduled launch time. Following the successful first live launch, Brown, an ex-Navy carrier pilot, described the sensation as 'much gentler than a cat shot'. Flight test data verified that indeed only two Gs longitudinal acceleration were experienced. Eight piloted launches were accomplished with amazingly few problems and a follow-on programme involving several additional launches was conducted in Germany.

Most of the challenge of the ZELL programme involved ground support equipment which had to be designed or modified to handle the booster/cradle installation, loading and unloading of the aircraft on the launcher and boresighting the booster. Several iterations of engine/booster exhaust gas deflector channels were tried before a successful configuration was developed. The hold-back fixtures were redesigned to eliminate interference with the landing gear. The final report contained the statement 'Zero-length launches of the F-104 aircraft have been demonstrated to be entirely feasible'.

■ F-104H

Designation given in 1964 to a projected Lockheed simplified single-seat version of the TF-104G (with an optical gunsight in place of NASARR) for export, but which was unbuilt. This model would have been a simplified F-104G with the Autonetics F15A NASARR fire control system eliminated and an optical gunsight and it was designed to be able to carry out both the interceptor and strike roles. Empty weight was 13,492lb and maximum overload weight was 28,440lb. This version was offered to Saudi Arabia, which preferred to buy the English Electric Lightning instead.

■ TF-104H

Designation given to a projected, but unbuilt, simplified two-seat version of the TF-104G with the same specifications as the F-104H, for export.

■ F-104J (Model 683-07-14)

Designation applied to 210 aircraft structurally similar to the F-104G but equipped as an all-weather interceptor and powered by a J79-1H1-11A turbojet built under licence by Ishikawajima-Harima. The first three F-104Js were produced and flight tested by Lockheed, after which they were dismantled and shipped to Japan. A further twenty-nine were assembled by Mitsubishi Jukogyo KK (Mitsubishi Heavy Industries Ltd) at their Komaki plant in Japan and by Kawasaki, from Lockheed components and 178 were built in two batches in Japan. The first Lockheed-built F-104J flew on 30 June 1961 and the first flight of a F-104J in Japan was made on 8 March 1962. Deliveries to the Nihon Koku Jieitai (Japanese Air Self-Defence Force/JASDF), took place during March 1962 to March 1965. The first aircraft, a J, was delivered to the JASDF in April 1962. By the end of 1962 thirty-two (twenty-four F-104Js/eight DJs) had been delivered; in 1963 seventy (sixty F-104Js/ten DJs); in 1964, ninety-eight (ninety-six F-104Js/two DJs), 1966 seven F-104Js; and a final batch of twenty-three F-104Js delivered in 1967.

■ F-104K toF-104M

Designations not assigned.

■ F-104N

Three Starfighters built as F-104Gs by Lockheed (683C-4045, 683C-4053 and 683C-4058) were delivered to NASA between August and October 1963 as F-104N supersonic chase planes (see Chapter 11).

■ F-104P to F-104R

Designations not assigned.

■ F-104S Model (CL-901)

Designation given to the multi-role, all-weather interceptor (caccia ogni tempo) version of the F-104G produced in Italy for the AMI for interception and interdiction/strike duties and for Turkey for interception. After flight testing some improvements on a modified RF-104G (61-2624), Lockheed received an Italian contract to modify two Fiat-built F-104Gs (MM6658 and MM6660, which were delivered to Lockheed in 1966) as prototypes for an advanced all-purpose Starfighter with improved capability both as an interceptor and as a fighter-bomber.

This entailed the removal of the M-61 20mm cannon and its ammunition can, replacement of these units with the Raytheon Sparrow missile control/CW radar system, addition of two new wing stores stations, pylons at BL104 for two underwing Raytheon AIM-7 Sparrow III radar-seeking missiles and/or two AIM9 Sidewinder missiles, incorporation of the fuselage-mounted stores stations at BL22, upgrade of the F15A NASARR radar to the R-21G configuration and integration of the Raytheon system with it. (Part of the radar development programme involved experimentation with different radomes, including a U-2 radome, which greatly changed the appearance of the F-104G).

The additional hard-points gave the F-104 a total of nine, one at the fuselage centreline, two at fuselage BL22, four wing pylon stations at BL75 and BL104 and two at the wingtips. The new Starfighter became a multi-mission interceptor/fighter-bomber capable of carrying widely varied weapons mixes. It could, for instance, be configured with four AIM-9 Sidewinders and two AIM-7 Sparrow IIIs for the Interceptor role, or up to ten M-117 750lb bombs or napalm tanks or rocket pods for the bombing mission. In this configuration, the 'lightweight' fighter exceeded 31,000lb gross weight. This increase in weight and a need to improve overall performance, led the fitting of the J79-GE-19 of 11,870lb static thrust and 17,900lb with afterburner.

The basic F-104G contained a fixed-frequency, hydraulic-driven AC generator. In order to provide power for the Sparrow system, a second such generator was added to the F-104S model. Auxiliary inlet doors were provided for the added air requirement by the J79-GE-19 engine. Two additional ventral fins were provided for stability. The F-104S model's Mach limit was increased from 2.0 to 2.2.

James Fitzgerald of the Lockheed Advanced Development Company recalled:

'The first Lockheed-modified F-104S (MM6658) was flown on 30 December 1966. The flight test programme afforded a number of avionics system challenges. The Sparrow missile control system had never been integrated with the NASARR fire control radar and the missile had never been as much as separation-launched from the F-104. Two F-86H Sabres were used during the flight test programme in roles as chase and target. As targets, they were RCS-enhanced by Lüneberg lenses mounted in their tails. The first F-104S did not contain the Sparrow missile control system and was used or aerodynamic tests, systems tests and weapons separation tests. The second (MM6660), was fitted with the complete Sparrow system and was the primary avionics/fire control system test vehicle. The test programme-was conducted during 1967 and 1968 and 71 flights were flown on the avionics aircraft alone. An additional 63 flights were flown on this aircraft in a follow-on programme to evaluate production avionics fire-control systems.

'Early in the programme, MM6658 was to launch a Sparrow at limit Mach 2.2 for separation purposes. Several earlier launches at lower Mach numbers had been successful. The only aircraft which could keep up with the S was the Navy's new F-4J. Since all missile firings in the programme were conducted at the Pacific Missile Test Range at Point Magu, it was no trouble to schedule an F-4J from VX-4. The acceleration characteristics of the two airplanes were considerably different from each other in the various subsonic regimes, resulting in an interesting 'drag race' but not-so-good chase photos. Just as the test airplane achieved Mach 2.2,

the second hydro-generator tripped off the line, removing power from the test missile and causing an abort. This was subsequently discovered to be a generator overheat caused by airflow stagnation in the (new, of course) shared cooling duct for the two hydro-generators. A slight redesign cured the problem.

'Initial missile-fire control integration testing included a 'three-plane captive' flight involving the avionics F-14S acting as interceptor, illuminating the target and missile with the fire control radar. An F-86H acted as a target and the systems F-14S as the missile carrier. The missile carrier airplane started in formation with the illuminator and after lock on, accelerated toward the target. By using the F-104 to carry the instrumented missile, it could act as the missile in flight by closing on the target, as data transmitted from the missile telemetry was monitored. All test missiles carried telemetry packages in lieu of warheads and ground telemetry stations were located at Lockheed Palmdale and at Raytheon's plant near Point Magu.

'After missile and fire control integration testing was completed, an ambitious series of planned line firings against drones was undertaken at Point Magu. They progressed from relatively benign tail-on aspect launches to the one we called 'FF-5', with the F-104 in a quartering head-on aspect at Mach 1.7 to an AQM-37 drone at supersonic speed. The first live shot scored a direct hit on the subsonic BQM-34 drone, exploding the drone's full tank and prompting test pilot Ken Weir to push for installation of a gun camera for the next launch, which we did. Remember, the missiles did not contain warheads and the idea was to recover the drones for re-use, not destroy them. We did, however, destroy or damage five with direct hits. The code word for a near miss was 'Boola' in the Point Magu control room and a direct hit was 'Boola-Boola'. We heard those terms on every shot. Ken Weir accounted for four of the drones, making him a near-ace. The FF-5 mission was particularly difficult, with a six second window between target acquisition and missile launch.

'On supersonic firings over Point Magu, the airplane frequently recovered at Point Magu due to low fuel. Both airplanes were unmarked except for a number, were painted in European camouflage and would land with a single Sparrow and a bare pylon opposite following a firing flight.

'One of the unplanned challenges which took place early in the development involved the Sparrow Line-of-Sight (LOS) signals we were recording as part of the test effort. They never seemed to work, at least did not show up on the oscillograph (yes, oscillograph) records. These signals were of very low (millivolt) magnitude and were crucial to the Sparrow antenna pointing accuracy. A very involved investigation took place and the bottom line was found to be conductive potting compound used in the missile pylon adapters. High level signals were not affected, but the LOS certainly were. This problem had to be solved prior to any live missile firings involving subsequent guidance.

'Overall, this was a highly successful fire control improvement and integration programme and some S models are still in service with the Italian Air Force.

'The first Italian-built 'S' flew on 30 December 1968. Total production by Fiat-Aeritalia ceased in March 1979 after 245 F-104S models, including 40 F-104S models for Turkey, had been produced.'

■ F-104S ASA (Aggiornamento Sistemi d'Arma – 'Weapon Systems Update')

In 1983 Italy decided to upgrade 153 of its F-104S models to ASA (Aggiornamento Sisterm d'Arrrux, or updated weapons system standard to enable the Starfighter to detect, track and shoot down low-level intruders. The original FIAR R21G/H radar was

replaced by Fiat R21G/M1 Setter with look-down/ shoot-down capability and fire control system. Selenia Aspide 1A medium-to long-range, radar-guided air-to-air missiles based on the Raytheon AIM-7E Sparrow AAM, replaced the Sparrows and fuselage rails were added for AIM-9L Sidewinder missiles. Improved IFF, more modern internal electronic countermeasures (ECM) systems and the addition of an automatic pitch control computer were also fitted. Provision was also made for a reconnaissance camera pod.

Flight trials of a modernized F-104S ASA demonstrator began in December 1984 and subsequently, 206 F-104S models were upgraded to F-104S ASA standard. By the beginning of 1995 the ASA still had 125 F-104 ASA models in its inventory among seven gruppi.

For air intercept sorties the F-104S typically carried an AIM-9L dogfight missile under the port wing, an Alenia Aspide 1A missile under the starboard wing and two wingtip tanks. In the fully loaded, but rarely used, interception configuration, the F-104S ASA carried four Sidewinders (two on fuselage rails, two on the wing tips), two Aspides and two drop tanks. All remaining F-104S ASA models were scheduled for replacement by the Eurofighter 2000.

The ASA/M upgrade (initially known as the 'ECO' - Estensione Capacità Operative upgrade, later Aggiornamento Sistemi d'Arma/Modificato – 'Weapon Systems Update/Modified') improved

TF-104G N104L *Renée* of Northern Lights
Aircraft, Inc. Initially retained by Lockheed as
a company demonstrator, this Starfighter was
used by Jacqueline Cochran to set World Speed
Records. It was then acquired by the KLu in
May 1965 as D-5702 and from 25 August 1980 it
was used by the Turkish Air Force.

reliability rather than combat enhancements on 49
F-104S-ASA and 15 two-seat TF-104G aircraft
from 1998 to ASA/M standard with GPS, new
TACAN and Litton LN-30A2 INS, refurbished
airframe and improved cockpit displays. All
strike-related equipment and the IRST ('IR-Sight',
forward the windshield) were removed.

CF-104 (CF-111)

Designation applied to 340 (CL-90) Starfighters
built under licence by Canadair, with the Orenda-
built J79-OEL-7 engine of 10,000lb static thrust
and 15,800lb with afterburner. The first 200 aircraft
(initially designated CF-111 by the Royal Canadian
Air Force) were built under a licence agreement
from Lockheed on 24 July 1959. Externally, these
aircraft were little different from the F-104G. They
retained provision for the removable refuelling
probe as fitted to US Air Force Starfighters, but
the R24A NASARR was optimized for the air-to-
air role and the Vulcan cannon was removed and
replaced by additional fuel tanks.

Other equipment was as specified by the RCAF.
This included a Vicon ventral reconnaissance pod
with four Vinten 70mm cameras and electronic
sensors manufactured by Computing Devices of
Canada. CF-104s also had larger tyres on the main
undercarriage and Dowty-patented liquid springs
with longer stroke. The first Canadair CF-104
was airlifted to Palmdale, California, where it first
flew on 26 May 1961. The first CF-104 to fly in
Canada was number four, which flew in August

that year. The last of 200 CF-104s for the RCAF
was completed in September 1963.

These were followed by 140 Canadair-built
F-104Gs as part of the Military Assistance
Programme (MAP). In Kongelide Danske
Flyvevabnet (KDF, Royal Danish Air Force) and
Kongelige Norske Luftforsvaret (KNL, Royal
Norwegian Air Force) service, ex-RCAF/CAF CF-
104s (and CF-104Ds) were modified to F-104G
and TF-104G standard respectively.

CF-104 (CF-113) (Model 583-04-15)

Designation applied to 22 CF-113 (later CF-104D)
two-seat advanced trainers and sixteen two-seat
advanced trainers (which, fitted with slightly
different equipment, were designated CF-104D
Mk.II) built by Lockheed for the Royal Canadian
Air Force (RCAF) (later Canadian Armed Services/
CAF). All were powered by the Orenda-built J79-
OEL-7 engine.

CL-1200 Lancer

Designation of a Lockheed Skunk Works second
generation project derived in 1961 from the F-104,
with the same fuselage, but with new, shoulder-
mounted wings of increased area and its tailplane
moved from the tip of the vertical and relocated
to the base of the aft fuselage. The CL-1200-1
was to have used an uprated version of the F-104
engine, the General Electric J79 with a later variant
known as the CL1200-2 to be powered by a Pratt
and Whitney TF-30 turbofan. Gross weight was
estimated at 35,000lb or 17.5 tons and top speed
at 1,700mph at 35,000 feet. Intended for the export
market as a concept for the lightweight fighter of
the 1980s and 1990s and in direct competition with
the Northrop F-5E Tiger II, Dassault Mirage F1,
Northrop YF-17 and the McDonnell Douglas F-4

Phantom, it was projected that CL-1200 deliveries could begin in 1972 but the aircraft finally lost out to the Northrop F-5E Tiger II in November 1970 and the Lancer never entered production. Lockheed had hoped to capitalize on its F-104 production experience through commonality of parts and systems and minimize expenses by reusing tooling, jigs and existing factory facilities. The USAF planned to buy at least one experimental Lancer under the designation X-27 (called the CL-1600 by Lockheed) for Mach 2.6 testing. The X-27 was to be similar in overall configuration to the Lancer, but was to feature modified engine air intakes of rectangular form. However, the X-27 programme received almost no US Congressional or Air Force support. Due to the lack of funding, no flight-capable aircraft were constructed. One full-scale mockup was built by Lockheed, although up to three fuselages had been converted before the shutdown of the project.

▮ CL-704 VTOL strike and reconnaissance aircraft

The F-104/VTOL (Vertical take-off and landing) project was first proposed in 1962. It would have seen the F-104G fitted with wingtip lift engine pods and Rolls-Royce RB.181 lift engines and a fuselage-mounted RB.168R main propulsion engine. Lockheed and Short Brothers and Harland of Belfast (who had pioneered VTOL with its 'flying bedstead' project) discussed the proposal in which the wingtip pods were to contain seven vertically mounted lift engines with detachable fuel tanks fore and aft of the stainless-steel powerplant bay.

Each lift engine was to have forward-facing inlet door that would adjust automatically for different air flow conditions. Swivel nozzles were to direct air flow downwards from the pods through a 15 degree arc on either side of the vertical thrust line. By deflecting the nozzles simultaneously, the pilot

would be able to control fore and aft movements while hovering. They would also be used, by differential deflection, for yaw control. Pitch control would be achieved by varying pitch settings between the four forward and three rear lift engines and through a pitch-control vane installed in the main engine exhaust system.'

The F-104G/VTOL programme never reached production because apart from the exceptionally high cost of fuel needed to blast the Starfighter off the ground, the advanced nature of the true-VTOL aircraft, the British made Hawker P1127 Kestrel, made the F-10G/VTOL virtually redundant at birth. (The P1127 design, which was evaluated by the Tripartite squadron consisting of US, RAF and Luftwaffe pilots, ultimately led to the highly successful Harrier VTOL jet.) (A larger-wing F-104 development was also proposed as an alternative to the MRCA (Multi Role Combat Aircraft) then being designed as a multinational European project.)

▮ X-27 (CL-1600)

In 1970 the US Air Force wanted to acquire a number of CL-1200 Lancers for use as high-performance-engine test aircraft. The USAF planned to procure one experimental Lancer, to be designated X-27. Similar to the CL-1200, the X-27 however featured modified engine air inlets of rectangular shape. The X-27 programme was terminated through lack of funding before any aircraft could be built.

NATO Operators

■ Belgium

Beginning in February 1963 the Force Aérienne Belge (FAé)/Belgische Luchtmacht BLu) received a total of 101 SABCA-built F-104Gs (one F-104G crashed before delivery) and twelve Lockheed-built TF-104Gs. These aircraft were assigned to four escadrilles/smaldeels (squadrons, or ème): the 349 ème and 350 ème of the 1 Wing de Chasse/l Jachtwing (interceptors), at Beauvechain/Bevekom and the 23 ème and 31 ème of the 10 Wing Chasseurs-Bombardiers/10 Wing Jager-Bommenserpers (fighter-bombers), at Kleine Brogel, for tactical strike and all-weather air defence, respectively. I Wing de Chasse/l Jachtwing began replacing its CF-100 Canucks with the Starfighter in 1963 and 10 Wing Chasseurs-Bombardiers/10 Wing Jager-Bommenwerpers received F-104Gs for the strike-attack role a year later. During the 1980s the Beauvechain and Kleine Brogel èmes converted to the General Dynamics F-16A/B. The 349 ème received its first F-16B on 26 January 1979 and the ème was declared operational in January 1981. 350 ème began conversion to the F-16 in July 1980 and was declared operational on the Fighting Falcon in the summer of 1981. The Kleine Brogel units meanwhile, retired the last of their Starfighters in September 1983. 23 ème received its first F-16s in

FX 12 of 350 ème/1 Wing, which was withdrawn from service on 8 November 1979; FX 30 of 349 ème/1 Wing, which was sold to Turkey on 17 May 1983 and FX 82 which operated with 349 ème/1 Wing and 31 ème/10 Wing before being WFU and stored on 21 October 1982. Stripped of all useful parts, it was shipped to the USA on 20 June 1989. It is now preserved at Planes of Fame Museum, Chino.

December 1981, being declared operational on the Fighting Falcon in March 1983. 31 ème became operational on the F-16 in 1984. The Belgian Air Force operated the type from 14 February 1963 to 19 September 1983; some survivors were sent to Taiwan (23 aircraft) and Turkey (18 aircraft). Thirty-eight F-104G and three TF-104Gs were lost in accidents and twenty-three pilots were killed.

FX 67, which was assigned to 10 Wing on 17 July 1964 and later was operated by 350 ème/1 Wing had several accidents during its career and was finally SOC in January 1987. It went to Taiwan in October 1990. FX 61 was issued to 23 ème/10 Wing on 8 June 1964 and later served with 1 Wing. WFU on 26 September 1983 and stripped of all useful parts, it was sold in December 1989 to the 'Tiger Air Force Museum'. It went to Kleine Brogel in 1992 for Battle Damage Repair Training.

Starfighters of NATO nations, together with jet fighters of RAF Germany, USAF and France. From top: USAF F-105D Thunderchief 00436 of the 36th Tactical Fighter Wing at Bitburg, Germany; RAF Gloster Javelin FAW.7 XH771/F; Koninklijke Luchtmacht (KLu, Royal Netherlands Air Force) F-104G D-8060, which was acquired by the Türk Hava Kuwetleri (THK, Turkish Air Force) in January 1982; RCAF CF-104 12815; Force Aérienne Belge (FAé)/Belgische Luchtmacht (BLu) FX 07, which was acquired from the Belgian Air Force by the RoCAF (Taiwan) in 1990; Luftwaffe F-104G DA+243 of JaboG 31 'Böelcke' and French Armée de l'Air Mirage IIIE 2-El.)

■ Canada

After the cancellation of the Avro Arrow programme it was announced in Ottawa on 2 July 1959 that the Canadair-built CF-104 had been selected to replace the Canadair Sabre Mk.6, which was suffering from a growing number of fatigue problems and the Avro Canada CF-100 Canuck, in the eight squadrons of the 1st Air Division in France and Germany. The Starfighter had faced stiff competition, from the Grumman F-11 Super Tiger, Hawker Siddeley Buccaneer S-2, Dassault Mirage IIIC, the Fiat G.91, the Northrop F-5A and the Republic F-105 Thunderchief. Its role would be Nuclear Strike and Photo Reconnaissance. Since the Canadian government wanted equipment to be fitted that was specific to RCAF requirements, it opted to manufacture the aircraft under licence in a Canadian factory rather than buy the aircraft outright from Lockheed. On 14 August it was announced that Canadair of Montreal had been selected to manufacture 200 aircraft for the RCAF under licence from Lockheed. In addition, Canadair was to manufacture wings, tail assemblies and rear fuselage sections for 66 Lockheed-built Starfighters that were destined for the West German Luftwaffe. The licence production contract was signed on 17 September 1959. In parallel with the production of the Starfighter by Canadair, Orenda Engines Ltd

CF-104 12701, the first of 200 CF-104 Starfighters for the RCAF, which first flew in July 1961. As the Canadair-built CF-104s were not armed with the M61 Vulcan cannon both the gun ports and the gun gas vents were faired over. The M61 cannon was retrofitted on CF-104s in 1971 when Canada changed its Germany-based Starfighters from nuclear strike to conventional ground attack.

acquired a licence to build the General Electric J79 engine (J79-OEL-7 rated at 10,000lb static thrust dry and 15,800lb st with afterburning) powered the CF-104. Optimized for the nuclear strike role rather than being a multi-mission aircraft, the CF-104 was fitted with R-24A NASARR (North American Search and Range Radar) equipment that was 'peaked' for the air-to-ground mode only. The main undercarriage members were fitted with longer-stroke liquid springs and carried larger tyres than the F-10G of the USAF. The CF-104 had the ability to carry a ventral reconnaissance pod equipped with four Vinten Vicom cameras. The 20-mm M61A1 Vulcan cannon and its associated ammunition were initially omitted from the CF-104 and an additional fuel cell was fitted in their place.

Lockheed sent F-104A-15-LO serial number 56-0770 to Canada to act as a pattern aircraft for CF-104 manufacture. It was later fitted with CF-104 fire control systems and flight control equipment and turned over to the RCAF, where it was assigned the serial number of 12700. Canadair rolled its first CF-104 (12701) out of the Cartierville plant

The first two CF-104s to fly at Montreal were 12703 and 12704, on 14 August 1961. CF-703 went to Denmark as R-704 in 1973. On 19 December 2010 it was shipped to the USA, arriving on 14 July 2011 at Maine for onward delivery to the Canadian Starfighter Museum at St. Andrew's Airport, Winnipeg, Manitoba.

■ **RCAF CF-104s 701-705 in formation.**

on 18 March 1961. It was the first of 200 built for the RCAF. The first Canadair-constructed CF-104 (RCAF serial number 12701) was airlifted to Palmdale, California in the spring of 1961, where it made its first flight on May 26. The second CF-104 (12702) also made its first flight at Palmdale. The first two CF-104s to fly at Montreal were Nos. 12703 and 12704, which both took to the air on 14 August 1961. Canadair built an additional 140 Starfighters for other NATO Nations. Enheat in Amherst, Nova Scotia built some components for the CF-104 programme.

Between January 1962 and September 1963, twenty-two dual seat CF-104Ds built by Lockheed were accepted by Canada. The very early Canadian Starfighter pilots were trained in the US until in July 1961 6 Strike/Reconnaissance Operational Training Unit at Cold Lake, Alberta became the first Canadian unit to receive CF-104/CF-104D Starfighters. (6 OTU was re-designated 417 Squadron on 23 March 1968.) Most CF-104Ds were used to train instructors first and then squadron pilots. A further sixteen CF104Ds were accepted in November 1964. The Canadian-built Starfighter was initially designated CF-111 by the RCAF and later changed to CF-104. They were designated CL-90 by the Canadair factory. This was changed to Canadian serial numbers 12701 through 12900. On 18 May 1970 they were re-serialled as 104701 through 104900. The Lockheed-built F-104A pattern aircraft was re-serialled from 12700 to 104700.

The 200th and last CF-104 (No. 12900) had been completed on 4 September 1963 and delivered to the RCAF on 10 January 1964. Many early production aircraft were modified to the standard of the last production machines. Following the

delivery of the last CF-104, Canadair switched over to the manufacture of F-104Gs for delivery to NATO allies under the provisions of MAP. By 1983, all single-seat CF-104s had been modified with the Litton LW-33 digital inertial navigation/attack system, which replaced the original LN-3 analogue inertial navigation system. The LW-33 was much more accurate and less expensive to maintain than was the earlier LN-3. In addition, the LW-33 had an attack function.

Beginning in 1983 the CF-104 Starfighters were replaced in Canadian Armed Forces service by McDonnell Douglas CF-18 Hornets. 439 Squadron was stood down on 1 July 1983. The last CF-104s were phased out of service by 441 Squadron at Baden-Söllingen on 1 March 1986. A number of former Canadian Forces single-seat CF-104 fighter-bombers and CF-104D two-seat trainers were transferred to Denmark and Norway after having been brought up to F-104G/TF-104G standards. Canada offered Turkey an initial batch of twenty CF-104s; later increased to 52, including six CF-104Ds. Twenty of these were sent to MBB at Manching in Germany in March of 1986 for inspection before being transferred to Turkey. The remainder were broken down for spares.

CF-104 12900 of 1 Air Division RCAF Europe, with the Vicon recce pod. ■

R-647 (63-16847) and FG-707/32707 (63-12707) of the Royal Danish Air Force at RAF Coltishall for the BoB Day on 14 September 1968. 707 last flew on 16 April 1986. In 1986 63-13647 was shipped to Taiwan for RoCAF service (as '4419') and was withdrawn from use on 7 March 1994.

Denmark

Beginning in November 1964, Kongelide Danske Flyvevadbnet (KDF, Royal Danish Air Force) received, under the Mutual Defense Assistance Act, 25 Canadair-built F-104Gs and four Lockheed TF-104Gs to equip two eskadrilles (squadrons) at Aalbørg. Esk 726 began replacing its F-86D Sabres in December 1964. Esk 723 began replacing its F-86D Sabres in January 1965. The first ten Starfighters were delivered to Aalbørg in a complicated operation that involved taking the F-104s on loaders through streets nearby after they had been offloaded at the docks. The remaining Starfighters followed in two more consignments, in December 1964 and in June 1965.

Surplus Canadian licence-built aircraft were transferred between 1971–73 (15 CF-104 and 7 CF-104D). In 1972-74 twenty-two ex-Canadian Starfighters (fifteen CF-104s and seven CF-104Ds,

with the latter being specially modified for use by Esk 726 in the electronic countermeasures role), were transferred to Denmark. On 1 January 1983 Esk 723 split into Esk 723-104 and 723-16, the latter transferring to Skrydstrup to receive the F-16. Esk 723-104 disbanded as a Starfighter squadron on 1 January 1984 and the new Esk 723 returned to Aalbørg on 30 March as the KDF's third operational F-16 unit. Some of Esk 723's Starfighters were withdrawn from service in November 1984, although one later returned to temporary service. On 30 April 1986 Esk 726 was disbanded and, with the exception of four aircraft temporarily retained for target-towing duty, the Starfighters were retired from Danish service. A total of 51 Starfighters were operated by Denmark before their retirement in 1986. Fifteen surplus F-104Gs and three TF-104Gs were transferred to Taiwan in 1987.

TF-104G RT-664 of Eskadrille 723 of the Royal Danish Air Force at Mildenhall Air Fete 1983. This ex-RCAF CF-104D (63-12664) was delivered in April 1965 to the Canadian 4th Wing in 1 Air Division at CFB Söllingen on 11 May 1965. Delivered to Denmark in May 1972, it was operated by Eskadrille 723 and later Esk 726 before being WFU on 20 February 1984. It was scrapped in May 2012. (Author)

Canadair-built F-104G R-698 (63-12698) of Eskadrille 726 On 3 December 1974 it crashed into the Skagerak during ship patrol. SK Lieutenant J. A. Hansen lost control after several tight manoeuvres at 1,500 feet altitude and he was killed.

TF-104G RT-681 63-12681 of Esk 723 at RAF Coltishall on 14 September 1968. In service with Esk 723 it crashed on 13 June 1975 due to a Compressor Stall. 2nd Lieutenant B. H. Johansen and 2nd Lieutenant J. T. Stentoft ejected safely.

Canadair-built F-104G R-752 of Eskadrille 723 which on 22 February 1971 crashed into the Kattegat due to engine failure after a compressor stall. The pilot, SK Lieutenant P. E. R. Anthonsen ejected safely.

A pair of Danish Air Force TF-104Gs taking off. RT-662, an ex-RCAF two-seater was wfu on 1 January 1984 and used for battle damage repair training at Skrydstrup from 1986 to September 1971. (Alf Blume)

F-104G FG-7151 of 336 'Olympus' Mira and 32720 of 335 'Tiger' Mira in anniversary scheme. These two Hellenic Air Force squadrons operated the Starfighter in the 114 Pterix (Wing) at Tanagra AB until on 21 December 1966 the 336 Mira moved to the 116 Pterix at Araxos AB. The 335 Mira continued flying from Tanagra until 1 June 1977 when it joined the 336 Mira at Araxos. 335 'Tiger' Mira Anachaitisis (Interceptor Squadron) deactivated in May 1992. 336 'Olympus' Mira Diokseos Bombardismou (Fighter-Bomber Squadron) deactivated on 31 March 1993, the official date for the withdrawal of the Starfighter from service in the Hellenic Air Force. FG-7151 is now exhibited at the Hellenic Air Force Museum at Dekelia (Tatoi), Athens.

Canadair-built F-104G FG-781 (64-17781) of the Hellenic Air Force. This Starfighter first flew on 8 June 1965 and went to the USAF on 19 August 1965 before going to Greece in December 1965 to operate with 335 Mirra. It was WFU in 1993 and was stored at Agrinion before being displayed at Nea Anchialos Airport (LGBL) from 2008. (Lockheed)

Greece

Deliveries to the Elliniki Vassiliki Aeroporia (Royal Hellenic Air Force) at Hellas of Canadair/Lockheed-built F-104G/TF-104Gs, began in March-April 1964 under the terms of the Military Defense Assistance Program (MAP). These aircraft were taken on the inventory of the 114 Ptérix Mahis (Combat Wing) for operation by one (later two) Dioseos Bombardismoy mire (fighter-bomber squadrons), 335 Mira 'Tiger' and 336 Mira 'Olympus'. 335 Mira at Tanagra became the first Greek Starfighter squadron in April 1964. From December 1964 to February 1965 nineteen Canadair-built F-104Gs were obtained by HAF and formed 336 Mira, based temporarily at Tanagra, in January 1965. This brought the number of Lockheed- and Canadair-built Starfighters supplied through MAP in 1964 to forty-five F-104Gs and six TF-104Gs. In 1972 nine more F-104Gs and one TF-104G, all previously operated by the Ejército del Aire, were received. Another 79 were received from Germany and seven from the Netherlands.

On 21 December 1966 336 Mira was relocated at Araxos Air Base (116 Ptérix Mahis) and became 336 Strike Squadron. 335 Mira of the 114 Ptérix Mahis remained at Tanagra Air Base until June 1977, when it moved to Araxos having retired the last of its F-104G/TF-104Gs and converting to the Mirage F1.

At the end of summer 1972 Flying Officer (later Wing Commander) D. Jannes was posted from 341 Mira to 336 Mira. 'At first, this was a surprise, but not a very pleasant one. After one and a half years and 280 hours on the F-5, I was being sent to Araxos on the F-104. At the time, I was beginning to master the F-5 and hold my own in air combat against the older people of the squadron. On top of that I had a very 'active' night life in the city of Volos. Then, the F-5 was the most manoeuvrable fighter at the time and we would hear terrible things about the F-104 such as 'It doesn't turn, it's impossible to get a good shot, at 3G's it starts shaking, etc'. It was with these thoughts that I arrived at Araxos.

'The 'tube', as it was called, was unique in taking 37% of the total lift from the fuselage and the rest from the wing and stabiliser! But it still flew! The cockpit with the C-2 ejection seat was relatively comfortable, unless you tried to reach the stick shaker, undercarriage siren safety switches, UHF/IFF/Auto Pilot safety switches plus a few others which were buried somewhere down below you and which became, after 1973 and the

Lockheed-built TF-104G TF-278 (22278) of the Hellenic Air Force.

▌ **F-104G FG-715 (32715) of the**
▌ **Hellenic Air Force.**

installation of Martin Baker seats, just a memory! The forward view was excellent. You can only see the last 10cm of the pitot tube to remind you that you are in a plane and not in a flight simulator.

'After starting the J79 and going through a swift process by communicating with the ground crew using all the fingers of your right hand, you are ready to taxi, all the time watching the engine gauges very careful. Throttle pushed just a little and the aircraft starts moving. You keep pushing the throttle and the squadron crew room becomes a blur. At the end of the runway, lined up, you go through the vital pre-take off checks and report to the tower 'canopy down - flaps down'. The big moment comes. You check the engine and you're cleared for take-off. You release the brakes and move the throttle from minimum afterburner....3, 4, 5 seconds, max afterburner and from that moment on you forget anything else that you've flown - F-5. T-33, T-37 or any other. 0-200 knots

in 16 seconds with 15,800lbs of thrust one metre behind you and the first time, believe me, you don't even see the 1,000 feet signs on either side of the runway. Then at 200 knots, you pull back and then it's u/c up. Keep low down at ten feet till the end of the runway where, at 370 knots, you pull 2-3 G's until the artificial horizon unlocks (it does so at an 82° climb angle!). You then level off at 3-3,500 feet over the end of the runway, hoping that the CO doesn't see you! At 0.9 Mach, initial climb rate is 50,000 feet/minute. Time from brakes release to 35,000 feet is less than three minutes! Well, the F-15 in the meantime will have reached 99,000 feet but we're talking about a 1954 design and the first flight of the G-model was in 1960 when the F-15 didn't exist, not even as a low voltage circuit in the memories of the McDonnell Douglas computers!

'With the F-104 you had a love hate relationship; nothing mid way. Very few people came to'hate it. For most, the F-104 has a special place in their hearts, no matter what they came to fly later - even the F-15. Look, it doesn't mean that the F-104 is the best plane. Certainly, aircraft like the F-16,

▌ **F-104G FG-715, TF-105G TF-278 (22278) and F-104G FG-720 (32720) of the Hellenic Air Force. The first**
▌ **37 F-104Gs were received in 1964 and equipped the 335 Mira and 336 Mira. Greece received 45 new-build**
▌ **F-104G and six TF-104s under the Military Assistance Program. These were supplemented by second-**
▌ **hand Starfighters passed on from other NATO air forces, including 79 from Germany, seven from the**
Netherlands and in 1972, nine from Spain. Greece lost thirteen Starfighters operationally between May
1964-September 1987

F-104G FG-090 (7090) of the 335 'Tiger' Mira, an ex-Luftwaffe aircraft.

F-18 and Mirage 2000 can do circles around an F-104. However, an F-16 pilot who will have reached 80-85% of the capabilities of his jet (the maximum figure for the average pilot) would make a minimum effort by comparison to that of an F-104 pilot and that's the key point in the philosophy behind the F-104. The pilot who flies the F-16 at 90% of its limits will come back thrilled. The pilot who approaches the same figure in the F-104 will come back really shaken, having done the Perfect Flight.

'The F-104 is particularly stable in close formation and all Starfighter pilots are experts in close formation flying - nine planes in diamond formation (display formation before 1979/80) occupy less space than a C-130! The CPM's were pure fun (back then as we were a Strike squadron we flew a lot of time alone) and in 1½-2 hours (with external tanks of course) we would fly all over Greece at 450-500 knots at 200-300 feet, or even down to 10 feet!

'The 'decisive' flight however was the air test. You went to the control room looking like 'Snake' Reaves, (Lockheed's Chief Test Pilot and perhaps generally accepted as the best F-104 pilot). Young technicians look at you in awe, the older ones in sympathy. After a little discussion on some details, things to note etc, you receive a freshly painted, fresh-from-inspection and clean (no tip tanks) F-104, ready for Mach 2.

'You did a take off as already described - for the benefit of the ground crew - and two minutes later you were at 33,000 feet (almost to the tropopause limit) over the sea off Zakinthos. After some stalls, flap checks etc, it was time for max afterburner.

Time from M 1.1 to 1.4 was usually under a minute because in this region the air intakes don't work too well, but then from M 1.4 to M2 or 121° CIT (ram air temp?) took less than 30 seconds. You had to be careful not to exceed 121 CIT otherwise something would start melting back there! You then had to brake and slow down because fuel state was on 'Bingo'.

'So, what's simpler; instead of doing a 180 turn and return to base at 35,000 feet, you make a zoom climb at 20-25° in full afterburner until, say, 78,000 feet, where you observe the certain roundness of the earth and the pitch black sky above. Keeping an eye on fuel, engine temperatures and the altimeter stuck at 45,000 feet, you return at 45-50,000 feet via Andravida (an F-4E Phantom base 50 miles East of Araxos). From there you are direct onto finals on Runway 36 at Araxos. Forbidding yourself the luxury of an overshoot due to your low fuel state, you touch down on the tarmac with a big smile on your face. The technicians are looking back angrily and gauging how much paint has been stripped off the nose cone and air intakes. Not bad after only fifteen minutes of flight!'

During 1981-82 Royal Hellenic Air Force acquired another one hundred Starfighters (52 F-104Gs, 16 RF-104Gs and 22 TF-104Gs from Germany and in May and July 1982, ten Fiat-built F-104Gs from the Royal Netherlands Air Force. Altogether, HAF operated 159 Starfighters. They completed 224,489 hours of flight in a period of twenty-nine years, from spring 1964 until spring 1993, while sixteen pilots were killed. 336 Mira of the 116 Ptérix Mahis at Araxos retired its last F-104G/TF-104G Starfighters in March 1993.

4-16 and 4-12 of 4° Stormo 'Amendo d'Aosta' of the Aeronautica Militare Italiana (AMI).

Italy

The Aeronautica Militare Italiana (AMI) received a total of 124 Fiat-built F-104Gs with which to equip its Starfighter gruppi (squadrons). The gruppi were organized into a stormo or wing). In turn, 24 TF-104Gs (twelve built by Lockheed and twelve co-produced) were also received by the AMI. Initially, the F/RF-104 Starfighter equipped four CI (Caccia (Fighter/Interceptor)/ CB (Caccia-bombardiere, or fighter-bomber) gruppi and two ricognizione (reconnaissance) gruppi. (Although the 101° Gruppo CBR of the 8° Stormo *Gino Priolo* at Cervia-San Giorgio received its first F-104G Starfighters in December 1964, the re-equipment order was cancelled and the reconnaissance unit reverted to the F-86F until replacement by the Fiat G91Y).

In March 1963 the 9° Gruppo CI, 4° Stormo *Amendo d'Aosta* became the first operational unit to receive the F-104G. In June 1963 the F-84F equipped 154° Gruppo CB at Brescia-Ghedi detached from the 6° Stormo *Alfredo Fusca* to receive F-104Gs, returning to the wing in September 1967 and temporarily operating some RF-104Gs 154° Gruppo began conversion to the Panavia Tornado in August 1982). In 1964 the 10° Gruppo CI, 9° Stormo *Francesco Baracca;* 12° Gruppo CI, 36° Stormo *Hefmu Seidl,* 21°

Gruppo CI, *53°* Stormo *Gugliemo Chiarini;* 23° Gruppo CIO, 51° Stormo *Ferrucio Sarafini* at Rimi-ni-Miramare (on 23 March 1973 23° Gruppo CIO moved from 51 ° Stormo to 5° Stormo *Giuseppe Cenni* at the same base); and the 102° Gruppo CB, 5° Stormo *Giuseppe Cenni,* also at Rimini-Mira-mare, received F-104Gs.

An OCU (Operational Conversion Unit) was also formed, when on 15 February 1965 the *20° Gruppo* re-formed at 20° Gruppo AO (Aadescramento Operativeo/OCU) *in the* 3° Stormo *Carlo Emanuele Buscaglia* at Grosseto. In 1972 the 132° Gruppo CR of the 3° Stormo *Carlo Emanuele Buscaglia* received F/RF-104G Starfighters, but it had to wait until 1977 before receiving Orpheus reconnaissance pods.

Beginning in February 1970 the AMI's F/ RF-104G Starfighters were supplemented by the much improved F-104S all-weather interceptor (caccia ogni tempo) version developed in tandem with Lockheed. Two hundred aircraft were built for the Italian Air Force and also for the Turkish Air Force. The AMI received two Fiat-built F-104Gs modified to F-104S standard by Lockheed (MM6658 and MM6660) and 204 Fiat-built examples (it should have been 205 but MM6766 was destroyed in an accident before delivery). The 9° Gruppo CI of the 4° Stormo *Amendo d'Aosta* at Grosseto, was equipped with

F-104G 6-12 of 6° Stormo 'Alfredo Fusca' over Verona.

F-104S models in February 1970, followed by the 22° Gruppo CIO of the 51° Stormo *Ferruccio Serafini* at Treviso-Isttana.

In December 1971 the 12° Gruppo COT of the 36° Stormo *Helmut Seidl* received its F-104S models. The 10° Gruppo COT of the 9° Stormo *Francesco Baracca* at Grazzanise received F-104S models in 1972. In the 5° Stormo *Giuseppe Cenni* at Rimini-Miramare the 23° Gruppo COT received the F-104S in March 1973, followed by November onwards, by the 102° Gruppo CB. By 1973 the 155° Gruppo CB of the 6° Stormo *Alfredo Fusca* at Istrana was also operating the F-104S.

These were replaced in 1984 as crews began their Tornado conversion courses. Additionally,

■ F-104Gs 3-23 and 3-41 of 3° Stormo 'Carlo Emanuele Buscaglia' in flight.

the 18° Gruppo Misto (mixed) of the 37° Stormo *Cesare Toschi* at Rapani-Bitgi, the 20° Gruppo COT of the 4° Stormo and the 21° Gruppo COT of the 53° Stormo *Gugliemo Chiarini* at Novara-Cameri also operated in the F-104S.

In 1984 Italy received some TF-104Gs from Germany to compensate the loss of a number of two-seaters since 1962. In the early 1980s six ex-Luftwaffe TF-104Gs were acquired and these joined the AMI inventory in 1988 after they were refurbished by Aeritalia in Turin. In total 104 F-104G, 21 RF-104G, 206 F-104S and 28 TF-104G aircraft were adopted by the Italian Air Force. In 1986 the AMI was the largest operator of Starfighters with eleven gruppi of F-104s. The 28° and 132° Gruppi CR of the 3° Stormo *Carlo Emanuele Buscaglia* at Vetona- Villafranca had a *Misto* (mix) of F/RF-104Gs (in July 1980 the 28° Gruppo CR (Cacria-Ricognizione/ fighter-reconnaissance) was taken off operations and assigned to training. The 12° Gruppo CI of the 36° Stormo *Helmut Seidl* at Gioia de Colle flew F-104Gs and the 20° Gruppo AO of the 4° Stormo *Amendo d'Aosta* at Grosseto operated TF-104Gs in the conversion training role.

To stay up-to-date the F-104S Starfighters received a number of modification programmes after the G versions had retired. Between September 1985 and November 1993 the 'ASA programme' (Aggiomamiento Sistema d'Arma), or 'updated weapon system' standard) modified aircraft (103 Interceptors and 48 Fighter Bombers). Twelve examples would each equip 9°, 10°, 12°, 21°, 22° and 23° Gruppo CI while another 18 examples, of the CB (Cacciabombardiere-Fighter Bomber) variant, served in the dual role, of interceptor and ground attack with 18° Gruppo CI/CB and 102° Gruppo (which converted to Tornado IDS in 1993). Some ASAs would also be issued to the operational conversion Gruppo, the 20°, operating mainly TF-104G. The Delivery of F-104S ASA Starfighters began in February 1987 with the first examples being issued to 23° Gruppo CIO of 5° Stormo *Giuseppe Cenni* at Rimini-Miramare. At the beginning of 1995 the AMI possessed 125 F-1 CHS ASA Starfighters, distributed among seven gruppi: 9° Gruppo CI, 4° Stormo, at Grosseto, 23° Gruppo CIO, 5° Stormo, at Rimini-Miramare, 10° Gruppo CI, 9°

F-104Gs 5-30 and 5-40 of 5° Stormo 'Guiseppe Cenni'. ■

**TF-104Gs of 20° Gruppo AO/COT
in 4° Stormo 'Amendo d'Aosta'.** ▮

Stormo at Capua-Grazzanise, 12° Gruppo CI, 36° Stormo at Gioa del Colle, 18° Gruppo Misto, 37° Stormo, at Trapani-Birgi, 22° Gruppo CIO, 51° Stormo at Revi-so-Istrana and 21° Gruppo CI, 53° Stormo *Gugliemo Chiarini* at Novarra-Cameri, twenty-five miles east of Milan. In 1989 the AM informed the Ministero della Difesa (Ministry of Defence), which was preparing a New Defence Model, that it should retain the F-104S ASA until it could be replaced by the EFA (European Fighter Aircraft, renamed Eurofighter 2000 in 1992 and later, in 1998, Typhoon II), of

which Italy committed to 165 aircraft. Discussions then began on a programme to extend its service life. Initially named ASA-2 and EVT (Estensione della Vita Tecnica - Technical Life Extension), the programme later received the designation ASA-M (Modificato - Modified).

The 'ASA-M programme' modified aircraft between July 1995 until December 2001. No improvement in the operational capacity was considered and the proposed radar and Aspide 1A missile guidance system improvements were discarded. As the ASA-M, the F-104 returned to

■ **F-104Gs of 36° Stormo 'Helmut Seidl'.**

■ **F-104Gs of 37° Stormo 'Cesare Toschi'.**

F-104Gs of 51° Stormo 'Ferrucio Serafini'. ■

its original function as a pure interceptor. All the fittings and functions enabling it to serve in the attack role were stripped out. Most notably, the AN/ALQ-70 self-defence system was removed to avoid any need to re-design the avionics compartment and the IR Sight and everything connected to the M61 Vulcan cannon were also eliminated. In January 1994 the Italian Air Ministry announced that it was to lease the Tornado ADV and consequently the ASA-M programme was given the official go-ahead, although the number of aircraft involved was reduced to sixty, including twelve two seaters.

The ASA-M prototype (MM6945, later MMX611) flew for the first time from Torino-Casselle on 31 July 1995. (The remaining TFs were upgraded to TF-104G-M between July 1995 and January 2001). Two-and-a-half years passed before the first series conversion reached an operational unit. By this time a number of the units which had been planned at the outset to receive these conversions had changed, for various reasons. The 22° Gruppo (part of the 51° Stormo at Istrana) had disbanded while 12° (of 36° Stormo based at Gioia del Colle) and 21° (of 53° Stormo, Cameri) had converted to the Tornado ADV. It was then decided to retain the last unmodified ASAs with the 9° Gruppo (4° Stormo at Grosseto) as it was to commence conversion onto the Eurofighter at Caselle in 2002. Deliveries of the ASA-M were

Aeronautica Militare Italiana Tornado 36-50 and F-104S 36-02 of 36° Stormo 'Helmut Seidl', Turkish TF-104G 9-029 and a USAF A-7D in formation in 1987.

to commence with the 23° and 18° (which by then had become a CI only unit) and 10° Gruppo. On 18 December 1997, MM6935, the first series ASA-M, was delivered to the 23° Gruppo (5° Stormo) at Cervia. Eight months later the re-equipment was complete and during the same period the 18° Gruppo (37° Stormo) at Trapani-Birgi received its first aircraft. January 1999 saw the turn of the 10° Gruppo (9° Stormo) at Grazzanise and by the end of the year, the 20° Gruppo (4° Stormo) had received the first of its planned four ASA-M. This Gruppo remained the main user of the TF-104 (the very last unmodified TF-104G served with RSV,

the test unit). Deliveries of the G-M variant began in November 1997 with the arrival from Alenia of MM54254, while the first conversion completed by the 4° RMV (MM54258) was delivered the following July. The last G-M arrived in August 2000, delivered by Alenia. The final ASA-M (MM6940) made its military acceptance flight on 21 December 2001, but remained at Caselle for tests. Alenia's connection with the F-104 ended in the summer of 2002 when the final aircraft inspection was completed.

The establishment of a Gruppo CI remained at twelve aircraft, each with a programmed annual

F-104ASA MM6847 4-54 of of 20° Gruppo, 4° Stormo 'Amendo d'Aosta' at Grosseto, making a 'fuel dump during a RAF Fairford departure in July 1999. (Roger Seroo)

use of around 200 flight hours, though since 1996 only ten had been assigned to NATO, which had air defence units permanently assigned. In collaboration with Tornado ADV units, ASA-M units continued to provide the national quick readiness alert (ORA) service with two or more (depending upon the alert status) aircraft. The Starfighters were ready to scramble within fifteen minutes, this being the new standard introduced in 1996. However, on a personal initiative Starfighter pilots still trained to the former standard of five minutes, as the F-104 pre-flight procedures permitted this. The heavy shifts and alert deployments involved in bolstering the southern flank of Italy following the Kosovo situation gradually ceased since the 'Allied Force' operation. With the ORAs benefiting from the Peace Dividend, only a couple of interceptors were ready round the clock in Italy, until the situation worsened again following the terrorist attacks in the USA on 11 September 2001.

Further delay to the Eurofighter programme and the suspension of F-104S ASA activity because of logistic incompatibility made the 9° Gruppo's transition onto the ASA-M inevitable and its first machine arrived at the beginning of January 2002.

By early 2000 the AMI's Starfighter inventory had shrunk to five F-104 units: 10° Gruppo CI

| **F-104ASA Starfighters of 4° Stormo 'Amendo d'Aosta' visiting Kleine Brogel, Belgium in 1999. (Peter Loncke)**

at Caserta, 9° Gruppo CI and 20° Gruppo AO at Grosseto, 23° Gruppo CIO at Ravenna and 18° Gruppo Misto at Trapani.

9° Gruppo/4' Stormo was the last operator of the ASA version, which stopped flying in December 2001. The unit received some ASA-Ms while waiting for the first Eurofighter 2000 deliveries in mid 2002. The 18th Gruppo at Trapani Air Force Base in Sicily became the 20th squadron to operate Eurofighter Typhoon in November 2012, joining squadrons in Grosseto and Gioia del Colle). The Starfighter stayed the front-line interceptor-fighter-bomber aircraft until 2004 when the AMI re-equipped its remaining three Gruppi (Squadrons) with F-16ADF Fighting Falcons leased from the American Government. This means that Italy flew the F-104 operationally for 42 years!

(Aggiornamento Sistemi d'Arma/Modificato - 'Weapon Systems Update/Modified') - 49 F-104S-ASA and 15 two-seat TF-104G aircraft were upgraded from 1998 to ASA/M standard with GPS, new TACAN and Litton LN-30A2 INS, refurbished airframe and improved cockpit displays. All strike-related equipment was removed and the IRST as well (the small unit known as 'IR-Sight', forward the windshield). The last Starfighters in combat service, they were withdrawn in October 2004 (the last unit was 10° Gruppo/9° Stormo, Grazzanise) and temporarily replaced by the F-16 Fighting Falcon, while awaiting Eurofighter Typhoon deliveries.

From the 1st to 10th September 1965 323 Squadron of the Koninklijke Luchtmacht (KLu) at Leeuwarden AFB hosted a two-way exchange with four Italian F-104Gs of 10° Gruppo, 9° Stormo 'Francesco Baracca' at Grazzanise and four Dutch Starfighters flew to Grazzanise together with one T-33. Two Dutch F-104Gs, including D-6657, a FIAT-built F-104G, in clean configuration with F-104G MM6572 4-44 are flying over the sea off Capri. D-6657 crashed at Havelte, Netherlands on 9 February 1978. The pilot was unharmed and but the aircraft was damaged beyond repair. On 1 April 1982 during manoeuvring at an airshow at Ghedi AB MM6572 (now in 6° Stormo, 154° Gruppo) hit a power cable during a high speed low pass. The pilot, Major Magg Rocchelli, who had ejected once before, again ejected safely.

Fokker-built F-104G D-8047, one of two F-104Gs first issued to the OCU on 24 April 1963 to commence flying. On 1 December 1981 this Starfighter crashed into the Waddensea 10 kilometres south of the Cornfield aircraft gunnery range on Vlieland, the Netherlands due to engine-failure. The pilot, Lieutenant Peer 'Doc' Donkerbroek (29) ejected safely. The remains of the aircraft were scattered over a sandbank and were brought over to the island by a Lynx helicopter of the Dutch Royal Navy.

The Netherlands

Altogether the Koninklijke Luchtmacht (KLu, Royal Netherlands Air Force) received 138 Starfighters, comprising eighteen RF-104Gs, 102 F-104Gs (including twenty-five F-104Gs built by Fiat) and eighteen Lockheed/co-produced TF-104Gs. The first Starfighter for the KLu to be assembled by Fokker flew on 11 November 1961 at Schiphol Airport, Amsterdam with company chief test pilot A. P. Moll at the controls. The first Fokker-built Starfighters delivered to the KLu (F-104Gs D-8013 and D-8022) were flown to Twenthe Air Base on 12 December 1962 by Kapiteins Okkerman and Janssen. These two Starfighters entered service with 306 (Reconnaissance) Squadron, which was in the process of replacing its Hunters and F-86K Sabres

and which initially also operated as the OCU for the Starfighter. The Operationele Conversie Unit (OCU), also known as the 'Dutch Masters' was established on 24 April 1963 and flying commenced using F-104Gs D-8047 and D-8049. A large proportion of the pilots for the OCU were not unsurprisingly drafted in from 306 Squadron.

In September 1963 306 Squadron received its first RF-104G but it was not until July 1964 that this squadron was fully operational on the RF-104G (one TF-104G - D-5811 - was assigned between 1966 and 1969). Its aircraft were then being equipped with Dutch-made cameras from De Oude Delfe. The squadron moved to Volkel on 3 September 1969. Beginning in November 1974, the RF-104G's cameras were being replaced by the Fokker-built Orpheus pod holding five TA-8M

Fokker-built RF-104G D-8125 of the KLu, which went to the Turkish Air Force on 30 November 1983.

cameras and one Infra-Red-Line-Scanner (IRLS) which enable reconnaissance at night. Previously the cameras had to be mounted inside the base of the fuselage.

The F-104Gs were operated in the all-weather interceptor role by 322 Squadron and 323 TACTESS (Tactisch Training, Evaluatie en Standaardisatie Squadron) at Leeuwarden, 1964-80. 322 Squadron had previously flown Hunter Mk.6s at Mokmer, Indonesia from August 1960 to August 1962, when it had disbanded. On 1 August 1964 the Royal Netherlands Air Force's premier fighter squadron re-formed at Leeuwarden with F-104Gs. Meanwhile, on 30 August 1963 323 Squadron flew its last Hunter sortie and it too converted to the Starfighter.

In April 1979 322 Squadron was partially stood down and its pilots began training with the locally raised Conversie Afdeling F-16 from April

Fokker-built F-104G D-8341 of 323 Squadron of the Koninklijke Luchtmacht (KLu, Royal Netherlands Air Force). This aircraft was lost at Wildenrath, Germany on 21 November 1978 when D-8341 collided with its forward cockpit section into the aft section of the D-8098. The pilot of D-8341 was killed instantly by this collision. (Dutch Defence Dept).

TF-104G D-5801 of the KLu. ∎

1980 onwards. (Conversion of 322 Squadron's pilots was completed on 1 May 1981 when the unit became the first in the KLu to achieve 'limited operational status' on the European-built General Dynamics F-16A/B, becoming 'combat ready' on 1 September). On 16 April 1979 323 Squadron absorbed most of 322 Squadron's pilots and F-104Gs and assumed the semi-official title 'No.645 Squadron' (arrived at by adding 322 and 323!) In August 1980 323 Squadron was stood down for F-16 conversion and it became fully operational on the Fighting Falcon on 1 April 1982.

Starfighters were operated in the fighter-bomber role by 311 and 312 Squadrons at Volkel. In June 1964 311 Squadron retired its F-84F Thunderstreaks and took delivery of the F-104G, operating the Starfighter until 1982. 312 Squadron retired the last of its Thunderstreaks on 1 December 1965 and began operating the F-104G Starfighter, which it continued to fly until 312 Squadron was stood down for F-16 conversion on 1 June 1984. F-16s began arriving on 16 July and 312 Squadron passed its F-104s on to the specially formed Vitfaseringsonderdeel (Phase-Out Unit), also at Volkel, with which the last Starfighter was withdrawn from service on 21 November 1984.

Two other Starfighter-equipped units, the CAV (Conversie AH-Weather Vlucht) and the TCA

Formation of KLu Starfighters with, nearest the camera, Fokker-built RF-104G D-8273 (which went to the Turkish Air Force on 8 March 1984) and then the Fiat-built F-104G D-6670, which went to the Greek Air Force on 7 May 1982: Fokker-built D-8084 and TF-104G D-5805, which last flew on 2 May 1984 and is now displayed at the KLu Museum.

(Transitie en Conversie AWX (all-weather), operated F-104Gs and TF-104Gs at Volkel 1968-84 and at Leeuwarden 1968-78, respectively. Altogether, the RNLAF lost 44 Starfighters in crashes or that were written off. Nineteen pilots were killed. On 21 November 1984 the KLu flew its Starfighter flight when F-104Gs D-8063 and D-8258 and TF-104Gs D-5803, D-5804 D-5810, flew formation for the last time in Dutch skies. The last KLu Starfighter flight (TF-104G D-5803) touched down at 10.49 hour on 26 November 1984 at Ypenburg.

F-104G FN-X (62-12240) which arrived in Norway on 26 October 1963. This Starfighter returned to USAF at RAF Sculthorpe, UK on 30 June 1981 and went to Turkey on 8 July 1981. Withdrawn from use (WFU) and without engine, it was scrapped in June 1983.

■ Norway

The Kongelige Norske Luftforsvaret (KNL, Royal Norwegian Air Force) was to receive two skvadrons (squadrons) of F-104s, but originally it took delivery of only enough Starfighters for one. (The remaining funds went instead to pay for the purchase of Northrop F-5A/B aircraft to enable Norway to obtain a larger number of aircraft - the second skvadron of F-104Gs earmarked for the KNL subsequently went to the Royal Hellenic Air Force). The KNL received sixteen Canadair-built F-104Gs in 1963 as part of the American MAP programme.

In 1965 the Royal Norwegian Air Force bought two RF-104s which were rebuilt to F-104G standard and in February 1966, one more single-seater, originally a F-104G model. All of the F-104Gs were modified to RF-104G standard for the all-weather fighter/interceptor (AWX) role with

Skv331 at Bødo. The first test flight was in August 1963 and Skv 331 became fully operational in 1967. However, following delivery of the RF-5 As for Skv717, the Starfighters reverted to the fighter configuration and served in the interception role until 1981 when crew training on the F-16 began. Skv331's surplus F-104Gs were despatched to Turkey in June and July 1981.

The KNL had lost its first Starfighter in 1970 (a two-seater) and as replacement, bought two ex-Luftwaffe TF-104Gs in 1975. It was high attrition in the Northrop F/RF-5 inventory however, that led to the disbandment in 1973 of Skv334, which then became the second Starfighter unit in the KNL. During winter 1973/74 Skv334 re-formed on the Starfighter at Bodø (later to be based at Rygge) with eighteen ex-Canadian Armed Forces' CF-104s and four CF-104Ds which were built by Canadair from June 1962 to November 1963. These aircraft were modified to carry Martin AGM-

F-104G-LOs FN-E (61-2629) and FN-B (61-2626) of 331 Skv, RNoAF on alert status (QRA) at Bardufoss AB in the Arctic Circle in 1969. Both went to the Turkish Air Force in 1981. (Erik Dahlen) ■

12C Bullpup air-to-surface missiles and operate in the anti-shipping role but Skv334 operated in this role for just one year. The CF-104/CF-104Ds of Skv334 were finally phased out during the winter of 1982-83 with replacement by F-16A/B aircraft.

Jan Mayer, Flynytt's (Norway's General Aviation Magazine) correspondent recalled a cold day in February during the seventies when they had an appointment with Olaf Frithjof Aamoth a Norwegian officer and pilot, who for a time was Inspector General of the Air Force. to learn some more about operations with F-104 in the north of Norway. 'We´re sitting in a conference room at NAKs headquarter in Tollbugata over mugs of coffee and Danish pastry, making small talk to find an end to start from. The building shakes a little every time a tram passes in the street below. The seventies were as close to a golden age in military aviation history as we´ll ever get. With 331 Squadron and F-104 we had a sharp and effective weapon. We had the almost daily intercepts of single missions close to our territory and we met large scale exercises that were directed towards American carriers in the Atlantic. It could happen that we, two single fighters intercepted swarms of 20-30 bombers on their way out. Occasionally we were the first to intercept and photograph new and exciting Soviet types as well.

'Let´s take a step back. The fighters didn´t operate alone, there would be a large organisation behind them. It was the Air Operations Centre (AOC) at Reitan that kept an overview of what was going on around us at all times. They had intelligence from the entire control and warning chain and saw the radar screens from all stations from Bodø in the east and all the way around the coast. There was a direct telephone line (hotline) from AOC to the air bases, wherever the fighters might be at the moment.

'At Bodø we had hangars blasted into rock at the east end of the airfield. Normally we had two fighters on 15 minutes alert and two more on one hour. The latter would be stepped up if the first were scrambled and the crew fetched at home or wherever they might be. The alert crew consisted of two pilots and line crew for making the aircraft ready and assist the pilots at start-up. The alert crew lived their lives beside the rest of the squadron. They resided and slept in the 'alert area' outside the hangars, accommodations that was suited for the purpose. There were bunks and a kitchen. Food was brought from the base mess and the crew prepared it themselves. It was plain luxury compared to what we had in the F-86 days. Then we lived in Nissen huts, even slept on the hangar floor at Banak and food was scarce at times. The pilots wore flight suits at all times, all they had to don at scramble was the survival suit.

'Aamoth sips some coffee and pauses before continuing, - At change of alert crew each day the,

F-104 4-16 of the 4° Stormo 'Amendo d'Aosta' and RF-104G (62-12234) FN-S in formation. On 10 September 1980 FN-S crashed on approach to Bodø in the sea near Helligvaer, approximately 17 nautical miles northeast of Bodø AB after a series of abnormal movements. It had been one of a pair of fighters on a mission to identify and photograph unidentified planes west of Lofoten. The pilot, Lieutenant Kare Haugvaldstad managed to eject, but was too low for the chute to open and he was killed.

F-104G FN-C (61-2627) of 331 Skvadron, Royal Norwegian Air Force shadowing a Tupolev Tu-24/126 'Moss' AWACS (airborne warning and control system) over the Baltic. This Starfighter arrived in Norway on 7 August 1963. It crashed on 21 July 1971 in upper Tolladal in Beiarn. The pilot, Lieutenant Atle Melling ejected safely with minor injuries. FN-C was on a training mission in a two-ship formation when the accident occurred. (RNWAF)

alert aircraft were started. They had designated bunkers and had electric power connected. All checks were performed, the inertia-navigator's platform was lined up. That took 7 ½ minutes. We had modified the equipment such that we could lock the platform and restart it in one minute, provided the aircraft was not moved in the meantime. The aircraft was ready for immediate takeoff. Then the pilots got a briefing from sector at AOC about the present situation which they plotted. There were codewords for this, if there was activity or quiet, as for the status on the surrounding airfields and alternates. A weather briefing was naturally part of it as well. The weather in the north of Norway is a story in itself, in winter and at night with gale force winds and blowing snow it could increase the flow of adrenalin considerably more than unknown aircraft.

'If the controller at sector registered activity that needed attention, the alert crew were usually warned and began preparing themselves. The line crew was roused if they were sleeping and the pilots donned their survival suits. If something developed they were stepped up at first – 'you may expect a scramble such and such.' Then the scramble would arrive on the hotline: 'This is Yankee, scramble two one-oh-fours, vector three two zero, angels three five zero, gate (climb in afterburner), contact Yankee channel one seven, back up ... 'The moment the controller started to read we pressed the alarm button. The line crew was awoken (if they were sleeping), we jumped into the survival suit (if we weren't wearing it already) and as soon as the controller concluded his message we got into the cockpit. We pressed the start button as we slid into the seat, fasten the harness, donned the helmet and plugged in and when the start sequence had concluded the inertia platform was lined up and ready to go. The tower was in the loop, hot scrambles needed priority. The fighters taxied out from the bunker and if the scramble was silent (without using the radio and thereby letting anybody know that something was going on), we got our clearance with lights, otherwise it was normal radio procedure. The alert area was at the east end of the runway so takeoffs were made to the west regardless, we could take off with 40 knot tailwind. It was only if there was no hurry that we bothered taxiing around and taking off the other way.

'After takeoff and established climb on the vector that AOC had given us, we called sector, checked in and were on our way. The controller would issue courses and other information he had to intercept the target. It was a piece of cake when he had both ourselves and the target on his radar screen and we squawked as designated. His computer would tell him all he needed and he would relay to us what we needed to do to get the target on our own radar. We usually got contact at thirty miles, the controller continued to talk us in while we kept track of the target on our own radar, adjusting course and speed such that the target followed a particular pattern across the screen.

'When we approached the target we would lock our radar on him. We would do that as late as possible. If the target was an 'Ivan' he would notice the lock on and might take evasive actions, like sudden alterations in course (jinks), gate stealing or simply jamming our radar. Getting to missile range we had to decide whether to fire weapons or to proceed close in for identification. (Firing in anger was luckily never required, but the alert aircraft were always armed with hot weapons). In daylight and nice weather identification was never a problem. In dark and/or in cloud it was a different story.

'We had a powerful light mounted behind the seat in the cockpit, but the only way to maneouvre it was by manoeuvering the entire aircraft. Getting visual contact, slide up along his side and light the target so we could decide what it was, read his tail number, sometimes photograph him and report type, registry, position, direction and speed to sector sometimes provided a solid challenge at night and in cloud. More than once I wanted an extra arm. The Russians were rarely out to help us and often flew with their nav lights off. We could get in close and suddenly discover that he had a wingman a little behind and off to the other side of us. Our own wingman was covering us from behind with his weapons. Then we would check fuel state, how much was left and report it to sector. We could then get ordered to return or to proceed to another target. We always kept close track of fuel remaining, that's an acquired reflex with fighter pilots. A usable alternate was usually the largest problem in peacetime operations, it would require something very special to launch if there weren't usable alternates within reach. The F-104 wasn't as difficult as the F-86 in this respect. We could actually reach Gardermoen with 3,900lbs

remaining over Bodø. The F-104 went like a knife through butter at Mach 0.9.'

With the supersonic interceptor, F-104G Starfighter, the Norwegian Air Force literally jumped a generation of fighters. The planes destined for 331 Squadron, arrived in Bodø harbour from the USA on a support-carrier in 1963. Unloaded by crane, the fighters were towed through the streets of the town to enter the airbase. Years later, two-seaters and a simulator arrived. Only the most experienced pilots underwent transition to the F-104 in the beginning and this contributed to an outstanding safety record, even if the area of operation would be the among the most demanding on the planet. The Starfighter was often referred to as the missile with a man in it and its performance was tremendous.

One late night in August finds Flynytt's correspondent sitting in a window seat on SK1345 to Trondheim watching the terminal building at Oslo Airport from the end of runway 01L, while the crew wait for takeoff clearance. The building looks like a modern rendition of a fairy tale castle with all it's different coloured lights at all its levels. How should such a motif be photographed so the fairy tale look would show? The thoughts are interrupted by the arrival of the clearance, the Boeing starting the takeoff roll. The lights along the runway edge move rearwards with increasing speed. Pilot Flying knows his craft, the rotation is almost imperceptible and we can once again experience the magic moment when the wings takes over the weight of the airplane and the runway edge and the lights fall away. The thoughts seek back to the day that just has passed...

'It takes one to recognise one. Olav Aamoth answers our suggestion that he must be one of the most eager aircraft enthusiasts we have ever met. We're sitting in the library in NAK's headquarters in Tollbugaten in Oslo and talk about the time when he was CO of 331-Squadron in Bodø at the end of the sixties. The table is full of notes, graphs and pictures. Both of us are coffee lovers, a thermos bottle and two mugs are also on the table. We have arranged this meeting to learn about a particular part of the work that was done at the squadron.

'When the F-104 arrived in 1963', Aamoth begins 'it was 331 Squadron that got the honour of operating it. In many ways it was a revolution in technology and performance. We went from navigation with watch, compass and map in a plane that could barely reach Mach 1.1 in a vertical dive from 40,000 feet to a weapon that was equipped with inertia navigation, map reading radar with terrain avoidance function and which could reach Mach 2.0 in a climb. High takeoff speed (it takes to the air between 190 and 210 K) and landing speed (long, flat final between 170 and 185 K). Turning radius nobody had even dreamt of also belonged in the picture. (Glidespeed without engine was 285 K and High Key for a dead stick landing was 20,000 feet). The fighter gave us a range of possibilities as well as a range of challenges for those who flew it and those who maintained it. At first it was put in the fighter-bomber role, the extreme speed and altitude performance were not interesting. The Canadian Forces further south in Europe utilized it in the strike role and if we may put it that way, with great success. This kind of utilisation wasn't even of academic interest for our headquarters. In 1965 it was apparent that the F-86K was completely insufficient as interceptor against the threats we were facing. We could neither reach nor follow the substantial Soviet traffic with Badger bombers down to our waters. And we were in no circumstance able to reach any of what was operating further north. We had no need for war, be it cold or warm to maintain daily tension. The Northern Norwegian winter weather supplied plenty of that.

He makes a short pause, leafs through some of the papers before continuing. 'It became apparent that F-104 would serve us better in the air defence role, particularly since our old F-86s were replaced with F-5s. In April 1967 I was appointed CO for 331 Squadron and part of my assignment was retraining it to an all weather air defence squadron (AWX). In November we had completed the transfer programme and were declared operational. The transfer programme included training in using our most important 'weapon', the Leica. This small, light and extremely good camera was standard equipment on board, but it posed a bit of a challenge to teach pilots not particularly interested in photography to use it. Remember, it was completely manual. You had to adjust shutter, f-stop and focus and snap pictures of the target, preferably several exposures with varying combinations of shutter and f-stop and simultaneously fly the fighter. No one attained operational status before they had turned in an approved film.

We interrupt: - From our own experience we remember intelligence briefs that drew up pictures of intense military activity all way up to the border east of Kirkenes on the Soviet side, particularly if

F-104G FN-R (61-2632) of 331 Squadron, Royal Norwegian Air Force shadowing a Tupolev Tu-16 'Badger F' off Norway. This Starfighter crashed on 18 December 1980 during a ground controlled approach to Bodø AB when it suffered a substantial loss of engine power. The pilot, Roar Strand realised he would not reach the runway and decided to eject and he landed with minor injuries in Valnesfjorden, the Starfighter coming down in deep water at Skjerstadfjorden, approximately 24 km east of Bodø AB. (RNWAF)

there were exercises in progress on our side. Could you expand on apparent threats?

'You may safely say that we experienced the Soviet superpower's ambitions to dominate the high seas as a threat. The fleet in the north was expanded and presence on all seas increased. At our latitudes we perceived it as an increase of traffic in transit to other areas and as increased exercise activity by Soviet's most modern aircraft types in our own close quarters. A scenario with attacks against the most northerly parts of our country to secure advanced bases and to improve defence of the Kola bases was an absolute possibility. Our practical area of interest was the coverage area of our radar warning system. - What Soviet aircraft were involved? - Even before the squadron was declared operational we were getting results. Training missions occasionally stumbled across 'Zombies' that flew through our training areas. The first good

pictures from our Leicas were duly celebrated the summer of 1967. During the next two years we encountered most of what the Northern Fleet, DA, Border Patrol or KGB operated. Most were of course comparatively simple targets, 'Badger', 'Bear' and 'Bison' in all varieties.

Some were slow like CUB on the 'milk run', others were high and fast as 'Blinder'. The most difficult were the ones that went low in ground clutter and the slow ones at high altitudes. A 'Badger' at Mach 0.6 at 40,000 feet made life troublesome for a 104-driver, particularly at night. I see that you're doubting, shouldn't a 104 manage a slow 'Badger'?

Remember that the fighter had high stall speed. At Mach 0.6 at that altitude it would barely be above stall speed and well behind the power curve. Aamoth continues. 'We knew there were things that flew above 'Backfire', not only U-2 and SR-71. Intelligence reports had for a long time described a Soviet 'U-2' and we were well acquainted with 'Mandrake' and 'Foxbat'. We wanted to encounter and photograph or engage such targets. By the way, 'Backfire' wasn't seen until long after the zoom programme was completed, but there were rumours.

A pair of RF-104Gs of the Royal Norwegian Air Force. '233' (62-12233/FN-P) (left), which arrived in Norway on 7 August 1963 returned to the USAF in England on 9 July 1981 and went to Turkey on 15 July 1981. '785' (64-17785 /FN-G) (right) arrived in Norway on 7 February 1966. It returned to the USAF in England on 30 June 1981 and went to the Turkish Air Force on 8 July 1981.

'We seem to remember some basic facts that up to 30,000 feet altitude man can manage by gradually substituting nitrogen with oxygen to maintain partial pressure. Over 30,000 feet you have to resort to pressure breathing to get sufficient oxygen. If we climb above 48,000 feet we will need a pressure suit, we recall from an old indoctrination.

'Absolutely correct' Aamoth replies. 'Of course our fighters have pressurised cockpits, but pressurised cockpits may fail or be shot apart. Anyways, pressurisation is lost if the engine stops. In peacetime we normally limit maximum altitude to 50,000 feet. He searches through the papers and produce a transparency with a graph. - Take a look at the fighter's flight envelope, he says. The K could only cover the lower part of it, up to Mach 1.0 and up to approximately 45,000 feet, slightly smaller than the 104 in military power; that is without the lighting afterburner (AB). You see that the 104 is largely limited to 50,000 feet and Mach 2.0. But if we swap speed for altitude we can reach higher. We know that light C-models have been zoomed to more than 100,000 feet. You may see from the graph that that such a high zoom is not very interesting for interceptions, there is no margin for manoeuvering, we have to stay below the 1.0 G stall line to be able to maintain altitude and have a small margin for manoeuvering. So we set out to determine how high we could reach and still fly

past the target with control in order to identify and photograph it.

'You actually wanted to develop tactics to utilise the 104´s zoom properties in order to intercept high flying Soviet targets. Hadn´t the Americans already developed methods for this? - Lockheed had considered the problem to some degree, but we couldn´t use their results directly. We knew that the Dutch had done extensive research and possessed some knowledge. The first we had to tackle was physiological safety for pilots that were to fly that high. When the planes were delivered, some MC3 pressure suits came with them. They had been duly stored at Kjeller. They had been in storage too long, some rubber parts had to be exchanged; they were uneconomical to repair.

'We bought three new ones. Dr. Vogt Lorentzen at FMI had studied problems pertaining to flight above 48,000 feet and enthusiastically wanted to participate in the project. He had good contacts at the American hospital in Wiesbaden. They supported the American operations with U-2 and SR-71 in these parts of the world. We were cleared by headquarters and together with Captain Langsrud from LFK we went to Wiesbaden in the fall of 1967. The Americans provided transport in an unbelievably cold C-47. The Americans were willing to help us with our new MC3 pressure suits. They had the necessary support- and test

CF-104D '4633' of 331 Skvadron RNoAF from Bodø AB. This Starfighter was taken on service by the RCAF on 23 March 1962 and operated in the test squadron at Cold Lake before being withdrawn from use on 23 May 1973 before it was sold to the RNoAF on 21 July. Withdrawn from service on 9 December 1982 it was stored at Sola AB until on 11 November 1987 it was used in an exchange deal and registered N104JR, went to the Combat Jet & Aerospace Museum at Chino, California where it was rebuilt. Its first flight was on 11 November 1987 at Mojave Field by NASA F-104 pilot Ed Schneider before joining its new owners, Combat Jets Flying Museum, Houston, Texas, which used the aircraft until 15 May 1992 when it was sold to the Experimental Aircraft Association at Oshkosh, Wisconsin. It was grounded early in 1993 and was bought by Mark Sherman in April 1996.

TF-104G '469' (63-8469) which arrived in Norway on 8 June 1975, transferred from 331 Skvadron to 334 Skvadron on 8 July 1981, WFU 334 Skvadron on 13 July 1982 and later was given to FMU, Gardermoen. RF-104G '629' (61-2629) which arrived in Norway on 7 August 1963, returned to the USAF in England on 30 June 1981 and went to Turkey on 8 July 1981.

equipment and access to a pressure chamber so we might test our equipment and train. Well home again we could proceed with the work. We adapted extra equipment to the plane's survival equipment. We also got in touch with RNeAF's department at Leeuwarden. They had done some work in the same field, had pilots in USA on Edwards as well as flown with Test Pilots School. They had put in a lot of work, on the practical as well as the theoretical side and had decided to go for some French equipment which in their opinion was better than the American.

'When did you start flying and who participated?

'We were ready for the next step in the fall of 1968. We, that is Johnsen, Westskogen and myself from the pilots and Staff Sergeant Thomassen from the Survival Equipment Section in Bodø went on our way to Wiesbaden in one of LKN's Twin Otters. We had our three pressure suits in the luggage. We had the suits fitted and tested them in the pressure chamber. We made climbs to 80,000 feet and explosive decompressions to 60,000 feet. The latter was mildly spoken a different experience, but the equipment functioned as advertised. On our way home we went through Leeuwarden to discuss experiences and establish a flight programme. The airport was actually closed due to construction, but our Twin Otter impressed by landing on the grass in front of the tower.

'We can see from the flight envelope that the problems you could encounter would be how the plane behaved at low indicated airspeeds.

It looks like you will be short of load factor for manoeuvering, we interrupt.'

'That is absolutely correctly observed, Aamoth answers. 'During a zoom manoeuvre the indicated airspeed could vary between 700 knots + down to zero in extreme cases. If the 104 got below 200 knots it required particular attention. Aerodynamic manoeuvrability is lacking and if the plane is not on a stable path towards lower altitudes and higher indicated airspeeds, the plane and pilot would be in serious trouble. Precise control with angle of attack and nice nurturing of the engine was paramount. We wanted to find out how high we could go and obtain operational results. The practical side of it was finding out how high we could maintain level flight for long enough to pass a target, identify and photograph it and then return to base.'

'Aamoth finds some pictures that were made at Survival Equipment Section in Bodø. They show a very young Westskogen being helped by Thomassen to don his pressure suit. The attire, if we may use such a word, looks like it belongs in a 'Flash Gordon' cartoon. Finally he puts on his Air Force blue flight suit over the pressure suit. The picture of the flyer in front of his aeroplane clearly tells that it hardly was comfortable attire. It looks cramped and with limited room for movement, which Aamoth acknowledges.'

'The helmet was attached to a rail around the neck and didn't have much room for movement. If you turned your head you would only see the inside of the helmet. It was poorly suited for what we intended to do, fly formation, observe and photograph to the side of the aircraft, he adds.

'How was the test programme put together?'

'First we had to test the aircraft. Then we would develop tactics we could use and then we wanted to establish a training programme for the rest of the squadron. All in all we flew 25 trips during the summer 1969, all together sixteen hours. The trips were shared between us three.'

'Aamoth leafs through his notes again and produces a map.'

'In order to obtain reasonably realistic and repeatable conditions throughout the test programme', he continues, 'we established a profile with a simulated intruder passing south west on the outside of Vesterålen and Lofoten. You see the stippled line on the map. We scrambled the fighter which for the occasion flew without external fuel tanks, only a pair of AIM9s (Sidewinders) on the Catamaran Launcher below the fuselage. The fighter should first get up, then accelerate to Mach 2.0 behind the target so that it might zoom up and complete the intercept. If you look at the flight envelope you will see that steady state maximum thrust envelope tops just below Mach 1.0. Then it decreases before it starts to rise against Mach 1.2 and won't reach the Mach 1.0 level before Mach 1.3. In words this means that drag increases faster than thrust from the engine in this speed segment and that it is necessary to trade altitude for speed to be able to accelerate further up to Mach 2.0. We managed that by climbing in afterburner with Mach 0.9 to 36,000 feet and then dive down again towards 20,000 feet to accelerate to Mach 1.4. Then we had the power to accelerate to Mach 2.0 and climb to 40,000 feet behind the target.'

'How did radar guidance from GCI fit into this picture?'

'We assume it would be GCI that were to scramble the fighter and would know where the target was?'

'You can see from the map that the fighter wasn't sent directly to the target. It needed time and room for climb and acceleration. You may view the map with respect to the graph in 'Standard zoom profile'. The tactic we developed was letting the interceptor climb on opposite course and with a 50 NM offset to the intruder up to 36,000 feet. We defined a gate (t=0) when we had a predetermined angle to the intruder and commenced the dive for acceleration. At gate plus 1:05 minutes at Mach 0.96 we commenced a turn into the intruder, altering course 110 degrees. At gate plus 2:20 minutes the speed had reached Mach 1.1 and we rolled out on course. At gate plus 3:45 minutes we reached Mach 1.4 and could commence climb again simultaneously with further acceleration. At gate plus 5:25 minutes we reached Mach 1.7 and commenced turn to pick up the intruder's track. The alteration in course now was 70 degrees. At gate plus 6:35 at Mach 1.8 we were parallel with the intruder. So at 7:05 minutes after gate we reached Mach 2.0 and 40,000 feet behind the intruder and might commence the zoom, pull up point (PUP) if we had radar contact. We flew the zoom by pulling 2.3G and lift the nose to 20 degrees above the horizon. Radar contact and very accurate flying were paramount. After pull-up the aircraft was in a ballistic trajectory for all practical purposes and without much opportunity for correction of the flight path. How far behind the intruder we established and started pull up, roll out distance (ROD), depended on the intruders'

RF-104G '626' (61-2626) which arrived in Norway on 7 August 1963, returned to the USAF in England on 30 June 1981 and went to Turkey on 8 July 1981. (Mike Freer)

airspeed. It varied from 4.5 to 10 NM for target speeds between Mach 1.4 and Mach 0.9. How long time we would have paralleling the intruder depended on how high he flew. We tested intercepts up to 70,000 feet indicated, that is 74,000 feet true altitude.'

'We mentioned GCI; there must have been some breaking of new ground at Reitan as well?'

'Absolutely, tactics were developed in cooperation with the controllers at Reitan. They had to develop new tools as well. Radar operators use an aid they call handy dandy. It's a transparent sheet they place over the radar screen. The sheet has lines that aid the controller with calculating the headings to be flown in the different segments to effect an intercept. The traditional technique assumed constant speed. The aid lines are then straight. Since the 104 accelerated the entire time, the lines become curved. We had to make entirely new handy dandies and train people in using them.'

'Did the rest of the squadron use the same programme for training? You had as we understand, no more than three pressure suits and they seemed to be individually adjusted? Aamoth shakes his head.'

'You touch the conclusion we reached. Fighter pilots in Northern Norway then as now operate largely over water during training and intercepts of Soviet traffic. To give them a remote chance of survival in case of an ejection and where it is largely probable that he will land in water, he needs a good immersion suit. This requirement could not be combined with the pressure suit, there existed no good combination. A typical intercept meant flying over ice cold sea more than half an hour and an intercept of a high flying intruder only meant no more than a minute and a half flying above 48,000

TF-104G '263' (62-12263) which arrived in Norway on 6 September 1963, returned to the USAF in England on 9 July 1981 and went to Turkey on 8 July 1981, where the Starfighter crashed on 4 April 1985.

feet. Further, the pressure suit was cumbersome to don and unacceptably uncomfortable to wear over prolonged periods on readiness. We concluded that we could train to 60,000 feet without particular aids provided time over 48,000 feet didn´t exceed 90 seconds. The aircraft and it´s systems had demonstrated reliability that permitted this. Actual intercepts needed special authorisation anyway.'

'The old general smiles in afterthought and adds; 'I have a special place in my memory for that aircraft. This work was clearly the apex of my work in my time as 104-driver. One felt like one mastered the heavens. The fighter had phenomenal power, it was a real hot rod and the engine got more powerful as the speed increased. At Mach 1.5 the compressor changed mode, the turbine RPM increased with 4% and acceleration increased further. What limited the engine and with that practical speed was compressor inlet temperature (CIT). That shouldn´t exceed 120 degrees. There was a reasonably large warning light in the cockpit that lit up in yellow if it got too hot there. We also had to watch the fuel diligently. We flew without external fuel and burned 450 pounds per minute during acceleration. The warning light for low fuel would usually come on during the turn away from the target. At that altitude there was little difference between full and idle thrust. We usually had 1,100lbs remaining when we landed in Bodø. The margins were small.'

'Aamoth collects his papers. - No Norwegian fighters have been higher. And, he adds, - it doesn´t look like they will get there again for some time.'

F-104G-LO FG-621 (61-2621) of the Turkish Air Force. This Starfighter crashed on 14 April 1978 near Akinci (Mürted) AB, Ankara. The pilot ejected safely.

Turkey

In 1965-66 The Türk Hava Kuvvetleri (THK, Turkish Air Force) received thirty-six new Starfighters (thirty-two single-seaters built by Lockheed and Canadair and four TF-104Gs) under MAP to equip two Filos (squadrons) at the 4th Ana jet Us Komutanligi (Main Jet Base Command) at Mürted and later the 9th Ana Jet Üs Komutanlığı at Balikesir. In 1972 eight F-104Gs and two RF-104Gs were transferred to Turkey from the Ejército del Aire (Spanish Air Force). Subsequently, the THK obtained from Italy twenty F-104Gs and, between December 1974 and mid-1976, forty F-104S interceptors, in batches of eighteen and twenty-two. At Mürted, the F-104S models replaced the last of the F-102A Delta Daggers in the fighter interceptor role and came under the command of 8 Wing, being operated by 182 Filo. At Balikesir in 1976, the F-104S entered service with 192 Filo. In 1976 Turkish Starfighters took part in the invasion of Cyprus.

Turkey signed an agreement late in 1980 with the Netherlands under which the Türk Hava Kuvvetleri was to receive forty ex-KLu RF/F-

Aeritalia-built F-104S 9-888 of 191 Filo of 9.AJU (Ana Jet Ussu/Main Jet Base) Turkish Air Force 1992 with fuselage weapon station. This Starfighter crashed on 22 October 1992 at Akhisar. The pilot was killed. Turkey directly purchased 40 new F-104S interceptors from Fiat in 1974–75 when the United States imposed an arms embargo on Turkey after the 1974 Cyprus intervention. The first batch of 18 delivered in 1975 was a gift from Libya and the second batch was delivered between 1976 and 1977, thereby becoming the only country that bought the F-104S. (Roel van Gestel)

104s. A token price of $75,000 for each aircraft was agreed between the two countries. Ultimately, the THK acquired a total of fifty-three Starfighters from the Netherlands, twenty-five F-104Gs, eighteen RF-104Gs (the photo-recce pods, however, were not included) and ten TF-104Gs) during 1980-84.

In 1980-81 F-104/TF-104Gs being phased out in Belgium and Germany, also began to arrive in Turkey. Seventeen F-104Gs came from Belgium during 1981-83, twelve F-104Gs and one TF-104G from Norway in 1981 and about 120 F-104Gs and twenty-eight TF-104Gs from Germany during 1983-89. In 1965 the Canadian government donated forty-four CF-104s and six CF-104Ds (all of which had equipped its 1st Canadian Air Division in Germany) to Turkey. After some minor modifications, these aircraft entered operational service with 181 nci Filo and 182 nci Filo, Inci Taktik Hava Kuvvetleri Komutanlığı (1st Tactical Air Force Command) at Diyarbakir, where they replaced the THK's obsolete F-100s in the close air support role.

By 1986, the varied collection of Turkish Starfighters equipped five Filos of the Inci Taktik Hava Kuvvetleri Komutanligi; the 141nci and

TF-104G 8-661 of the Turkish Air Force.

142nci Filoler at Mürted, the 182nci Filo and the 191nci and 192nci at Balikesit. At Bandirma, the 6th Ana Jet Us Komutanlığı operated two filos of F-104s (161 Filo, in the close support role and 162 Filo, in the ait defence tole). By 1993 only the 8th Ana Jet Us Komutanligi 181nci and 182nci Filo and 9th Ana Jet Üs Komutanlığı 191st Filo (F-104S - interdiction role), 192nd Filo (F-104G - air defence mission) and 193rd Filo (F/TF-104G - this unit was the OCU for all THK F-104 pilots), at Diyatbakir and Balikesir respectively, were still operating the Starfighter. All remaining Starfighters were replaced by the General Dynamics F-16 Fighting Falcon in 1993-94. The F-104 was finally retired from Turkish service in 1995.

Turkish Air Force F-104G 62-12324 at Mürted on 22 July 1974.

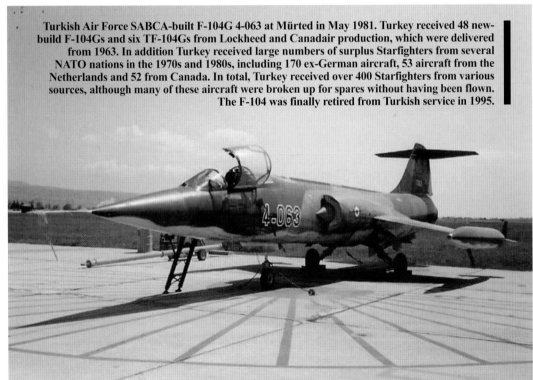

Turkish Air Force SABCA-built F-104G 4-063 at Mürted in May 1981. Turkey received 48 new-build F-104Gs and six TF-104Gs from Lockheed and Canadair production, which were delivered from 1963. In addition Turkey received large numbers of surplus Starfighters from several NATO nations in the 1970s and 1980s, including 170 ex-German aircraft, 53 aircraft from the Netherlands and 52 from Canada. In total, Turkey received over 400 Starfighters from various sources, although many of these aircraft were broken up for spares without having been flown. The F-104 was finally retired from Turkish service in 1995.

F-104G 20+36 'Bavaria' of JaboG 32 from Lechfeld on the last F-104 flight of JaboG 32 on 18 April 1984.

▌West Germany

The first German Starfighters were F-104Fs, which were used initially at Luke AFB, Arizona and George AFB, California, attached to the 4512th, 4518th and 4443rd Training Squadrons of the 58th Training Wing to train a cadre of instructors and later pilots and ground crews. Training of F-104 pilots in the USA ended in March 1983 when the

▌ **Lockheed-built F-104G-LO**
DA+710 (63-13243)

Luftwaffe Starfighters were withdrawn from service with the USAF's 69th TFS, 405th Tactical Training Wing and the Starfighters were handed over to Waffenschule 10 (WS10) at Nörvenich.

In all, Germany received a total of 915 Starfighters. These were made up as follows: 30 F-104Fs, 96 F-104Gs and 136 TF-104Gs from Lockheed; 255 F/RF-104Gs from the North Group, 210 F-104Gs from the South Group, 88 F-104Gs from the West Group, 50 F/RF-104Gs from the Italian Group and 50 F-104Gs from MBB. All told, Germany lost 281 Starfighters.

Luftwaffe and Marineflieger Service (See Chapter 4.)

Marineflieger RF-104 21+21 of MFG 2 at Mildenhall Air Fete in June 1983. This Starfighter was later sold to the Greek Air Force. (Author) ▌

Marineflieger F-104G 23+24 with a 'Kormoran' anti-ship missile. ▌

1st Canadian Air Group

Everyone has to have a great and timeless love in their life. I shamelessly admit to having two and they live in complete harmony with each other. The first is my wonderful wife of thirty years. The other is merely the most beautiful aircraft to ever grace the skies, the Lockheed F-104 Starfighter. The durable love affair started in the early 1960s when I first saw this striking machine with its pencil-thin fuselage and tiny canard-like wings was consummated in 1972 when I first flew the jet and endures to this day, nearly 2,400 flight hours later. Many aircraft have been christened with nicknames over the years by those who work with them and the F-104 is no exception. The Americans and Germans like to call it the 'Zipper' or the 'Zip'. We would occasionally refer to it in jest as 'the aluminium death tube', or 'the Flying Phallus', hut more often than not, we would just call it 'the 104' or by its given name, 'the Starfighter'. Somehow it seemed so appropriate - an elegant name for an elegant aircraft. One just couldn't conjure up a derisive name from those who flew her. Other airplanes got 'Thud', 'Hog' and 'Aardvark', not so the 104. I never heard anyone in the pilot community call it 'the missile with the man in it'. That was pure press hype and Lockheed had an excellent sales promotion and PR department. Perhaps more to the point, I never heard a pilot call it 'the widowmaker' and I don't know a self-respecting 104 pilot who would. This is because none of us who flew her blamed her for the relatively high accident rate incurred during 104 operations, especially during the early transition days. For the most part, the demanding role of the 104 in NATO was the main reason for the elevated accident rate, not the aircraft itself.

Lieutenant Colonel David L. Bashow (left), who retired from military service in 2004 after a 36-year career as a Royal Canadian Air Force fighter pilot, a senior staff officer and a military academic. His flying time includes nearly 2,400 hours in the CF-104/F-104G and he is a graduate of the USAF/GAF Fighter Weapons School and the US Navy's Top Gun School at the postgraduate level.

The Royal Canadian Air Force (Canadian Armed Forces from 28 February 1968 by consolidating the Army, Navy and Air Force) ultimately received 200 CF-104s and 38 CF-104Ds. Replacement marked a change of role from air defence to nuclear strike. Operating in the strike role, the CF-104 carried a single high-yield tactical nuclear weapon on the centreline. This weapon could have been delivered using a LABS toss manoeuvre, or in a low-level laydown attack. After the Canadian government's rejection of the nuclear role in 1968, CF-104s were assigned to conventional ground attack and in 1974 the M-61 cannon 20mm Vulcan cannon was installed and the fairing was removed from the cannon port. Twin bomb ejector rack carriers and multi-tube rocket launchers were installed.

One hundred and thirty nine CF-104/CF-104Ds were partially disassembled and flown in C-130

CF-104 104704, which made it first flight at Cartierville on 14 August 1961, was used by AETE (Aerospace Engineering Test Establishment) and 448 (Test) Squadron at RCAF Station Cold Lake, Alberta, throughout its RCAF career is seen here firing a salvo of CRU-7 rockets during air-to-ground gunnery practice at the Cold Lake range in 1974. This Starfighter, which also carried out tests for LAH-3 rocket pods, ended its career as a battle damage repair airframe.

Line-up of RCAF Starfighters with CF-104
104771 and 104779 nearest the camera, 104771
went to Denmark on 24 November 1973, as
R-771 and later became a decoy at Tirstrup
Air Base. It is displayed at Aalborg Air Base.
104779 suffered an engine fire on takeoff
from Baden Söllingen on 9 September 1975.
Captain J. E. McGillivray safely ejected. It
was his second ejection of his career.

Hercules transport aircraft to form eight squadrons of 1 Air Division in Europe - six nuclear strike in Germany and two photo-reconnaissance in France, beginning in December 1962 with 427 'Lion' Squadron, 3 Wing at Zweibrücken,. The two other squadrons in 3 Wing - 430 'Silver Falcon' and 434 'Bluenose', were also re-equipped with the CF-104, in April 1963. Re-equipment of the two Sabre Mk.6 squadrons in 4 Wing at Baden-Söllingen - 422 and 444 Squadrons - were equipped in May and July respectively. Starfighters for 430 'Silver Falcon' and 421 'Red Indian' Squadrons in 2 Wing at Grostonquin, France proceeded in September and December 1963, respectively. However, on 5 February of 1964, even before France withdrew from NATO (in 1966) French bases had to be evacuated following the French-US disagreement on the storage of nuclear weapons. 2 Wing was disbanded and its two CF-104 squadrons were transferred; 421 moving to 4 Wing and 430 moving to 3 Wing. The two photo- reconnaissance Squadrons, 441 'Silver Fox' and 439 'Sabre Toothed Tiger' which had operated the last RCAF Sabres in Europe until they were retired on 14 November 1963, were formed at 1 Wing in Marville, France in January and March 1964 respectively. These two squadrons were designated in the photo-reconnaissance role, but they could also be used as strike fighters with conventional weapons. Marville was closed by March 1967 and 1 and 3 Wings in Germany absorbed the Starfighters of 439 and 441 Squadrons, which re-located to Lahr. On 31 March 1967 434 Squadron

at Zweibrücken and 444 Squadron at Baden-Söllingen were disbanded, reducing CF-104 strength to four nuclear strike squadrons and two tactical reconnaissance squadrons.

Nos. 421 and 422 Squadrons at Baden-Söllingen continued as 4 Wing until 1970 when the Canadian government decided to reduce the strength of the Air Division to only three squadrons and to relinquish its nuclear strike role in favour of conventional attack. 1 Air Division was re-designated 1 Canadian Air Group; 422, 427 and 430 Squadrons were disbanded. 439 and 441 Squadrons replaced all but 421 Squadron in 4 Wing at Baden-Söllingen. Of the remaining three squadrons, 421 and 441 were committed to converting to ground attack roles, leaving 439 Squadron to continue tactical reconnaissance missions. 417 Squadron at Cold Lake continued as a CF-104 Operational Training Unit. CF-104 air operations at Lahr ceased in 1970, when it became a Canadian Army base, but 1 Canadian Air Group Headquarters remained there, co-located with the Canadian Forces Europe Headquarters. The airfield at Lahr remained operational for air transport operations as well as being a deployment base for the CF-104s from Baden-Söllingen.

'Noise was a part of the unique personality of the 104' recalls David Bashow. 'It made distinctive sounds that manifested themselves on engine run-up and on the overhead break. On run-up, the 15,000lb thrust General Electric J79 engine made an unearthly shriek that was dubbed 'the moose call' because it sounded exactly like a moose in rutting season and became cause for nervous banter during the moose-breeding season in northern Alberta where we were based. The very thought of one of those beasts charging our jets on the button of the runway conjured up an unpleasant image. Perhaps even more distinctive was the unique, supernatural moaning sound like the wail of a wounded banshee, made by the 104 in the overhead break for landing. Sometimes it's a pity to let science get in the way of romanticism. Unfortunately, both the moose call on engine run-up and the moaning in the overhead break had technical explanations. The 'moose' was due to a rapid repositioning of the engine inlet guide vanes and the 'moaning' I am told was due to disturbed airflow over the engine air bypass flaps. But to those of us who flew her and lived around her, this was just more 104 magic.

CF-104 104797 in formation with a Canadair Sabre Mk.6 of 412 'Falcon' Squadron RCAF. This Starfighter was sold to Turkey in 1986.

'Takeoff was child's play. You engaged nose-wheel steering and plugged in the afterburner, which gave a smooth, positive light in seven stages. The stick was just held in the neutral position until approximately 20-25 knots below the computed takeoff speed when back pressure was applied. From then on, flight was (usually) inevitable. Throttle response was truly awesome. Unlike some other jet aircraft, fuel control units metered JP-4 to engine and afterburner such that you never had to worry about overtemping the engine, the net result being that you could bang the throttle around as much as you wanted. A real stop-go lever. Also, unlike today's high bypass engines spool-up time was very rapid; the resulting thrust changes instantaneous. The power

was thus always there when you needed it and this was a tremendous advantage when flying close formation and also for making rapid corrections to airspeed in any phase of flight where this was required, such as in the landing pattern or when dropping bombs, where speed accuracy is vital. Often, today's bypass engines produce significant delays from throttle movement to engine response, a condition that requires some forethought to compensate for on the part of the pilot. This was certainly not a problem with the 104.

'I personally had the relatively unique experience of flying the jet in both temperature extremes, starting with three years as an instructor (after a long tour in Germany) in Cold Lake, Canada, where we had square tyres and -40°F

CF-104s' 104845 and 104887 in formation. The latter was sold to Denmark in 1971. On 18 August 1982 it crashed at Fjernislev after an instrument failure. LTC T. Peterson successfully ejected.

weather for weeks on end in winter. We used to joke that we had eleven months of winter and one month of bad skiing, but it wasn't far from the truth. The good news was the remarkable effect the cold air had on jet engines. One of the parallel runways at Cold Lake is 12,000 feet long and I can remember that on afterburner takeoff on a -40°F day in a 'clean' (no external stores) aircraft, you could have 450 knots on the clock by the end of the runway. The most difficult part was getting the landing gear locked up by its limiting speed of 260 knots after takeoff. If you hesitated even a second after nose wheel rotation, you were going to get an overspeed.

'In marked contrast to this experience were memories of operations in the Arizona desert as an exchange instructor at the USAF/GAF Fighter Weapons School. Over the years, I suppose I've flown just about every configuration the 104 has to offer, but as an antithesis to the clean jet

in the wintertime Cold Lake, the dart-tow ship in summertime Phoenix springs to mind. This consisted of two wingtip tanks, a wing pylon tank and the dart rig itself, a cumbersome target device that looked like a huge foil paper airplane that was reeled out in flight under the left wing. On a 140°F runway temperature day, the takeoff roll was spectacular and guaranteed to make a devout Christian out of even the most practised atheist. You can joke about your 'gravel sniffers in the nose' to sense nose wheel rotation time; this situation really called for it. I'll never forget that tyre fail speed was 239 knots and at that temperature and configuration, takeoff speed was around 235. The jet ended up clawing her way into the air, waging a personal war with Sir Isaac Newton for every inch of altitude gained. It was always a near thing and happiness was staggering away into the heavy summer desert air with the gear safely tucked up and the runway behind you.

All this for the privilege of letting someone shoot at you.

'Landing was always an impressive, though usually straightforward event. The approach speeds were fast by anybody's standards, but you got used to the speed just like anything else. Normal landing configuration was with LAND (full) flap selected and a long, flat final approach was flown at 175-180 knots with touchdown at 155-160 minimum. To these basic speeds were added extra knots for any fuel over 1,000lb, crosswinds, gusty winds, external stores, mother, wife, kids and so on. In short, it was not at all unusual to add 20 knots to the basic speeds. Boundary Layer Control (BLC) was added to the razor wings to lower landing approach and touchdown speeds with LAND flap selected. Because the BLC was only effective down to about 82 per cent engine rpm, the aircraft was unusual in that it was routinely landed with power on. When instructing, we

CF-104 104732 of 6 ST/R OTU (Operational Training Unit) from Cold Lake. This Starfighter crashed on 30 April 1982 with 417 OTS, Cold Lake when it went into a flat spin after loss of control during Air Combat Training ACT on a Fighter Weapons Instructors Course (FWIC). The pilot, Captain Dave Ghyselincks ejected safely.

threatened dire consequences to the novice who pulled the power to idle prior to touchdown, since this would result in an abrupt loss of both BLC and lift, usually on one wing before the other and at best, a bone-jarring arrival on the runway. In reality, as long as the pilot smoothly and slowly reduced power to idle, there was no controllability problem.

'Landing patterns could also be flown with TAKEOFF (half) flap configuration at slightly higher approach speeds than LAND flap, but BLC roll-off was not a factor to worry about. A flapless landing, however, was both an emergency

and a memorable experience, especially at night. Final approach/touchdown minimum speeds were 230/195 knots respectively, plus additives. You flew a long flat final where you were going like a scalded cat and felt like you were continuously on the ragged edge of disaster Descent rate was around 800 feet per minute and we tended to fly final on a combination of both airspeed and angle-of-attack (AOA) indications. I remember very distinctly a caution Pilot's Notes that sternly warned at no time to allow the rate of descent on a flapless approach to exceed more than 2,000 feet per minute as recovery would require more than 400ft of altitude.

'In *all* cases, the aircraft was landed with crab on and you just kicked it straight with nosewheel steering on the post-landing roll. As you can well imagine, increased stopping power was highly desirable and provision was made for this with a big 16t diameter drag chute and an excellent anti-skid braking system. If these didn't work, or we had a takeoff emergency or a slippery runway, we had an arrester hook mounted under the aft fuselage that snagged a cable at the end of the runway. And if *that* didn't work, well then it really wasn't your day. We almost never attempted aerodynamic braking. After all, how efficiently can you aerodynamically brake a pencil?

'Stalls and spins were another flight area approached with great caution. Due to the aerodynamics of the high T tail, the aircraft was prone to a phenomenon known as pitch-up at high AOAs. Beyond a certain point, this pitch-up was uncontrollable and resulted in severe gyration (or even structural failure) of the aircraft and a large loss in altitude before recovery to level flight. It was possible to develop stall angles of attack very readily and rapidly during abrupt manoeuvres, even though relatively small amounts of stabilizer were used. In supersonic flight, the usual stall

warnings were inadequate to prevent excessive AOA and an Automatic Pitch Control (APC) was therefore provided which initiated corrective action at the proper time to prevent reaching an AOA high enough to cause pitch-up under any operating condition. These warnings took the form of a stick shaker and a kicker, which abruptly kicked the stick forward. It was, in effect, both a built-in buffet warning and an artificial stall that occurred ahead of the aerodynamic stall. Stalls were never practised to completion; recovery action was initiated at either shaker or kicker action, depending on configuration and stalls were *never* practised below 25,000 feet AGL.

'Spins were violent, gut-wrenching manoeuvres and intentional spinning was prohibited. A friend of mine had a wild tide one day when one of the main landing gear doors accidentally deployed in supersonic flight during air combat practice. Although he executed a brilliant recovery, the thrill factor was so high that it was several minutes before he was capable of coherent speech.

'Because of the jet's rather awesome out-of-control characteristics, pilots generally developed a phobia about flying slow in it at all. At the Weapons School, I would routinely demonstrate a confidence zoom to zero airspeed. Actually, it was perfectly safe under pre-ordained conditions of centre of gravity and fuel weight. The trick was to recover very gently, using a very conservative maximum reading on the APC gauge and rolling the aircraft towards the nearest horizon. Ailerons were very effective well past the stall. In reality, if the pilot were just to take his hands *off* the controls in the vertical stall condition, the aircraft generally knew what it wanted to do better than the pilot did and would usually recover to a recognizable flight attitude from which a full recovery could be easily made. This would *not* want to be done low to the ground though. Altitude losses in out-of-control situations in the 104 were formidable. For example, ejection was a checklist procedure if recovery was not affected by 15,000 feet AGL.

'The 104 was a relatively sophisticated aircraft in its heyday and possesses relatively advanced components and systems. As pilots, we used to marvel at the seemingly incongruous effect activation of a given button or knob would have on a supposedly unrelated system in the aircraft. Examples of this are legion, but one that comes to mind was running up engine power from idle to retract a stuck windshield rain remover! There were so many of these quirks and foibles that 104 students became just a little gullible to say the least and from this situation was born the legendary 'Order of the Thruster Thumpers'.

'Now the 104 had explosive canopy jettison thrusters, rather phallic in appearance, mounted on each side of the canopy sill just about abeam the pilot's head. These thrusters would explosively blow the canopy clear of the aircraft in an emergency, or as part of the ejection sequence. The 104 also had warning lights and a horns test switch that illuminated all advisory, caution and warning lights in the cockpit, while making appropriate noises. The switch was replicated in the rear seat instructor's position of the two-seat trainer and activation of this test function was a standard part of the pre-start check. Preying on student vulnerabilities, one instructor very early in the programme thought he would have some fun with his charge by reviewing the various idiosyncrasies of the aircraft and then suggesting that if the warning lights would not go out when the test switch was released, pounding either one's fists or another blunt object vigorously on the thruster would remedy the errant lights. In reality, the instructed simply held down his own test switch in the rear seat and did not release it when the student released his in the front, until a suitable display of strenuous physical activity had been elicited. The hardest part of this whole operation was keeping a straight face. Our ground crew were wonderful and often reinforced the myth by either helping with the pounding or offering a substitute items such as the screwdriver to take the stress off the student's poor tired fist. We didn't manage to get everybody, but there were some memorable achievements, including general officers. Once an instructor found that he 'had a live one', this foible was judiciously reinforced by other instructors throughout the course, just to increase credibility. At the end of the course, the most deserving souls were awarded a trophy with a 'nice having you' caption, inducted into the 'Order of the Thruster Thumpers' and sworn to secrecy for all time.

CF-104 104726 which served with 6 (ST/R) Operational Training Unit at RCAF Station Cold Lake, Alberta. was operated by 417 (ST/R) Squadron at CFB Cold Lake when it crashed on 14 January 1969 during a routine night training mission in a three-aircraft section over the Primrose Lake Weapons Testing Range. Lieutenant R. B. Kaiser of Victoria, British Columbia, who had reported 'fuel problems' and said he was dropping to a lower altitude to burn off excess before returning to base was killed. Kaiser's body was found near the wreckage the following morning. His squadron commander, Lieutenant Colonel Kenneth Thorneycroft, had this assessment of the situation: 'Putting it bluntly, the thing glides like a brick shithouse.' Kaiser's last communication with the base had him descending through 1,500 feet. 'The only thing a pilot can do when his airspeed drops...at that altitude is get the hell out of the airplane,' Thorneycroft said. (Andy Graham via Stephen Fochuk)

'Another idiosyncrasy of the aircraft created one of my fondest memories of the 104. There were just too many 'T- and 'D'-shaped handles in the cockpit to activate various systems such as rudder pedals, canopy jettison, emergency hydraulics, the drag chute and a number of other items and a lot of them looked uncomfortably alike. During September 1975 our squadron deployed for two weeks to Kleine Brogel, Belgium while our runway in Baden, Germany was being resurfaced. One day I was leading a four-ship flight on a nearby bombing range and had a very senior squadron officer as my Number Two. I had already finished my post-start systems checks and was waiting for the rest of my flight to check in, when I glanced over at my Number Two just in time to see the drag chute come streaming out! Cunning devil that I am, I plumbed my brain to recall if this was a new post-start check procedure, knowing full well it wasn't. The next thing I heard was a meek little voice coming from Two (who didn't think I could see him) saying that he was having a 'small problem' and would have to abort.

'Later investigation on my part with the ground crew revealed that this rather absent-minded senior had been adjusting his rudder pedals with the drag chute handle! To make matters worse, 'our hero' reputedly attempted to hush up this minor embarrassment by offering the ground crew a keg of the finest Belgian beer if they would keep a lid on the event. Being both enterprising and honourable chaps, they agreed, took the beer and then, because the story was just too juicy to suppress, promptly blabbed it all over Western Europe! The fall from grace in the hero trade can be swift and brutal!

'Because the flying weather in Central Europe, the most common home of 104 operations, can be particularly grim, the aircraft had to be optimized for instrument flying. Although navigation aids consisted merely of the inertial navigation system, TACAN and, to a certain extent, the ground mapping radar, the instrumentation itself was first class. Although it didn't have a Horizontal

CF-104 104706 passing Hohenzollern Castle. This Starfighter ended its career as a battle damage repair airframe.

Situation Indicator (merely a bearing pointer and Distance Measuring Equipment) the attitude indicator in the Canadian version made up for it. It was an enormous 5in sphere, grey over black with the compass headings etched in the sphere itself and it was your 'own little world'. It really spoiled you on Ground Control Approaches to minimums in particularly rotten weather. The Rhine Valley was especially bad in winter, with half-mile flight visibility being routine. Needless to say, at final approach speeds in excess of 180kts one's flying had to be precise and accurate.

'The inertial navigation system was a very primitive variant, although it was the last word when it emerged. We used to joke that the hamsters were getting tired out on the treadmill when it acted up, which was often. Later, it was replaced with the excellent Litton LW-33 system during the aircraft's twilight service years.

'The F15A radar (not to be confused with the F-15 Eagle) had both air-to-air and air-to-ground modes. Although the air-to-air mode was extremely primitive by today's standards it was still a useful tool in the hands of a skilled operator. However, the air-to-ground radar was really first class.

'Raw as opposed to processed radar returns were provided, so one had to become good at interpretation, but once this was mastered, you could navigate (and even bomb) off it with a very high degree of accuracy. Unlike synthetically processed radar returns, which can look like a photograph, the F15A radar in a ground-mapping mode was only straightforward when flying over large lakes, coastlines or large, distinctive cultural centres such as cities. At other times, such as flying over mountainous terrain, one had to take such items as the radar's line of sight and subsequent impact on the scope presentation into account. Good radar navigation in the CF-104 was quite an art form.

'The low-level characteristics of the Starfighter were incomparable. Due to its exceptionally clean lines, it created very little form and parasitic drag and the high wing loading, although detrimental in hard-turning air combat engagement, ensured an extremely stable flight at high speed 'on the deck'. In fact, the 104 cut through turbulence like the proverbial hot knife through butter. The air-minded German public loved the aircraft. Since so many NATO nations including Germany flew the 104, I think she became a symbol of the Alliance to them. However, adverse publicity during the high accident rate period of its career was extensive enough to inspire the Teutonic sense of humour. They joked that if you wanted to own a 104, just buy an acre of land anywhere in Germany. Sooner or later...

'At any rate, when all was working properly, the airplane did outstanding work in the low-level high-speed environment. When it didn't, you had to think fast, since the 104 had the glide ratio of an anvil strapped to a manhole cover.

'A friend of mine is the source of one of my favourite 104 stories. He was motoring along at low level one day in the Moselle area of Germany when he suffered a catastrophic bird strike that totalled the engine, necessitating an immediate ejection from the doomed machine. Apparently, every warning light and horn in the cockpit came on. His statement to the accident Board of Enquiry is a classic: 'I looked inside the cockpit, saw all those pretty lights and just *knew* I'd won a hundred free video games, but didn't think I'd hang around to play them.'

'Night flying was downright pleasant in the 104, with good cockpit lighting and excellent visibility. The Canadian version had completely red cockpit lighting and I remember being bitten by that once on a night low-level radar navigation route. I had marked some reference lines on my map in red ink. I soon found out that the net effect of red lines under red lighting was invisible lines. Brilliant. The GAF/USAF version had more conventional white lighting. Night formation was a rather dicey business on a dark night since there was no strip lighting and what external lights that were available were very limited. What lights we had consisted of white, amber, red and green ones strategically located on the sides of the fuselage and either on the wingtips or on the tip tanks. The trick was to arrange all these lights into some predetermined geometrical pattern when nothing else was available. Night formation takeoffs and landings were not normally a problem though. On takeoff, the rosy glow of the aircraft afterburners provided a great deal of reflected light, although it sure could get dark in a hurry when afterburner was deselected. In a landing configuration, the lead aircraft's landing lights tended to bathe his machine in enough light to provide easy reference to normal daytime formation hues. An afterburner

takeoff at night was a treat to the eyes. The rosy glow of the afterburner plume, which extended 30-40 feet behind the aircraft, was evenly interspersed with white shock diamonds of hot gasses. Very impressive.

'Over the years and in service with various nations, the 104 acquitted various different forms of camouflage war paint. However, the Arizona birds spent their lives in natural aluminium and two of them were what we considered our airshow steeds, the ones we most liked to show off. They were actually used in the F-104/Yeager spin sequence in the movie, *The Right Stuff*. One of the crew chiefs was a fanatic. He continuously polished the jet with jeweller's rouge; he even shone the nozzle feathers of the tailpipe after landing. This guy used to walk behind you with a rag and scowl at pilots who put fingerprints on his beloved during the pre-flight walk-around. We used to call it 'the grape' in air combat training, since it was so shiny it could be seen for miles earlier than anything else and the guy flying it tended to get eaten alive during those close encounters of the finest kind.

'In Air Combat manoeuvring (ACM), the aircraft displayed limited turning capability due to its high wing-loading, but *great* acceleration. Only the F-105 and perhaps the F-111 were in a similar wing-loading league with the 104. Almost all the other fighter or fighter-bomber types with which we routinely practised ACM tended to have much lower wing loading. We would capitalize on the aircraft's aerodynamic properties with 'hit and run' type tactics, not allowing ourselves to enter a hard turning engagement with a superior turning fighter. Although an occasional deviation from this norm by a highly experienced air combat pilot to capitalize on an adversary's mistakes was possible, in most cases, violations of the hit-and-run principle resulted in a severe drubbing for 104 pilots. 'Turning and burning' was just not its forte. It took acres of airspace to turn the jet around at combat speeds and it's no wonder that ex-104 pilots who now fly the redoubtable CF-18 Hornet have likened this worthy successor's close-in, hard-turning fighting capabilities to 'a knife fight in a telephone booth'. Still, the 104 could turn where we needed to turn, down in the high-speed, low-level environment and this was due to the better turning and engine performance in the denser air at lower altitudes. Few people realize that a 'clean' 104 below 5,000 feet MSL in full afterburner could *sustain* a seven 'G' turn. The trouble was, in full burner, you couldn't sustain it very long before you ran out of gas, fuel flows being *very* high at low level. A typical ACM mission might not last more than 30-40 minutes, of which perhaps only about ten minutes actually involved combat. With less than 6,000lb of fuel in a typical ACM configuration and a fuel flow rate probably eight or nine times that in pounds-per-hour (PPH) in afterburner, one does not have to be Albert Einstein to realize why fuel control was (and is) such an essential element of air combat.

'In this day and age, sophisticated weapons systems such as those on the CF-18 and the Panavia Tornado can deliver all types of ordnance with utterly reliable accuracy, with varying degrees of automation. The 104 was very much a manual system, where individual pilot skill determined the outcome of each and every bombing, rocketry and gunnery event. Recent strides in weapons delivery technology are marvellous - a real aid to the fighter pilot, but we developed a tremendous sense of accomplishment in honing our skills on the 104 in manual release modes. We got very good and also very competitive. Canadian 104 pilots did very well in international NATO bombing and gunnery competitions during the aircraft's heyday. Although I'm sure Kelly Johnson at the outset never envisaged this beautiful aircraft as a bomber, the excellent high-speed, low-level characteristics of the jet made it a rock-solid, stable platform for delivering various types of ordnance. Unfortunately, about 4,000lb of conventional munitions was about the most she could reasonably be expected to carry.

'Typically, our deliveries tended to be low and fast, allowing minimum exposure time, this in deference to anticipated heavy enemy defences in the Central European scenario and the typically low ceilings and reduced visibility of the sodden, pewter skies prevalent in this part of the world. Delivery parameters usually varied from level up to 10 degrees of dive and delivery airspeeds from 450-550+ knots - the faster the better. We used to have an elaborate betting system for quarters or German marks on the results of a lot of our bombing range missions. For example, each bomb dropped or rocket fired and best overall score with the gun would be worth a quarter. This is not to imply that our fighter pilots were a bunch of high stakes gamblers - very little money actually changed hands when you consider a typical range mission would mean about six practice bombs dropped, three or four practice rockets fired and several gun passes. Furthermore, it was unusual for any one individual to 'sweep' the competition. Anyway, rivalry was often fierce amongst the experienced and I can remember days when four or five 'bull-eyes' or 'shacks' (direct hits) were not good enough to finish you in the money. (Gary, if you are reading this, you still owe me 50 cents.) Not bad, when you consider that anything inside about 140 feet was a qualifying bomb. You had to be good, or there went the kid's lunch money.

'Unfortunately, the 104 garnered a reputation over time as a 'killer' aircraft and it is time that this unfair reputation was put squarely in perspective. In fact, it was an extremely honest aircraft and as long as it was flown within the boundaries of its flight envelope and was treated with respect, it was utterly dependable. When the 104 entered service with NATO in the early 1960s, the technology afforded by the aircraft was a quantum leap over the earlier vintage jet aircraft then in service and it took some time for the operators and maintainers

CF-104 104798, which in 1966 struck a forested hill on a low level mission. Flight Lieutenant D. C. Lawson failed to eject and was killed.

to come to grips with this new technology and the unique demands it made on pilot and technician alike. The Canadian accident fate is comparable to that of the other NATO members who operated the 104. Although 113 of the 238 CF-104s produced were destroyed in accidents during its Canadian service, it must be remembered that this record represents 25 years of continuous service in a very demanding environment. Thirty-seven Canadian pilots forfeited their lives on CF-104 operations. Needless to say, this record says a great deal for the escape system of the aircraft and there were a great many successful ejections, even in marginal conditions. The biggest accident cause factor was the role to which the jet was exposed - the high-speed, low-level arena where opportunities to err are legion. Since the jet was only equipped with one engine, if you *lost* that engine at low altitude, you were in a world of hurt.

'Some years earlier, I reviewed all the 104 accidents that had occurred in the NATO

CF-104 104751 of 6 ST R OTU at Cold Lake in 1962. This Starfighter was sold to Turkey in 1986.

consortium and it is truly amazing how few were attributable to unexpected mechanical failures. Most took place in the 104's early service days when various teething troubles were being ironed out and the aircraft experienced a rash of recurring catastrophic engine failures due to bird strikes at low level. It wasn't a devious airplane. It just demanded respect and punishment for a major transgression was often swift and fatal. By and large, 104s did not kill pilots. Pilots killed pilots and 104s.'

About 110 CF-104/CF-104Ds were lost in accidents, out of 239 delivered - a loss rate of no less than 46 percent. However, Canadian CF-104s probably had the highest-flying time of any country operating the Starfighter. At the time of retirement, average airframe times were in the order of 6,000 hours as compared to 2,000 hours for the Luftwaffe. In all, thirty-seven pilots lost their lives flying the Canadian Starfighter. Unfortunately the CF-104, the fastest aircraft to serve in the RCAF, was not as manoeuvrable as many other types of aircraft. At low level this lack of manoeuvrability could be dangerous if a pilot was not paying close attention. Canadian pilots excelled with the Starfighter, some being considered among the best pilots in NATO.

The first fatality was Flight Lieutenant John Richard Mulhall serving with 6 STR (Strike and Reconnaissance) OTU Cold Lake, Canada who ejected from his CF-104 (102742) on 10 August 1962. He sustained fatal injuries when the parachute disintegrated in the aircraft fire area.

Flight Lieutenant Clarke W. 'Tex' Gehman ejected from CF-104 Starfighter 104764 on 1 November 1963: 'I was maintenance test pilot at Cold Lake, Alberta and tasked this day to do a very simple flight to try and locate which fuel tank probe was causing erroneous readings. I was briefed to apply accelerations in all directions (including deceleration). A rapid throttle retard caused my engine to flame out and resist relighting. Later investigation revealed an improperly seated 'O' ring ruptured with the ram effect of the reduction in fuel demand.

'My ejection sequence was from about 1,000 feet AGL and very slow for the 'Zip', something like 250 knots. The craft was in full shudder and sinking rapidly as only that machine could do. My first impression was that the 1/3 second for everything to happen was taking a very long time to get done. Then a rapid light/dark/light/dark vision of the world as I tumbled rapidly heels over head. As the 'chute opened, I swung fore and aft, putting my heels above the horizon then falling back as the lower edge of the chute collapsed into itself. This only happened a few times until I tugged the risers and it immediately stabilized into a very nice descent. I was able to turn and watch my ride take its 'dirt nap'. Very sad to see.

'It was then that I heard the rushing of the wind in the trees below me and realized that I had had my helmet and mask torn from my head. And it was on very tight! Landing in the trees at a sideways speed of 20-25 knots taught me what a bowling ball must feel like. I wished

that I had retained my seat survival pack instead of releasing it on its lanyard as we were instructed to do. (Since revised, I believe, due to my post incident comment.)

'I did not touch the ground, was hung about twenty feet up in trees with my survival gear strung out in the trees above me. I got myself down and felt great to be on terra firma once more.

'As an aside, it was later revealed that although I was only fourteen miles from the base, the control tower did not pick up my Tx on guard. It was heard by the pilot of another 104 and relayed. This bit makes me think that I was perhaps quite a bit lower than the 1,000 feet when I had decided to 'step over the side'. I was rescued by helicopter a very short time after and made it to Friday beer call only a little bit late. My only injuries were a lump on the side of my head from tree impact and a scored eyeball and forehead from the microphone in my mask as it was torn off over my head.

'A while later, the test establishment was doing some trials from a modified T-33 when the pilot noticed that something flew over his nose after the seat was fired. The something was the rocket motor tube from the seat. Fortunately all parts were recovered and it was found that the nozzle of the rocket had been installed backwards, so instead of putting the thrust through the centre of gravity, it made a pinwheel out of the seat/ man (in this case 'dummy'). My seat was never recovered, but having watched an ejection from very similar speed and sink rate as I had, mine was very different. The one I saw was picture perfect, straight up seat ride and smooth parachute opening. Unfortunately just as we were cheering his success, the fireball came up and got him. For this reason, although it can't be proved, I suspect that I rode a faulty rocket.'

On 11 May 1964 Flight Lieutenant Len J. 'Speed' Bentham of 3 Wing at Zweibrücken ejected from his CF-104. 'My rudder failure occurred at about 200 feet above the ground in France about thirty minutes from 3 Wing in Zweibrücken. There was a very severe yaw to the left and the rudder pedals could be pushed without the normal resistance in either direction without results. The only way direction could be maintained was to introduce about 20 degrees of bank to the right. I gained altitude and flew back to 3 Wing in this attitude. After informing the tower of my problems I made four or five attempts to land but on each approach I could not hold the centre line and had to go around. Since the rudder

CF-104 104811 flown by Flight Lieutenant L. J. 'Speed' Bentham of 3 Wing at Zweibrücken suffered a disconnection of the rudder linkage during flight on 11 May 1964. Bentham ejected using his C-2 seat.

pedals gave absolutely no resistance and produced no effect I was afraid I would have no nose wheel steering and no brakes and technical people on the ground could not assure me that they would be available. Since there was a strong crosswind at 3 Wing I decided to try an American base which was not too far away and the runway was more into wind. On my approach to this base I realized I was over a heavily populated area and my fuel was getting very low. Rather than risk a flame-out and still unsure if I could land safely I decided to proceed to the bail-out area which was only a few minutes flying time away and eject. The ejection went as expected and the aircraft went into the ground vertically with no resulting fire. When the investigating team arrived at the wreckage they found the rudder hydraulic control access panel at eye level and discovered one control rod disconnected giving full power to the opposing rod. A very simple investigation.'

Thirty-two-year-old Flight Lieutenant Harry Ruault Stroud, of 421 Squadron RCAF at Baden-Söllingen ejected near Karlsruhe on 16 November 1964 from CF-104 12856. 'The problem was jamming of the inlet guide vanes in the closed position due to the use of improper lubricant. After a TACAN letdown from 35,000 feet (high cloud that day) power was demanded to level off. It was not forthcoming. From the time of problem identification to my feet on the ground was 43 seconds. Most aircraft have a glide ratio of eleven in the horizontal to one in the vertical. The CF-104 is similar but different with a glide ratio of

Remains of the ejection seat of CF-104 104856 of 3 Wing at Zweibrücken after Flight Lieutenant Harry R. Stroud's successful bailout using the C-2 ejection seat on 16 November 1964. Engine failure due to inadequate maintenance was judged to be the cause of the accident.

eleven in the vertical to one in the horizontal. That baby was going nowhere but down.'

On 9 June 1965 Flying Officer Garry Sanderson of 6 STR OTU at Cold Lake was on his first solo on type and the engine failed, '(probably as a result of trying to digest something it wasn't designed to handle) in final turn.'

'My chute opened at about treetop height, (belatedly, as I had a death grip on the D handle and didn't let go until the still-attached seat bashed me in the head to indicate that it might be a good idea to do so). I still have the D handle tucked away somewhere, gathering dust, along with the slightly scorched handle from the control column. My wife has long since discarded the bent and twisted turbine blades that were kept because, 'Someday I'll make knives out of these'.

Flight Lieutenant 'Al' E. A. Seitz twice ejected during his service with the RCAF. His first ejection was on 8 July 1952 when the engine of his F-86E Sabre quit in the North Sea (in the area called The Wash). The flameout occurred after an hour's flight. He glided from 30,000 feet to 20,000 feet before ejecting. His dinghy did not inflate because the stopper was rusted! He spent 1:45 minutes in the North Sea (not as warm as the Mediterranean but at least not the high waves). He was picked up by a US Navy Albatross and returned to North Luffenham where he was based with 439 Squadron. His body temperature was beginning to drop. Both times he had reached the point of thinking that he wasn't going to be

rescued and he said once accepting that he had an amazing sense of peace. He returned to Canada in December 1953.

On Friday the 13th of August 1965 he suffered engine failure very shortly after take-off from 'Decci' [Decimomannu, Sardinia]. He was scheduled to return to 4 Wing after having had week long bombing practice at Decci. His aircraft landed in pieces on an island in the Mediterranean where a prison was located. Meanwhile Al had noticed an onshore wind and kept his parachute attached hoping to land on soil rather than in the water as had happened to him when he ejected from an F-86 Sabre! However the cord from himself to his dinghy was not strong enough to withstand the wind and it broke resulting in it going off with the parachute and Al landing in the Gulf of Assinara. He spent nineteen minutes parachute time and thirty minutes in the water. He was picked up by Sardinian fishermen who were heading in to port due to the strong winds. He was given artificial respiration on the boat and was hospitalized in Cagliari for a few days. Pneumonia was a possibility due to the salt water irritation in his lungs. He did suffer a hairline crack in his neck. At the time of Al's 104 ejection his wife Millie was on the base at 4 Wing with their daughters, then aged 5 and 7. 'The deputy Squadron commander came to tell me that Al had bailed out and the dinghy had been sighted (they didn't know that Al wasn't in it!). It seemed like such a long time before there was any more word before I was informed that he was in the hospital at Cagliari. Eventually he returned with a neck brace on.'

Flight Lieutenant E. A. 'Al' Seitz of 4 Wing at Baden Söllingen who successfully ejected from CF-104 104738 on 13 August 1965 after an engine failure in flight.

On 4 May 1973 Captain John B. Croll of the 417 OTS at Cold Lake made a high speed, ultra low altitude ejection from the CF-104. 'During a training flight, I had gotten into a fairly steep dive angle for a simulated weapons release and was having trouble with the pullout due to the operation of the automatic pitch control (APC) system (stick kicker). I finally overpowered the kicker, but the pullout was so low that the aircraft clipped the top ten feet off a sixty foot spruce tree. The impact with the tree, at an aircraft speed of about 500 knots, caused extensive aircraft damage. The shock of the impact, including the shattering of the canopy, caused me to begin to lose consciousness (grey-out and tunnel vision) and I initiated ejection before blacking out. The windblast at 500 knots ripped off my helmet as soon as the seat departed the aircraft, knocked me unconscious and caused considerable facial injuries. Fortunately, all the automatic ejection features worked and I landed in the trees after only a couple of 'swings' in the parachute (as recounted by my wingman later on, since I was unconscious and unable to enjoy the ride!). I woke up about twenty minutes later and

recall that the forest seemed very quiet, with the birds singing softly in the trees and a peaceful lull over everything. In my initial dazed state, I actually thought that I had died and that this was heaven. At that moment, my wingman flew overhead in his CF-104, looking for evidence of my survival. As soon as I saw him I recall being very happy that there were CF-104s in heaven and that I would be able to continue flying! As it turned out, I recovered from my injuries and had a successful flying career over the next thirty years.

On 27 November 1980 at the end of a three day local exercise 38-year-old Captain Ralph Edward Harrison was piloting CF-104 'Hawkeye 27' from the CFB at Baden-Söllingen. 'On returning for a full stop landing, IFR recoveries were in process and I was cleared for a vectored Ground Controlled Radar Approach. GCA called me one mile from the glide path and I lowered full flaps and increased fuel flow because of the extra drag and then that's when the banging started, really loud clanging, banging. It didn't feel like explosions; more like as if someone was hitting the aircraft with a sledge hammer and at the same time the 104 rolled violently left and right three or four times. There were about three to five bangs and with each bang the Starfighter rolled back and forth. At the same time the warning panel lights and the master caution light would flash like a pin-ball machine but the only one that stayed on was number 2 generator failed. With each bang the panel would light up and then go out but I couldn't catch up with it to see what lights were flashing and that moment I declared an emergency. The engine instruments looked normal to me and no fire warning lights came on. Then almost immediately there was a tremendous explosion which really vibrated the aircraft and fumes entered the cockpit. I called GCA that I was ejecting [in level flight at approximately 1,600 feet AGL and approximately 200 knots]. 'As I was IFR and in cloud I kept the 104 steady with my right hand and pulled the 'D' ring with the other hand. As the 'D' ring was travelling up I released the control stick and used both hands to continue pulling. The canopy blew off with very loud bang and the shoulder straps pulled me back quite quickly. I saw the instrument panel and the canopy bow flash by and at the same time there was a very, very loud roar probably caused by the wind blast and the rocket motor in the ejection seat. I would estimate the time from the start of the banging to ejection was between 10 to 15 seconds.

I felt I was tumbling backwards. The roaring ceased and I remember thinking this is where the chute should open. I felt a gentle tug and I could see I had a good chute. Almost immediately I came out the clouds. I was sitting straight up and down with no oscillation of the chute. I would estimate I was about 1,500 feet above ground. At this time I was aware my knees were hurting and the flying suit was torn around the knees. I don't remember how I received these injuries. I was having difficulty in breathing and I realized the problem was my mask was still on and then I removed it from my face. Knowing I would be landing soon, I released the seat pack which is attached to the parachute and to the Mae West by a lanyard and I felt a tug when the seat pack reached the end of the lanyard and deployed but the line broke and I helplessly watched the pack fall to earth with the dingy opening.

'The wind started to drift me towards woods which were near a freshly ploughed field. I pulled on the back parachute lines which set a drift away from the trees. About 200 feet I started to go right towards that ploughed field. The drift was slow and I managed a soft landing. I released the chute right

away. I laid there for a few minutes rubbing my knees until the pain went away. The crash occurred over farmland six nautical miles from the south runway of CFB Baden-Söllingen, near the village of Muchenschop.

'By this time I was drawing a crowd. The aircraft explosions had alerted their attention to me. Two nice ladies found my seat pack and brought it to me but they didn't stick around. A gentleman from the local village came to me a put his hand on my shoulder and in German told me I was going to be alright but he didn't stay either. I think there were trying to tell me something. Then I realized I had on a shoulder holster with a pistol in it (the pistol was carried as a part of the exercise and it was unloaded and the firing pin had been removed). Perhaps

On 27 November 1980 CF-104 104807 (far left) in 421 'Red Indian' Squadron RCAF formation crashed while on approach to CFB Baden-Söllingen following a local base exercise sortie when it suffered a fire and explosion near the village of Muckenschopf, approximately 6 nm south of the base. The pilot, Captain Ralph Harrison ejected at 1,600 feet AGL, suffering injuries to his knees. The cause was an improperly installed fuel line fitting.

that's why they didn't want to keep me company! I opened the seat pack and found the emergency radio but the container for the radio had been bent on impact and I couldn't get it out. About fifteen minutes later a German ambulance arrived and took me to the base. I believe someone in the local village must have called for the ambulance. I ended up with contusion/ abrasion to each knee, with a right chip fracture of the patella and a marked hemarthrosis [a bleeding into joint spaces]. I had no other bruises not even from the parachute straps.

'As for the cause of the accident, the Board of Inquiry found that during a routine check prior to 807's last flight a technician did not properly torque the fuel reference pressure line hose fitting which had been disconnected during this maintenance check. As a result due to aircraft vibration this fuel line fitting worked loose somewhere during the last phase of my flight and fuel pooled between the fuselage and engine. To give the Starfighter more lift on landing when full flaps are selected, hot compressed air from the last stage of the engine compressor is directed over the flaps. The temperature of this hot air is 900°F. When I lowered full flaps this hot air probably ignited the fuel air mixture which in turn ruptured other fuel lines. The explosion probably blew out the first fire but as other fuel lines were ruptured more explosions occurred and the fate of the aircraft was sealed. Witnesses on the ground

who were directed to the Starfighter because of the explosions stated there was a large plume of fire at the tail end of the 104. The aircraft flew for another two nautical miles where it flamed out due to fuel starvation and crashed in an open field. As for my injuries it was caused by either coming in contact with the canopy bow or collision with the seat during man/seat separation. The Board found that the 'D' ring cable should have been cut as soon as the ejection seat ejector straps function but there was enough of delay to cause a man/seat collision. Other words I was still holding the 'D' ring when I was pushed out of the seat and then I could have swung around and made contact with it. A modification to the timing of the 'D' ring cutting was ordered but I have no idea if it was actioned. Also modes were ordered for the seat pack lanyard and the container for the emergency radio. Again, I am not aware if this was done too.' Harrison 'was 'unserviceable' for eleven weeks and then returned to flying.

A particularly tragic accident occurred when the five Starfighters of 431 Squadron Canadian Air Demonstration Team was performing at the USAF Rhein-Main Air Base open house on 23 May 1983. The air base shared runway facilities with Frankfurt International Airport. As the four-plane diamond formation passed the show line, the solo aircraft flown by 27-year-old Captain Alan Stephenson in the 439th 'Sabre-Toothed

CF-104 104762 at the Mildenhall Air Fete in May 1981. It was with 421 'Red Indian' Squadron RCAF when it crashed on 9 June 1981 after striking trees during a simulated tactical delivery. The pilot, Lieutenant Kerry G. Cranfield ejected safely. On 4 June 1982 Captain Cranfield, now on 417 Squadron ejected safely from CF-104 104892 at Cold Lake after an in flight fire during an air-to-ground range mission due to improper maintenance when a broken afterburner fuel line caused a massive engine fire. (Author)

Tiger' Squadron at Baden-Söllingen prepared to perform two 360 degree turns with the last turn being a slow fly by. During the last turn, speed was reduced to 350 knots and in order to line up on the show line, Stephenson pulled a little tighter to prevent overshooting. At this point the aircraft appeared to pitch up and departed controlled flight as the nose pointed down. Stephenson pulled the aircraft away from the airfield to let it crash into a forest but unfortunately it crashed and exploded onto highway B43, a major road passing through a forested area within the city only a half kilometre from the city's main soccer stadium and adjacent to tennis courts where a tournament was being held. Parts of the exploding aircraft landed in the tennis courts and the engine, in particular, destroyed many cars in the nearby parking lot. Miraculously, no one was injured at this location but Pastor Martin Jürges and four of his family of five died in a car on highway B43 which was engulfed in the fireball. A niece that was able to escape the car

died 81 days later from severe burns. Captain Alan Stephenson ejected safely.

Brigadier General Dave Jurkowski, a Canadian Air Force jet pilot for thirty years, recalled. 'Like those before us in the 'Sword' (F-86 Sabre), 'Clunk' (CF-100 Canuck) and real war fighter eras, Canadians strapped into CF-104 Starfighters daily and consistently demonstrated the highest levels of combat effectiveness, achieving top scores on Annual NATO Tactical Evaluations and winning NATO-wide weapons and reconnaissance competitions. In the early 104 days, Canadian fighter pilots were well-trained to fly long-range, high speed, low level, visual or - more often - all-weather missions to deliver nuclear 'buckets of sunshine' to selected targets well into Warsaw Pact territory. A number of squadrons were also unsurpassed in their ability to fly reconnaissance missions. The DNA for both skill sets were handed down to those who continued to fly the 'Zipper' in the conventional role after the transition to the conventional role in the early '70s. As a consequence we were well trained to deliver conventional weapons at 540 KIAS (Knots Indicated Air Speed) a few hundred feet above ground level (AGL) on selected targets with tolerances of plus or minus three seconds and plus or minus 100 feet either side of designated bomb impact point. While we flew with the LN3 inertial navigation system in the early days we really relied on watch-map-ground techniques to make our time-of-day deliveries. And we were good at it.

'And so, it was serious business. That said there were many lighter moments and this is one 'war story' worth telling from which lessons might still be learned.

'Believe it or not, one of a handful of principles to which many fighter pilots subscribe is humility. The willingness to be on 'receive' rather than 'transmit' is critical to understanding one's abilities and shortcomings in air-to-air combat or while racing along a few hundred feet AGL in poor visibility at 900 feet a second. You'd better know exactly where you are and what you're doing. You'd better be constantly in the self-analysis mode if you erred. But sometimes, it was hard to be humble, especially when you were a young CF-104 pilot cut loose in Europe; especially when you were taught high speed, low-level navigation techniques over tough European terrain by the best in the business: reconnaissance (recce) trained RCAF pilots like Bud Berntson, Dan Graham, Larry Kinch, Roy DeWolfe and Gord Dejong.

'Now many nasty things have been said about 'Click click, you're dead' recce pilots and of course, I agree with all of them. That said, these luminaries in the mysteries of high speed navigation for snapshot sake had to be exceptionally accurate in capturing their targets in their camera pod at just the right time and angle in any kind of weather and on the first go. The information on their filmstrips and in their analytical minds would be critical to a post-strike assessment in a real war. These squadron Magellans were legendary, unbeatable and always on time with a quality product.

'As a newcomer to 439th Tactical Fighter Squadron (the 'Sabre Tooth Tigers') in the Cold War January of 1973, I listened attentively to the brain trust of recce nav techniques on a squadron that had recently re-roled from the recce to conventional weapons delivery mission. On the south 'marguerite' - dispersal - in Baden-Söllingen, I learned to build my strip maps using best terrain masking and nav checkpoints in countries where all the villages, church steeples and autobahns looked the same. Like my mentors, I learned to cut my maps as narrow as possible to force myself to fly accurate ground tracks and to minimize cockpit administrivia at 500 feet AGL at 540 knots over unforgiving terrain, checking six for commie

bogeys and still drop qualifying bombs from 200 feet AGL.

'I was becoming so confident finding my way around Europe at low altitude, I was able to cut my maps a whole two inches wide and roll them on pencils just like my teachers. I would often test myself by cutting my map with no headings, just minute marks and still make it to my equivalent 'EQ' targets within acceptable limits. I even learned to fly a map cut down the track line itself with only one side to cross-check for landmarks.

'Map preparation was an intensely personal craft. Once these 1:250,000/1:50,000 sets were built, you never, never let them go astray. One good reason was the Duty Ops Officer. When taking our turns pulling that non-flying duty day, some of us simply had to be amused by way of compensation for not flying, I suppose. Woe to the unsuspecting pilot who was foolish enough to leave his maps on the ops desk while he checked and donned parachute, helmet and spurs (Yes, spurs. But that's another story). Reason? Some of us held a secret but rapidly accessible cache of pre-cut autobahns, cities and lakes which we quickly glued on or near the flight path of the unguarded map. We'd also look for opportunities to take a felt-tipped pen to change 3's to 8's and 1' to 4's or 7's on headings for added spice! Many a cockpit had been awash in adrenalin and dismay as the owner of these vulnerable maps strained vainly through the ubiquitous haze for non-existent track checks. Ah, the good old days before digitally displayed maps!

'Now wise to the world, there was no question in my simple mind that I was well on my way to becoming a regular high-speed, modern day Jean Cabot of Central Europe renown.

'Then it happened; during the late summer of 1973. It was a single ship, low level, three EQ counter-clockwise sortie around Munich in pretty good weather.

'Notwithstanding our nav skill prowess, it was always prudent to dial in the TACAN frequencies of suitable Brit, US and Luftwaffe air bases along the route in case of emergencies. The bearings and distances of the non-precision Tactical Air Navigation (TACAN) systems could always be useful for a swift recovery in this single engine fighter. A reliable but occasionally fallible system.

'Turning south from a westerly heading with the German Air Force (GAF) Base Fürstenfeldbruck on my left, I could see the tree line on the banks

CF-104 104702, which was accepted by the RCAF in 1961, spent its whole career flying with CEPE (Central Experimental and Proving Establishment), 448 (Test) Squadron and AETE (Aerospace Engineering Test Establishment). It flew as a chase plane for Lockheed built Starfighter 12700 piloted by Wing Commander Robert A. 'Bud' White, who set the Canadian altitude record of 100,110 feet on 14 December 1967. Renumbered as 104702 after unification in 1968, the X on the tail was AETE's 'squadron' marking. SOC in 1983 it was put on display at the Joe Hoffner Memorial Park at Grand Centre, Cold Lake, Alberta.

of the north/south Leck River through the haze on my right. All was 'in ordnung' at 800 feet AGL and 450 knots ground speed. But strangely, the 'Fuersty' TACAN showed on the nose for a scant ten nautical miles. It ought to have been off my left wing for about 15 nm! I double and triple checked my ground references and quickly confirmed I was bang on track. After the distance ran down to five, then quickly to zero NM, no airfield emerged out of the haze. Must have been the occasional '40 degree lock-off' error. Another navigational mystery solved. A confident sigh of relief.

'But, pre-occupied with not running down an air base which might have been on the nose, I had instinctively slowed and was now some thirty seconds late! Unacceptable! And tough to make up in just a few minutes before the next leg. Too easy! I'll just make up time by accelerating and cutting the next corner of my slick two-inch wide map over familiar territory. Approaching the point where I had planned to turn east, then south, then west, I would instead, fly south off my map, turn

west at the appropriate time and regain track and time.

'Now in life, there are reasons for everything. Rules of Engagement. Hard and soft decks in air-to-air combat training. Standard Operating Procedures. Squadron Flying Orders. All there for good reason. So too are circuitous turns to the east, south and then to the west: Kaufbeuren! A GAF C-160 transport base!

'Happily making up time now at over 900 feet per second, I was jolted to see the Kaufbeuren control tower and runway at 90 degrees to my flight path on the nose at about 2 nm - a scant 12,000 feet and closing rapidly! No time to turn short. The best I could do was, well, just hope for the best!

'As if I could tip toe unnoticed around Kaufbeuren in a screaming 'Zipper' and - good grief - a large bright yellow squadron tiger painted on my tail! I did the only thing I could: quickly descended to below control tower catwalk, 'stroked' the afterburner, pulled hard left at 7g and ripped eastbound between the active runway and taxiway. I could see GAF C160s with their props turning moving about the airfield. I swear I saw exclamation marks and 'vas ist los?!' word balloons over their flight decks.

'Burner cooking and now heading east in the weeds at near supersonic speed in a sea of acute awareness, I clearly heard the heavily accented tower controller calmly transmit on Guard frequency for the whole world to hear: 'Nize goink Tiger! Skip Hit!'

'Normally reserved for successfully lobbing napalm into a 50' x 200' 'skip pit' target on controlled weapons ranges, the expression seemed mildly droll on an active airfield. Anyway, how could he have seen the tiger on my tail when all he could possibly see was the inside of my cockpit?!

'My career was surely ended! How could I have let this happen? And just when I knew where I was! And just when it would be tough to learn more!

'Back home an hour later, I waited nervously for the phone call which would signal the airspace violation, but more worrisome, the revelation to my colleagues. Derision would follow. My ego was already sore. Fate was cruel but unfair!

'The call never came, but did I learn something? Yes indeed. At least three things: don't get ahead of your headlights in life; there's a reason for

CF-104 12838 of 439 'Sabre Toothed Tiger' Squadron in yellow and black Tiger scheme striping at the 104 'meet' at RAF Greenham Common in the summer of 1977. (Air Portraits)

everything; and, there's still enough paper to go around for maps wider than two inches!

'I was never uncertain of my position again. Well, hardly ever.'

In the spring of 1986 the Canadian Armed Forces retired the Starfighter from its inventory. The rest of NATO followed suit and as Dave Bashow says 'the aviation world is a slightly sadder, lesser place for her passing.'

CF-104s 104824 and 104837, (which were sold to Turkey in 1986); 104843 (which became a damage repair airframe) and 104868 (which was destroyed in a hangar fire in 1984) of 439 'Sabre Toothed Tiger' Squadron at the Tiger meet at Gütersloh on 27 August 1982. (Thomas Westhoff-Düppmann)

Winning Their Spurs

Chapter

8

No matter what you call her, 'the F-104', 'one-o-four', the 'missile with a man strapped to it', she was quite an aircraft! A mistress, a temptress, she could lure the Belgian Starfighter pilots from a warm hearth, soft arms, hobbies, week-ends and even holidays, if she was 'available' to be flown.

ADC (Adjutant Chef, or Warrant Officer) Jan Govaerts, 350 ème /l Wing, a 2,500-hour veteran Belgian Air Force F-104 pilot.

The Force Aérienne Belge (FAè/Belgische Luchtmacht (BLu) received one hundred F-104Gs and twelve TF-104G two-seaters for initial training and instrument ratings. Jan Govaerts, who began the conversion course on the Starfighter at Waffenscule 10 at Jever, Germany and then became a member of 350 ème and an instructor, recalls that the Starfighter, of which his total time was 2,511 hours on type: 'Whatever she was called or whatever people thought of her, depended on what colleagues were flying - aircraft such as Fougas, Marchettis, Alpha-Jets, Mirages or transports. Mirage pilots regarded the F-104 Starfighter with disdain. Some of the Training Command instructors thought that to he threatened with a tour on F-104s was worse than being assigned to the salt mines! In West Germany Inspektor-General Johannes Steinhoff of the Luftwaffe called the 104 'a most exceptional aircraft'. Germany, one of the great users of the plane, put 916 Starfighters into the line, but lost 270 of them in crashes, killing 110 pilots. A sorrowful record but they were not alone.

'The Belgian Air Force had to recruit pilots to fly the Starfighter, which, as the Chief of Staff pointed out, was 'a very sophisticated aircraft with lots of electronics and so complex we can put this aircraft only in the hands of experienced pilots'. And this was why the first requirement to fly the Starfighter was 2,500 flying hours on jet aircraft. So far so good, but with all the polemics in the press and the fact that not all the Belgian pilots available were eager to fly an aircraft with such a background, the BLu was running short of candidates. This then was the main reason why the Tactical Air Command decided to recruit non-commissioned officers (NCOs) to fly the F-104! In 1963 an effort was made to stop recruiting

F-0104G FX-1, the first F-104G for the Force Aérienne Belge (FAé)/Belgische Luchtmacht (BLu), touches down after a routine test flight at Lockheed's desert jet base at Palmdale, California on 14 November 1951. This was the only Belgian F-104G to be produced and assembled by Lockheed. FX-01 was issued to 350 ème/1 Wing on 14 February 1953 and was used as instructional airframe at Saffraanberg from 1955 to March 1958.

NCO pilots. One general said that the 'IQ' of the NCO was not high enough to master an aircraft like the Starfighter. Another general said an NCO pilot flying one of my Starfighters - over my dead body!'

'At first, starting in 1963, Belgian pilots were trained at OAF Nörvenich air base near Cologne. Later on, in 1964, Belgian pilots like myself received their training in the Waffenschule 10 at GAF Jever, after having passed the ground school at Twenthe, in the Netherlands. The aircraft used were the F-104F and, from 1965, the (T)F-104G. The first one was really a flying rocket for high-speed performance. It had a limited instrument panel, no sophisticated electronics and no external load could be put on the wings. The second one permitted us to fly on instruments! Each pilot flew seven transition stages totalling six and a half hours and included a supersonic flight lasting 45 minutes, instrument and formation flying, a Mach 2 run and a solo test flight before soloing.

'The Mach 2 run used up much fuel! The F-104G started with 5,825lb but after start-up, taxi and run up, just 5,400lb remained and after take-off, acceleration on full power to 450 knots (in sixty seconds), fuel remaining was 4,830lb! Climbing on maximum power at 450 knots until Mach 0.9 and maintaining this speed until 36,000 feet (time, 95

seconds) used up another 700lb. After accelerating to Mach 2 at 36,000 feet fuel remaining was 2,705lb. Flying at Mach 2 at 36,000 feet for two minutes would leave 1,465lb remaining (at 50,000 feet the time would be 4min for the same fuel consumption). Returning to base at economical speed left 715lb of fuel remaining and a missed landing, overshoot, then landing, would leave 215lb of fuel remaining.

'Following successful completion of the seven transition stages the pilot then joined either 349 ème or 350 ème to begin Transition training on the F-104G (ten missions), followed by a radar transition (plus or minus ten missions), after which he attained operational status. When Belgium got its two-seaters in 1966, 1 Wing de Chasse/1 Jachtwing at Beauvechain began its own conversion unit called the 'Flight-TF', followed by 10 Wing Chasseurs-Bombardiers/10 Wing Jager-Bummenwerpers at Kleine Brogel. All technical information was then given by the Technical School at Saffraanberg near St. Truiden. When we started with our own 'Flight-TF' we used the same programme for new pilots with more than 2,500 hours jet experience and in the case of those with less than this requirement, twelve transition flights.

'In 1967 transition of the pilots to (T)F-104 instructors began. In 1968 instrument rating was

F-104Gs FX 05; FX 02 and FX 03 at the SABCA factory roll out. FX 05 of 349 ème/1Wing crashed at Samee-Dochamps on 20 June 1968 after power loss during a return flight from Bitburg to Beauvechain. Cdt Henri Vandegaer (Wing Ops) ejected successfully. FX 02 suffered several minor accidents in service, including a lightning strike at Beauvechain on 27 March 1975, the pilot, Adjutant Bart Boeykens was unhurt. It transferred to 3 ème/10 Wing on 6 June 1978 and was sold in January 1987 to RoCAF.

accomplished in the (T)F-104. Previously, it had always been done on the T-33 Shooting Star. In the early seventies, when we had very young pilots with an average of 300 hours' flying experience, we intensified this programme with more formation instrument flying and radar handling. As such, the pilot arrived in the squadron ready to start his operational transition with forty hours' F-104 experience.

'In the whole of my career (ten years instructor on F-104s), we experienced a few things that did not go right for four student pilots. One was a former fighter-bomber pilot who never did fly solo on the F-104. Pilot number two was a former instructor who ejected from a Starfighter during his training and who then decided to resume his career as an instructor! Pilot number three walked up to me after a formation training exercise and told me frankly, 'This is it. I can't follow it as it is too difficult for me.' I appreciated this very much since he was honest!

'Pilot number four was a former member of the 'Red Devils' on Fouga Magisters and an instructor. He was posted to 1 Wing but did not like flying the Starfighter. We soloed him for flying in the F-104 at night. The weather conditions were ideal but his recovery using GCA wasn't! He was too high

on the glide path and the controller gave him the call to overshoot. Panic-stricken, he continued on regardless and put his aircraft on the runway too steep and too fast. The undercarriage completely broke off and the Starfighter skidded along the

From 14 till late May 1973 there was a squadron exchange between 350 eme/1 Wing and Lightning F.3s operated by 111 Squadron at RAF Wattisham. F-104G FC 04 was TOC at Gosselies in April 1963, being flown to Beauvechain by Lieutenant Colonel Steve Cailleau (Wing Commander) for official acceptance ceremony of first 1 Wing F-104G. It went to 350 ème on 19 April. It suffered several minor accidents and an engine bay fire at Kleine Brogel on 13 July 1976 and thereafter was used as a loading training airframe at 10 Wing. It went to Beauvechain in August 1990 for gate guardian duty in front of the Officers Mess. (Serge Bonford)

runway on its belly. The amazing thing was the following day we looked over the runway and there was not a trace of a skid! The crippled one-o-four had skidded on the white centreline for about 8,000ft without leaving any marks whatsoever. Only when the speed had slowed did it leave the centre line in a shallow turn, to come to a stop close to the grass. The F-104 burst into flames and the minute the fire crew arrived, the ejection seat fired. The poor pilot fled in shock and some 500 yards away, stopped at the Louvain-Namur road waving his arms in the air. A driver stopped and picked him up and returned him to the base. The driver was a former fighter pilot who had been a member of 1 Wing!'

Typically, the Belgian Starfighters of 349 Escadrille/Smaldeel (Squadron, or ème) and 350 ème of 1 Wing de Chasse/1 Jachtwing at Beauvechain/Bevekom and 23 ème and 31 ème of 10 Wing de Chasseurs-Bombardiers/10 Wing Jager-Bommenwerpers at Kleine Brogel, were very adaptable. They were used in the fighter role as well as the fighter-bomber role. This way the aircraft and their very expensive equipment were never idle. It is interesting to note that the electronic equipment represented about 40 per cent of the total cost of the aircraft. The total cost of a F-104G at that time was 108 million Belgian francs. For a TF-104G Belgium had to pay 110 million Belgian francs.

Lieutenant Colonel Steve Cailleau became the first Belgian pilot to fly solo on the F-104G, at Edwards AFFS, on 24 June 1961. Two years later, on 18 April 1963, Lieutenant Colonel Cailleau, the 1 Wing de Chasse/1 Jachtwing commander, landed the first F-104 (FX 04) at Beauvechain. Next day Major Marcel Legrand, 350 ème Commander, made the first flight from the base, in FX 04.

Captain Georges Castermans was the first Belgian pilot to eject from a F-104, when he banged out on 16 July 1963. Bernard Neefs, the SABCA production test pilot, also had cause to eject, when he did so during an acceptance test on 21 November that same year. Jan Govaerts remembers the production test pilot: He was one of the first three Belgian pilots to qualify on the Starfighter in the USA and soon after left the Air Force to become a test pilot. As a member of the Auxiliary Squadron he was permitted to fly at weekends and even during weekdays. One day he flew an operational mission with 350 ème. Two pairs of F-104s took off for a sweep over Belgium. The first pair was composed of Captain Marcel Vanderstockt and Bernard Neefs was his wingman. The second pair consisted of ADC Willy Van de Perre and myself. The weather at take-off was not good and we were expecting very bad visibility with haze. Shortly after take-off we were informed that the weather over Beauvechain was rapidly deteriorating from a 'green' airfield state to 'yellow'. The two pairs rejoined the overhead position and since Mister Neefs was not used to flying in marginal weather conditions, Willy and I decided to let the other pair land first. The weather by now was really deteriorating and the control tower people suggested that we descend individually! Neefs went in first, followed by Vanderstockt. Both landed safely on Runway 04 left. When I started my letdown the weather state changed to 'amber'. While in the GCA approach and committed to landing, the state changed again, this time to 'red'! Thanks to my knowledge of instrument flying and experience in bad weather conditions, I made the runway alright and landed safely.

'Willy Van de Perre was next and he was told he could have only one try. Visibility was practically nil thanks to the haze. Poor Willy missed the runway and he had to overshoot. By this time his fuel state was so low that he told GCA that he was, 'Pulling up and bailing out!' As he reached 2,000 feet, the Kleine Brogel GCA, on stand-by to help Beauvechain, told Willy, 'We have definite contact with you. Fuel permitting, come in and land here. Our weather state is still 'yellow'. Van de Perre set course tor Kleine Brogel and landed there without further incident.

'Later that day, when the weather improved again, Willy Van de Perre flew his F-104 back to home base where he received a serious scolding from the wing commander, Lieutenant Colonel Marcel Legrand. The CO said, 'You should not have said that you were pulling up and bailing out!'

'Willy was really flabbergasted. After saving a valuable aircraft he was not even worth some sort of congratulation.

'When I reached the dispersal after having parked my aircraft I entered the pilots' room and saw my friend Bernard Neefs trying to drink a cup of coffee. I asked him, 'How did it go?' He looked at me and replied, 'You know, it scared the hell out of me. From now on I have the utmost admiration for you fighter pilots flying in weather like this. Never again. I will stick to flying at my test unit with 'blue' conditions -unlimited visibility and no clouds!' This was the last time we ever saw Bernard Neefs on the squadron. On 7 November 1965, the same year the above story happened, he crashed in a light aircraft at Genes, Italy and was killed.'

On 30 April 1964 His Majesty King Baudouin paid an official visit to 1 Wing de Chasse/1 Jachtwing at Beauvechain and he received his pilot wings from Lieutenant General Jan Ceuppens, Chief of Staff, Belgian Air Force. Twelve years earlier, Prince Baudouin, as he then was, had been taken aloft in a Meteor Mk.7. On 18 August Captain Pierre Tonet piloting FX 66 became the first of twenty-four Belgian pilots to be killed flying the F-104, after he entered a loop during a test flight at SABCA Gosselies and crashed onto a hangar at the base. The first squadron pilot to die was Captain Jacques Verhulst of 31 ème, on 27 January 1965 when FX 77 crashed between Helmond and Deurne (the Netherlands) during a low level navigation flight.

On 21 September 1965 the Air Defence Competition saw the first participation by 1 Wing de Chasse/1 Jachtwing's Starfighters. The team,

F-104Gs FX 40 and FX 17 of 350 ème/1 Wing in flight over the North Sea. FX 17 was TOC at Gosselies on 16 September 1963 and FX 40 was TOC at Gosselies on 25 August 1964. FX 17 was sold to Turkey as 9-039 on 16 July 1983. FX 40 was also sold to Turkey, as 083 on 25 February 1981.

FX 66, which crashed onto a hangar at Gosselies on 18 August 1964 during a looping maneouvre. The pilot, Captain Pierre Tonet the CEV/Gosselies-SABCA production test pilot was killed.

which was led by Captain Georges Castetmans and composed of Captain Piet Hallaux and Captain Emiel Baestaens and five non-commissioned pilots; ADCs Francois Bodart, Leo Mommens, Georges Goussens and Thierry Grisard took first place. Altogether, twenty-nine ADCs (non-commissioned officers - including ADC Jan Govaerts, the first Belgian pilot to log 2,000 hours on the F-104, on 24 February 1975) flew the Starfighter in the 1 Wing de Chasse/1 Jachtwing at Beauvechain and sixteen in 10 Wing Chasseurs-Bombardiers/10 Jager-Bommenwerpers at Kleine Brogel. All of them had more than 2,500 hours' jet experience, which was quite normal since they were never called away to a desk job. It is remarkable that none of the forty-five non-commissioned officers who flew the Starfighter were killed. In 1965 NCOs were no longer recruited into the Belgian Air Force. (The last two were pensioned off on 31 March 1987!)

There were other highlights in the 1960s. On 12 October 1965 the first air-to-air firing took place at Solenzara in Corsica. Jan Govaerts recalls: 'In the early days of the Starfighter we had to qualify pilots in shooting air-to-air and air-to-ground. The air-to-air period rook place annually in Corsica on a North-South axis east of the island. One month before going abroad every squadron had to exercise the pilots on the targets with the cine-gun camera above a more or less deserted area of Belgium. For air-to-air we commonly used a towed flag as a target with the Meteor and other jets, but in 1965 we were going to make use of a new system, known as the dart. At the time we did

not know that it was going to be such a pain in the arse! It was some sort of 'tetrahedron' fitted to the port wing. Next to it was a pylon tank in which the release mechanism was housed with 1,500 feet of cable. Extra fuel was carried in a tank under the starboard wing. The four wings of the dart were made of plywood covered by metallic sheets to reflect radar, in order to be able to lock on the target before shooting our Vulcan gun. Once in the air there was no danger of hitting the towing aircraft since the weight of the cable and the dart combined put it much lower. Due to its position, the dart could move up and down a few inches and ground clearance was such that care had to be taken on the takeoff run. The F-104 with a dart on the wing was limited to 15 degrees of flap (a mechanical stop on the flap lever reminded the pilot that using full flap was impossible!), this meant that the take-off had to be calculated to the 'nth' degree in a rather flat attitude! If we didn't, the dart fins would touch the ground and pieces fly off.

'On 12 November 1965 Captain Georges D'Hert took off and pieces of one of the fins went straight through the gap between the wing and aileron. The shock to the system was such that the dart failed to reel out! Once safely airborne, the pilot flew to the towing area, reeled out the dart

ADC (Adjutant Chef or Warrant Officer) Jan Goeverts of 350 ème/1 Wing.

F-104G FX 06 of 350 ème/1 Wing at Solenzara, Corsica with air-to-air gunnery practice firing dart attached, in 1965. On 6 April 1977 this Starfighter crashed during a practice bombing run over Vlieland after hitting a dune during pull-up. The pilot, Captain Fritz Hartmann of 31 ème/ 10W was killed. (Jan Goeverts)

and the F-104s could start their exercise. On return the tow-ship had to fly at 1,500 feet parallel to the runway to release the cable and permit the dart to fly into the ground. Mostly it did not skid down but crashed, which made it difficult for the armament officers to check if any scores were made on the fins with coloured 20mm ammunition.

'During four gunnery periods in Corsica I towed twelve times and six were successful. For example, on 27 October 1966, when I reeled out the dart, a hook came loose and flew into the rudder of my aircraft. Another time the reel-out was successful, but once behind the aircraft, the dart starred performing barrel rolls. Landing was another thing. Since we could not lower full flap we had to fly a higher approach speed - instead of the normal 175 knots we had to increase this to 195 knots plus fuel reserve, 5 knots/1,000lb of fuel. Returning with 2,500lb fuel left, the airspeed had to be 210 knots. The standing order therefore was 'No landing with the dart!'

'On two occasions in Corsica, the blasted thing did not come out and on 19 October 1965, Willy Van de Perre had to drop the whole system on the beach. Next day I experienced the same problem and I had to drop the system too. Some days later back at Beauvechain Captain Min Degraeve landed successfully with a hang-up. It was then decided that if they had a hang-up, experienced pilots could land the tow-ship with the dart still attached. On a later occasion an inexperienced pilot was mistakenly told to tow the dart. On

the way out to his Starfighter the strong wind whipped his notes for dart towing off his kneepad. He recovered the notes but they were now out of sequence. The first action should have been 'Reel out the dart', 'troubleshooting when stuck etc' and finally, 'emergency drop of the system'. Instead, 'emergency drop of the dart' appeared first and one and a half hours later a valuable piece of equipment was dropped into the sea!'

Peter Loncke, a F-104 ground technician, recalls: 'Most of the 10th Fighter Bomber Wing armament people came from the F-84F Thunderstreak to be converted onto the F-104 Starfighter. The leading edge of the F-104 wing was as sharp as a razorblade and more than once did I see people walk in with their forehead cut open after they had run into the wing! They used to load the .50 calibre machine guns in the nose of the F-84F, but the Starfighter, with its M61 Gatling Gun, was a plane our of the next century. The M61 gun was mounted in the left side of the Starfighter in front of the air intake and permitted easy access for maintenance. Compared to the .50s of the Thunderstreak, the M61 needed very little maintenance. The system had a built-in 'Gun Purge System' to blow out gases left by the fired 20mm rounds. This system took compressed air from one stage of the engine and blew all the gases out of the bottom of the gun compartment. To get the gun system operational you had to use 80 per cent thrust from the engine. This was checked by the armament people each time an aircraft left the maintenance hangar after an overhaul.

DUCT INSPECTION ACCESS

CAUTION
CHECK FOR FOREIGN
OBJECTS OR FORGOTTEN
TOOLS IN DUCT BEFORE
CLOSING DOOR

FINGER HOLES
PULL HERE

TORQUE FASTENERS
90-135 IN. LBS

F-104G FX 47 served on 23 ème/10 Wing and 31 ème/10 Wing. In 1989 it was stripped of all useful parts and on 15 July 1991 was presented to the Royal Army Museum (Aeronautical Department).

'One day in Corsica, one of the returning F-104s had a gun problem. The weather was not so good and it was late in the afternoon when the chief of the armament shop, ADC Cop, decided to check the system out on the flight line. He put on his raincoat and went to the aircraft, whose engine was already running. The pilot would rev up the engine to 80 per cent and fire the gun to see where the problem was. A voltmeter was connected to the firing contact of the gun to see if the 250 volt DC arrived at the firing contact. ADC Cop stood next to the gun in front of the air intake. (As all of this was done quickly, no intake covers were placed over the left air intake). The engine was using 80 per cent of its power and the Adjutant Chief standing next to the gun was sucked against the air intake! He lost his raincoat and his false teeth! No other harm was done as the engine was shut down immediately. The engine was taken out and inspected for damage. They found his rain coat inside the engine but his false teeth were never found!'

Also in Corsica (on 25 April 1978), FX 35 went to the range and fired a 2.75 inch rocket at a ground target made up of old car tyres. The rocket hit one of the tyres and one of them went

straight up in the air, right into the air intake of the F-104. It crashed into the Mediterranean. Second Lieutenant (Sous Lieutenant, or pilot officer) Freddy Antheunis, who ejected was rescued by a French SAR helicopter and arrived back wet but safe.

On 13 April 1966 the first flight of a (T)F-104G at Beauvechain took place with Captain Luc Declerck at the controls. Also, Captain Xavier Janssens flew Minister of Defence Charles Poswick in a (T)F-104G. On 30 January 1967 the first 'zoom' flight in Belgium took place when Lieutenant Colonel Etienne Barthelemy, Wing Commander, 1 Wing de Chasse/l Jachtwing, reached 62,000 feet in an F-104G Starfighter. On 14 March 1968 Major Marcel Lamproye and Lieutenant Colonel Etienne Bathelemy reached a record height of 80,000 feet in a Starfighter. Two weeks later, on 28 March, this record was beaten by Commandant Ludovic Forgeur, when his Starfighter reached 82,500 feet.

Jan Govaerts recalls: 'In 1967 a Starfighter squadron exchange between 349 ème and a Turkish squadron at Mürted near Ankara was planned. To avoid problems, the Wing Commander Flying sent two pilots - Major Georges Philippot and myself, both of 350 ème, on ahead on 7 March to prepare the groundwork. This was the first time that 1st Wing Starfighters had flown so far and it called for some intensive route planning. The two F-104s were equipped with only two extra fuel ranks. Our departure was delayed due to mechanical

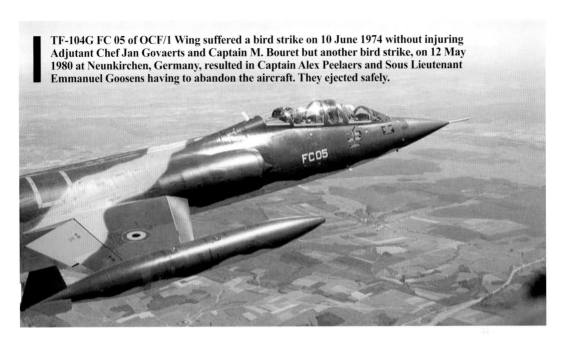

problems and we finally took off two hours late, at 1200 hours. This meant that the local time in Turkey was 1400 hours. We kept this in mind. We reached Grosseto near Rome after one hour fifty minutes flying time. Being in a hurry, we had no time to stop and eat and took off again one hour later for Tanagra near Athens, a flying time of one hour forty minutes. The Greeks were very friendly and offered us overnight hotel accommodation, but Major Philippot explained that we had to leave as soon as possible.

'We took off again and once we were above the Aegean we headed east at 30,000 feet for Izmir on the Turkish coast. Far above the horizon we could see the first signs of sunset. What worried me most, given the tension between the two countries, was the handover from Greek radar to Turkish radar. We radioed Athena control; we are leaving your zone now. Thank you for your co-operation.' Next, 'Joker' radar, this is 'Echo-Bravo 121'. How do you read?' Silence! We verified our radio and frequency and repeated the message. Still nothing! Darkness was descending and I asked my boss to put his navigation lights on steady dim because from now on I was going to fly in close formation. We had about an hour to go, thirty minutes of which would be in darkness. From time to time we called 'Joker' radar, without success! Luckily, our LN3 navigation system seemed to be working nicely and it gave us accurate information about Mürted distance and heading. All this time we

wondered if Greek radio had passed on our flight plan. (Much later we learned that the Turkish radar station normally closed down at 1715 hours but left a watch to listen out on certain frequencies, including ours. The watch heard our frequent calls but did not speak English.)

'After one hour of flight with the last ten minutes in complete darkness, I began to wonder if we would have to bail out. We had only about thirty minutes' fuel left and no ground control. And, were Mürted expecting us? My total flying hours on the F-104 at this time was 353 and I prepared for the first time to eject. All of a sudden a heavenly voice on the earphones indicated that Turkish radar were aware that we were overhead. Then I noticed through the scattered low clouds a concentration of lights. It was Ankara. Even without control we could descend, aim for the capital and from there fly on to Mürted. It was not difficult to pick out the airfield lights of Esenboga and I knew from the navigation charts that from there on in I had to fly in a westerly direction for Mürted. I called the CO and gave him my idea. His reply came back like a cold shower. 'We don't go down by ourselves. We need effective radar control!' I told him bluntly, 'If you don't go down, I will.' This seemed to convince him and he proposed to follow me in close formation. Throttle back, speed brakes out, I started to descend towards Ankara. The Hell with ground control. We broke cloud and levelled off at 5,000 feet.

'Mürted were expecting us, but not after 1700 hours. Major Bosran of the Turkish Air Force was waiting for us at Mürted but at 1700 hours had given up waiting for us and he drove home in his Volkswagen. On the road to Ankara he suddenly heard the unmistakable scream of the J79, jumped out of his car, ran to the nearest telephone booth and called the Mürted control tower to tell them to turn on the runway lights. My greatest worry was the surface wind. Landing downwind in a Starfighter is not that easy! I hoped that if there was any wind, it came from the east. Another thing was a 7,000 feet mountain nearby.

'We had made a thorough study of the local terrain before leaving home base and this is what saved us. We turned on finals and landed without any problems. Minutes later we saw the flickering lights of the crash crew accompanied by a Volkswagen 'Follow Me'. On stopping engines we were surrounded by Turkish ground-crew whom we could not understand, but Major Bostan arrived and talked to us in English. He welcomed us and was so excited that we had arrived at night and with no control in a visual circuit. He even added that the pilots on the base never flew when there was more than four eighths cloud and avoided flying at night. Next morning we flew home via Tanagra, where the Greeks were amused when we told them of our experience with the Turkish Air Force!

'The mess at Tanagra was closed so we still had not eaten when we took off for Grosseto, Italy.

Rome radar controlled us and steered us straight into a storm front with lightning, hail, snow and strong turbulence. Before entering the storm I went into close formation with Major Philippot. Seconds later my Starfighter experienced a power loss. A split second look at my instruments revealed that the exhaust nozzles were wide open. I pulled my emergency handle to close them again and resumed my close-in position. The approach and landing at Grosseto continued without further problems and we landed safely. Finally, we were going to eat! However before I could enter the mess I was called back to the flight line. An Italian crew chief had checked my aircraft and found nothing wrong. Static electricity had caused the exhaust nozzles to open. We got airborne again and headed for Belgium. Halfway I changed frequency and asked the chief controller, a neighbour in married quarters, to do me a favour and ask my wife to prepare me a big juicy steak. I was starving!'

10 Wing at Kleine Brogel never experienced a fatal or disastrous crash on landing. But it had to endure two major crashes during the take-off run. Most of the time the F-104G fighter-bombers from Kleine Brogel had to take off heavily loaded, as required for their low-level mission. Four extra fuel tanks on the wings and a bomb dispenser did not make acceleration easy. Every inch of the runway was needed to get the Starfighter into the air. Runway markers helped the pilots to check their rotation and lift the nose off at the time to become airborne. On 4 April 1968 1st Lieutenant

FX 52 which operated from 1964 to 1983 first with 23 ème and then 31 ème, was involved in a mid-air collision with FX 11 on 10 November 1981 but the pilot, 1st Lieutenant Yvan Janssens managed a perfect emergency landing at Kleine Brogel.

Lineup of F-104Gs of 23 ème/10 Wing with FX 42 nearest the camera, which crashed at Vlieland on 30 September 1970. The pilot, Sous Lieutenant Paul van Edom was killed.

Leonard 'Jim' Van Roy of 23 ème took off in FX 75, retracted the undercarriage and climbed to twenty metres. During the war in the Belgian Congo, Leo had earned himself the nickname 'Death' because of his armed sorties in a T-6 Harvard against rebels. Suddenly FX 75 dived towards the runway. Van Roy pulled up, but the Starfighter hit the runway in almost horizontal level. The pylon tanks exploded, Van Roy lost control and ran through the landing lights at the end of the runway. He started tumbling in the overrun and stopped in a field. Van Roy was killed. The accident was caused by a defect in the stabilisation system. About a year after Van Roy's crash, on 24 September 1969, halfway down the runway, Captain Guido Ghys of 31 ème in FX 71 noticed that he had insufficient engine thrust and abandoned the takeoff. He followed the emergency procedure by the book, but then his luck ran out. One after the other the emergency brake system failed and the aircraft continued straight ahead off the runway into the overrun, started tumbling when crossing the Peer-Kleine Brogel road and caught fire. Ghys reacted very quickly by using his ejection seat the moment his aircraft began breaking up and just before the aircraft was about to cross the road. The seat went out at about 90 degrees but the parachute had no time to open and he was found in a swamp outside the airbase, seriously injured and choking, but alive. Badly injured, he was confined to a wheelchair.

'From 1 May 1969 the Starfighter display team known as the 'Slivers' began representing the Belgian Air Force and displayed at international and national air shows and 'open houses' in Europe. Beauvechain was represented by Major Marcel Legrand, Major Bill Ongena and Captain Francois Jacobs, while from 10 Wing Chasseurs -Bombardiers/10 Wing Jager-Bommenwerpers at Kleine Brogel came Major Hadelin D'Hoop, 23 ème commander (killed flying a Starfighter on 9 September 1965), Captain Kamiel Goossens and Captain Wilfried De Brouwer.'

In 1969 Major Steve Nuyts and Adjutant Chef Palmer De Vlieger from 350 Squadron of the Belgian Air Force were selected to form a demonstration duo flying with F-104G Starfighters. One technician was also appointed to the team. On 14 May 1969, at graduation ceremony at Brustem AB, this new two-ship F-104 Starfighter aerobatic team performed its first demonstration. The name of the team was derived from famous Lockheed test pilot Glenn 'Snake' Reaves who proclaimed the F-104 prototype aircraft as the 'Silver Sliver' because of its long shiny fuselage and stubby wings. This nickname was also used by the Belgian pilots and so they decided that 'Slivers' was the appropriate name for the team. The 'Slivers' Starfighters were painted in two tones of green and tan with grey on the underside. The team's logo was painted on both intakes of the team aircraft. In 1972 this logo was replaced with the 'Slivers' inscription painted in white. The logo was replaced, since poor quality red paint in the logo would lose its colour after only a few flights. The 'Slivers' display was concluded with a crossing manoeuvre at speeds from 550 to 750 km/h. The pilots used the edge of the runaway for their display axis while crossing, with one of the pilots flying over the grass and the other over the runaway. At their crossing their separation distance was only approximately 2 metres apart. In July 1975, the 'Slivers' were disbanded, as Major Steve Nuyts was recalled for other duties and there were no other candidates to replace him. Up until that point, the 'Slivers' had performed 68 official demonstrations in five countries including Belgium, United Kingdom, Germany, France and Italy.

Legendary Belgian Air Force 'Slivers' Aerobatic Team member, William 'Bill' Ongena often performed a touch-roll-touch in a F-104G, a plane that was infamously difficult to control at lower speeds. Until Bill actually performed the manoeuvre, it was said to be impossible, though clearly it wasn't. Bill was the first of very few pilots to successfully perform it, though many

▌ **FX 14 getting airborne. This Starfighter crashed on takeoff at Dion-le-Mont on 20 July 1970. Major Guy Paulet was killed.**

subsequently tried, with some dying in the trying. Wolfgang Czaia once commented: 'He would approach the runway with gear and take-off flaps extended, touch-down briefly, apply full power and pull up to about 50 feet while initiating a roll on his upward trajectory. Then came a power reduction, possibly speed brake extension to slow down and descent to another touch-and-go. With the landing gear down, full aileron travel (20°) was available, producing a sufficiently good rate to complete a 360° roll without the nose dropping dangerously low. (With landing gear up, the aileron throw was only 10°). It was strictly a 'show' manoeuvre to demonstrate the controllability of the airplane and had no practical application. After Belgian pilot Jacobs was killed during a practice flight, the maneouvre was prohibited.' Bill Ongena tragically passed away, in of all things, a car accident, well before his time.

Ferry Van Der Geest flew the RF104 in the Royal Netherlands Air Force until the last day of F-104 operations. His squadron got the 104 in 1963 and

FX 11, which on 10 November 1981 with 350 ème was involved in amid air collision with FX 52 and crashed near the Dinant Dominican Abbey. Major Theodoor Theeuwen was found dead near the Mobelco plant at Neffe after his ejection seat chute became entangled. ▐

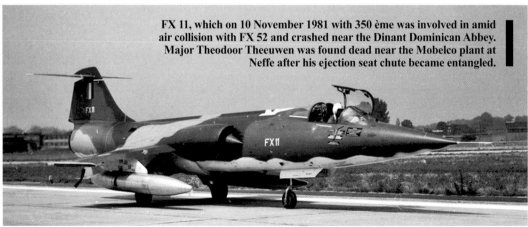

she was replaced in in 1984 by the RF16. He was with 306 squadron from September 1983 until May 1987. He only flew the 104 for 1.5 years with a total of around 320 hours. But according to him, as a young fighter pilot he had enough adventures with the 'Spillone' (Italian for 'needle') to fill a book. Ferry's comment: 'This famous touch-roll-touch was only performed in Belgium, one day a pilot had an afterburner (AB) blow-out and he crashed on the second touch, killing himself in the process. It is an extremely dangerous manoeuvre with no room for error whatsoever. The average touchdown speed is at around 175 knots and the use of AB is totally mandatory. So far no one has ever done something like this afterwards.'

Hans Van Der Werff flew the 104 in the Royal Netherlands Air Force, his total flight time on the F-104 is 2400 hours, though it's worthwhile to note that the RNAF uses actual flying time instead of block time, so for an apples to apples comparison with other pilots from other air forces, adding 10% is in order. Hans flew the 104 from 1968 until 1980. He was instructor-pilot, instrument rating examiner and test-pilot. From 1974 until 1979 he was the official demo-pilot for the F-104G for the Royal Netherlands Air force and he participated in over 100 flying displays. Hans' Comment: 'I did this manoeuvre (touch-roll-touch) a couple of times myself during training for my airshow. As you probably know I was the F-104 demo pilot for the Royal Netherlands Air Force from 1974 until 1979. Air-staff prohibited me from doing the manoeuvre after a USAF pilot crashed doing the same thing. Subsequently I would do a 'dirty roll' without touching. To do the manoeuvre it actually takes as much guts as skill. The low speed/low altitude was the main problem. And then the extended gear made the roll-rate a lot less. Also, because the roll was started in a climbing attitude, you had to take care that the roll ended slightly nose down to start the landing within the limits of the runway.'

The 'Slivers' gave their last performance on 11 July 1975.

On 6 June 1969 His Majesty King Baudouin visited No. 1 Fighter Wing at Beauvechain and expressed a wish to take the controls of a Starfighter for the first time. ADC Jan Govaerts recalls: 'It was not the fact that His Majesty wanted to fly the F-104 for a mission which included a high performance climb followed by a Mach 2 run that started a controversy, but the question, 'who is going to pilot the sovereign?

'At this time the flight (T)F consisted of a commanding officer and four NCO instructors, so it would have been normal to take the expert pilot with the most experience and that's where the 'shoe pinched'. ADC Leon Hanson was the most experienced bur was refused because he was an NCO! So, the commanding officer of the flight, Commandant Leo Lambermont, was chosen. This caused yet another problem. He was a very skilled instructor on Stampe/Vertongen SV4b in the Elementary Training School and had taken command of the flight (TF) at Beauvechain two days earlier and was not used to flying the Starfighter from the back seat. (T)F-104G FC-09 was going to be manned by the Commandant in the back seat with His Majesty King Baudouin in the front seat. To make things easy for our sovereign, a second twin-seater (FC-01) was going to fly in formation with FC-09. This was to be flown by the wing commander, Lieutenant Colonel Georges Castermans and myself.

'The weather was not too good with inversion reducing visibility to a minimum. The airfield state varied from amber to red but on top of the inversion, at 5,000 feet, we would have clear sky.

'After the pro-flight briefing we walked to our aircraft. The dispersal area was crowded with military personnel, journalists and high-ranking officers. Leon Hanson assisted HM with the strapping-in procedure and off we went.

'Take-off was made with full afterburner and we initiated a climb at Mach 0.92. At 5,000 feet we were on top of the inversion and the deep blue sky was clear of cloud. At 36,000 feet we turned left towards Bitburg, still in afterburner and we accelerated to Mach 2. At this point Leo Lambermont got excited and called over the radio, 'The King is Mach 2. The King is Mach 2!'

'It was time to get out of the afterburner range and proceed to home base. There was very little fuel left since the twin-seater had no external ranks and had only 4,500lb on start up! The weather state did not improve and we made an individual descent with a GCA (Ground Controlled Approach) for landing. We were down again with a very happy King after thirty minutes!

'Colonel Paul Dewulf, the station commander, walked up to me and told me that he was very sorry that we NCOs could not participate in the reception in the officers' club. Thirty minutes later he called me and told me to hunt down some NCOs since there were not enough officer pilots available to present to His Majesty! Sometime later twelve of us NCOs arrived at the officers' club. It was quite crowded and suddenly, the journalists and photographers were asked to leave the club and King Baudouin then asked the station commander to be presented to some of the pilots - the oldest,

the longest serving, the one with the most flying hours, the one with the most children, etc. Every time the CO looked at me and I pointed out one of the NCOs and even myself. Surrounded by twelve NCOs, His Majesty turned around, looked at one of the generals and said, 'Dear general, I thought you told me this morning that there were no non-commissioned officers flying the F-104!'

'The day that began so wonderfully well, was going to end with a tragedy. The same afternoon the weather cleared and Beavechain was going to participate in a fly-by over Brussels to commemorate the 25th anniversary of the 6 June 1944 'D-Day' invasion. 349 ème and 350 ème put up twelve Starfighters with two spares. One of the pilots was Major Wally D'Haese, visiting Staff pilot 1W, formerly of 349 ème. His aircraft was started when Wally experienced some trouble with his electronic equipment. There was little time left before the order to taxi, so he called the leader and said that he was going to take one of the spares. After the show over Brussels, Georges Castermans, the Wing Commander Flying, made a fly-by over the base with his wingmen at 2,500 feet at 450 knots. Overhead the base the unexpected happened. During the fly-by the aircraft encountered some turbulence and in Wally's aircraft (FX 55), the left undercarriage came out, ripping off the left flap and part of the wing. (In these early years of the F-104, the undercarriage was activated by hydraulic pressure and not locked up mechanically.) Miraculously, Wally was able to control his crippled aircraft and master it at a lower speed. Lots of pilots in the air gave him good advice over the radio. It was then decided to make Wally fly to the less populated area of Florennes and eject. One thing seemed to be overlooked. No-one told Wally to climb to a higher altitude. He maintained 2,500 feet. After Beauvechain, two F-104s remained with him. One was piloted by Andre Desmittere and the other by Andre Tribel, his wingmen in the formation. Suddenly, we heard them cry out, 'Bail Out, Bail Out!' Wally had ejected without telling his wingmen. Things went so fast. They noticed the aircraft diving down and never saw the seat fire.

'Airmen at Florennes starred to search the crash area and finally found the pilot with his parachute unopened. When he had changed from his original aircraft to the spare Wally must have forgotten to connect his parachute lanyard, which in the case of a bail-out pulls the ripcord automatically when the pilot is kicked out of the seat. Highlighted in the Pilot's Notes under 'bail-out', it says 'Try to beat the system....

'Thirteen days later, on 19 June 1969, FC-09 took off again in the hands of a student pilot, 1st Lieutenant Henri Loots in the front seat and instructor ADC Leo Mommens in the back seat. The mission was the same as 6 June - take-off on full afterburner and accelerate to Mach .9 to initiate the climb. It was a very impressive manoeuvre in the Starfighter. First you had this terrific increase in speed and then the pull-up. It was like putting the F-104 on its tail. Pulling back on the stick had to be done with a smooth but continuous jerk. At briefing we told the students never to check forward again at this speed. In FC-09, Loots did and the Starfighter started porpoising - a violent manoeuvre around the transversal axis which never seems to end. This movement is really scary with the nose going up and down the horizon. To stop it, by two white parachutes blossoming out. The whole thing took a couple of seconds but when Leo Mommens told the

story it took him an hour! Remarkably, the location where Henri Loots came down - at Mont St. Guibert - was the same place where on 13 March 1956 he had crashed his Meteor NF11! It was during a night mission and his two engines both flamed out after water in the Kerosene had frozen up his fuel filters.

'The F-104 was not an ideal 'dog-fighter'. Moreover it was a 'hit-and-run' fighter, which was due to its tremendous climbing speed and ability to accelerate to whatever speed was needed. This does not mean that as a fighter pilot you were unable to defend yourself against an aggressor. 'Air Combat Manoeuvring' held no secrets for us in 1 Wing at Beauvechain, but there were limits. One of these limitations was the ultimate angle of attack where the aircraft is no longer able to respond and flips over in the 'pitch-up' attitude, followed by a difficult-to-control spin. The book even said: A spin revolution will result in a loss of about 1,800 to 2,000 feet with each revolution taking five to six seconds and producing rare of descent of approximately 18,000 feet per minute. The aircraft should be abandoned if rotation has not stopped by 15,000 feet above ground level!'

F-104G FX 47 at Solzanara, Corsica during air-to-air firing exercises. FX 47 was TOC at Gosselies and issued to 23 ème/10 Wing on 25 April 1966. It suffered a Cat.2 at Kleine Brogel on 30 October 1981 when it lost part of the nose wheel during take-off. Lieutenant Yvan Janssens was unhurt. It went to 31 ème/10 Wing on 1 July 1982 before being stripped of all useful parts in 1989 and being presented to the Royal Army Museum (Aeronautical Department) on 15 July 1991. (Peter Loncke)

'An ingenious system prevented the F-104 from going into pitch-up. At a certain angle of attack the stick started 'shaking', warning the pilot that he was approaching a critical condition. This 'shaking' started at high angles in level flight and also in accelerated stall conditions, i.e. dog-fights, as well! If the pilot disregarded this 'shaking', seconds late the 'kicker' fired, pushing the stick forward with a jerk. On their first solo the F-104 pilots had to get acquainted with this 'shaker' and 'kicker'. There was an unwritten law that pilots had to take off with the 'Auto Pitch Control Switch' in the 'off' position to avoid inadvertent 'kicker' on take-off. Once the gear was up and the F-104 safely climbing away, we called the wingman to check his 'APC.

'In normal flying without flaps and on rake-off with flaps the pilot could have a 'shaker' and a 'kicker'. With the flaps in 'landing position' there was only a 'shaker' and no 'kicker'! On two occasions the Belgian Air Force lost a Starfighter because the pilots engaged in a dogfight with a Mirage with their flaps in the 'landing position' (to turn steeper). Both their aircraft went into 'pitch-up'. There was no 'kicker' to warn them and they had to eject!'

'Pitch-up resulted in the loss of three Belgian Air Force Starfighters. The first occasion was on 14 December 1966, when Major Emmanuel Kennes, CO, 350 ème, was killed after his Starfighter (FX 16) went into a pitch-up on the break. On 20 April 1967 Second Lieutenant Pierre Rassart of 349 ème ejected safely in a pitch-up after experiencing problems in a dogfight with a Mirage V.

'The third and last Belgian Starfighter lost as a result of 'pitch-up' occurred on 26 January 1971 when Captain Luc Declerck experienced pitch-up in FX 01 and had to eject using his C-2 seat. Declerck was to recall the events of this day twenty-seven years later in a conversation with Jan Govaerts:

'Some details of the mission I flew for 350 ème that day are not very clear any more bur essentially it is still there as if it happened yesterday. The pain in my back, which is unbearable at times, is more than an aid to memory. I took off on a 'freelance' interception mission under radar control. After two successful intercepts, the job was done. I set course to home base at 32,000 feet, when all of a sudden I noticed an acceptable target some 2,000-3,000 feet below. I had an ideal attack position and I decided to have a go! Seconds later, I was engaged in a dogfight. During a steep turn to the right with a bank of 60 degrees with manoeuvring flaps and the engine at the gate with full afterburner, the nose of my Starfighter pointed steeply above the horizon. It looked like a spin but I knew better; this was 'pitch-up'! Since the aircraft moved to the right, I pushed left full rudder and moved the stick fully forward. I selected 'flaps up' and shortly after, went back to 'rake-off flaps'. At this time the instruments were impossible to read. Everything was shaking very badly! The 15,000 feet of the Dash. I flashed through my mind and I remember having seen 16,000 feet on the altimeter. My position was above the Ardennes. Good heavens, there is no more flying. I grabbed the D-ring between my feet and pulled.'

'The ring fired two initiators. One ejected the canopy, the other started pre-ejection functions. In three tenths of a second this happened: Metal stirrups pulled Declerck's feet close to his body and held them until time of man-seat separation. Knee guards rotated into position to prevent his legs spreading and to counteract the effects of airloads. Arm support webbing flipped up and prevented outward movement of his arms. Moving up the rails, the seat hit a striker and - one second later - Declerck's lap belt was released, foot retention cables cut and the pilot seat reel operated.

'Forcible separation was actuated pyrotechnically by a windup reel behind the head rest. Sequenced with the lap belt release, the webbing was drawn taut between the head rest and the lip in two tenths of a second 'pushing' Luc Declerck out and away from the seat one second after ejection.'

Luc Declerck continues: 'Soon after I regained consciousness and saw lots of things twirling around me. I raised my eyes heavenward and saw, a few feet above, my ejection seat - my guardian angel, my angel in need.

'This was it. Free fall! Was this possible? Should it be like this? I moved both my hands towards my back to touch the parachute. Good heavens - nothing! It gave me a nauseating feeling. So this was it. No parachute. My career was going to end. So where was the film of my past life? Where was it? Everyone talks about it. Why couldn't I see it?

'Beat the system. Oh yes, another thing in the Dash-1 marked in bold face. I gave a jerk on the D-ring of the parachute. There was a jolt and the parachute blossomed out above my head. I was going to survive!

'Was there anything else to do? The morning weather forecast gave gusts in the area of up to 35mph so I thought I had hotter keep my bono dome on, but I decided to get rid of my oxygen mask. Below 15,000 feet I didn't need oxygen any longer. Of course then I realised why I need not have worried. The parachute would have opened automatically once 15,000 feet altitude was reached! How could I have been that stupid? I decided to keep my spurs on and would drop them when closer to the ground, but the survival pack had to be activated now. 1 pulled the handle and saw the dinghy blossom up below me! Wrong again! The whole pack dropped away out of sight. Did I make a mistake again?

'The ground came up very near now. Spurs away. I had the impression of falling horizontally. It was either the slope of the terrain or the wind that gave me this idea? Jesus! I missed the roof of a farmhouse by inches and I had to avoid a barbed wire fence. Bringing my feet up, I cleared this last obstacle. I should not have done this because I hit the ground very hard, so hard that two visors of my helmet slid down. I was so nervous that I had difficulty opening the quick releases of the parachute harness and the wind was so strong that it dragged me away from the spot.

'Once the releases were open I bundled up the parachute. It was all over now. I finally felt safe. The farmhouse I had missed by inches was a haven of refuge and the landlady offered me a much appreciated drink. It took me seconds to phone the authorities and I hoped that my aircraft had not caused anyone any harm when it crashed. Good news, it had crashed in open country and the wreckage was spread over a good square mile. People even found my spurs and my survival pack. Later that evening I was back in 350 ème, hurt, but in high spirits! My back injury is another story!'

Jan Govaerts pays tribute to the General Electric engine that powered the Starfighter: 'The good old J79 was a marvellous engine, powering the Starfighter like a rocket. With the afterburner going and with very little fuel remaining, you could really put the 104 on its tail and zoom it up. As far as I know in the Belgian Air Force, we never experienced an airborne engine failure. To take off we had to go full forward on the afterburner and this is where the fun started. There was only one way to light the afterburner and that was the 'good way'! With the pilot burner blazing in the exhaust the afterburner had to light and give you the 'kick in the ass', if you set the throttle position correctly! If not, the nozzle opened and instead of having thrust, it gave you the impression of

slowing down! Sometimes, it confused pilots so much that they aborted take-off. Sometimes they returned and said, 'This aircraft does not go into the afterburning range properly.'

'So, one day in good old 'three-fifty squadron' a pilot on his return from a mission noted in the Form 700 that his F-104 had difficulty going into afterburner. Short of aircraft that day the CO, Major Georges Casrermans took note of this, looked round and told ADC Guy Famenne to take the aircraft to the runway and perform an afterburner check. Guy was the youngest recruit in the smaldeel, with very little experience on the F-104!

'The aircraft, FX 18, was not serviced and had some 1,200lb of fuel remaining. Guy went to the hangar, picked up a test sheet and climbed into the aircraft. He did not strap in, started the aircraft, taxied out and had the safety pins of the launchers removed. After the control tower gave him clearance, Guy was told to go ahead with his test. He lined up on Runway 04 left, ran up the engine twice, taking note of the instrument readings and opened up the engine again. He lit the afterburner and went full afterburner (without any problems), released the brakes and let go!

'Noting down the readings was a matter of seconds and suddenly, he had a strange feeling. 'Boy, this aircraft was screaming down the runway and by God, he noted 180 knots on the airspeed indicator!' This was flying speed! Guy pulled the throttle back into full idle, got hold of the nose wheel steering and moved his hand forward to pull the drag chute. 'Blast! This aircraft was not serviced and there was no chute!

'OK, no sweat. He could always take the barrier, but once again a shiver went down Guy's spine. He had not strapped in and taking this barrier at high speed without straps would have killed him! So guy did the only thing that was left to him. He hit the brakes and hit them continuously. Luckily for him there was sufficient wind to help him aerodynamically and he was able to turn off the runway on the last intersection. Two aircraft were at that point on standby to line up for rake-off on 22 right and one of the pilots told Guy that smoke was curling up from his wheels! Guy acknowledged and kept taxiing. He came to a full stop right in front of the dispersal to have his launcher pins put in, when his tyres blew up! His squadron commander was a very interested bystander!'

This was not the end of F-104G FX 18's troubles, as Jan Govaerts explains: 'The F-104 was really

not an aircraft to crash land, so no-one ever tried. On landing, the Starfighter's nose had to be put down gently on the runway at the correct speed and nose wheel steering had to he engaged so that no shimmy was experienced. Pilots therefore had to avoid stalling the nose. Now, since the tail section of the Starfighter was a good target for crosswinds, the steering was very necessary to keep a straight line. Releasing the control in order to remove the shaking nose was the best solution. Another solution was to release the drag chute in order to lift the load on the nose but in doing this the terrible crosswind would take over and force the aircraft to one side of the runway. When the speed slows down the rudder control gets less and less effective, so that the pilot engaged the nose wheel steering again with the same result, very heavy nose wheel steering.

'On 23 May 1978 1st Lieutenant Jean-Luc Storder in FX 18 experienced a very heavy nose wheel shimmy-on landing. Part of the undercarriage broke away and the Starfighter turned over onto its back, trapping him in his cockpit. The fire crew were able to release him only after breaking the canopy with a crowbar. Jean-Luc managed to crawl out without injury. He was lucky. He must have looked death in the face and had a narrow escape!'

On 10 April 1981 the last official flight of the Beauvechain Starfighters of 350eme took place when Captain Philippe Callandt, 1st Lieutenants' Bart Boeykens, Mark Bongartz and Luc Van Landeghem flew the mission. A few months later, on 30 November, the first Belgian F-16 landed at Kleine Brogel.

'On 21 October 1982 ADC John Lemmens became the first and only Belgian Air Force pilot to log 3,000 hours on the Starfighter. The last flight of a Belgian Starfighter took place on 26 September 1983 when Captain Aerts (in FX 99) and ADC John Lemmens and 1st Lieutenant Steens (in FC-11) landed at Koksijde. Lemmens finished with the most flying time on the F-104, with 3,007 hours. Next was Commandant Fernand Dasseville, with 2,757 hours. I was third highest with 2,522 hours. Ten of the NCOs in Beauvechain were instructors on the F-104 and what is more, in the F-16 era, two NCOs of 10 Wing Chasseurs-Bombardiersl 10 Wing jager-Bommenwerpers became instructors on the Fighting Falcon at Kleine Brogel. Such was the situation in the early sixties. Later, in the seventies, considering the experience we had on the Starfighter, the Belgian Air Force accepted young pilots with barely 300 hours' flying total.

The final tribute to the Starfighter goes to Jan Govaerts: 'The F-104 used to be the hottest fighter for so many years and she could truly he flown high, wide and handsome. Some of her shortcomings were doubtless the result of inexperience on the part of those who designed and tested her and the political pressure that was exerted in the early years. In the hands of a capable pilot the Starfighter could chalk up respectable gunnery scores on towed targets. It was a good, stable, weapons platform and handled well under instrument flying conditions. Accidents happened, hut these never made us professionals dislike the Starfighter.

'One thing is certain; many genuine tears were shed into many a beer when the old gal's wheels were chocked and her big turbine wound down for the last time.'

Operational History
World-Wide Military Operators

F-104J Starfighters of 207 Hikotai of the Nihon Koku Jieitai (Japanese Self-Defence Force) passing Fuji-san.

■ Japan

In Japanese service the Starfighter, or the Eiko (Glory), as it was known, equipped seven Hiko-tais (squadrons) of the Nihon Koku Jieitai (Japanese Air Self-Defence Force, or JASDF), 1966-86. Altogether, 210 F-104J air-superiority fighters and twenty F-104DJ operational trainers entered service with the JASDF The first unit equipped was the 201st Hiko-tai, a provisional training unit, at Komaki Air Base on 22 March 1962, which after receiving its full complement of F-104Js, moved to Chitose in northern Japan in September and began training that December. Next to equip with the F-104J was the 202nd Hiko-tai, at Nyutabaru AB on Kyushu. Next, the 203rd Hiko-tai was activated on 25 June 1964 and it began assuming an alert mission in December.

F-104DJ trainers and F-104J single-seat models await delivery to the Nihon Koku Jieitai (Japanese Self-Defence Force) in the pre-flight hangar at the Mitsubishi Heavy Industries' Komaki plant near Nagoya. (Lockheed)

F-104DJ trainers and F-104J single-seat models of the Nihon Koku Jieitai (Japanese Self-Defence Force).

On 22 January 1965 the 203rd Hiko-tai received its first 'hot' scramble. These three Hiko-tais were followed by two more Hiko-tais - the 204th and the 205th (the latter activated on 28 December 1964). On 20 December 1965 the 206th Hiko-tai was activated and on 31 March 1966 the 207th Hiko-tai was activated, both squadrons forming the 7th Wing. Their alert mission began on 22 August 1967. The 201st and 203rd Hiko-tais formed the 2nd Air Wing, the 202nd and 204th Hiko-tais, the 5th Air Wing and the 205th Hiko-tai became a part of the 6th (Composite) Air Wing.

201 Hikotai F-104Js 46-8581, 76-8709, 38-0542 and 38-0543 from Chitose Air Base flying over Japan. (photo via JASDF Chitose Air Base)

F-104Js 46-8646 and 46-8640 in mirror aerobatic formation.

All seven Hiko-tais' F-104Js used operationally by the Nihon Koku Jieitai were optimized for the airborne interception role, normally carrying four AIM-9 Sidewinder AAMs and two underwing fuel tanks (no other stores were carried as the Japanese constitution bans weapons and aircraft with an offensive capability).

On 12 June 1981 the JASDF reduced its Starfighter Hiko-tais from seven to four squadrons, leaving 165 F-104J/F-104DJs to be operated by the 202nd and 204th Hiko-tais at Nyutabaru, the 203rd at Chitose, the 205th at Komatsu and the 207th at Naha. Beginning in December 1981 the F-104Js were progressively replaced by Mitsubishi-built F-15J/-15DJs. Some 27 F-104Js and five F-104DJs (the latter were used for spare parts) were acquired by the Nationalist Chinese Air Force on Taiwan. The last F-104J were retired by the 207th Hiko-tai at Naha in March 1986 and

F-104J '689' (76-8689) of 204 Hikotai of 5 Kokudan at Tsuiki AB leading an echelon formation in 1984.

sent to the Air Proving Wing at Gifu for storage. A number were converted to drone aircraft. During service from October 1962 to 1986 only three Starfighters were lost (including a mid-air collision accident.)

F-104Js 36-8533, 36-8648; 46-8640nand 46-8591 taxiing out.

203 Hikotai F-104Js 38-516, 46-8623 and 56-8671 from Chitose Air Base flying over Japan. (photo via JASDF Chitose Air Base).

In Jordan from 1967 until 1983 the F-104 equipped
9 Squadron RJAF at Prince Hassan Air Base and 25
Squadron RJAF at Mwaffaq Salti.

Royal Jordanian Air Force F-104s on
display in Jordan.

Jordan

Jordan acquired 29 F-104As and four F-104Bs
delivered under the Military Assistance Program
in 1967; 15 and three of which respectively, were
formerly operated by the Nationalist Chinese Air
Force in Taiwan until late in 1966. Initial deliveries
to the Al Quwwat Aljawwiya Almalakiya
Alurduniya (Royal Jordanian Air Force) were
begun in the spring of 1967, to 9 Squadron at
Prince Hassan Air Base. Two days before the June
1967 Six-Day Arab-Israeli war the US removed the
F-104s temporarily to Turkey. After the war ended
the US refused to return the Starfighters to Jordan

but after it appeared that King Hussein might turn
to the Soviet Union and accept MiG-21s, the US
relented and agreed to supply Jordan. Reissue of
the (now refurbished) F-104As and four F-104Bs
to 25 Squadron at Mwaffaq Salti Air Base began
in mid-1969. One of the Jordanian Starfighters
saw combat during the failed coup against King
Hussein in November 1972. The F-104/Bs were
gradually replaced by the Northrop F-5E Tiger II
and the last Starfighters were finally replaced by
Dassault Mirage FICJs in 1982-83.

■ 252

PAF F-104A 56-0803 and 56-0805, an ex-83rd FIS Starfighter at Hamilton AFB, San Francisco which was sent to Pakistan on 21 June 1961, where on 9 Squadron, it was lost on 10 July 1968 due to a ground fire in the starter unit which became uncontrollable and burned out the aircraft. The pilot, Squadron Leader Asif Iqbal, escaped unhurt.

▍Pakistan (see Chapter 10)

Pakistan remained an important ally of the United States through the Cold War and was the first non-NATO country to equip with the Starfighter after Soviet premier Nikita Khruschev threatened to drop a nuclear bomb on Peshawar following the U-2 incident on 1 May 1960. In August 1961 the PAF received ten refurbished F-104As and two F-104Bs, all supplied under the US Military Defense Assistance Program (MAP), to protect the city from high flying Soviet bombers. At PAF's request, all its F-104As were refitted with the M-61 Gatling 20mm gun. The more powerful GWE- J79-11 engine was also installed on the aircraft. This made the Pakistan F-104s somewhat unique: they had the gun and being the lightest of F-104 series with a more advanced J79 engine enjoyed the best thrust-to-weight ratio.

PAF Starfighter leaving for an ▍
operational sortie.

The PAF Starfighters were the first Mach 2 capable aircraft in Asia. Even in Europe at this time, most countries were still flying subsonic aircraft and many questioned Pakistan's ability to fly and maintain such a sophisticated aircraft as the F-104A/B. The only Pakistan Air Force (PAF) unit to be equipped with the F-104 was No. 9 Air Superiority Squadron, which became an elite unit, its personnel handpicked from F-86 Sabre squadrons. The in-commission rate of the F-104 during the first five years of service was over 80% and all its systems performed with high reliability. The fighter was employed in the air-to-air role by the PAF and was used extensively for aerial gunnery against both banner targets and the Dart targets with excellent scores. In strafing attacks the M-61 gun was superbly accurate.

9 Squadron lost only one Starfighter during training when Flight Lieutenant Asghar 'pitched up' and went into an uncontrollable spin during an air combat training sortie. He ejected safely at high speed and received major bruises. This F-104A was replaced under the MAP programme. Also, Flight Lieutenant Syed Khalid managed a 'dead stick' landing after an engine flame out in another F-104A.

By September 1965 when hostilities broke out with its immediate neighbour India the PAF had

Flight Lieutenant Asghar Khan pilot proudly poses with his Starfighter. ▌

only 150 aircraft (including 102 F-86Fs), while the Indian Air Force (IAF) possessed approximately 900 aircraft. PAF Starfighters were used throughout the wars with India in 1965 and in 1971 (see Chapter 10). During the 1965 Pakistan-India War they flew a total of 246 hours and 45 minutes while during the 1971 War the F-104s flew a total of 103 hours and forty-five minutes. The F-104 Starfighters remained in service with Pakistan Air Force for twelve years and flew 11,690 hours Late in 1972 the PAF decided to phase the F-104 out of service after the inventory had been decimated as a result of a US Government arms embargo which made it increasingly difficult to maintain a reasonable in-commission rate on the F-104A/Bs.

▌ **F-104A 56-0798 of the Pakistan Air Force on display at the Pakistan Air Force Museum at Faisal AB, Karachi.**

■ Spain (which joined NATO in 1982)

Under the terms of the Military Assistance Program (MAP) Spain received in 1965, eighteen C.8 and three CE.8 Starfighters (Canadair-built F-104Gs and Lockheed TF-104Gs respectively). These served with a single squadron in the Ejército del Aire (Spanish Air Force) which operated these aircraft at Torrejón between February 1965 and 31 May 1972. As 61 Escuadrón (Ala no.6), the F-104s were operated February-April 1965, when the unit was renumbered 161 Escuadrón (Ala no 16). On 29 November 1967 the unit was renumbered 104 Escuadrón (Independent) and operated as such until 27 May 1971 when it became 104 Escuadrón (Ala no.1^2) (for just five days) then finally, 122 Escuadrón (Ala no.1^2). The F-104G/TP-104Gs

Canadair-built F-104Gs (C.8) 63-2720, 63-2279 and 63-2717 of the Ejército del Aire (Spanish Air Force) in formation.

were replaced in service by two squadrons of the F-4C Phantom II and in 1972 the Spanish Starfighters were returned to the USAF for transfer to Greece and Turkey. In 1972 eight P-104Gs and two RF-104Gs were transferred to Turkey, while Greece received nine F-104Gs and one TF-1040 previously operated by the Ejército del Aire. Spain was unique among the European operators of the Starfighter since it never lost an aircraft during their 17,060.35 hours of operational use; which owed much to the fact that they were used only in its intended role of an interceptor and mainly in very good flying weather.

Eighteen C.8 and three CE.8 Starfighters (Canadair-built F-104Gs and Lockheed TF-104Gs respectively) served with the Ejército del Aire, March 1965-May 1972. These C.8 Starfighters - 62-12733, 62-12716, 62-12715 and 62-12720 - are from 161 Escuadrón (Ala n.il6), which operated these aircraft at Torrejon from April 1965 until 29 November 1967, when the unit was renumbered 104 Escuadrón (Independiente/Ala n.il2). (Lockheed)

104-12 and 161-14 of 104 Escuadrón at Torrejón AB in 1968. The Ejército del Aire (EdA) Starfighters had the distinction of operating without a single accident during their seven years of service. . In May 1972 all twenty-one Spanish Starfighters were returned to the USAF for transfer to Greece (ten) and Turkey (eleven).

Taiwan

Altogether, the Republic of China Air Force (RoCAF) of Taiwan received a total of 281 Starfighters: 46 F-104As; eight F-104Bs; six F-104Ds; 115 P-104Gs (including 37 from the Luftwaffe, 14 from Belgium (used for spare parts) and three from Turkey); 49 TF-104Gs (including 27 ex-Luftwaffe machines following the closure of its Starfighter training facility at Luke AFB, Arizona, nine ex-BLu (Belgian Air Force) two-seaters (used for spare parts) and three ex-KDF - Royal Danish Air Force - two-seaters); 25 RF-104Gs (including three ex-Luftwaffe aircraft); and 27 ex-JASDF F-104Js and five F-104DJs under the 'ALISAN 9' project in 1978 (five of the F-104Js were used for spare parts).

The first two Starfighters (F-104B-5-LOs) were delivered in May 1960 and were serialled 4101 and 4102 respectively. Between August and September that year seven F-104As were received and in October, two more F-104B-5-LOs were delivered. (A fifth F-104B, 57-1296, was delivered in October 1963 as an attrition replacement - four F-104As and two F-104Bs being lost in crashes 5

May 1961-10 October 1964 and eight pilots killed.) A further hatch of fifteen F-104As was delivered between late November 1960 and early January 1961. All these Starfighters were used to equip No.8 Squadron as part of the 3rd TFW at Ching Chuang Kang (CCK) Air Base in central Taiwan.

RoCAF TF-104 with instructor and trainee pilots.

From 1961 to 1962 and in 1964 a number of F/TF/RF-104Gs, fitted with Martin-Baker Mk.7A ejection seats were ordered. The first Canadair-built Starfighter for the RoCAF (63-12728) first flew on 7 October 1964 and was given the serial 4333. The Gs were used to re-equip 8 Squadron at Ching Chuang Kang (CCK) Air Base and also to replace the Sabres of Nos. 7 and 28 Squadrons. On 13 January 1967 four Republic of China Air Force F-104Gs engaged a formation of eight MiG-19s of the People's Liberation Army Air Force over the disputed small archipelago of several islands called Kinmen or Quemoy, administered by the Republic of China. Major Hu Shih-lin and Captain Shih Bei-puo each shot down a MiG-19. This marked the first uncontested F-104 combat victory in the world. One F-104 did not return to base and its pilot was listed as MIA.

RoCAF Starfighters lined up for as far as the eye can see. F-104G 4312 (62-12215) crashed on 1 June 1992 due to a stall during landing. 4310 (62-12260) crashed on 4 December 1967 in unknown circumstances.

F-104Gs 4344 (64-17770) and 4319 in late grey camouflage of 8 TFS of 3 Wing ROCAF at Hsinchu AB in 1989. 4344 scored a J-6 (MiG-19) kill on 13 January 1967 with an AIM-9B AAM. This Starfighter is displayed at the RoCAF Academy in Taipei, Kaosiung.

President Nixon's visit to Mainland China in 1978 resulted in much closer ties with the United States while the introduction of more modern aircraft to Taiwan was delayed for fear of upsetting the Communist regime. As a result, Taiwan broke off diplomatic relations with the US and it was forced to source its Starfighters from further afield. They came not just from NATO nations, but also from Japan and Taiwan was able to replace its aging F-100A Super Sabres with, albeit, somewhat 'weary' Starfighter aircraft. The 'new' F-104s replaced the F-100As in 41 Squadron of the 2nd Tactical Fighter Wing at Hsinchu and Starfighters were also issued to Nos. 42 and 48 Squadrons and to Nos. 7, 8 and 28 Squadrons of the 3rd TFW. Four of the ex-JASDF Starfighters were lost, including

one while en route from the overhaul facility at Ping Tung South to Ching Chuang Kang (CCK) Air Base. On 5 December 1990 the commander of the RoCAF was killed when 4511 reportedly disintegrated during flight.

At the end of 1986, Starfighters still equipped three interceptor/strike squadrons and one reconnaissance squadron. By early 1994 the surviving Starfighters were operational with the 41st, 42nd and 48th Tactical Fighter Squadrons of the 499th Tactical Fighter Wing at Hsinchu (with F-104Gs); the 7th, 8th and 35th TFSs of the 427th Tactical Fighter Wing (F-104G) and the 28th, a training unit (with a mix of TF-104Gs and F-104Gs), at Ching Chaung Kang (CCK) Air Base; and the 12th (Reconnaissance) Squadron

Ex-Luftwaffe TF-104Gs 4178 (61-3082) and 4179 (61-3083) at the head of the long line of RoCAF Starfighters. Both these TF-104Gs are displayed in the military cemetery at Li Jia (Martyr's Shrine) at Tai Tung City.

(operating as part of the 6th TRG with RF-104Gs) of the 401st Tactical Composite Wing (largely equipped with the F-5E Tiger II), at Taoyuan.

After serving with the RoCAF for thirty-eight years, the F-104 was officially withdrawn from service. The first F-104 unit removed from service was the 427th TFW, which started to convert to F-CK-1s in 1993. Then in May 1997 the 499th TFW at Hsinchu AB started to replace its Starfighters with Dassault Mirage 2000-5s for the interceptor role. Before F-104s' retirement, the 12th TRS was the sole F-104 operator and the unit was relocated from Taoyuan AB to Hsinchu AB. The last two operational RoCAF Starfighters, TF-104G 4186 and 4196, departed Hsinchu for CCK on 8 May 1998 for the decommissioning ceremony held at Ching Chuang Kang Air Base (AB) on 22 May. CCK air base is home to the 8th TFS, the

flyable and were cannibalized for spare parts only. In its heyday, the F-104 equipped the 7th, 8th, 28th TFS of the 427th TFW at CCK AB, the 41st, 42nd, 48th TFS of the 499th TFW at Hsinchu AB and the 12th TRS at Taoyuan AB.

As the RoCAF is more conservative compared with other air forces in the free world, those lavish overall special paint schemes seen at special occasions in foreign countries were a rarity in Taiwan and the F-104 retirement ceremony is no exception. Nonetheless, seven F-104s were painted with fin markings corresponding to the seven former Starfighter squadrons to mark this event. The first F-104G of the RoCAF, 4301 (62-12250), featured the 'Wolf' squadron badge of the 7th TFS. F-104A 4253 (56-0833) came out of the 'Alishan 6' project and sported the 'Flying Dragon' marking of the 8th TFS. Although now with its

Canadair-built 4342 (64-17764) in the RoCAF which crashed on 24 July 1984 45 NM west of Ching Chuan Kang AB. The pilot, Chang Tsong-Tien, was killed.

first RoCAF squadron to operate the F-104. Now equipped with the F-CK-1 Ching Kuo (aka IDF), the 8th TFS took delivery of its first F-104s (A and B models) on 17 May 1960. It was for this reason that the ceremony was held at CCK, rather than Hsinchu AB, where the last operational F-104s had been based.

The RoCAF's F-104 programme was run under the code name 'Alishan' (Mountain Ali), from Alishan 1 to Alishan 11. The RoCAF had acquired 247 F-104s through the 'Alishan' Programme. These F-104s were mostly second-handed, their sources including USA, Canada, Germany, Japan, Denmark and Belgium. The versions ranged from F-104A, B, D, G, J, DJ, RF-104G, to TF-104G. Some of these aircraft obtained were not even

engine stripped, 4253 used to be equipped with the J79-GE-19, the most powerful engine ever used by the F-104A. TF-104G 4147 (61-12236), which had accumulated 6000 flying hours before it retired, was painted with the 'Baby Dragon' badge of the 28th TFS on its fin. However, its serial number was wrong and should be 61-03030. The three aircraft just mentioned were gate guards of CCK AB. So it is likely that 4147 got the wrong serial number when it was refurbished for this event. Joining the display during the ceremony, TF-104G 4186 (63-08458) retained its 'Peeping Yellow Lion' of

Ex-Luftwaffe F-104G 4400 (67-22517) and RF-104G 4375 (63-13254) ready for takeoff. 4400, which was modified to RF-104 LOROP 'Stargazer' is displayed at a park in Xihu Township, Chyanghua County. 4375 is on Gate Guard duty at Hualian AB (RCYU).

the 12 TRS and had the distinction of being one of the two last flying RoCAF Starfighters. F-104G 4378 is another 'problematic' aircraft because its serial number should be 63-13260, rather than 65-13260 shown. Its fin was painted with the 41st TFS marking for this occasion, although it was converted to RF-104G after it had been delivered to the RoCAF and served with the 12th TRS. TF-104G 4193 (63-08467) wore the 'Eagle' badge of the 48th TFS. Also converted to RF-104G, F-104G 4400 (67-22517) was applied with the 'Snake and Maple Leaves' marking of the 42nd TFS.

The retirement ceremony was presided over by the RoCAF Commander-in-Chief, General Hsien-Jung Huang. At the beginning of the ceremony, a four-ship formation consisting of one AIDC F-CK-1B (Ching-Kuo)/(Indigenous Defence Fighter), one RF-5E, one F-16B and one Mirage 2000-5Di, made a low-level flypast salute. But for safety concerns, none of the F-104s performed aerial demonstrations. The highlight of the show was provided by TF-104G 4186, with the 499th TFW Commander Major General Kuang-Yueh Geh in the back seat, which fired up its J79 engine for the last time and slowly taxied to the apron where the ceremony was held. Major General Geh then presented an F-104 model to the RoCAF C-in-C, signifying that RoCAF Starfighters had finally come into history after accumulating 380,000 flying hours in total. After the ceremony, the RoCAF hosted a reception in a hanger, where F-104G 4371 (63-13249) was displayed.

Ex-Luftwaffe TF-104G 4186 (63-8458) of the RoCAF.

The 'Wicked One'

Even before its introduction to combat the Starfighter had gained such a reputation in the IAF that it was known as the 'hadmash', 'scoundrel' or 'wicked one.

Since Partition of British India in 1947, Pakistan and India remained in contention over several issues, not least the disputed region of Kashmir. On 5 August 1965 between 26,000 and 33,000 Pakistani soldiers crossed the Line of Control dressed as Kashmiri locals headed for various areas within Kashmir. Indian forces, tipped off by the local populace, crossed the cease fire line on 15 August. Initially, the Indian Army met with considerable success, capturing three important mountain positions after a prolonged artillery barrage. At that time the Pakistan Air Force (PAF) had about 140 combat aircraft, mostly American-built, including the F-104As of 9 Squadron. Pakistan acquired its Starfighters as a direct result of the Soviet downing of an American Lockheed U-2C spy plane that had been based at the US airbase at Badaber (Peshawar Air Station) on 1 May 1960. On 28 April the U-2C

was ferried from Incirlik Air Base in Turkey to Peshawar airport by pilot Glen Dunaway. Fuel for the aircraft had been ferried to Peshawar the previous day in a US Air Force C-124 transport. A US Air Force C-130 followed, carrying the ground crew, Central Intelligence Agency pilot Captain Francis Gary Powers and the back-up pilot, Bob Ericson. On the morning of 29 April the crew in Badaber was informed that the mission had been delayed one day. As a result, Bob Ericson flew the U-2C back to Incirlik and John Shinn ferried another U-2C from Incirlik to Peshawar. On 30

A line of PAF F-104A Starfighters. Squadron Leader Bhatti flying 56-0879 nearest the camera, on 4 December 1971 claimed an Indian Air Force Su-7 'Fitter' over Amritsar. This Starfighter is preserved on pole at PAF HQ Chaklala, Islamabad.

April, the mission was delayed one day further because of bad weather over the Soviet Union. The weather improved and on 1 May, 15 days before the scheduled opening of the east–west summit conference in Paris, Powers took off in 56–6693 on Operation 'Grand Slam' to overfly the Soviet Union, photographing targets including the ICBM sites at the Baikonur Cosmodrome and Plesetsk Cosmodrome and then land at Bodø in Norway. The U-2 flight was expected and was hit by an S-75 'Dvina' (SA-2 'Guideline') surface-to-air missile and crashed in Sverdlovsk.

The incident severely compromised Pakistan's security and worsened relations between it and the United States. Understandably annoyed at the Pakistanis for allowing the Americans to use their country as a base for espionage missions, the Soviets threatened to target Pakistan for nuclear attack if such activities continued. Taking the threat seriously, the United States agreed to provide Pakistan with enough surplus F-104A interceptors to equip one squadron.

The first three pilots selected to undergo type conversion in the United States included Squadron Leader Mervyn Sadruddin, Flight Lieutenant Mervyn Middlecoat and Flight Lieutenant Alauddin 'Butch' Ahmed. Sadruddin was sent to George AFB, California, east of Los Angeles) and spent time with 434 TFS, 479 TFW. This was part of 'on the job' training as an executive officer for a squadron for six to seven months. Towards the end of the stay he transitioned to F-104s and flew about 22 hours on the aircraft while in the USA (4-6 hours on dual and rest solo). Since the F-104As in US service were nuclear weapon capable, USAF considered stripping the aircraft of this equipment before allowing Sadruddin to go solo but later decided against this. During this timeframe Sadruddin also became the first Pakistani to fly at Mach 2. The other two pilots went to an Air National Guard unit in South Carolina for type conversion. The fully assembled aircraft were sent by ship to Pakistan where they arrived at Karachi harbour in August 1961.

Before these newly delivered Starfighters could scream through Pakistani skies at Mach 2, they had to undergo a more mundane journey i.e. travel on Karachi roads from the harbour to PAF Station Drigh Road (now called PAF Base Shahra-e-Faisal). This was done by towing aircraft with tractors during the night, with pilots sitting in the cockpit during this journey to apply aircraft brakes if necessary. The time also marked the arrival of USAF test pilot Major Swart Nelson who checked out the three PAF pilots after which the aircraft were ferried to PAF Station Sargodha (now PAF Base Mushaf).

At Sargodha these aircraft re-equipped PAF's 9 'Griffins' Squadron which was re-formed on 15 August 1947 just a day after Pakistan's independence. In 1961 the squadron was the last operational unit still flying Sea Fury aircraft while all other PAF squadrons had converted to jets. Perhaps to compensate its oldest squadron for such neglect, it was decided by Air Headquarters to equip it with the first Mach 2 capable jet in PAF's inventory. Squadron Leader Sadruddin took over as the squadron commander of the re-equipped 9 Squadron with Flight Lieutenant Alaudin Ahmed as his flight commander. Other pilots included Flight Lieutenant Jamal A. Khan, Flying Officer Farooq F. Khan, Flight Lieutenant Hakimullah, Flying Officer M. M. Khalid, Flight Lieutenant Arif Iqbal, Flight Lieutenant Hashmi, Flying Officer Amjad Hussain and Flying Officer M. Akbar. The squadron was at the same time joined by two US Air National Guard pilots, who along with the already converted first three PAF pilots helped convert other PAF pilots to F-104s. That PAF senior commanders literally led from the front is demonstrated by the fact that the Air Marshal Asghar Khan (PAF C-in-C at the time) and some other senior officers attended the relevant ground school and undertook number of familiarization flights on the aircraft. The conversion course included 2-3 weeks of academic classes followed by a few rides in F-104Bs and final check rides in a single seater. Once the pilot was qualified, an initial training period consisting of 40-50 sorties commenced. This included navigation, formation flying, gunnery, air combat manoeuvring and interceptions.

F-104s clearly surpassed the F-86F Sabres in PAF inventory in terms of performance and represented the cutting edge of aviation technology at that time. Although the Sabre was loved for its beautiful handling and manoeuvrability, Starfighter's performance remained unmatched till the induction of F-6 and Mirage aircraft later in the decade. Though very advanced at the time, the avionics of the aircraft suffered from limitations inherent with late 1950 and early 1960s technology. The impressive sounding Infra Red (IR) sight and

Airborne Intercept (AI) radar had very limited tactical applications. The IR sight was rudimentary and hardly provided information which could be useful to the pilot in a real tactical situation. The aircraft's AN/ASG-14T1 fire control system which incorporated AI radar suffered from severe ground clutter at low level and the very limited firing envelope of early AIM-9B Sidewinders seriously constrained firing opportunities in combat. During the period 1961-65, PAF F-104s training mostly included GCI controlled High and Low level interceptions during day and night, Low Level Navigation/Strikes, ACM/Tail Chase, Zoom Climbs for very high level interceptions and Dissimilar Air Combat Training missions against F-86 aircraft. However PAF's night Low Level interception Capability was very limited due to non availability of low level radar coverage.

Although the F-104As were intended to defend Pakistan against high-flying Soviet bombers coming over the Hindu Kush Mountains, their actual combat use would be under quite different circumstances. The PAF's fighter force comprised 102 F-86F Sabres and twelve F-104 Starfighters, along with 24 Martin B-57 Canberra bombers. B-57s flew 167 sorties, dropping over 600 tons of bombs. Three B-57s were lost in action, along with one RB-57F electronic intelligence aircraft. However, only one of those three was lost as a result of enemy action. During the war, the bomber wing of the PAF was attacking the concentration of airfields in north India. In order to avoid enemy fighter-bombers, the B-57s operated from several different airbases, taking off and returning to different bases to avoid being attacked. They would arrive over their targets in a stream at intervals of about fifteen minutes, which led to achieving a major disruption of the overall IAF effort. The unknown Pakistani flying ace, '8-Pass Charlie', was named by his adversaries for making eight passes in the moonlight, to bomb different targets with each of the B-57's bombs.

Facing the PAF was the Indian Air Force (IAF), with about 500 aircraft of mostly British and French manufacture. In January 1957 India placed a large order for the Canberra; a total of 54 B(I)58 bombers, eight PR.57 photo-reconnaissance aircraft and six T.4 training aircraft were ordered, deliveries began in the summer of that same year. Twelve more Canberras were ordered in September 1957; as many as thirty more may have also been purchased by 1962.

The IAF had also begun to acquire MiG-21Fs, new Soviet interceptors capable of Mach 2, but only nine of them were operational with 28 Squadron in September 1965 and they saw little use. On 1 September Pakistan launched a counter-attack, called Operation 'Grand Slam', with the objective to capture the vital town of Akhnoor in Jammu, which would sever communications and cut off supply routes to Indian troops. Attacking with an overwhelming ratio of troops and technically superior tanks, Pakistan made gains against Indian forces that were caught unprepared and suffered heavy losses. India responded by calling in its air force to blunt the Pakistani attack. The next day, Pakistan retaliated, its air force attacked Indian forces and air bases in both Kashmir and Punjab. India's decision to open up the theater of attack into Pakistani Punjab forced the Pakistani army to relocate troops engaged in the operation to defend Punjab. The war saw aircraft of the Indian Air Force (IAF) and the Pakistan Air Force (PAF) engaging in combat for the first time since independence. The IAF was flying large numbers of Hawker Hunter, Indian-manufactured Folland Gnats, de Havilland Vampires, English Electric Canberra bombers and a squadron of MiG-21s.

PAF's reconnaissance fleet consisted of RT-33 aircraft which were ill-suited for any recce missions in a high threat area. Therefore F-104s were used to escort any such recce missions and a pair of F-104s had to criss-cross the slower RT-33 to maintain formation. On at least one such mission the PAF formation came across an IAF Hunter formation which appeared to be returning to its base. The IAF Hunter formation promptly scattered and the PAF F-104s being deep into Indian territory with an RT-33 to escort decided not to pursue matters. An innovative solution to the recce problem was found when two seater F-104Bs were used as recce birds with the pilot in the back seat holding a hand held camera. The F-104B would fly extremely

low, pulling up slightly near the target airbase and go inverted, allowing the pilot in the back seat to get a better view for recce photos. Pakistan used the F-104As primarily for combat air patrols, usually consisting of two Sidewinder-equipped F-86F Sabres, with a Starfighter to provide top cover. The F-104s occasionally provided escort to PAF Martin B-57B Canberra bombers or reconnaissance aircraft and sometimes flew high-speed photoreconnaissance missions themselves.

On 3 September a CAP of two PAF Sabres was bounced by six IAF Gnats with PAF air defence controller scrambling a F-104 flown by Flying Officer Abbas Mirza to the aid of the Sabres. The IAF Gnats scattered on sighting the charging Starfighter, *Pajh oye...104 eeee* ('run...it's a 104') is how Squadron Leader Brij Pal Singh announced the arrival of the Starfighter. In the meantime another F-104, flown by Flight Lieutenant Hakimullah, was vectored to aid the fight. It arrived after the Gnats had already split. Perhaps mixing this Starfighter with the first one or realising that there are now two F-104s, Squadron Leader Brij Pal Singh concluded that safely egressing to India was not possible and landed at a nearby disused airfield at Pasrur in Pakistan. The incident is recalled by Flying Officer

Flight Lieutenant Aftab Alam Khan and Squadron Leader Mervyn Middlecoat flying inverted in F-104B 57-1309 on a reconnaissance mission over the Indian airfield at Halwara on 9 September 1965. This Starfighter is preserved at the PAF Academy, PAF Risalpur AB. (PAF artist Hussaini) ■

Abbas Mirza: 'I was on air defence alert in the cockpit (877) when I got the order to scramble. The weather was very hazy. The visibility on the ground was about two miles and in the air it got worse reducing to about a mile or so. There was no cloud; in other words an ordinary September day. I was airborne within two minutes and made an accelerated climb to 15,000 feet and 500 knots IAS. The GCI (Ground controlled radar) directed me to head immediately towards the Sialkot sector as two F-86s were engaged in air combat against six IAF Gnats. The F-86 pair was led by Squadron Leader Yousuf Ali Khan and his wing man was Flight Lieutenant Khalid. Yousuf asked his wing man to return to base as on Khalid's aircraft one drop tank had failed to jettison. Yousuf was now alone against the six Gnats.

'GCI urged me to accelerate to 600 knots as the situation against Yousuf was getting increasingly precarious. I must add that the brilliant manoeuvring of Yousuf had kept the Gnats at bay for over ten minutes in spite of being damaged in the vertical fin and rudder area. I was asked to descend to 12,000 feet and then 10,000 feet and was informed that I was about five miles away from the fight and advised that the fight was taking place 12 o'clock to me. In the meanwhile another F-104 was scrambled with Flight Lieutenant Hakimulah in the cockpit and was fast approaching the area. Suddenly, just ahead, about a mile or so I saw below me the F-86 in a tight turn to the right followed by the six Gnats. The lead Gnat was about 1,000 feet behind Yousuf and the rest in a line astern formation. I initially thought the Indian aircraft were Hunters but when I saw them a bit closer they turned out to be Gnats.

'Unfortunately since I was doing in excess of 500 knots when I had initial contact with the fight while the dogfight was around 200 or so I could not slow down fast enough to engage the enemy immediately, instead I decided consciously to pass in front of the F-86 to show Yousuf to hold on and to the Indians that reinforcements were on hand. I shut down my afterburner and simultaneously pulled up in a classic yo-yo manoeuvre to maintain the height advantage and also to slow down so as to keep the enemy in sight. The Gnats upon seeing me entering the melee immediately broke away from Yousuf and headed back towards the border. In the meanwhile Flight Lieutenant Hakimullah had been manoeuvred into the area and he was close to Pasrur airfield (disused by PAF) which

was about five or six miles away from the area of engagement. One of the Gnats (Birjpal) saw the second F-104 as well and decided against taking up a fight against two F-104's and landed his aircraft at Pasrur airfield. Had he known that neither Hakimulah nor I had visual contact with him till he was about to land he may have got away safely but I guess personal safety got the better of him. In the meanwhile as I reached the top of my yo-yo (16,000 feet) and began to descend, I lost contact with the Gnats because of very poor visibility and also because the Gnat is an extremely small aircraft

F-104A 56-0877 piloted by Flying Officer Abbas Mirza makes a low buzz after forcing an Indian Air Force Folland Gnat to land at Pasrur airfield on 3 September 1965. (PAF artist Hussaini)

and difficult to spot from a distance even in good visibility. I stayed in the area for another thirty minutes under the guidance of GCI but no other Indian aircraft entered to engage me. GCI informed that Yousuf had landed safely in Sargodha but he had to engage the runway barrier placed at the end of the runway as he had lost hydraulics brakes and lowered his undercarriage through the manual system. His aircraft had suffered tail damage and some other non critical battle damage. (The aircraft was recovered and subsequently flew again in the war.)'

The first IAF air strikes on PAF bases took place on the morning of 7 September. It was at 05:30 hours that the first IAF strike on PAF's Sargodha airbase was detected when the formation six six IAF Mystères was already pulling-up to attack the airfield. An F-104A flown by Lieutenant Amjad Hussain Khan was vectored by ground control to intercept the raid. According to Lieutenant Amjad he got behind two Mystères which were exiting on a heading of 120 degrees at about 100 feet AGL. He fired an AIM-9B at one of the Mystères which hit the ground after leaving the launcher. Closing in he fired at the Mystère with his gun and saw hits on the aircraft. The second Mystère meanwhile broke into the Starfighter forcing Amjad to make a high speed yo-yo and attack again. The Mystère turned into him again forcing another yo-yo with afterburners engaged. The Starfighter climbed to 13-15,000 feet and then dived to make another attack on the Mystère. This time the Mystère pilot did not see the F-104, with the Starfighter diving and closing in at 540 knots and opening canon fire at a range of

the Hawker Hunter fighters were superior in both power and speed to the F-86 according to Air Commodore Sajjad Haider, who led the PAF's 19 Squadron in combat during the war.

Group Captain Mohammed Shaukat-Ul Islam recalls; 'In November 1964 I was posted to 11 (F) Squadron, commanded by Squadron Leader M. M. Alam at Sargodha. I became operational in August 1965 and was allowed to take part in the 6-23 September 1965 war with India. I considered myself very lucky to have taken part in the war as a Flying Officer with only about eighty hours on the F-86F with a grand total of about 400 hours. At the outbreak of the war 11 Squadron was tasked to carry out a dawn strike against the Indian Army

F-104A 56-0803 of the Pakistan Air Force which was delivered to 9 Squadron on June 1961 was lost on 3 September 1964 when it struck the ground while pulling out of a low altitude practice strafing pass. The pilot, Flight Lieutenant Tariq Masood, was killed.

3,000 feet. The Mystère exploded when the range was 1,000-1,500 feet and before the Starfighter could pull up to clear the explosion, it flew through the resulting debris. The F-104's controls froze and aircraft stopped responding, going into a left bank. At this point about 75-100 feet AGL Lieutenant Amjad Hussain ejected from the aircraft and landed near a village receiving a hero's welcome from the villagers and made back to Sargodha airbase by a bicycle, a horse and a helicopter!

During the 1965 conflict the PAF was out-numbered by around 5:1. The PAF's aircraft were largely of American origin, whereas the IAF flew an assortment of British and Soviet aeroplanes. It has been widely reported that the PAF's American aircraft were superior to those of the IAF, but according to some experts this is untrue because the IAF's MiG-21, Hawker Hunter and Folland Gnat fighters actually had higher performance than their PAF counterpart, the F-86 Sabre. Although the IAF's de Havilland Vampire fighter-bombers were outdated in comparison to the F-86 Sabre,

in Chamb-Jurian sector with two formations of 8 x F-86 aircraft. Each aircraft carried 32 x 5.75-inch rockets and 1,800 x .50 inch ammunition. We exhausted all the weapons on the convoy of the Indian army and returned to Sargodha safely. As it was a surprise dawn strike we faced only small arms fire from the enemy. By the time I landed and cleared the runway my aircraft flamed out because of shortage of fuel.

'On 9 September four F-86Fs were tasked to provide a low level escort mission for three B-57 bombers attacking a train carrying ammunition at Gadro. The bombers carried out four attacks each and all seven aircraft remained within heavy ack-ack fire for about fifteen minutes. All aircraft exited low level after successful delivery of weapons. The three bombers recovered at Peshawar and we four fighters came back to Sargodha safe and sound. It was my first experience to remain within such heavy anti-aircraft fire for such a long time.

'On 11 September, I in a formation of four F-86F's took part in an escort mission at day time to give air protection to a train carrying ammunitions from Lahore to Sialkot sector. It might sound very easy but to give protection to such a slow moving train by so fast moving aircraft at low level by four aircraft for such a long time was very demanding. The train reached its destination and got its cargo off loaded.'

On one occasion a faint sign of what might have been an ambush effort by the IAF was seen. On 11 September Flight Lieutenant Hakimullah was orbiting over Indian territory, low on fuel he was about to turn for Pakistan when PAF radar at Sakesar, monitoring IAF transmissions, reported two sections of IAF fighters reporting visual contact with the Starfighter. Hakimullah spotted two Gnats below him and as he was placing his sights on one of the Gnat he noticed that he was outside the firing parameters of AIM-9B missile. This necessitated bit more repositioning, as he heard the missile tone PAF radar warned him of two more contacts diving at him. He looked up and saw two MiG-21s diving at him. Hakimullah broke into them which took him further inside India. Given his fuel state he broke in the opposite direction and engaged afterburner. Egressing he saw two more MiG-21s approaching him head-on. Diving down with afterburners engaged he broke the sound barrier, although the MiGs tried to pursue, the Starfighter was able to outrun the MiGs. Crossing over to Pakistan, Hakimullah zoomed up to 25,000 feet and reduced power. It was obvious that the Starfighter would not make it back to Sargodha with the remaining fuel and the pilot elected to make a power-off approach to the disused airstrip at Risalwala. The Starfighter made a touch down at Risalewala with the engine flaming-out as the aircraft turned off the runway.

On the night of 13/14 September Squadron Leader Mervyn Leslie Middlecoat achieved the first blind night interception in an F-104, firing a Sidewinder at a Canberra from a distance of 4,000 feet and reporting an explosion, but failing to obtain a confirmation. Another Starfighter was lost on September 17, when Flying Officer G. U. Abassi tried to land in a sudden dust storm, undershot the runway and crashed in a ball of fire. Miraculously, he was thrown clear, still strapped in his ejection seat and survived with only minor injuries.

On 16 September Group Captain Mohammed Shaukat-Ul Islam took off from Sargodha as Squadron Leader M. M. Alam's wingman to carry out a high level offensive patrol mission deep inside Indian territory. 'We were flying in battle formation at 23,000 feet between two Indian Air Bases, Halwara and Adampur. The aim was to invite the Indian fighters to come and fight with us. We could take such a venture because by then the PAF already had established air superiority over the IAF. It was about 2 pm with clear blue sky when our ground controller from a radar station transmitted that two IAF Hunters had taken off from Halwara and were approaching to intercept us. When they came in sight we jettisoned our drop tanks and entered into close air combat. The air battle became intense and under such high 'g' manoeuvres I could not stay on the tail of my leader. As it turned out, my leader shot the No.2 of the other formation and their leader shot me. My aircraft caught fire and I ejected through the shattered canopy at about 12,000 feet. I lost consciousness for a couple of seconds and by the time I got my senses back I was floating in the air and that the small parachute was pulling out the bigger one. As I settled down with my parachute I

F-104A 56-0868 of the Pakistan Air Force taxies in after a sortie. This Starfighter was lost on 17 September 1965 when Flight Lieutenant Ghulam Abbasi crashed due to disorientation of the pilot while landing in low visibility (sandstorm) undershooting the runway at Peshawar. The aircraft exploded, Abbasi was thrown clear and slightly hurt. Flying this aircraft on 6 September 1965 Flight Lieutenant Aftab Alam Khan claimed a Mystère IV-A shot down by AIM-9 overhead the Rahwali airfield.

Squadron Leader Mian Sadruddin (first commander of 9 Starfighter Air Superiority Squadron, PAF), followed by Squadron Leader Mervyn Leslie Middlecoat, lands Pakistan's first Starfighter, F-104A 56-0802, at Sargodha airfield in 1962. On 13 November 1963 this Starfighter crashed when it 'pitched up' and went into a spin. Flying Officer Asghar Shah ejected safely at high speed and received major bruises. (PAF artist Hussaini)

saw a Hunter with streaming fuel and crash with a big explosion. The Hunter pilot was shot in the cockpit. When I looked down to locate my probable landing spot, I noticed with horror that a man in uniform was pointing a .303 rifle at me and a civilian was aiming a double barrel shot gun. I heard three shots and within seconds my feet touched the ground. I got up, released the parachute and was surrounded by a crowd of people. The name of the place was Taran Taran. The local police rescued me from the crowd and took me quickly to a nearby Police Station and then to a hospital. I was bleeding profusely from my back. A doctor operated on me and showed me a .303 bullet taken out of my back. Next day I was taken to IAF Base, Adampur and flown by the AN-32 to Delhi and admitted in the CMH. The cease-fire was declared on 23 September when I was still in the CMH. Later, I joined another pilot and a navigator of the B-57, which was shot down by AA fire on 15 September in a night raid over IAF Base Adampur. We three returned to Pakistan after being released in a prisoner exchange in February 1966.

'In the war of 1965 I flew a total of nineteen missions including the Air Defence missions day and night up to 16 September. The story as a PoW was a different chapter of my life. However, I can say that the IAF treated me very well. In the later days when I joined the Bangladesh Air Force in 1972, I had the opportunity to visit the IAF as official guest and met many friends whom I came in contact as a PoW. After returning from India I was posted back to 11 Squadron. From then on it became

my passion to be a master in the air combat. In my later days I could fly the F-86 like a toy and used to manoeuvre it to its design limits. In the early sixties we used to comment by saying that a pilot who had not flown the F-86 did not enjoy the charm of fighter flying. I was later posted to 14 Squadron, Dhaka and 26 Squadron, Peshawar where I continued flying the F-86F. In 1968 the PAF introduced the F-86E and soon it became a very popular fighter aircraft. I continued flying both models till 1970 and logged about 1200 hours on the F-86F and E combined. In total I had flown thirteen types of aircraft in my career including the MiG-21MF and the F-5.'

The two countries have made contradictory claims of combat losses during the war and few neutral sources have verified the claims of either country. The PAF claimed it shot down 104 IAF planes and lost nineteen of its own, while the IAF claimed it shot down 73 PAF aircraft and lost 59. According to one independent source, the PAF flew 86 F-86 Sabres, ten F-104 Starfighters and twenty B-57 Canberras in a parade soon after the war was over. Thus disproving the IAF's claim of downing 73 PAF fighters, which at the time constituted nearly the entire Pakistani front-line fighter force. Indian sources have pointed out that, despite PAF claims of losing only a squadron of combat craft, Pakistan sought to acquire additional aircraft from Indonesia, Iraq, Iran, Turkey and China within ten days of the beginning war. But this could be explained by the 5:1 disparity in numbers faced by the PAF. India retained much of its air force in the East, against the possibility of Chinese intervention and as a result the air forces were quite evenly balanced in the West.

During the 1965 war 9 Squadron was commanded by Squadron Leader Mervyn Leslie Middlecoat who, as a flight lieutenant, was, with Squadron Leader Mian Sadruddin, one of the two pilots to land the first pair of PAF Starfighters at Sargodha in 1962. India had radar cover above 5,000 feet, which made it virtually impossible for the Starfighter to achieve surprise, while subsonic aircraft operating under radar cover could easily defend themselves. At first, most thought that the chance of a real war breaking out between the two countries was high and morning Combat Air Patrol (CAP) was flown before dawn. The F-104s would fly to 30,000 feet and patrol the area near the disputed territory of Indian-held Kashmir.

India claimed that the F-86 was vulnerable to the diminutive Folland Gnat, nicknamed 'Sabre Slayer.' The PAF's F-104 Starfighter was the fastest fighter operating in the subcontinent at that time and was often referred to as 'the pride of the PAF'. However, according to Sajjad Haider, the F-104 did not deserve this reputation. Being 'a high level interceptor designed to neutralise Soviet strategic bombers in altitudes above 40,000 feet,' rather than engage in dogfights with agile fighters at low altitudes, it was 'unsuited to the tactical environment of the region.'

On 6 September two Starfighters from Sargodha, with Flight Lieutenant Aftab Alam Khan, leading and Flight Lieutenant Amjad Hussain Khan as his wingman, were vectored by Sakesar Radar towards four IAF Mystères engaged in bombing and rocket attacks against a stationary passenger train at Gakkhar railway station near to the border with Kashmir. What followed was the first combat kill by a Mach 2 aircraft and the first missile kill for the PAF when a PAF F-104A shot down an IAF Mystère IV. It was also proven that the F-104 and the Sidewinder missile were an effective weapon system at low altitude. Flight Lieutenant Aftab Alam Khan recalls: 'I was informed that the IAF had crossed the Pakistan border and were attacking ground positions approximately 80 nautical miles south of us. This meant that India had actually decided to start an all-out war. We were immediately vectored and were soon over the site where the Indian aircraft were attacking. While dawn was breaking at 15,000 feet, it was still dark down below I asked for permission to descend to ground level, hut was denied. The reason given was that radio contact would he lost. I, however, decided to descend and leaving

my wingman at 15,000 feet to act as radio relay, I dived down and headed towards some flashes. As I reached the area, I was surprised to see that I was flying head-on into a formation of four IAF Mystère IVA aircraft that were attacking ground targets I was shocked more than I was surprised, as I felt a wave of anger leap through me. I had to shoot down these aircraft. I jettisoned my external fuel tanks and started to engage the Mystères as they turned into me. Manoeuvring started at treetop level I kept my eyes 'glued' on the target. I could feel the strain under high Gs, looking over the tail of the aircraft, keeping the enemy in sight and skimming the trees at high speed. One mistake and I would have hit the ground. If I had lost sight of the Mystères the fight would have been over. The F-104 with the afterburner blazing at low altitude was responding very well. I used the high-speed take-off flaps to improve the turning capability as required. The 'stick shaker' was a big help in flying the aircraft to its limit. The Mystères would have no problem keeping the F-104 in sight because of its afterburner.

'After some hectic manoeuvering, I was positioned behind two aircraft, but the other two were still not visible. I then spotted them, further ahead. Joy leapt though me. I aimed my weapons and decided to shoot the first two with missiles and the next two with guns. I fully realized that a confidential order prohibited me from using the missile below 10,000 feet. However, I was sure the missile could he used effectively at any height provided the targets could he discriminated from the background heat sources. A distant increase in missile tone ensured this. I set the wingspan of the Mystère IVA and started to recall the missile-firing checklist. Check Ranger, Check Tone, Check G's, Squeeze the trigger and hold.'

'I aimed the missile at the nearest aircraft and heard the loud pitched missile tone. The sight indicated that I was in range. With all the other requisite firing conditions met, I squeezed the trigger and kept it pressed. I waited, only to note that the missile had not fired. As I looked towards the left missile, I saw a big flash and the missile leaving the aircraft. The missile had taken, as stipulated in the manual, approximately $8/10^{\text{ths}}$ of a second to fire after the trigger had been pressed but in combat, this seemed like an eternity. The flash of the missile blinded me for a few seconds. The radar controller [Flight Lieutenant Farooq Haider from Sakesar radar] who was also monitoring the radio of the Mystères immediately informed me that one

Mystère had been shot down and that another had been damaged. I was then at once instructed to turn tight and pick up visual contact with the other Mystères, which were exiting. I turned as directed but could not see them. On landing back, I was informed that the dogfight had taken place overhead the Rahwali airfield where low-powered radar was located. The Mystère wreckage had fallen close by. The other three had got away.'

In one of the early attacks, Flight Lieutenant Arif Iqbal in an F-104 was about to fire at a Mystère IVA, when he suddenly saw a PAF F-86 flight appear between him and the IAF aircraft and shoot down the Mystère. During an Indian attack on Sargodha air base, however, Flight Lieutenant Amjad Hussein Khan who had missed his chance the day before made amends. He made visual contact with the IAF Mystères and headed toward them. By the time he caught up with them, the Indian aircraft were 6-8 miles away from Sargodha, flying at 150-200 feet in a south-easterly direction towards India. As the Mystères jettisoned their drop tanks, Khan positioned himself behind one of them and released a Sidewinder missile, which went straight into the ground. The Mystère then began to dogfight with the Starfighter, which used its superior climb and acceleration to raise the combat from ground level to about 7,000 feet to gain room for manoeuvre. Khan fired his cannon and was delighted to see the shells hit the Mystère. The IAF pilot, Squadron Leader Ayamada Bopayya Devayya of 1 Squadron IAF, showed commendable courage in staying with

the F-104 and despite being mortally wounded, scored several cannon strikes on the Starfighter. Amjad Hussain Khan managed to eject at low altitude. He had reason to be grateful that his F-104 did not have the original downward-firing ejection seat - otherwise, his subsequent award of the Sitara-i-Jurat would probably have been posthumous. (Six F-104 pilots received gallantry awards during the 1965 war). This was the only Starfighter to be lost through enemy action in the 1965 war. During attacks on Rawalpindi and Peshawar by IAF English Electric Canberras that night, three F-104s tried to intercept them but failed to get a target acquisition because the bombers were too low.

At around 0515 hours on the morning of 7 September a large number of PAF F-104s and F-86s flew CAP in the vicinity of Sargodha waiting for the IAF to attack. The F-104s were assigned the outer perimeter, while the F-86s were kept closer to the airfield. The first IAF attack, at 0530, by six Mystère IVAs of 1 Squadron, got through without being intercepted. Six Hawker Hunter F.56s of Nos.7 and 27 Squadrons IAF carried out the second attack on Sargodha, at 0610 hours. The third attack was made

The first Starfighter encounter with the Indian Air Force in the Indo-Pak war of September 1965, when at 0525 hours, 6 September, Flight Lieutenant Aftab A. Khan destroyed an IAF Mystère IVA of 1 Squadron IAF and damaged another. The engagement marked a new era of dog-fighting at very low altitude. It was the first combat kill by any Mach 2 aircraft and the first missile kill for the PAF. (PAF artist Hussaini)

at 0947 hours, by four Mystères of 1 Squadron IAF and a fourth and final attack on Sargodha was carried out by two Mystères at 1030 hours.

Flight Lieutenant Aftab Slam Khan continues: 'The pilots of 9 Squadron competed fiercely; to undertake as many combat missions as they could, never missing a chance to close with the enemy looking for combat. In the days that followed, the F-104 pilots noted that whenever they got airborne, the IAF grounded all its aircraft. This made it very difficult for the F-104 pilots to engage the enemy during the day. Flight Lieutenant Muchtaq, my brother, flying an F-104 in the same squadron, made contact with the enemy, only to note that as he approached the target, the IAF Hunters disengaged well in time. Flight Lieutenant 'Mickey' Abbas in an F-104 had a similar episode. This experience would he repeated for the F-104 pilots for all daytime interceptions. I personally patrolled in a lone F-104, at 30,000 feet, deep inside Indian Territory over the two Indian fighter airfields of Adamput and Halwara fur one hour and there was no response from the Indian side. This was total air superiority and it displayed the supremacy of the Starfighter.

'At medium and high altitudes the F-104 ruled the sky. The IAF refused to challenge the Starfighter. But below 5,000 feet a fierce battle raged between the F-86 and the IAF fighters, mainly the Hunters and Gnats. The F-86 was the workhorse of the PAF. It was under-powered, outnumbered and outgunned. Nevertheless, the F-86 pilots showed great courage as they fearlessly engaged their opponents and displayed an unusual skill for air combat, achieving an excellent kill ratio. The F-104, by controlling the sky at medium and high altitude, had reduced the workload for the F-86s to the extent that the numbers were manageable. The F-86s could now hold their own against the enemy at low altitude.

'Immediately after the start of the war there was an urgent need for a high-speed reconnaissance aircraft. The PAF RT-33 was rendered obsolete with a speed of less than 400 knots. It was liable to be shot down as it crossed the border. At night we did standby duties, one bout in the cockpit and one bout off. In the off time I would go and receive the B-57 pilots returning from their bombing missions over Indian airfields. The battle damage from these missions needed to be assessed. I suggested to the Base Commander that if he authorized a recce mission by the F-104, I would have a photograph on his table by noon next day. He ordered the mission.

'Low flying was not a part of the F-104 war plan - no training had been conducted hut while demonstrating the aircraft, I noticed that the Starfighter flew very well at low level. I planned the mission at 600 knots (10 miles/minute). Low flying was normally done at 420 knots in the F-86 squadrons. For the photograph I went to town early morning and bought a film for my personal Yashica 120 camera. I then requested Squadron Leader Middlecoat, the squadron commander, if he would allow me to fly while he took the pictures. He agreed. The mission was flown in an F-104B dual seater [57-1309]. Ten miles a minute made the DR navigation very easy. Over flat terrain, the height of the aircraft was lowered until Squadron Leader Middlecoat said that downwash was hitting the ground. This height was then maintained - a thrilling experience. We pulled up, slightly offset from the airfield. Pictures were taken and a visual recce made. The photographs were placed on the Base Commander's table, as promised. The missions that followed were with bigger and better cameras but I was always told to fly. The F-104 had a new role.

'The reconnaissance flights revealed that the forward IAF bases had only approximately forty aircraft each at Adampur and Halwara and even fewer than that at Pathankot. Where were the rest of the IAF aircraft? This got me thinking and I went on to study the map. Moving further east from the Indian airfields of Adampur and Halwara were Agra and Delhi. These airfields were 350 nautical miles from Sargodha. There was no attack aircraft in the PAF inventory that could reach these airfields flying at low level. If an aircraft approached at a high altitude level, it could easily be intercepted. I therefore presumed that the Indians would have the bulk of their aircraft at these bases and because they were sure they could not be attacked, the aircraft would be in the open. The F-104A's J79-11A engine was very fuel-efficient. This gave the PAF F-104s an extended range capability. I marked the route and was surprised to note that if we took off with four tanks and jettisoned them as they went empty, we could reach these bases while maintaining a speed of 540 knots at low level. It would also allow us to make two gun attacks, exit at 600 knots to the border; climb to attain height and land back with 1,000lbs of fuel remaining. The plan looked like a very exciting possibility to me. I thought of 'Pearl Harbor'; complete surprise could be achieved. I stayed up all night, made the

Flight plan and next morning made the proposal to my Squadron Commander. He told me that he was against submitting the proposal, as it was too risky. I then took the plan to the Wing Leader who had been my instructor on the Harvard T-6G. He said that it was a good plan but refused to take it any higher. I then went to the Base Commander. He said he liked it, but he would not make the proposal to the high command. There was nobody else to go to. Immediately after the war, The Air Chief ordered a high altitude recce mission of the airfields at Agra and Delhi. This was to be flown by the B-57F (Droopy), a four engine Fanjet modified B-57 that had replaced the U-2 and was flown by Pakistani pilots. The recce Flight revealed that Agra and Delhi were sprawling with aircraft. If the F-104 had attacked Delhi and Agra, it could have been a historic day for the PAF, as well as for the IAF to remember. This was the greatest chance missed by the PAF and the F-104. After the war I had a chance to discuss the plan with the Air Chief, he said that he would have definitely ordered the attack if it had been brought to his notice.'

The 1965 war ended with 9 Squadron flying 254 sorties of which 246 were day and night air defence, four escort and four counter air. Mostly; the missions flown were Air Defence and Air Superiority operations, but 42 were at night against IAF Canberra B (I) 58s. The Starfighter's rudimentary AN/ASG-14T1 fire-control radar system met the Soviet high altitude bomber threat of the Cold War era for which it was designed, but it could not illuminate small targets against ground clutter. The standard high-speed intercept tactic employed by PAF F-104 pilots was to approach their targets from below, with a typical height differential of 2,000-

3,000 feet, against a target they wished to acquire at a range of 10-15 kilometres. This limitation was well known to the Canberra jet bomber pilots of the IAF. They adopted a standard hi-lo-hi profile to minimize the threat of interception. During most of their inbound and outbound flight over Pakistani territory the IAF Canberra B (I) 58s of Nos. 5 and 35 Squadrons would stay below about 1,000 feet during their approach and exit phases. This posed a difficult night interception problem. The PAF F-104s had, in these circumstances, to be used in an unconventional low-altitude intercept profile that severely challenged the capabilities of its airborne radar. To pick up low-flying bombers on their scope, the F-104 pilots had to get down to about 300-500 feet ASL to point their radars upward and clear of the ground clutter at the IAF bombers. The problem was exacerbated by the Canberra's tail warning audible alarm that would go off the moment an F-104 got to near astern position and enable the bomber to take timely evasive action to shake off its pursuer.

PAF's tactics during the war included single or pairs of Starfighters providing top-cover to CAPS of F-86s. In addition F-104's radar based fire control system meant that it was the only fighter in PAF's inventory which could take up the role of a night interceptor against IAF Canberras with any degree of credibility. In this role too, the F-104s were limited by lack of a comprehensive low level radar network and the technology limitations of its onboard radar which suffered from ground clutter and limited search area. While most F-104s operated from Sargodha, a pair was deployed every night to Peshawar to provide night air defence over northern Pakistan. The night intruding IAF

■ Four Pakistan Air Force F-104As in formation.

Canberras were warned of F-104s presence by the Indian ground control radar at Amritsar and its own tail warning radar. On warning of an approaching F-104 the IAF Canberras would resort to sudden change in height making it difficult for F-104s to keep track of the target. The usual IAF method was to approach Pakistan at medium altitude of 25-30,000 feet and then descent to low level to approach the target. On target the IAF Canberras would pull-up to 8-10,000 feet to avoid flak and then egress at low level climbing up to medium level after crossing into India. Given PAF's own night counter attack missions, IAF had deployed its Canberra at airbases deeper inside India and therefore range considerations were important while flying the hi-lo-lo-hi mission profile just described. PAF's counter to this tactic was to extend the arc F-104s would patrol at, hoping to intercept an IAF Canberra when it climbed to medium altitude while egressing from Pakistan. CAPS of one or two F-104s and F-86 Sabres were flown against each wave of intruding Canberras. It was hoped that the Sabre although lacking any night capability could act as a deterrent using GCI and infra-red homing heads of its Sidewinder missiles to detect and attack the Canberras at night.

'The F-104 was the only night fighter with the PAF' says Flight Lieutenant Aftab Alam Khan. 'Its radar was good for high altitude, line astern missile attack, but was unusable below 5,000 feet, because of ground clutter. Also, if the target started to turn, it was not possible to deliver a missile attack. These were the limitations of the system. The IAF Canberra bombers would operate at night, usually below 500 feet. One aircraft would drop flares while others bombed the targets. After delivering their ordnance they would exit at low altitude, but as they approached the border, the Canberra's would start climbing. At this time the F-104's would be vectored for the intercept. The IAF had also installed tail warning radars on their Canberras. As the F-104 started to get into a firing position, the bombers would start a defensive turn and radar contact would be lost. Twice, I had made radar contact but as I closed into missile range, the aircraft executed a defensive manoeuvre.'

The first positive contact between an F-104 and a Canberra took place on the night of 13/14 September when Squadron Leader Middlecoat fired a Sidewinder on a Canberra in a blind intercept. An explosion was seen at a range of 4,000 feet but no confirmation was possible as the encounter took place over Indian territory.

An F-104 was lost on 17 September when Flying Officer G. U. Abasi landed short of the runway when Peshawar airbase was under a dust storm; miraculously the pilot still strapped in his seat was thrown clear of the crash and survived without any major injuries. In another incident Flight Lieutenant Amjad Hussain intercepted an IAF Canberra near Lahore and positioned himself neatly behind it, only to experience short circuiting of the gun – missile selection switch rendering both weapons unusable. Amjad then flew alongside the Canberra with the IAF pilot looking at him. Other squadron pilots recalled watching a long gun camera film of this incident.

On the night of 21 September, Squadron Leader (later ACM) Jamal A. Khan, flying F-104A 56-874, intercepted an IAF Canberra B(I)58 at about 33,000 feet. He executed a perfect 'textbook' attack and shot it down with a AIM-9B Sidewinder near Fazilka, inside Pakistani territory. The bomber pilot, Flight Lieutenant Manmohan Lowe, ejected and was taken prisoner but the navigator, Flying Officer A. K. Kapor, who could not eject, was killed in the action. (The British-built Canberra B (I) 58, unlike its American counterpart, the Martin B-57, which the PAF used, had no ejection seat for the navigator). The Canberra pilot stated that the tail warning radar made very annoying beeping sounds at low level, therefore, he had switched it off and he had forgotten to switch it on again as he had climbed out. This was the first kill achieved by an F-104 at night after a number of near misses. Although the F-104 made only one night kill, it did prevent the enemy from doing damage. The threat or fear of the F-104, forced the Canberras to

operate at low altitude levels, once over Pakistani airspace. This prevented the attacking pilots from making determined attacks. They did not, or could not properly identify their targets and thus dropped their bombs at random, doing little or no damage.

'As the war progressed' says Flight Lieutenant Aftab Alam Khan, 'a radar controller assigned to the army gun radar unit told me that the army radar could see the IAF Canberras very clearly at night, but the track length was limited to approximately twenty nautical miles. I realized that this was good enough for the F-104 to make an interception. With its high speed it could position behind the target very fast. Once this was done, the F-104 could be aligned with the help of its infrared (IR) gun-sight for a missile or a gun attack. The Canberra tail warning radar was ineffective at low altitude. To get the system working only a radio had to be installed in the army radar unit. The war ended before the system was made effective and put into practice.

'Flying the high speed F-104 at night in wartime conditions was hazardous. The environment was as hostile and dangerous as the enemy. When there was no moon, the nights were pitch-dark, as the blackout was complete. Haze and poor visibility was common. The runway lights were switched on once the aircraft was about to pitch out for a landing. We were lucky if we could see the airfield lights on downward and turning base. The landing conditions were severe. The TACANs were not aligned with the runways. There were no approach

lights, IFS or VASI. It was under these conditions that Flight Lieutenant Ghulam Abbasi, while making an approach, crashed short of the runway. The F-104 was destroyed, but miraculously, he escaped and survived to fly again.

'A cease-fire had been agreed and the fighting was to stop at 3am on 23 September 1965. I was told to confirm the same from the air. The visibility was excellent but it was like a dark night. From 30,000 feet I could see the firing along the bomb-line. It looked like a ping pong match. Exactly at 3am the firing started to slow down and then it stopped completely. I made the report and was ordered to land back at the home base. As I came on final approach, I noticed the runway was tilted to the left. I turned left and I was no longer aligned with the runway. I approached in a zigzag manner and decided to go-around and try again. I guess the stress; fatigue and landing conditions were creating illusions. I asked for my squadron commander, who came immediately. I explained the problem and he gave me the necessary instructions. The next approach was worse, after which I had fuel left for two attempts. I tried again and I was told to overshoot. My squadron commander then told me to eject on the downwind. He was getting the helicopter airborne. Now, I had only 200lb of fuel left, just enough for one last approach. At this time the air traffic controller requested permission to switch on the entire airfield lights, as the war was over. As soon as this was done, my senses returned to normal and a safe landing was carried out. Thus ended the 1965 Indo-Pak War. The F-104 and myself had seen the start and we saw the finish; a lucky and historic coincidence.

'Pakistan got the better of the IAF, with odds of 1:6 or 150:900. Air superiority was maintained day and night. The genius and courage of Air Marshal Nut Khan and F-104/F-86 team had made this possible. Undoubtedly the F-86 was the workhorse, but the F-104 had a very special task. The PAF pilot/F-104 team had created a situation where the IAF pilots did not have the will to fight the F-104. When the F-104 was 'up', the IAF was 'Down on the Ground'. This removed a major portion of the threat. The Starfighter and its pilots had contributed immensely to achieving this victory. The pilots fought very aggressively, never losing an opportunity to engage the enemy by day or night. Working long hours and flying under difficult flight conditions, the maintenance crews and the F-104s deserve a special accolade: not one technical abort

or snag affected a mission! The F-104 was flown by determined pilots, maintained by efficient crew and supported by dedicated radar controllers. This made a tremendous team that helped win the battle for air superiority for the PAF. The F-104 Starfighter was in a 'class of its own'. Superlative' to say the least. Without the dozen Starfighters the outcome of the dozen Starfighters the outcome of the war may not have been so good. It definitely was a pleasure, a thrill and the ultimate experience to fly the F-104 in combat.'

The 1965 Indo-Pak war lasted barely a month. The PAF lost 25 aircraft (eleven in air combat), while the Indians lost sixty (25 in air combat). Air superiority was not achieved and was unable to prevent IAF fighter bombers and reconnaissance Canberras from flying daylight missions over Pakistan. Thus 1965 was a stalemate in terms of the air war with neither side able to achieve complete air superiority. Most assessments agree that India had the upper hand over Pakistan when ceasefire was declared. The war proved that Pakistan could neither break the formidable Indian defences in a 'blitzkrieg' fashion nor could she sustain an all-out conflict for long. Pakistan Air Force on the other hand gained much credibility and reliability among Pakistan military and international war writers for the successful defence of Lahore and other important areas of Pakistan and heavy retaliation to India on the next day. Some pilots were scrambled six times in less than an hour on indication of Indian air raids. Pakistan Air Force along with the army is celebrated for on Defence Day and Air Force Day

Wing Commander Arif Iqbal and Squadron Leader Amanullah in 56-0874 carrying out a surprise attack on the IAF airbase at Utterlai on 11 September 1965. During the 1971 Indo-Pak War, Arif Iqbal piloting 56-0874 destroyed an Alizé aircraft of 310 Squadron of the Indian Navy. (PAF artist Hussaini)

F-104A 56-0807 of the Pakistan Air Force. This Starfighter was lost on 15 April 1968 due to an in-flight fire. Flight Lieutenant Ghulam Abbasi died in the accident.

in commemoration of this in Pakistan (6 and 7 September respectively).

Pakistan ended the war having depleted 17 percent of its front line strength, while India's losses amounted to less than ten percent. Moreover, the loss rate had begun to even out and it has been estimated that another three week's fighting would have seen the Pakistani losses rising to 33 percent and India's losses totalling fifteen percent. PAF lost two Starfighters during the conflict. These losses were not replaced by the US given the arms embargo imposed on Pakistan and 9 Squadron therefore was left with only eight F-104s and two F-104Bs after the hostilities. In addition PAF faced the problem of dwindling spare parts stocks for the aircraft which were also embargoed and had to be sourced from third party sources and black market. During this period one F-104A aircraft (tail number 56-805) was written-off in 1967 in a ground accident. During aircraft start-up the starter unit did not disengage automatically due to an electrical failure and became overheated due to high RPM and caught fire. This fire spread to the engine and the aircraft was switched off. Despite efforts by fire tenders the aircraft was completely burnt. Yet another F-104A (56-807) was lost in 1968 when Flight Lieutenant Ghulam Abbasi had a fatal crash while practicing low level aerobatics near Mianwali. It is believed that during this practice mission he faced multiple technical problems which the Board of Inquiry could not exactly pinpoint.

Flight training during this period added more emphasis on low level night interceptions, which was not routinely practiced before the 1965 war. This was made possible by PAF's acquisition of some low level radars which were deployed to cover important areas and valuable points. To test the effectiveness of this radar system extensive night training was carried out for F-104 pilots and radar operators. In addition air combat training

missions were flown against other PAF aircraft. With the induction of Chinese F-6 (MiG-19) in PAF and PAF's increasing experience of flying Soviet built aircraft in the Middle East, comparison between the types was increasingly common.

The F-104 was ill-suited to the type of air combat likely in South Asia was well illustrated in the 'Feather Duster' report which the United States Air Force (USAF) completed in 1965. The study evaluated various USAF aircraft including F-104Cs against MiG 15/17 type aircraft (simulated by F-86H Sabres). The study included defensive and offensive setups of various US fighters against F-86Hs. In case of USAF Starfighters the study concluded several lessons which unsurprisingly pointed to the type's very limited capability to engage in a manoeuvring fight. Out of 29 sorties where an F-86H acted as an offensive aircraft (positioned line astern and higher speed) a kill was scored on 21 occasions with the F-104's defensive manoeuvres like the break, turns or hard pull-ups being unsuccessful. The only manoeuvre which allowed F-104s to disengage on some of the occasions was an accelerating diving spiral. In an offensive set-up, F-104s key advantage turned out to be its small size which from certain positions made visual detection of the attack very difficult. In cases where the F-104 tried to follow the F-86H's defensive manoeuvre, it ended up overshooting the target. The report summarized by saying:

'As with the F-105, if a rear hemisphere missile/gun attack by MiG15/17 type aircraft is observed by defending F-104 aircraft, max acceleration 0-1G diving separation is recommended. If the attack is observed too close for this type of separation, a diving accelerating spiral employing rapid roll rates is effective. The F-104 has an excellent chance to subsequently re-engage undetected visually by the enemy. If attacking threat is carrying missiles, the accelerating dive, if delayed until missile launch range, must rapidly generate angle-off prior to attempting escape. The F-104 has little success in forcing overshoots through the use of breaks, hard turns, high G rolls or scissors manoeuvres. In attacking with the F-104, an outstanding advantage is its small frontal silhouette. The F-104 attack should be pressed at supersonic speed, 1.1-1.3 Mach, to ensure closure before the defender's turn forces an overshoot. Both in attacking and defending with the F-104, once supersonic separation has been effected, initiation of climb must be delayed at least 1-2 miles to prevent MiG15/17 type aircraft from cutting off in vertical plane.'

Given its ageing RT-33 aircraft based reconnaissance capability PAF attempted to use F-104s high speed performance for such missions. During 1968-69, at least one of the two F-104Bs was modified to carry Swedish made reconnaissance cameras (TA7M) in the rear seat. There were three cameras in one set of equipment, two oblique cameras and one vertical, with the vertical camera installed in the centre and oblique cameras installed on either side of vertical camera. This setting provided a total photo coverage angle of 170 degrees. This gave the F-104B the capability to look deep inside the enemy territory from a safe distance with coverage area depended on the height at which the aircraft would be flying. This modification flew quite a few trial missions before the war and the results were very encouraging. Although during the later 1971 war, the three available Mirage-IIIRPs were considered sufficient and the recce modified F-104Bs did not fly a recce mission.

Another important modification was installation of radar homing device on a single F-104A aircraft. This device called SLARD (Short range Low Altitude Radar Detection) and alternately Radar Locator (RALOR) was sourced through an American source and initial trials were carried on a twin engine communication plane. Based on results of such trials it was decided to fit an F-104A aircraft with this equipment. Aircraft tail number 56-875 was modified with this equipment (near the war perhaps due to maintenance related issues the equipment was removed from 56-875 and installed on 56-804). Initial trial fitting on the aircraft made the cockpit very uncomfortable for the pilot and was also considered a safety hazard in case of an ejection. Such issues were resolved during the testing phase which included extensive missions against various PAF radars. The SLARD had two sensors on the right and left of the nose cone. The device had a pick up range of about 7-10 miles at low level. The display in the cockpit would indicate the location of radar about 30 degrees either side from the nose of the aircraft. A vertical line/mark would appear after every two to three seconds to guide the pilot about exact location of the target radar with reference to the aircraft.

The F-104s also had an infrared (IR) sight however its pick up range was too short to be of any operational use. After the 1965 war, a serious effort was made by PAF engineers to improve its performance. These efforts did succeed in increasing the pickup range from less than half a mile to seven-eight miles against a single jet engine source by cooling the IR cell with liquid Nitrogen. The modified system did give the pilots good pick up ranges but because of ice formation, the system would clog and shut down. It required good 15 minutes for the ice to clear and the system to start functioning again. Unable to find a satisfactory solution to the problem, the effort was finally abandoned.

Yet another major modification was to make the under wing fuel tank station a weapon station capable of carrying Sidewinder missiles. Both the

F-104As 56-0798 and 56-875 taking off on a mission. 56-875 is preserved on a pole at PAF HQ Chaklala, Islamabad-Chaklala. (PAF artist Hussaini)

F-104 A and B versions that Pakistan had acquired had four external stores positions, one on each wingtip capable of carrying either an external jettisonable fuel tank or a Sidewinder missile and one under each wing capable of carrying a jettisonable fuel tank only. Of these external store stations, the wingtip station was much cleaner and far less drag producing than the under wing station. For all operational missions, when Sidewinder missiles were carried, the pilots had either to fly with no external fuel tanks at all or carry them on the under wing station.

Operationally the ability to carry both wingtip tanks and Sidewinder missiles was considered very desirable. It was thought that the underwing stations could be modified to carry Sidewinder missiles. After the 1965 war, efforts were made locally for this modification. PAF's technical staff was able to fabricate a set of Sidewinder launcher racks for the under wing station and also completed other necessary modifications like wiring, sighting and emergency jettisoning etc. After thorough ground and flight testing, a number of live firing tests were carried out and the modification was declared successful. The entire fleet of F-104s was then modified at PAF's main engineering depot at PAF Base Faisal.

As India-Pakistan tensions mounted around mid-1971, a number of pilots with previous F-104 experience were sent to Jordan for regaining currency on the aircraft, while pilots returning recently from Jordan were reposted to 9 Squadron. In Jordan PAF pilots could also undertake Dissimilar Air Combat Training with Jordanian Hunters (given the significant presence of the type with IAF). When war with India broke out on 3 December some of the F-104 pilots were still in Jordan and had to return home as quickly as possible.

Once again, the IAF outnumbered the PAF by nearly 5 to 1. More significant, however, the qualitative advantage enjoyed by the PAF in 1965 had been considerably reduced. Indian and Bangladeshi and international sources consider the beginning of the war to have been Operation 'Chengiz Khan' (inspired by the success of Israeli Operation 'Focus' in the Arab-Israeli Six Day War) when Pakistan launched pre-emptive air strikes on eleven Indian airbases in north-western India, including Agra, 300 miles from the border on the evening of 3 December (the Moslem Sabbath) at about 1740 hours. But, Pakistan put up no more than fifty aircraft. As part of the pre-emptive strikes, No. 9 Squadron was tasked for deep penetration strikes close to dusk against TAP airfields and radar stations at Amritsar, Faridkot and Bernala using guns only. The aim was to degrade their performance by damaging or destroying the antennas using the Starfighter's Vulcan cannon, affecting IAF capability to interdict PAF raids on the forward airfields. Further strikes were to be carried on these and other radar installations such as the one operating from Bernala from 4 December onwards. A total of 183 bombs were dropped rendering the Indian airfields useless for six hours to six days.

Wing Commander Arif Iqbal and Squadron Leader Amanullah were to strike the Faridkot and Squadron Leader Amjad and Squadron Leader Rashid A. Bhatti the Amritsar radar station. Arif and Amanullah got airborne from Sargodha just before dusk on 3 December and set course at low level. During ingress to the target Amanullah maintained tactical formation on the starboard side of Arif, keeping 20 degrees behind the line abreast position. Few miles from the target Arif pulled up but could not spot the airfield due to limited visibility conditions as it was getting dark. Amanullah instead of pulling up kept low and went down to 100 feet and spotted the runway. Amanullah recalls: 'I went further down and on the side of the runway (small abandoned airfield of British time) I saw radar vehicles and one temporary camouflaged shelter with a light aircraft. While Arif was orbiting on top still unable to spot anything, I made a 360 turn to line up with side of the runway where all vehicles were parked and made strafing attack with long burst firing 66 rounds per second with the 104's Gatling gun. I managed to hit the target, made another 90-270 degrees turn and made a second pass. After the second pass I exited. Arif had left before I did therefore I was independent and alone. When I was exiting it was dark and I did not see Ravi and continued west 270 and passed south of Sargodha and when I pulled up it was over Indus River closed to Mianwali. I realised then and set course back for Sargodha. When I came to land, as it was the initial moments of war, the Ack Ack of Sargodha opened on me. I went round shouted at Sargodha ATCO and came back and landed. Base Commander was waiting for me and hugged me since I had come back late. He told me that I have hit an Indian light aircraft at Faridkot (announced by Indian radio). They did not say anything about radar, but the radar was silent after the attack throughout the war. Arif came back without firing while I had expended closed to 400 rounds.'

The first raid on Amritsar radar was carried out at 1710 hours by two F-104A aircraft lead by Squadron Leader Amjad Khan, with Squadron Leader Rashid A Bhatti as his wingman. Amjad was flying the specially equipped radar locator F-104A (56-804). Both the aircraft took off from Sargodha Air Base configured with two fuel tanks on pylon stations and two Sidewinder missiles on wing tips. The radar was located and engaged successfully and it went off the air. Next morning, 4 December, pilots were informed that the radar is back on air. Another mission was planned for 0500 hours with Bhatti as lead (in F-104A 56-804) and Amanullah as his wingman. As the formation arrived over the radar, heavy ack-ack opened up. The pilots decided to stay low and make a 180 degree turn to re-attack. While turning and pulling up, the Amanullah spotted a Gnat trying to level behind the Bhatti (lead) with all guns blazing. Amanuallah gave out a warning 'Gnat behind you, exit' with the lead punching his tanks and going full afterburner. While trying to position himself behind the leading F-104A, the Gnat pilot had not noticed the wingman. With Bhatti's F-104A now pulling out of range at supersonic speed, Amanullah positioned himself behind the Gnat and after getting a locked-on tone fired the AIM-9B Sidewinder missile. While the missile was homing on, the Gnat broke right and the missile exploded under its belly. Amanullah saw

F-104A 56-0804 of the Pakistan Air Force over the Himalayas. 804 was modified with SLARD (Short-range Low Altitude Radar Detection and RALOR (Radar Locator). On 4 December 1971 Squadron Leader Amanullah Khan claimed an Indian Air Force Folland Gnat F.1 over Amritsar radar. Next day this Starfighter was shot down by AAA fire in the Amritsar area. Squadron Leader Amjad Hussain Khan, who was attacking a radar installation, ejected, but was captured. Amjad Hussain is the only pilot who was shot down in both the 1965 and 1971 wars. (PAF)

some parts of the Gnat flying off but did not see it crash. After the attack, the wingman also broke-off and headed home.

While flying back Bhatti looked at his wingtip tanks which were stuck and had not jettisoned. Since he was going supersonic the aileron got stuck, which happens because of tortional effect of the tanks on the aileron. Bhatti popped up his speed breaks and the aircraft came out of turn and he was able to safely exit.

Wing Commander Arif Iqbal claimed a HAL HAOP-27 Krishak military observation aircraft. The PAF admitted to losing just three aircraft and the onset of night prevented any further advantage the attackers may have had. In an address to the nation on radio that same evening, Prime Minister Indira Gandhi held that the air strikes were a declaration of war against India and the Indian Air Force responded with initial air strikes that very night. These air strikes were expanded to massive retaliatory air strikes the next morning and thereafter which followed interceptions by Pakistanis anticipating this action. This marked the official start of the Indo-Pakistani War of 1971. Indira Gandhi ordered the immediate mobilisation of troops and launched the full-scale invasion. This involved Indian forces in a massive coordinated air, sea and land assault. Indian Air Force started flying sorties against Pakistan from midnight. The main Indian objective on the western front was to prevent Pakistan from entering Indian soil. There was no Indian intention of conducting any major offensive into West Pakistan.

Another strike was planned on Amritsar radar station at noon on 4 December. This was Rashid Bhatti's third mission and he flew as No.2 to Squadron Leader Amjad Hussein Khan, who once again was flying the specially equipped F-104A

with SLARD. While crossing at low level, Bhatti spotted two Su-7 'Fitter's crossing above them at approximately 3,000 feet Bhatti warned Amjad about the Su-7s, who by this time had also visually picked them up. Amjad manoeuvred to settle behind the lead Su-7 with the second Su-7 trying to come behind Amjad. Bhatti warned Amjad over R/T of the other Su-7 closing behind him, but being focused on trying to track the lead Su-7, he did not respond immediately. All this time Bhatti was also manoeuvring to get behind the second Su-7 to shoot it down before it could shoot down Amjad. With the second Su-7 now even closer to the Amjad, Bhatti gave a tactical call to 'break right' and this time Amjad immediately responded. With Amjad now out of danger, Bhatti closed in on the second Su-7 and after getting a Sidewinder lock-on tone, fired the first missile from a distance of 4,000 feet. Bhatti saw the missile hit the Su-7 and the aircraft crashing to the ground. Bhatti then tried to close in on the lead Su-7 and after getting a locked-on tone fired his second Sidewinder. Bhatti failed to notice if his second Sidewinder also hit its mark, as in the process of closing in on the lead Su-7, he was also fumbling with switches in the cockpit, trying to jettison his external fuel tanks. The fuel tanks failed to jettison and with emergency selection, only the right pylon fuel tank got released. Now with the left pylon fuel tank almost full the aircraft was uncontrollable due to asymmetric conditions at very high speed (550-600 knots). Bhatti however managed to control the aircraft and informed his leader. After crossing the border, Lahore Radar was also informed and Bhatti was cleared to climb to safe altitude and reduce aircraft speed as per procedural requirements. The aircraft recovered safely at Sargodha Air Base.

A fourth mission was planned for 5 December at 13:30 hours with Squadron Leader Amjad as leader and young Flight Lieutenant Samad A. Changezi as his No. 2. Intelligence had reported the position of this radar at a road going towards Amritsar airfield. The pilots approached the target from the south and Amjad made a strafing pass. In the first pass Amjad hit an antenna and realized it was a wooden decoy when he saw it splinter. Right at that moment he saw the actual antenna rotating on the right. Changezi also confirmed the contact on the right. The formation did a turnaround and attacked again, hitting the antenna. This time the radar station was struck successfully and it went off the air for the second time. During the exit, Amjad's aircraft (56-804) was hit by anti-aircraft guns deployed around the radar station. He turned towards Pakistan, hoping to recover when his wingman gave an ejection call, confirming that fire was spreading. Amjad successfully ejected and was taken prisoner.

On 6 December the squadron was ordered to move to PAF Base Masroor, Karachi. For the rest of the war the squadron performed day and night Air Defence and Counter Air Operations from this base. It was at PAF Base Masroor that the squadron received nine F-104s provided by the Kingdom of Jordan in support of Pakistan during the 1971 war. These Starfighters were ferried by RJAF pilots (along with some PAF pilots) to Masroor on 13 December from where they operated for the remaining period of the war. When the Jordanian Squadron pilots were about 200 miles out from Karachi, a PAF Starfighter formation led by Squadron Leader Amanullah got airborne to escort them to Masroor as they were not armed. Amanullah was in formation with Major Ihsan Shurdom and Awni Bilal to guide them for landing while orbiting over head to give them top cover.

As the war progressed, the Indian Air Force continued to battle the PAF over conflict zones, but the number of sorties flown by the PAF gradually decreased day-by-day. The Indian Air Force flew 4,000 sorties while the PAF offered little in retaliation, partly because of the paucity of non-Bengali technical personnel. This lack of retaliation has also been attributed to the deliberate decision of the PAF High Command to cut its losses as it had already incurred huge losses in the conflict. Though PAF did not intervene during the Indian Navy's raid on Pakistani naval port city of Karachi, it retaliated with bombing the Okha harbour destroying the fuel tanks used by the boats that attacked. In the east, the small air contingent of 14 Squadron was destroyed, putting the Dhaka airfield out of commission and resulting in Indian air superiority in the east. While India's grip on what had been East Pakistan tightened, the IAF continued to press home attacks against Pakistan itself. The campaign settled down to series of daylight anti-airfield, anti-radar and close-support attacks by fighters, with night attacks against airfields and strategic targets by B-57s and C-130 (Pakistan) and Canberras and An-12s (India).

By 1971 the MiG-21 had become numerically the most important fighter in the IAF, with 232 in service, enough to equip nine squadrons. Hindustan Aeronautics Ltd had been producing improved model MiG-21FLs under licence. In addition, the IAF had six squadrons of Soviet-built Sukhoi Su-7BM supersonic fighter-bombers. The PAF had three squadrons of French-built Mirage IIIEJs from an unidentified Middle Eastern ally (who remains unknown) and three squadrons of Shenyang F-6s (illegal Chinese copies of Russia's supersonic MiG-19F), which the Pakistanis had improved with British Martin-Baker ejection seats and American Sidewinder missiles. In addition, the Pakistanis had replaced their older model F-86Fs with five squadrons of a far more potent version, the Canadair Sabre Mark 6, acquired via West Germany and Iran. The F-6s were employed mainly on defensive combat air patrols over their own bases, but without air superiority the PAF was unable to conduct effective offensive operations and its attacks were largely ineffective. During the IAF's airfield attacks one US and one UN aircraft were damaged in Dacca, while a Canadian Air Force Caribou was destroyed at Islamabad, along with US military liaison chief, Brigadier General Chuck Yeager's USAF Beech U-8 light twin.

Sporadic raids by the IAF continued against Pakistan's forward air bases in the West until the end of the war and large scale interdiction and close-support operations and were maintained. Indian Canberras flew a strategically important sortie against the Karachi oil tanks. This had the effect of helping the Indian Navy in their own operations, a series of missile boat attacks against the Pakistani coast.

On 8 December Flight Lieutenant Manzoor Bokhari intercepted an IAF Canberra B (I) 58 and shot it down during a low-level chase. On 10 December Wing Commander Arif Iqhal and Squadron Leader Manzoor Bokhari took off from Masroor Air Base in search of Indian Navy OSA boats towards Okha base along the southern coast. As they were searching for the OSA boats Arif spotted a Breguet Alizé ASW aircraft of the Indian Navy (one of twelve supplied for 310 Squadron aboard the carrier Vikrant) at low level. Settling behind it in gun range, Arif shot it down into the sea over the Gulf of Kutch with a gun burst. Lieutenant Commander Ashok Roy, Lieutenant H. S. Sirohi and ACO Vijayan, were killed. The F-104 formation safely recovered at Masroor. On the morning of 11 December, Wing Commander Iqbal with Squadron Leader Amanullah as his wingman took off from Masroor for a Fighter Sweep mission.

On 6 September 1965 Squadron Leader Amjad Hussein Khan in F-104A 56-0877 fired his cannon at a Mystère IVA. Amjad, certain that the stricken Mystère was doomed, broke off to look for other Mystères. As he tried to get behind one. While crossing the Mystère's tail the Starfighter rammed into the Mystère. His controls frozen, Amjad ejected with barely enough time for the parachute to blossom fully. This was the first and only Starfighter to be lost in action in the 1965 war. The pilot of the Mystère, Squadron Leader Ajjamada Bopayya Devayya of 1 Squadron IAF had survived the first volley of bullets and he chose to fight on but he was unable to eject. His body was found intact, thrown clear of the wreckage and was later buried by the villagers. Amjad Hussain was awarded the Sitara-i-Jur'at soon after the war. Ajjamada Devayya was posthumously awarded the Maha Vir Chakra in April 1988. (PAF artist Hussaini)

The aim was to catch any fighters taking off from the IAF base at Utterlai. Navigating at low level the Starfighter formation pulled over the Utterlai air base completely undetected and noticed two HF-24 Marut's lined up on the runway for takeoff. Amanullah aimed for one of the HF-24 and fired 170 rounds in one single burst, destroying the aircraft. As Amanullah pulled up and positioned for another attack, he saw Arif, who was below him, firing at the other aircraft. Amanullah shifted his aim into an aircraft pen and fired another burst. The formation exited the area at low level and safely recovered at Masroor.

On 13 December the PAF became the only nation to use the Starfighter in air-to-air combat, when two F-104s flying at low level towards Indian airfields or port installations bordering the Gulf of Kutch were intercepted by two MiG-21FLs of 47 Squadron from Jamnagar. The two F-104s were tasked to strike IAF's airfield at Jamnagar. Wing Commander Mervin L Middlecoat one of the veterans of the 1965 War was to lead this mission with Squadron Leader Tariq Habib as his No.2. The formation ingressed for the strike at low level, with the Starfighters configured with wingtip tanks and two Sidewinders under the wings. Close to the target the formation pulled-up to 2-3,000 feet with target offset to their right by 2-3 miles in order to line up for their strafing runs. For some reason Middlecoat who was leading the strike, banked to the left while target was on the right. Habib gave him a call to correct this. Repositioning for the strafing run resulted in formation spending another minute or two near the target area. After repositioning when formation was again going in for a strafing run, Middlecoat gave Habib a call saying that a missile has been fired at him. Habib cleared his six but did not see anything. Moments later while exiting and over the Gulf of Kutch, Habib got a call from Middlecoat saying that he has been hit and is ejecting. Habib inquired if he could make it to overland but he replied in the negative. Habib saw Middlecoat ejecting and the Starfighter going into the water while inverted. At that moment Habib noticed a MiG-21 to his right. As he pulled up to convert behind the MiG-21 his auto-pitch control malfunctioned and the aircraft nose started oscillating. After disengaging the APC Habib safely exited from the area. Later from various published Indian accounts it transpired that two IAF MiG-21's had intercepted the Starfighters while they were lining up for the strafing run. The

lead MiG-21 flown by Flight Lieutenant Bharat B. Soni had fired a K-13 Atoll missile at Middlecoat's F-104 which missed but was able to close-in for a gun kill. Cutting inside the Starfighter's turn and closing to 300 metres, Soni fired three bursts from his GSh-23 cannon and then watched the stricken F-104 pull up. Middlecoat ejected and parachuted into the shark-infested Gulf of Kutch. Soni called for a rescue launch, but no trace of his opponent was found. Middlecoat was declared MIA. Flight Lieutenant Arun K. Dutta, another MiG-21 pilot, was awarded the claim of having shot down Flight Lieutenant Samad Changezi. Both Wing Commander Middlecoat and Flight Lieutenant Samad Changezi were awarded the 'Sitara-e-Jrat' (approximately equivalent to the British DFC).

PAF Base Masroor was a very important target for IAF attacks and used to come under regular night attacks by IAF Canberra bombers. Due to the difficulty faced in launching missions from the base, while under attack at night, it was decided that two F-104s should be positioned at PAF Base Faisal for night Air Defence Missions as an alternate airfield. On 16 December Squadron Leader Rashid Bhatti and Flight Lieutenant Samad Changezi were detailed to move to PAF Base Faisal with two F-104A aircraft. These aircraft were out of the nine F-104s that came to Masroor from Jordan on 13 December. The Jordanian Starfighters lacked the special modifications, carried out by PAF on its Starfighters, enabling them to carry two Sidewinders on under wing weapon pylons in addition to two on the wingtips. Due to lack of this modification, Bhatti and Samad had no choice, but to fly these aircraft for night air defence with guns only and carry fuel on wingtip tanks for extended range. The main idea being that at night PAF wanted the IAF raiding bombers to know that Starfighters are in the air leaving them with a very uncomfortable position to continue their planned attacks. Both Bhatti and Samad took off from PAF Base Masroor for PAF Base Faisal on 16 December at 1600 hours. After landing at Faisal the pilots completed necessary operational requirement to organize the Air Defence Hut in tents and both aircraft were made ready for the night mission.

On the last day of the war, 17 December, when 9 Squadron's Starfighters clashed with MiG-21s of 29 Squadron, Squadron Leader I. S. Bindra claimed an F-104, though in fact it escaped with damage. In a later fight over Umarkot, Flight Lieutenant N. Kukresa made a similar premature claim on an F-104, but when he was attacked in turn by another Starfighter, Flight Lieutenant A. Datta blew it off his tail, killing Flight Lieutenant Samad Ali Changezi. Squadron Leader Rashid Bhatti and Flight Lieutenant Samad Changezi were ordered back to Masroor. While preparing to return they received instructions from Air Defence Command to fly a CAP around Mirpur Khas and Chor area before landing back at Masroor. Both pilots started a CAP in the designated area. Samad was flying the Starfighter 56-767 and Bhatti 56-839. After an hour, while both pilots were planning to return to Masroor for landing, they heard a call from Badin Radar Station, informing them of two bandits, flying at 10,000 feet and heading in their direction. The radar controller asked if they would like to engage them, Bhatti replied affirmative. Radar controller started passing on the instructions to establish contact with the bandits. As the Starfighter was approaching near the targets in battle formation, Samad who was on Bhatti's left established contact with one of the IAF MiG-21s coming from opposite direction. Samad broke off from his lead and tried to manoeuvre behind this MiG-21. Meanwhile Bhatti (lead) also picked up both the MiG-21s and tried to position behind them. Now the situation was such that Samad was behind one MiG-21 trying to close in within gun firing range (about 3,500 feet) with the second MiG-21 trying to close in on Samad. At this time Bhatti saw the second MiG-21, while still diving and turning, fire one missile at a very high angle-off at Samad. This missile missed Samad's aircraft. At this moment Bhatti called Samad that one MiG-21 is behind him and has fired a missile which was a miss. Bhatti told Samad to jettison his fuel tanks and go full afterburner (full throttle) and disengage. Since Samad was very excited trying to get within the gun firing range of the MiG-21 he ignored Bhatti or was not very attentive in the heat of the situation. The second MiG-21 fired another missile which was a direct hit and Samad's Starfighter exploded in the air. He had no time to eject and was killed instantly. Bhatti by now had closed in behind this second MiG-21, but both the MiG-21s made a hard turn to the right and headed east towards their base. Due to low fuel and lack of any air-to-air missiles, Bhatti also turned towards own base and recovered at Masroor. This was the third and final Starfighter loss of 1971 war.

While no MiGs were downed by Starfighters during the war, one was reportedly shot down by an F-6 on 14 December and another MiG-21 lost a dogfight with a Sabre flown by Flight Lieutenant Maqsood Amir of 16 Squadron on 17 December. The Indian pilot, Flight Lieutenant Harish Singjhi, bailed out and was taken prisoner.

Although the PAF scored a three-to-one kill ratio, destroying 102 IAF aircraft and losing 34 aircraft of its own, the war was only three days old when East Pakistan fell. After just thirteen days, on 16 December, the war between India and Pakistan ended when Pakistan agreed to Indian demands for an unconditional surrender. The Indian victory was achieved with significant help from the Soviet Union. Although there was a US Government embargo on arms sales to both India and Pakistan (which had been in force ever since the 1965 war began), no consideration was given to the fact that India, a long-time ally of the Soviet Union, barely used any American military equipment and the sanctions exclusively degraded the combat potential of only the Pakistani armed forces. At least one Tupolev Tu-126 'Moss' AWACS (Airborne Warning and Control System) aircraft, which would effectively have observed every move the PAF made or intended to make, was detached, with its crew, to serve with the IAF during the 1971 war. Indian ECM effectively knocked out the Pakistani ground radar and communications network.

Hostilities officially ended at 1430 GMT on 17 December, after the fall of Dacca on 15 December. India claimed large gains of territory in West Pakistan (although pre-war boundaries were recognised after the war), though the independence of Bangladesh was confirmed. India flew 1,978 sorties in the East and about 4,000 in the West, while PAF flew about thirty and 2,840. More than 80 percent of the IAF's sorties were close-support and interdiction and about 65 IAF aircraft were lost (54 losses were admitted), perhaps as many as 27 of them in air combat. Pakistan lost 72 aircraft (51 of them combat types, but admitting only 25 to enemy action). At least sixteen of the Pakistani losses and 24 fell in air combat (although only ten air combat losses were admitted, not including any F-6s, Mirage IIIs, or the six Jordanian F-104s which failed to return to their donors). But the imbalance in air losses was explained by the IAF's considerably higher sortie rate and its emphasis on ground-attack missions. The Instrument of Surrender of Pakistani forces stationed in East Pakistan was signed at Ramna Race Course in Dhaka on 16 December 1971.

The United States supported Pakistan both politically and materially. President Richard Nixon and his Secretary of State Henry Kissinger feared Soviet expansion into South and Southeast Asia. Pakistan was a close ally of the People's Republic of China, with whom Nixon had been negotiating a rapprochement and where he intended to visit in February 1972. Nixon feared that an Indian invasion of West Pakistan would mean total Soviet domination of the region and that it would seriously undermine the global position of the United States and the regional position of America's new tacit ally, China. Nixon encouraged countries like Jordan and Iran to send military supplies to

F-104A 56-0798 of the Pakistan Air Force on display at at the Pakistan Air Force Museum at Faisal AB, Karachi.

Pakistan while also encouraging China to increase its arms supplies to Pakistan. Nixon requested Iran and Jordan to send their F-86, F-104 and F-5 fighter jets in aid of Pakistan. Ironically, late in 1972 the PAF decided to phase the F-104 out of service after the inventory had been decimated as a result of a US Government arms embargo which made it increasingly difficult to maintain a reasonable in-commission rate on the F-104A/Bs.

Summary Of All The Starfighters Operated By PAF And Their Fate

Induction	Tail No.	Remarks
5 Aug 1961	56-802	Lost on 9 November 1963 when the aircraft went into spin. Flying Officer Asghar Shah ejected.
5 Aug 1961	56-803	Lost on 3 September 1964 during a low pull-out. Flight Lieutenant Tariq Majeed died in the accident.
5 Aug 1961	56-804	Lost on 5 December 1971 due to AAA. Flight Lieutenant Amjad Hussein ejected
5 Aug 1961	56-805	Lost on 10 July 1968 due to fire while on ground. Pilot Squadron Leader Asif Iqbal survived.
5 Aug 1961	56-807	Lost on 15 April 1968 due to an in-flight fire. Flight Lieutenant G. U. Abasi died in the accident.
5 Aug 1961	56-868	Lost on 17 September 1965 due to pilot getting disoriented while landing in low visibility (sandstorm) undershooting the runway at Peshawar. The aircraft exploded, Flight Lieutenant Ghulam U. Abbasi was thrown clear and was only slightly hurt.
5 Aug 1961	56-874	Preserved at PAF Base, Sargodha.
5 Aug 1961	56-875	Mounted at PAF Base Chaklala.
5 Aug 1961	56-877	Lost on 7 September 1965 after a mid-air collision with IAF Mystère. Flight Lieutenant Amjad Hussein ejected.
5 Aug 1961	56-879	Mounted at PAF Base, Masroor.
8 June 1964	56-773	Lost in air combat on 12 December 1971. Pilot Wing Commander M. L. Middlecoat died after the ejection.
1 March 1968	56-798	Preserved at PAF Base, Faisal.
5 Aug 1961	57-1309	Preserved at PAF Academy, Risalpur.
5th Aug 1961	57-1312	Preserved at PAF Museum, Faisal.

Shooting for the Stars

With its short wings and T-tail, the F-104 epitomized the features that caused inertial coupling. A marginal dog-fighter against the other century-series fighters, it was designed only to get to high altitude fast and pass by the enemy at high enough speed to avoid a dog-fight and a retaliatory missile. It was never intended to be a dogfighter; instead, it was a greyhound built to nip at the butt of the pit bulls as it passed by.

NASA research pilot Milt Thompson poses in front of an F-104. (NASA Photo)

Lieutenant Commander Milton Orville Thompson USNR (4 May 1926-6 August 1993) better known as Milt Thompson, was an American naval officer and aviator, engineer and NASA research pilot who was selected as an astronaut for the USAF X-20 Dyna-Soar programme in April 1960. After the programme was cancelled on 10 December 1963, he remained a NASA research pilot and went on to fly the X-15 rocket plane. He flew 23 different types of aircraft as a research pilot from 1956 to 1965, after which he remained at NASA in several management positions. He became Chief Engineer and Director of Research Projects during a long career at the NASA Dryden Flight Research Center.

On Monday 27 August 1956 at the National Advisory Committee for Aeronautics (NACA) High-Speed Flight Station (HSFS) at Edwards AFB, California several employees anxiously watched as crew chief Dick Payne made sure that 45-year old test pilot Joseph Albert 'Joe' Walker was properly strapped in, in the cockpit of No. 7, YF-104 55-2961,the High-Speed-Flight's first Starfighter. 'It was one of those days you read about in travel brochures' says Roy Bryant, B-52 Project Manager. 'The temperature was in the high 80s, with a slight breeze and a deep blue sky accented by high, thin wisps of clouds truly a 'chamber of commerce' day in the land of the X-planes. As Walker taxied the aircraft off the ramp onto the dry lakebed runway for take-off, anxiety began to build. Soon the canopy closed, the pilot moved the throttle forward and the aircraft responded to the thrust of its powerful state-of-the-art jet engine.'

'Joe' Walker, who was born on 20 February 1921 and raised on a farm in Washington, Pennsylvania and graduated from Trinity High School in 1938 flew the Lockheed P-38 Lightning fighter and F-5A Lightning photo aircraft (a modified P-38) on weather reconnaissance flights in World War Two. While in Cleveland, Walker became a test pilot and he conducted icing research in flight, as well as in the NACA icing wind tunnel. He transferred to the High-Speed Flight Research Station in Edwards in 1951. By the mid-1950s, he was a Chief Research Pilot. Walker worked on several pioneering research projects. He flew in three versions of the Bell X-1: the X-1 #2 (two flights, first on 27 August 1951), X-1A (one flight), X-1E (21 flights). The X-1A's loss of control at Mach 2.4 in December 1953 (when Chuck Yeager recovered from a subsonic inverted spin and landed successfully) and the crash of the X-2 in November 1956 (in which

Captain Milburn Apt was killed), had been caused by inertial coupling. Joe Walker had encountered inertial coupling during high roll rates on an October 1954 flight of the X-3 aircraft. That same month, several F-100As were lost when they broke up in flight. One of the pilots who was killed was George Welsh, North American chief test pilot. It appeared that the accident had been caused by inertial coupling. When Walker attempted a second flight in the X-1A on 8 August 1955 the rocket aircraft was damaged in an explosion just before being launched from the JTB-29A mother ship. Walker was unhurt, though and he climbed back into the mother ship with the X-1A subsequently jettisoned. Other research aircraft that he flew were the Douglas D-558-I Skystreak #3 (14 flights), Douglas D-558-II Skyrocket #2 (three flights), D-558-II #3 (two flights), Douglas X-3 Stiletto (twenty flights), Northrop X-4 Bantam (two flights) and Bell X-5 (78 flights). Walker was the chief project pilot for the X-3 programme. Walker reportedly considered the X-3 to be the worst airplane that he ever flew. In addition to research aircraft, Walker flew many chase planes during test flights of other aircraft.

'This first NACA Starfighter flight' continues Roy Bryant 'lasted approximately thirty minutes and it ushered in a legacy that would span portions of five decades, ending 3 February 1994. It was the legacy of the Starfighter. The F-104 was developed for a primary Air Force mission.

However, as history would show, it also would become perhaps the most versatile aircraft ever to grace the skies over the Mojave Desert and to reside in the hangars of the NACA/NASA unit at Edwards AFB. From the first flight to the final farewell fly-by more than 37 years later, the F-104 served NACA/NASA faithfully in four major areas: basic research in the transonic and high supersonic regions; as an aerodynamic test-bed facility to obtain data for projects/experiments quickly and at low cost; as an airborne simulator for the X-15 and lifting body programmes; and in a support role as safety/photo chase or to maintain pilot proficiency in high-performance aircraft. On a few rare occasions, test vehicles were launched or dropped from one of the aircraft.

'Eleven aircraft saw duty in the NACA/NASA F-104 fleet. Each provided valuable support in one or more of these areas. The results were significant contributions to the Center's and Agency's overall mission and goals. The Department of Defense and industry also reaped significant benefits from the data acquired by these aircraft. Important benefits were realized early in the Starfighter legacy when the Center's F-104-961 was the only instrumented F-104 aircraft remaining; the contractor and Air Force had lost all their instrumented F-104 aircraft in accidents.

'An agreement was reached whereby the HSFS conducted a major test programme to investigate inertia or roll coupling phenomena believed to be responsible for many aircraft losses. That investigation led to a mass of data turned over to the manufacturer and the Air Force and publication through NACA Research Memorandums.

'A subsequent test programme investigated the engine flame-out problem that plagued the early F-104 aircraft. The cause was determined to be asymmetrical airflow into the engine compartment from the inlet ducts. As a result, a vertical duct-splitter was installed at the engine face to balance the inlet airflow and thus alleviate the problem. Later this aircraft was outfitted with a jet reaction control system. This was done to augment an earlier programme that used the X-1B rocket aircraft to give the pilots experience in flying these systems. This was important because the X-15 would have this type of control system for use at low dynamic pressures (high altitudes). During this programme the Starfighter successfully performed zoom climbs to the 90,000-foot region. This work with reaction controls provided the first research experience for pilots controlling an airplane at dynamic pressures below 20 lbs per square foot where conventional controls lose their effectiveness'.

Between August 1956 and October 1963 NACA/NASA acquired eight F/TF-104 Starfighters second-hand from the USAF. These (plus three F-104Ns which arrived in 1963 and three ex-Luftwaffe machines which followed in the summer of 1975) were used for a variety of

| YF-104A 55-2961 (N818NA) which was acquired in August 1956 and operated by NASA until 18 November 1975.

roles, including basic research of the transonic and high supersonic regions and as aerodynamic test bed facilities to obtain data for projects and experiments quickly and at low cost, as well as an airborne simulator for the X-15 and lifting body programmes. They were also used in a support role as safety/photo chase or to maintain pilot efficiency in high performance aircraft. On a few, rare occasions, they were used to launch or drop test vehicles. NACA's first use of the Starfighter was to investigate inertial or roll coupling, a new phenomenon which primarily was a result of the new aircraft configurations which appeared in the late 1950s.

NACA successfully identified the F-100A's catastrophic inertial coupling characteristic by flying 45 F-100 flights to define the limits. Ultimately, an enlarged vertical tail was installed to enhance directional stability and roll damping. This success led the Air Force to offer one example of each new century series fighter to NACA to conduct a similar independent evaluation exercise. With its short wings and T-tail and all the weight confined within a short distance of the aircraft centreline, the F-104 Starfighter epitomized the features that caused inertial coupling.

In August 1956 NACA received its first Starfighter (the seventh service test YF-104A) when it took delivery of 55-2961 (which was originally numbered 018, later N818NA). An agreement was reached whereby the NACA High Speed Flight Station at Edwards conducted a major test programme using N818NA with Joe Walker as project pilot, to investigate inertia coupling

phenomena believed to be responsible for many Starfighter losses. This investigation produced a mass of data. A subsequent test programme investigated the engine flame-out problem that plagued the early F-104 Starfighters. The cause was determined to be asymmetrical airflow into the engine compartment from the inlet ducts. As a result, a vertical duct-splitter was installed at the engine face to balance the inlet airflow and thus alleviate the problem.

The US Air Force really wanted their F-104 back after the evaluation but NACA was reluctant and finally the US Air Force agreed to let NACA keep 55-2961. (This Starfighter was operated by NASA until November 1975.) Later, N818NA was fitted out with a jet reaction control system to augment an earlier programme that used the X-1B rocket aircraft to give pilots experience in flying these systems. During this programme the Starfighter successfully performed zoom climbs to the 90,000 feet region. This work with reaction controls provided the first research experience for pilots controlling an aircraft at dynamic pressures below 20lb per square foot where conventional controls lose their effectiveness.

The second Starfighter to be delivered was 56-0734 on 7 October 1957 and it received the NASA number N820NA. There followed a major programme to obtain boundary-layer-transition measurements in full-scale flight on this aircraft. This Starfighter was acquired initially to determine whether natural laminar flow could be achieved at supersonic speeds using an optimum airfoil surface. To obtain the desired data, HSFS personnel installed pressure instrumentation and temperature gauges on the outside surface of the left-hand wing. The leading edge flaps were deactivated and a fibreglass glove installed to maintain the original contour and smooth surface of the wing. Neil Armstrong made the first flights in this investigation which were continued by Milton O. Thompson. The optimum airfoil surface was achieved by applying a fibreglass coating on the right wing of N820NA, which was subsequently shaped and smoothed to achieve an almost perfect airfoil surface. Thermocouples were installed in the fibreglass layer to measure the surface temperature and in this manner determine whether the airflow over the surface was laminar or turbulent. Turbulent flow imparted more heat into the fibreglass than smooth laminar

JF-104 (YF-104A) 55-2961 (N818NA) during ground testing reaction control system (RCS)

flow. Surprisingly, the investigation worked as conceived - laminar flow was achieved on the fibreglass-coated wing over the forward 25 to 30 per cent of the wing. The standard left wing was also instrumented and revealed a much lower amount of laminar flow. 56-0734 was then used in measuring boundary-layer noise on a smooth polished nose cone that was substituted for the production nose cone, an experiment that provided data to compare with wind tunnel data for calibration purposes.

NASA needed to test the Mercury capsule drogue chute which was to be deployed at supersonic speed to stabilize and decelerate the capsule prior to deployment of the main recovery chute. There was no convenient way to test and demonstrate the operation of this chute and so Dryden proposed using a modified F-104A. NASA therefore requested the loan from the US Air Force of an F-104A that had been modified with a weapons rack under the belly of the aircraft.

On 13 April 1959 56-0749 (1037) became the third Starfighter to be acquired by NASA when Neil Armstrong ferried the supersonic jet from Lockheed's Palmdale, California facility to NASA's Flight Research Center where it was equipped with special instrumentation and re-designated as a JF-104A. (It subsequently received the NASA number, N824NA.) Initially it was configured with a centre-line launcher system to serve as a launch platform for parachute test vehicles and experimental sounding rockets. Later, it was used for mission support, pilot proficiency and as a chase plane for other research aircraft. In all, seven NASA pilots flew the airplane 249 times. The weapons rack could be extended below the aircraft, allowing large rockets or missiles to be fired without endangering the aircraft. It was the only Starfighter to be modified in this manner. NASA used N824NA to carry a bomb-shaped simulated Mercury capsule to the planned speed and altitude for operational deployment. The dummy capsule would contain instrumentation to measure the deployment loads and a drogue chute with its associated deployment hardware. The dummy capsule weighed as much as the Mercury capsule, roughly 1,800lbs. NASA calculated that they could launch the dummy capsule at 70,000 feet at Mach 1.2 or greater. The dummy capsule was intended to impact the Edwards bombing range and then be reusable for successive launches. Joe Walker flew this series of flights.

56-0749 was next configured for the Alsor programme to launch a large balloon, ten feet in diameter, to 1,000,000 feet altitude using a rocket mounted on the extended launch rack. The purpose was to measure the density of the atmosphere at a location on the X-15 flight track that would allow researchers to calculate the true altitude airspeed and dynamic pressure of the X-15 after a mission. Programme pilot Milton O. 'Milt' Thompson described this endeavour as 'not very successful, but interesting.' The programme proposed to deploy a balloon stowed in the nose-cone of a rocket. It would be propelled up to perhaps a million feet and then the balloon would come out of the rocket nose-cone, inflate and then begin its descent. The balloon would then be tracked with radar, its descent measured and from that air density would be compute. The programme began with a near-vertical launch of the rocket carrying the balloon. At peak altitude, estimated to be in excess of 800,000 feet, the nose cone would separate from the rocket and the balloon would be deployed. It would be inflated by a drop of water inside the balloon that theoretically would vaporize at the near vacuum pressure at these altitudes. The balloon would be tracked by radar and its descent measured. From this, HSFS personnel could compute air density. Altitudes of 600,000 feet were achieved on three occasions. HSFS personnel, however, were never able to track

the balloons on any of the trial launches after the nose cone separated from the rocket. Thompson said. 'We tried to impart as much energy into the rocket as possible before we launched it. We did in fact achieve altitudes of almost 700,000 feet. The basic manoeuvre was a real high-altitude loop (typical launch conditions M = 1.4 near 60,000 feet at the vertical flight condition). We were never able to track the balloons after the nose cone separated from the rocket, so we just don't know what happened to the balloons.

On 20 December 1962 Thompson was scheduled to evaluate weather conditions over Mud Lake, Nevada in JF-104A-10-LO 56-0749 call sign NASA 749 in preparation for the launch of an X-15 rocket plane over that area a few hours later. Weather flights were critical because go/no-go decisions were based on real-time observations made along the planned flight path. Thompson described the day: 'The morning of my weather flight was a classic desert winter morning. It was cold, freezing in fact, but the sky was crystal clear and there was not a hint of a breeze - a beautiful morning for a flight.'

Thompson strapped himself into the JF-104A cockpit, taxied to the runway, took off to the northeast and climbed to cruising altitude. Visibility was clear all along his route. Upon returning to Edwards, Thompson configured the JF-104 so he could practice simulated X-15

landings on the clay surface of Rogers Dry Lake. With fuel remaining in the Starfighter's tanks, Thompson began practicing simulated X-15 approaches to the dry lake bed. X-15 pilots used the F-104 to practice landing approaches. The two aircraft were almost the same size and with speed brakes extended and the flaps lowered, an F-104 had almost the same lift-over-drag ratio as the X-15 in subsonic flight.

During his first approach Thompson cut the throttle, extended speed brakes and began a steep, descending turn toward a runway marked on the lakebed's surface. Decelerating, he lowered the flaps and held 300 knots indicated airspeed as he dived toward the airstrip. The jet lost altitude at a rate of 18,000 feet per minute until he levelled off at 800 feet, lit the afterburner and climbed away.

When Thompson extended the F-104's flaps for the second simulated X-15 approach, he was at the 'high key' - over Rogers Dry Lake at 35,000 feet and supersonic. As he extended the speed brakes and lowered the flaps, NASA 749 began to roll to the left. With full aileron and rudder input, he was unable to stop the roll. Adding throttle to increase the airplane's airspeed, he was just able to stop the roll with full opposite aileron. Thompson found that he could maintain control as long as he stayed above 350 knots (402 mph) but that was far too high a speed to land the Starfighter.

JF-104A (F-104G) 56-0749 (N824NA) with ventrally-mounted Air Launched Sounding Rocket (ALSOR), which was acquired on 13 April 1959. NASA test pilot Milton O. Thompson ejected from this aircraft on 20 December 1962 after an asymmetrical flap condition made the jet uncontrollable.

In October 1957 NASA acquired on loan, two ex-USAF F-104A single seaters (F-104A-1-LO FG-734 56-0734, pictured and 56-0749) for use in the NACA HSFS (High Speed Flight Station) programme, Dryden (56-0749 crashed in 1962). On 10 January 1961 'NASA 734' was transferred back to the USAF and was converted to QF-104A standard, which was finalized on 14 May 1962. On 1 August 1963 the aircraft was finally shot down during a drone-mission by a BOMARC missile after 114 drone flights by the 3205 Drone Squadron.

Bell X-15 No.3 (66672) with F-104 56-0817 chase plane. This Starfighter is on loan to the Pacific Aviation Museum from the Museum of Aviation at Robins AFB, Warner Robins, Georgia.

He experimented with different control positions and throttle settings and recycled the brake and flaps switches to see if he could get a response, but there was no change. He could see that the leading edge flaps were up and locked, but was unable to determine the position of the trailing edge flaps and came to the conclusion that the trailing edge flaps were lowered to different angles. Thompson knew he was in serious trouble and wasn't sure he could land safely. It slowly dawned on him that he might have to eject.

In a last-ditch effort, Thompson radioed NASA-1 - the Flight Operations office - and urgently asked for fellow research pilot Joe Walker, who was suiting up for his X-15 mission.

'Trouble?' Walker asked.

'Right, Joe,' said Thompson.

'I told Joe the symptoms of my problem and he decided that I had a split trailing edge flap situation with one down and one up. He suggested I recycle the flap lever to the up position to attempt to get both flaps up and locked. I had already tried that, but I gave it another try. Joe asked if I had cycled the flap lever from the up to the takeoff position and then back again. I said no. I had only cycled the flap lever from the up position to a position just below it and then back to the up position. Joe suggested we try it his way. I moved the flap lever from the up position all the way to the takeoff position and then back to the up position. As soon as I moved the lever to the takeoff position, I knew I had done the wrong thing. The airplane started rolling again, but this time I could not stop it. The roll rate quickly built up to the point that I was almost doing snap rolls. Simultaneously, the nose of the airplane started down. I was soon doing vertical rolls as the airspeed began rapidly increasing. I knew I had to get out quick because I did not want to eject

supersonic and I was already passing through 0.9 Mach. I let go of the stick and reached for the ejection handle. I bent my head forward to see the handle and then I pulled it. Things were a blur from that point on.'

'She's going, Joe!' he called.

Ominous black smoke rose over California's high desert and there was no sign of a parachute. Della Mae Bowling, the pilot's office secretary at NASA's Flight Research Center was crying as fire trucks raced across the vast expanse of Rogers Dry Lake toward the crash scene. But Della Mae and others were to learn that what might have been a terrible tragedy turned out instead to be a triumph of piloting skill.

'After four complete rolls, Thompson ejected while inverted. He felt a terrible pain in his neck as the seat's rocket motor blasted him free of the airplane. His body was whipped by air blast and he began to tumble wildly. After rocket burnout, he separated from the seat but soon realized he was still holding onto the ejection handle. His parachute opened promptly as soon as he released his grip. Floating gently down from 18,000 feet, Thompson saw the airplane plummet nose-first into the desert and explode on the Edwards bombing range. He was breathing rapidly and felt lightheaded and slightly breathless. After several failed attempts to activate his bailout oxygen bottle, he unfastened his mask and breathed the thin, but fresh, air. He landed softly, gathered up his parachute and walked to a nearby road. He hiked to the road and shortly a farmer came by in a truck and asked if he could give him a ride. Thompson took the offer and the farmer brought him back to the Center.

Thompson wrote, 'It was only 7:30 am and still a beautiful morning.'

At NASA-1, the mood was grim. Thompson hadn't had time to inform anyone that he was ejecting and nobody saw his parachute. Their faces bearing shock and tears, NASA employees stared at the column of thick, black smoke rising in the distance. NASA chief of Flight Operations Joe Vensel hopped in a car and sped across the lakebed toward the crash site, expecting the worst. To his surprise, he found Thompson waiting calmly by the roadside, apparently unharmed. An investigation revealed that the accident had most likely been the result of an electrical malfunction in the left trailing-edge flap. The investigating board, headed by Donald R. Bellman, gave Thompson high marks for his actions. 'Throughout the emergency,' the board's report read, 'the pilot showed superior skill and judgment, which contributed materially to his own safety and to the understanding of the causes of the aircraft loss.'

On 16 December 1959 meanwhile, 57-1303, a two-seat F-104B became the fourth member of the NASA fleet and was numbered N819NA. With the addition of this two-seater, another dimension was added to the Center's research capability: that of carrying instrumented individuals and/or experiments in the back cockpit with a safety pilot flying the aircraft from the front cockpit. As a result numerous bio-medical experiments were conducted, many of which were applicable to the space programme and the medical community. First assigned to Ames Research Center, this Starfighter was acquired by Dryden where NASA headquarters had decided to concentrate all of its high-performance aircraft research programmes. One such programme was the development of instrumentation and a mini-recorder to monitor the pilot's physiological parameters (heart and respiration rates, oxygen consumption and pulse wave velocity). Recording the pulse wave velocity provided definition of the time delay in the pulse wave travelling from the heart to an extremity, in this case the little finger tip. These data allowed the researchers to measure and predict the pilot's workload. A spin-off from the biomedical experiments was a 'spray-on electrode' used in obtaining in-flight electro-cardiograms that was developed by the staff along with an atomizer spray gun, used to attach the electrodes and capture the signal wire. Another major spin-off of this programme was the real-time ambulance electro-cardiogram capability currently in use by paramedics in major cities worldwide. Other programmes included the development of an in-flight mass spectrometer to analyze the respiratory exhalation (each breath) and a liquid cooled garment which incorporated the use of a frozen backpack in the cooling process. The initial programme using a Ground Command Guidance (GCG) system, which was the forerunner of the Remotely Augmented Vehicle (RAV) capability currently used at Dryden, also flew on this aircraft. A rather unique programme used to demonstrate the capability of the GCG system was the Focused Boom experiment. This experiment, affectionately known as 'Big Boom,' required that a ground track profile (loaded in a ground-based computer) and certain pertinent parameters, uplinked to instruments in the front and aft cockpits, be flown so that the energy from the sonic boom generated would be focused on a specific area on the ground. The F-104 was remotely deployed to Michael Army Airfield at Dugway, Utah for this programme and used the Ely, Nevada, radar-tracking site to support these flights.

In December 1959 F-104B-10LO 57-1303 was transferred to NASA and assigned the NASA number of '819'. It served until 1978, when it was finally retired.

A milestone was achieved in the Starfighter legacy on 14 October 1970 with a total of six flights in a regular workday (first flight take-off time 8:45 am, flight six landing time 4 pm.). Kudos to crew chief Don Guilinger and his crew for keeping pilots Tom McMurtry and Hugh Jackson airborne. This was the second time within five weeks that the team had accomplished this feat.

The F-104B was used to conduct some zero-g experiments, initially involving a small tank designed to supply fuel continuously under zero-g conditions. It was also used for indirect viewing experiments using a periscope in the rear cockpit. At hypersonic speeds the windshield of an aircraft can exceed 2,000°F and needs heavy and specialized glass to withstand the enormous temperatures. If the windshield could be done away with and replaced with, say, a periscope for pilot viewing, then a large saving in weight could be achieved. It was found that the field of view was an outstanding 180 degrees laterally and about 60 degrees vertically. Apart from exaggerating the stereoscopic effect and causing some errors in depth perception and the need for the pilot to keep his head and eyes pressed against the eyepieces during elevated g manoeuvres, the system was quite successful and test pilots used it to make step simulated X-15 unpowered landings.

The F-104B also enabled an instrumented individual to be carried in the rear cockpit with the safety pilot flying the aircraft from the front cockpit. As a result, numerous biomedical experiments were carried out in the F-104B, many of which were applicable to the space programme. One such programme was the development of instrumentation and mini-recorder to monitor the pilot's physiological parameters (heart and respiration rates, oxygen consumption and pulse wave velocity). Recording the pulse wave velocity provided definition of the time delay in the pulse wave travelling from the heart to an extremity, in this case the small fingertip. These data allowed researchers to measure and predict the pilot's workload. A spin-off from the biomedical experiments was a 'spray-on-electrode' used to obtain flight electrocardiograms that was developed by the staff along with an atomizer spray gun. Another major spin-off was the real-time electro-cardiogram currently used in ambulances by paramedics all over the world.

Other programmes included the development of an in-flight mass spectrometer to analyse breathing and liquid-cooled clothing. The initial Ground Command Guidance (GCG) system, the forerunner of the Remotely Augmented Vehicle (RAV), was also tested on this Starfighter. The Focused Boom Experiment was a unique programme used to demonstrate the capability of the GCG. This experiment, affectionately known as 'Big Boom', required that a ground track profile (loaded in a ground-based computer) and certain pertinent parameters, data-linked to instruments in the cockpit, be flown so that the energy from the sonic boom generated would be focused on a specific area on the ground. The F-104 aircraft was deployed to Michael Army airfield at Dugway, Utah, for this programme and used the Ely, Nevada, radar-tracking site to support these flights.

The first four Starfighters had all been acquired through loan agreements between NACA/NASA and the Air Force. The fifth Starfighter to be acquired, on 27 December 1966 was F-104G 56-0790, which was numbered N820NA, although it needed modification and was not put into operation until April 1968. In addition to its support role at NASA, 56-0790 also made a major contribution to research as a test-bed aircraft, being used in the acquisition of the baseline data used in the development of the Centre's aircraft agility techniques programme. In response to an informal request from the Federal Aviation Agency (FAA), the initial flights to investigate the wake vortices of jumbo jet aircraft were flown with this F-104 probing the wake of a C-5 Galaxy. The data obtained on these flights were used as the criteria to establish an inertia minimum separation distance for aircraft trailing jumbo jet aircraft. (A major programme to investigate various wake vortices characteristics was later completed by NASA and the FAA.)

For almost twenty-two years, until 21 April 1978 NACA, which became the National Air and Space Administration (NASA) on 1 October 1958, operated no less than fourteen F-104 Starfighters of various descriptions. Three of them were purpose-built NF-104As and three F-104Ns and were used on a variety of tasks in support of NACA/NASA space research projects. NASA ultimately expanded to include the Lewis Aeronautical Laboratory, the Ames Aeronautical Laboratory and the High Speed Flight Station, later the Flight Research Center and then the Dryden Flight Research Center. Dryden primarily specialized in high-speed flight with aircraft such as the early X-series. Lockheed received a contract from the

USAF Air Research and Development Command in 1962 to modify three F-104A-10-LO Starfighters (56-0756, 56-0760 and 56-0762) to Aerospace Trainer Aircraft configuration for use in training candidate astronauts at the USAF Aerospace Research Pilots School (ARPS). Designated NF-104s, they were inexpensive trainers that would expose students to altitudes above 100,000 feet. Like the X-15, the NF-104s had small directional thrusters in the nose and wingtips for attitude control up where normal controls had no effect. The three NF-104A Starfighters were F-104G models modified for use in training candidate astronauts at the USAF Aerospace Research Pilots School (ARPS) at Edwards. The three Lockheed-delivered F-104Ns and eight other Starfighters delivered to NASA and designated F-104N, were primarily used as supersonic chase planes. During the period 27 August 1956 to 21 April 1978 at least nineteen different pilots (sixteen from Dryden), two from Ames and one from the USAF) flew the Starfighter during its NACA/NASA career. Included in this total are Apollo astronauts and X-15, lifting-body, XB-70A Valkyrie and YF-12 pilots.

In order to attain altitudes at which the reaction control system would function, each NF-104A received a Rocketdyne LR121/AR-2-NA-1 liquid fuel auxiliary rocket engine that used JP-4 fuel and hydrogen peroxide as an oxidizer to produce 6,000lbs of thrust. This was mounted at the base of the fin above the jet pipe of the J79-GE-3B turbojet, which was retained. The rocket engine was throttle controlled from 3,000 to 6,000lb

All three NASA F-104Ns flying in formation on 24 October 1963. (NASA)

F-104/N 603C-45053 (012) N812NA
the second of three F-104N supersonic
chase planes acquired by NASA, on
1 October 1963, in its original NASA
colour scheme at Edwards AFB,
around 1966. N812NA was used until
3 February 1994. (AFMC)

thrust with approximately one minute 45 seconds' burn time. A hydraulically driven fuel boost pump replaced one of the electric pumps to provide JP-4 to the rocket engine following the loss of the AC generators in the ballistic portion of the flight profile. The NF-10A had its original vertical fin replaced with the larger fin used on the TF-104G, wingspan was increased by four feet to 25.94 feet; a metal nose cone replaced the plastic one. To further save weight, all non-essential equipment, such as the Vulcan cannon, AN/ARC-66 UHF radio, AN/ASG-14T-1 fire control system, ILS, braking parachute and auxiliary wingtip tanks,

were removed. The two UHF radios which replaced the original were lighter, single-channel units with one mission frequency and one guard. The power output was about two watts and therefore had very limited range. It was not uncommon during the test programme for a pilot to run out of peroxide at altitude, lose control and come spinning back into the atmosphere unable to communicate with test directors because of these radios. New batteries for high-altitude power, an AN/APX-46 IFF system, special instrumentation, a Collins 718 radio, a pressure tank for cockpit pressurization and a reaction control system, were installed. The wingtips were extended two feet and the engine air inlet shock half-cones, modified.

To enable the astronauts to get the feel of the hydrogen peroxide controls with which they would steer their space craft, each NF-104A was provided with control thrusters at the nose, tail and wingtips. Reaction control thrusters were added in the test nose boom with pitch and yaw vanes and on the wingtips for roll control. A separate 'stick' controller was installed on the instrument panel for the reaction control system. A three-axis reaction control damper system was also added, sharing the thrusters with those of the primary control system. These systems also used hydrogen peroxide for fuel. Internal tanks were added for the peroxide. With the reaction control system, a student could control the NF-104 on a zero-G trajectory through the thin atmosphere at the edge of space for about eighty seconds. The pilot wore a pressure suit; without engine power at that altitude there was no cockpit pressurization. The empty weight of the NF-104 A was only 13,400lb and gross take-off

The tail unit of F-104N '812' (N812N)
which was retired on 3 February 1994.

weight just 21,800lb. The first NF-104A (56-0756) was delivered to Edwards AFB on 1 October 1963, the second (56-0760) on 26 October and the third (56-0762) on 1 November.

James P. Fitzgerald of the Lockheed Advanced Development Company recalled: 'One episode just prior to the first planned rocket engine firing on 56-0762, the first modified and primary flight test airplane nearly made a widow of our shop foreman's wife. Frank Harvey had just completed a visual inspection of the rocket motor nozzle and was descending the access stand when test pilot Jack Woodman, per the test card, depressed the rocket timer 'Clock Reset' button in the cockpit. The rocket motor immediately ignited. Once Jack got it shut down, we engineers unrolled the prints right under the airplane and discovered to our horror that a sneak circuit had been designed into the clock reset wiring which applied power directly to the turbo pump valve when the clock was reset. A diode solved this one and we pressed on.

'Everything, including the fuel, was packed into a small, high fineness ratio fuselage, with short wings and tails to minimize frontal area and drag.

It was great from the aerodynamic performance standpoint but it had some other insidious effects. The mass of the aircraft was concentrated close to the roll centreline, while the damping from the wing was minimized for the same reason. When the aircraft made a turn, its angle of attack (the angle between the airflow and the wing) would change. Under certain specific conditions of speed, altitude and roll rate, the plane's stability would decrease and it would suddenly go out of control.

'The typical mission profile for the NF-104A involved a level acceleration at 35,000 feet to

Commandant Deatrick, student Loh and instructors Rider and Rhodes by NF-104A 56-0760. Colonel Eugene Peyton Deatrick Jr., born 17 November 1924, was Commandant of the USAF Aerospace Research Pilot School at Edwards Air Force Base,. Deatrick flew 402 combat missions in the A-1E Skyraider in the Viêtnam War and was responsible for the rescue of Lieutenant Dieter Dengler USN, who had escaped from a prison camp after six months of captivity. NF-104A 56-0760 was lost on 10 December 1963 when Colonel 'Chuck' Yeager narrowly escaped death.

■ NF-104A zoom-climbing over the Mojave Desert.

Mach 1.9, ignition of the rocket motor at nearly full rated thrust, start a shallow climb while continuing to accelerate to Mach 2.1, a rapid 3.5G pull-up into a steep climb at 50 to 70 degrees pitch altitude and 11 degrees alpha. The J79 afterburner would normally blow out at about 70,000 feet, followed by the main engine at 80,000 feet. The rocket motor continued to run until fuel starvation (as mentioned, about two minutes' total). At this point the airplane was well over 100,000 feet and reaction controls were exercised to effect a push-over and re-entry manoeuvre. J79 restart was initiated at 40,000 to 35,000 feet and following restart, return to base (RTB). It was standard practice upon return from a flight above the stratosphere to conduct a precautionary simulated flame-out approach to landing. Many times pilots landed with 400-500lb of fuel remaining, which in the F-104 represents the proverbial 'fumes'. The test programme consisted of 42 flights between 9 July and 29 October, the average duration of which was 34 minutes due to the mission profile. Some of the challenges involved in this programme were several redesigns of the reaction control system stick to provide the proper 'feel', development of a technique to bleed the hydrogen peroxide fuel lines prior to rocket motor ignition to preclude late light offs and development of the accel/pull-up technique to optimize zoom altitude. On one test flight, the reaction control

system was inoperative and because of the ineffectiveness of the normal control surfaces, an unplanned pitch-up and spin resulted during the zoom recovery. This incident emphasized the need for the reaction control system for recovery. Since JP-4 and hydrogen peroxide are hypergolic, any fuel leaks were, of course, intolerable.'

George J. Marrett, born in Grand Island, Nebraska in 1935 was a second lieutenant attending flying school when he saw an Air Force colonel wearing an orange flying suit and a dress military hat with 'scrambled eggs' on the visor. His spurs were clinking and clanking as he walked. Then and there George knew that he wanted to fly the Starfighter. He got his chance in December 1963 when he was selected to attend the Test Pilot School at Edwards Air Force Base. 'Our class had ten Air Force pilots; two Navy pilots, two NASA pilots and one pilot each from Canada and the Netherlands. We all wanted to be part of the Space Age even though our very presence here put us in competition with NASA. The Air Force had initiated its own manned

George J. Marrett, author of
*Sky High in a Starfighter: My climb to
the top in the F-104.*

space programme with the Boeing X-20 Dyna-Soar, a single-seat space vehicle scheduled to make its first flight in 1966, just three years away. All X-20 pilots would be graduates of Yeager's school and actually fly their spacecraft from liftoff to an unpowered landing on Edwards' Rogers Dry Lake. NASA astronauts, on the other hand, returned to Earth in a capsule suspended from a parachute and landed in the ocean.

'Yeager was instrumental in changing the curriculum of the test pilot school to include spaceflight training. The name of the school was also changed to Aerospace Research Pilot School, though it was commonly referred to as 'Yeager's Charm School'. He still had the golden touch: Yeager seemed to have a credit card enabling him to tap into the Air Force budget and there seemed to be no limit to what he could spend. His motto appeared to be 'Follow me. I will put the Air Force in space.' It was widely understood that whoever first pushed the NF-104 to its maximum performance was certain to set a world record for altitude achieved by an aircraft taking off under its

own power. In 1961 the Soviets had set a record of 113,890 feet with the E-66A, a rocket-powered variant of the MiG-21 fighter. Some US X-planes had flown higher, but they had to be carried aloft by a Boeing B-52.

'In 1963 Lockheed began shakedown flights on the NF-104 with company test pilot Jack Woodman. After a few months the programme was turned over to Major Robert W. 'Smitty' Smith at the Air Force Flight Test Center (AFFTC), flying out of the Fighter Branch of Test Operations. [On 15 November 1963 56-0756, in the hands of Major Robert W. Smith, climbed to 22.5 miles (118,860 feet); an unofficial world altitude record from a ground take-off at Edwards AFB]. A year later, when I was assigned to the fighter branch, I did a little off-the-record dog-fighting against 'Smitty'. By disabling the safety system that prevented loss of control at high angles of attack and high Gs, he could fly the F-104 near its aerodynamic limits. You couldn't beat 'Smitty' in an F-104.

'To reach maximum altitude, the pilot accelerated the NF-104 at full power to maximum speed and

Colonel (later Brigadier General) Charles E. 'Chuck' Yeager, who by 1952 had been named the commandant of the USAF Aerospace Research Pilots School (ARPS) at Edwards AFB, in the cockpit of one of the School's three NF-104Ns modified for use in training candidate astronauts. (AFMC History Office)

NF-104A-L0 56-0756 zoom-climbing over the Mojave Desert, its Rocketdyne rocket motor at full 6,000lb thrust. 56-0760 is now on display at the USAF Test Pilots School. (NASA/AFMC History Office)

then pulled up into a 'zoom climb.' In a zoom, the more energy you could build up during acceleration - and the more precisely you could maintain the optimal climb angle - the higher the airplane would climb when it coasted to the top of the zoom. On 6 December 1963 'Smitty' reached 120,800 feet [in 56-0756] on one zoom - not an official world record because it was a test flight and the official monitors were not in place. Optimum climb angle for the aircraft turned out to be between 65 and 70 degrees, which, added to a 14-degree seat cant and a five-degree angle of attack, left the pilot reclined at an angle of about 85 degrees. You couldn't see the ground from that position, so all zoom manoeuvres were made on instruments. On one flight, 'Smitty' tried an angle of 85 degrees, but he lost control and tumbled, going over the top upside down. The aircraft entered a spin but he recovered. 'Smitty' was fearless.'

'Chuck' Yeager had taken NF-104A 56-0760 up three times to get a feel for it and on 10 December 1963 he was scheduled to fly two zoom flights in preparation for an all-out record attempt the next day. During the morning flight he reached 108,700 feet, but Yeager felt the Starfighter could be taken much higher. On the afternoon flight his test profile called for him to accelerate to Mach 1.7 at 37,000 feet, light the rocket engine to accelerate to Mach 2.2 at 40,000 feet and then climb at 70 degrees. He climbed to 35,000 feet, about 100 miles from Edwards at the bottom end of the San Joaquin Valley near Fraser Peak and headed for Rogers Dry Lake at 37,000 feet in afterburner. Yeager was flying at more than Mach 2 when he fired the 6,000lb thrust rocket in the tail. Passing 60,000 feet as expected, the afterburner flamed out, oxygen-starved in the thin atmosphere. Later, when he reached 40,000 feet, Yeager planned to enter a shallow dive to permit the compressor blades to windmill in the rush of air, working up the required revolutions enabling re-ignition in the lower air. He shut down the engine and let the rocket motor carry him over the top at 104,000 feet. By this time he was climbing at a steep 70 degree angle. As the aircraft passed through 70,000 feet, ground control informed Yeager that he had less than the desired angle of climb. He applied the reaction controls to get back on the flight path, a technique he had used before. But on this flight he was at a lower altitude (101,595 feet) and the reaction controls were not yet effective. There was a higher dynamic pressure on the control surfaces, meaning the horizontal tail would have been more effective. Now, as the angle of attack reached 28 degrees, the NF-104's nose pitched up (something which had happened in the morning flight). Yeager used the small peroxide thrusters on the nose to try to push it down but the nose refused to lower (the stabilizer had frozen into the climb position) and the NF-104 fell off flat and went into a spin. 'Bud' Anderson, flying the T-33 chase plane, saw Yeager 'coming down like an autumn leaf off a tree'. The NF-104 was falling 'so flat and so straight' that Anderson could circle him and 'kind of corkscrew down with him'. They went through about 14,000 feet and Anderson said, 'Hey Chuck, that's enough. Get out.'

A mile above the desert and falling like a manhole cover, Yeager's engine had wound down to the point where it stopped and locked at about

NF-104A-LO 56-0760, one of three Starfighters modified in 1963 to be used in the USAF astronaut training programme conducted by the Aerospace Research Pilot School at Edwards AFB, California. They were fitted with a 6,000lb thrust Rocketdyne AR-2 auxiliary rocket engine above the jet-pipe, 2 feet wingtip extensions, the enlarged vertical surfaces of the F-104 and hydrogen peroxide control thrusters at the nose, tail and wingtips. (Lockheed-Martin Skunk Works)

40,000 feet. (The data recorder later indicated that the Starfighter made fourteen flat spins from 104,000 feet until impact on the desert floor. Yeager stayed with the aircraft through thirteen of these spins before he ejected safely at 8,000 feet - he hated losing an expensive aircraft but there was nothing more that he could do). Yeager ejected. The seat functioned normally and out went Yeager upwards at 90 mph. However, following seat-man separation, the seat, which still had a residual fire in the back from the rocket charge, became entangled in his parachute risers, or shroud lines and the risers began smouldering. Fortunately, the lines had not burnt through and the chute opened, much to Yeager's relief, but the popping motion dislodged the seat and the tube end of the rocket motor, which was glowing red hot, smashed into Yeager's pressure suit faceplate, hitting his left eye. The blow broke the faceplate and deposited unburned rocket propellant inside the helmet. Burning material on the seat ignited the rubber seal around Yeager's helmet and in the 100 per cent pure oxygen environment inside the pressure suit it 'erupted like a blow torch'. Yeager's head was engulfed in flames and smoke. He could not breathe, nor could he see out of his left eye. Yeager thrust his gloved hand into the open faceplate and tried to scoop in air to breathe but the rubber-lined glove caught fire. Instinctively, he pushed up the visor on what remained of his helmet, an action which automatically shut off the oxygen feeding in from the emergency bottle. The aircraft hit the ground in a flat attitude and Yeager landed a short distance from the wreckage. Within a few minutes a helicopter and flight surgeon arrived. Yeager had second-degree burns on the left side of his face and neck and on his left hand and a cut on one eyelid. Yeager was hospitalized for a month while surgeons treated his severely burned face and hands. He also lost the tips of two of his fingers using a knife to cut off his burning glove). The loss of an NF-104 was not the only bad news that day: Secretary of Defense Robert S. McNamara announced the cancellation of the X-20. The Air Force lost a manned space programme and the Air Force put a hold on his spending.

George Marrett recalls: 'The two surviving NF-104s were grounded pending an investigation, so I wouldn't get to fly one. But the standard Starfighter was still the hottest airplane in the Air Force inventory and I wanted to get into it. As a new student, I got my first flight in the back seat

NF-104A zoom-climbing over the Mojave Desert. ■

of an F-104 with an instructor, Major Frank E. Liethen, as he conducted a functional check flight, or FCF. Regulations called for an FCF any time major maintenance had been performed. The FCF pilot would fly the repaired aircraft at the limits of its envelope to determine that it was safe for student pilots to fly. Only the most experienced pilots were asked to fly these potentially hazardous flights. Liethen had been the outstanding student in his class at test pilot school. After a year as a project test pilot at Nellis Air Force Base in Nevada, he returned to Edwards to attend the new space school. After graduation, he became an instructor in the school. He applied to become a NASA astronaut, but he was turned down - too tall. Just as he graduated from space school, the Dyna-Soar program was cancelled. His only chance for a spaceflight was the Air Force programme called the Manned Orbiting Laboratory, or MOL. Unfortunately, the MOL (cancelled in June 1969) was on the drawing board at the time and crew selection was years away.

'The Starfighter could be a handful and had a terrible safety record; many pilots had been killed flying it. So as Liethen performed manoeuvres in the F-104, tickling the pitch-up boundary, I held the control stick ever-so lightly in my hand. He talked on the intercom as he flew, but I watched him like a hawk.

'As a student, my zoom flight would be the high point of the twelve-month course and my last flight. I'd take the F-104 (not the rocket-powered NF but a standard -104) to the rarefied atmosphere above 80,000 feet.

'On the day of the flight, I was sweating profusely, having spent an hour and a half in a full pressure suit. Wearing the helmet and faceplate was like looking at the world from inside a fishbowl. And the helmet was almost as wide as the canopy. I could move my head only a few inches from side to side before the helmet bumped against the plexiglass. As I sat cooking in the Mojave Desert sun, I felt confident. I'd logged thousands of hours in Air Force fighters, from the F-86 Sabrejet to the F-101B Voodoo. But I'd never flown a Starfighter to 80,000 feet - 'Angels 80,' military pilots call it. I'd flown the F-104 often in the previous months to get the feel of it. But you always have little doubts when you're trying something that you've never done before.

'If I overcorrected at the top of the zoom, I'd be uncontrollable in seconds. Lieutenant Patrick 'Pat' Henry, a Navy pilot in the class just ahead of mine, lost control at the top of the zoom, entered a spin and eventually ejected. If I were not precise in my planning and control, I'd share his fate. If the engine failed to restart as I was coming down, I'd be committed to a flameout pattern.

'The tower's call interrupted my thoughts. 'Zoom 5, you're cleared onto Runway 04 to hold.'

'Sweat was dripping into my eyes, but it would be cool up where I was headed. A quick glance to my left confirmed that my chase aircraft, an F-104 with the call sign 'Zoom Chase,' was in position and ready for takeoff. He'd chase me until the pull-up point and then, as I descended through about 30,000 feet, he'd rejoin in formation in order to accompany me through the traffic pattern. He'd check the airplane's exterior, be ready to offer any assistance I might need and help keep me clear of other airborne traffic, since I'd be focusing most of my attention on the instrument readings.

'The J79 gave its characteristic howl and roar as I eased the throttle full forward and back again to idle.

'Zoom 5, winds are calm, you're cleared for takeoff,' the controller said.

'No time for other thoughts now. I got a good afterburner light and then pushed the throttle up to maximum afterburner. The acceleration pressed me against my parachute. Control stick aft at 100 knots (115 mph), nose wheel raised at 150, airborne at 175. Landing gear up before 250 knots or I'd rip the gear doors off. Then flaps up. Passing 400 knots, I raised the nose slightly to start my climb and throttled back out of afterburner. Then I started a turn to the east and climbed at 450 knots, waiting for the Mach to build to 0.85.

'The chase pilot radioed that my Starfighter looked fit to continue. Climbing toward the morning sun, I had only a few seconds to enjoy flying this beautiful aircraft. It was no time to daydream; I had to focus on the test mission. Climbing at 0.85 Mach, I levelled off at 20,000 feet, passing abeam the Three Sisters Dry Lake. It was time to dump cockpit pressurization and inflate my pressure suit. If my pressure suit failed at this low altitude, I would have plenty of time to repressurize the cockpit, abort the mission and return to Edwards. Slowly the suit inflated. I felt like a fat man in a telephone booth.

'On the way to 35,000 feet, I could see Baker's Dry Lake in front of me. The lake bed was about 100 nautical miles east of Edwards and my turning point for the run back in the supersonic corridor - airspace where speeds over Mach 1 were legal. I made a gradual 180-degree turn to the left, glancing over my right shoulder to confirm that my chase was still in position.

'Rolling out, I pointed the nose toward the town of Tehachapi. Moving the throttle forward, I selected maximum afterburner, easing the control stick forward ever so slightly to unload the one G of level flight and help the Starfighter ease through the transonic zone. The airplane passed Mach 1.0 with no physical sensation. The Mach needle was really climbing fast now: 1.3…1.4…

'I tried pushing the throttle harder against the forward stop, hoping to get every last pound of thrust from the engine.

'Mach 1.7…1.8.

'The F-104 was at its design speed now and the Mach number was climbing fast. At an indicated airspeed of 675 knots, I started a gradual climb to 38,000 feet. What a tremendous feeling to be going faster and faster. The chase aircraft was miles behind me now. Mach 2.1…2.15… I let the Starfighter accelerate as long as I dared - I wanted every bit of energy I could get. The more speed I built up, the more altitude I'd get over the top.

'One last glance at the checklist. I had pencilled a reminder for myself when I reached this point: 'Check gloves.' Just before he started his pull-up, my classmate, Captain Jerry G. Tonini, had the thumb of one of his gloves start to balloon. Fortunately, he caught it in time. Had the glove popped open, he would have lost all suit pressure. If that had happened, he would have lost consciousness in a few seconds and crashed.

'The compressor inlet temperature was approaching the limit: 155 degrees Celsius (311 Fahrenheit). A last check on fuel showed just under 1,200lbs, the minimum before starting the zoom in order to recover with a safe reserve at Edwards. Go for it, I thought. Pull up. At that moment the image of Yeager wrapped in bandages flashed before my eyes.

'I pulled back on the stick gently, entering the climb at a rate of 1 G per second. When the G meter reached 3.5, I kept the pressure constant and I focused on the attitude indicator in the centre of the instrument panel. As I reached 40 degrees of pitch, I began slowly easing off the backstick pressure and held 45 degrees. I monitored the exhaust gas temperature (EGT) - I didn't want to overtemp the engine.

'Quickly I glanced at the altimeter. The needles were spinning too fast to read. I'd passed 60,000 feet; EGT was at maximum: 615 degrees Celsius. I began to retard the throttle to hold EGT constant. Passing 67,000 feet, I brought the throttle back into idle cut-off. The engine shut down and started to unwind; at this altitude, if I left it running, even at idle, it would overtemp.

'I held the 45-degree climb angle until the angle of attack reached eight degrees, then pushed forward on the stick. Minimum indicated airspeed over the top was 120 knots, the lowest speed at which there was still enough air flowing over the horizontal tail to ensure the tail would be effective. I felt weightlessness coming on. Even though my shoulder harness was firmly tightened and locked on the ground, I felt my pressure suit lift off the ejection seat and my helmet touch the canopy.

'Just approaching the peak of the climb, I treated myself to a sweeping view of Earth. Most of the flight so far had been 'head in the cockpit, fly the gauges.' The sky was very dark blue - almost black. I could see the Pacific Ocean in front of me, although still a hundred miles away. There was smog in the Los Angeles basin down to the left and at my right I saw the San Francisco Bay area. Sightseeing was over; I had to return to business. I'd topped out at Angels 80. It was so quiet I thought I could hear my heartbeat.

'I held zero G until the Starfighter had pitched over into a steep dive. I put the speed brakes out and airspeed started to build up fast as the light brown Mojave Desert came back into view. I was now diving straight down, with Rogers Dry Lake directly below me. Passing 35,000 feet, I restarted the engine.

'The EGT started to rise - I had a good light. With the engine running, I started a turn back to the Edwards runway when I was startled by a silver flash on my faceplate. Then I realized it was a drop of sweat.

'I passed my landing reference point at 25,000 feet directly above Edwards' Runway 04, where I had started the flight about a half-hour before. I'd be landing out of the same dead-stick pattern that the X-15 used: 300 knots indicated airspeed and in a 20-degree dive. Base leg altitude was 15,000 feet, but I had flown the pattern many times before and felt quite comfortable. Rolling out on high final at 6,000 feet, I had the 15,000-foot runway directly in front of me. I started the stick coming back for the flare and lowered the landing gear at 250 knots. I checked to ensure the gear was down and locked just before touchdown at 190 knots.

'The tyres squealed as they burned rubber on the painted white line that crossed the runway at the 10,000-feet-remaining marker. As I lowered the nose gently onto the runway and pulled the drag chute handle, my chase sped past me in a low approach.

'With sweat dripping into my eyes, I looked up at the contrail my zoom had etched against the blue desert sky. I had returned safely from the edge of space.'

In June 1971 the third NF-104A (56-0762), suffered an explosion at Mach 1.15 while at 35,000 feet. The explosion was caused by a failed O-ring which allowed leaking hydrogen peroxide into the Starfighter's rear fuselage. Captain Howard C. Thompson, the pilot, was able to safely land the aircraft but it had lost half its rudder and rocket motor. In any event the programme was nearing its end, so 56-0762 took no further part in training. Combined, the first and third NF-104A flew a total of 126 flights, the last being made on 20 December 1971. 56-0760 is now on display at the USAF Test Pilots School.

NF-104A (F-104A) 56-762 which was delivered to NASDA on 1 November 1963 and w/o in June 1971.

On 8 June 1966 Joe Walker flew F-104N 013 as part of a formation of aircraft that were powered by General Electric engines. The other aircraft - all provided by the Flight Test Center - were the No.2 North American XB-70A Valkyrie, piloted by Alvin S. White the North American test pilot and Major Carl C. Cross a new USAF Flight Test Center project pilot; a US Navy F-4B Phantom from Point Magu flown by Navy Commander Jerome P. Skyrud with radar intercept officer E. J. Black sitting back seat; a YF-5A flown by John Fritz, a General Electric test pilot; and a T-38 Talon flown by Peter Hoag and Joe Cotton. Clay Lacey the famous aerial photographer was hired by General Electric to photograph the formation from a Lear Jet.

The formation, consisting of the F-104N and YF-5 A off the XB-70A's right wing and the T-38 and the F-5B off the left, flew a racetrack pattern around Edwards. Suddenly, Walker's F-104N pitched up and rolled to the left, toward the Valkyrie. 013 continued up and over the XB-70A's wing, colliding with the twin vertical tails, severely damaging the right tail and tearing off the left tail. The Starfighter broke in two and exploded in a ball of flame following the collision and burned as it fell towards the Mojave Desert. Walker had no time to eject and was found dead

in the cockpit still strapped to his seat. Aboard the Valkyrie, neither White or Cross had felt the collision. White even thought that two other aircraft in the formation had collided. The XB-70A flew on for sixteen seconds then suddenly rolled off to the right and appeared to enter a spin, finally impacting in the desert twelve miles north of Barstow. White managed to eject after some initial difficulty with his escape capsule. Cross died in the aircraft cockpit.

Many theories as to the cause of the accident were aired. One theory blamed strong local vortices near the wingtip that sucked the F-104 into the Valkyrie. The accident investigation board finally concluded that Joe Walker, who was married with four children, had misjudged the position of his horizontal tail relative to the downward deflected tip of the XB-70A wing (which complicated judging relative separation or clearances between the two aircraft). As he flew in formation the Starfighter's tail touched the downward deflected tip of the XB-70A wing, which then caused this aircraft to pitch up and roll over the wing and hit the two vertical tails.

'As a result of the quest to fill the vacancy left in the NASA Starfighter fleet by the loss of F-104 No. 813' recalls Roy Bryant, 'another Starfighter, 56-0790, was acquired on loan from

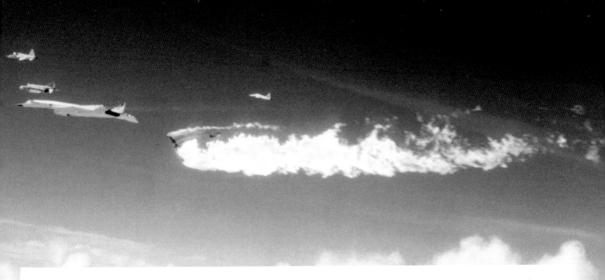

On 8 June 1966 a formation led by the No.2 XB-70A Valkyrie, piloted by Alvin S. White, North American test pilot and Major Carl C. Cross USAF was flown from Edwards AFB, California. The other aircraft were a NASA F-104N flown by Joe Walker; a USN F-4B Phantom flown by a crew from Point Magu; a YF-5A flown by John Fritz, a General Electric test pilot; and a T-38 Talon flown by Peter Hoag and Joe Cotton. Clay Lacey, the famous aerial photographer, was hired by General Electric to photograph the formation from a Lear Jet. The formation flew a racetrack pattern around Edwards. Suddenly Walker's F-104N pitched up and rolled to the left, towards the Valkyrie, continued up and over the XB-70A's wing, colliding with the twin vertical tails, severely damaging the right tail and tearing off the left tail. The Starfighter broke in two and exploded in a ball of flame following the collision and burned as it fell towards the Mojave Desert. Walker had no time to eject and he was found dead in the cockpit still strapped to his seat. The XB-70A flew on for a few seconds then suddenly rolled off to the right and appeared to enter a spin, finally impacting in the desert 12 miles north of Barstow. White managed to eject after some initial difficulty with his escape capsule. Cross died in the aircraft cockpit. (NASA/AFMC History Office)

the Air Force in December 1966. However, it did not become available for duty until April 1968 because it was due for a major inspection, which had to be completed first. In addition to performing in a support role, this F-104 also made major contributions to research as a test bed aircraft. A significant research contribution was the acquisition of the baseline data used in the development of the Center's aircraft agility techniques programme. In response to an informal request from the Federal Aviation Agency (FAA), the initial flights to investigate the wake vortices of jumbo jet aircraft were flown with this F-104 probing the wake of a C-5 aircraft. The data obtained on these flights were used as the criteria to establish an interim minimum separation distance for aircraft trailing jumbo jet airplanes. (A major programme to investigate various characteristics of wake vortices was later completed by NASA and the FAA.) Of special significance were accomplishments that reflected the performance of the aircraft maintenance and instrumentation crews (Nick Massimino/Bill McCarty and Al Grieshaber/Harvey Price respectively).

During the period 10 April 1969 to 19 December 1969, Dryden flew a total of 134 missions,

including ninety flights for data on six different research projects. These flights were accomplished in 176 regularly scheduled work days, only 138 of which were available for flight because of down time to accomplish a Time Compliance Tech Order (TCTO) and to install an experiment. The bottom line: During this eight-month period there were no aircraft or instrumentation problems.

'Even on a day when there were no research or support flights scheduled, Center pilots would find a reason to fly the Starfighter. Such was the day of Friday 11 April 1975. The previous day it had rained and now, although cloudy, the sky was clearing. It was an ideal setting for an airborne photo mission. One young enterprising pilot, Gary Krier, recognized the 'knock of opportunity' and seized the moment. Quickly he organized and obtained approval to fly the mission. By 8:30 am you could look out at the DFRC staging ramp and see five blue-and-white Starfighter all in-line and ready for the mission at hand. At 9:15 am the first Starfighter was airborne, followed in rapid order by the remaining four aircraft. The fifth Starfighter became airborne at 9:35 am.

'During the mission the aircraft were flown in several different formations with the photographer in the T-38 photo chase busily photographing. It was a photographer's dream come true. The mission also included formation fly-bys to the delight of the Center's employees. The mission lasted just over an hour. Participants in this operation were: Fitz Fulton/Ray Young, flight-test engineer (F-104-819 [303]), formation leader, Bill Dana (F-104 [811]), Tom McMurtry (F-104 [812]), Einar Enevoldson (F-104-818 [961]), Gary Krier (F-104-820 [790]) and Don Mallick and photographer Bob Rhine in the T-38.

On Wednesday 2 July, a sunny morning in 1975, the NASA Starfighter fleet took on an international flavour with the arrival of three West German F-104G's (two had been built by Lockheed [in West Germany] and one in Holland). A 'NASA Blue flyby' at 10:15 am was the climax to a journey that began six days earlier at Jever Air Base in West Germany for four of the Flight Research Center's elite test pilot cadre, Tom McMurtry (824), Bill Dana/ Einar Enevoldson (825) and Gary Krier (826). An appropriate ceremony was held on the NASA ramp where the pilots were duly honoured for their achievement. With these newer versions of the F-104, replacement parts were more readily available, making these aircraft easier to support and keep flying. Thus the NASA Starfighter legacy continued into the 1990s.'

On 18 November 1975 F-104A N818NA (55-2961), NASA's first Starfighter, with Chief Test pilot Don Mallick at the controls, was flown off to a place of honour at the National Air and Space Museum in Washington DC. It was a fitting tribute to an aircraft which during its illustrious career had been flown at speeds greater than Mach 2 and at

■ **F-104 '812' flight with T-38 chase in 1975.**

altitudes above 85,000 feet (26,000 metres). From the initial stability and control handling qualities evaluation and propulsion programmes (research to obtain data on the basic F-104 aircraft) to the last test bed experiment flown, this Starfighter provided invaluable aerodynamic data. In addition to the roll-coupling evaluation, interaction of non steady twin-inlet flow study, jet-reaction control programme and many others, N818NA flew the Panel Flutter Flight-Test programme to obtain in-flight data about the aerodynamic phenomena known as Panel Flutter. This programme also compared these data accurately with the results of wind-tunnel studies.

Another programme on this Starfighter obtained flight test verification of wind-tunnel data on two configurations for reducing base drag (retarding forces). This 'Two-Dimensional' Base Drag reduction experiment also demonstrated devices for breaking down major vortices, thereby also reducing base drag. In a separate programme, N818NA was used to study and develop the low-lift/low-drag landing technique used by pilots during the X-15 rocket research aircraft and Lifting Body programmes, thereby contributing tremendously to those two significant milestones. N818NA even served as an airborne simulator of landing patterns and approaches for the pilots who flew the X-15 and the wingless vehicles.

N818NA had devoted 59 per cent or 1,444 flights to obtaining data for research programmes. Nineteen different NACA/NASA pilots had flown this Starfighter during these missions. Three of the pilots, including Neil Armstrong, the first astronaut to walk on the moon, in 1969, were Apollo astronauts. Seven, including Joe Walker, who holds the unofficial altitude record of 354,200

feet (107,960 metres) flew the X-15 and four flew the X-15 above the 50-mile altitude necessary to qualify as winged astronauts. Six flew one or more Lifting Body Vehicles tested at Dryden.

The retirement of F-104 N820NA on 1 June 1977 followed after a career spanning nine years and 1,022 total flights. It had first been a research test aircraft and then enjoyed a second career as a support aircraft along with N811NA and N812NA. Dryden's F-104 N820NA logged a total of 1,022 flights, including 308 flights to obtain data for research programmes. In its role as a research test aircraft, it gathered data for a number of experiments that made significant contributions to the aircraft community. From the initial Profile optimization experiment (Phase 1) to the last instrumentation validation test, N820NA provided invaluable aerodynamic data.

The Profile Optimization experiment consisted of two phases in which state-of-the-art, strapdown inertial systems would be flown aboard the aircraft. The computer was programmed to optimize a predetermined parameter and performed this operation in real time by providing the pilot with steering commands in the display system of the aircraft. Data gathered during this experiment advanced strapdown inertial system technology as applied to terrestrial vehicles. This experiment also provided operational experience with an airborne digital computer for its use as a research tool in the investigation of control, guidance and airborne simulation technology. In addition, this experiment yielded an especially interesting data point. For one test, a top speed of Mach 2.0 at 50,000 feet was the objective. However, N820NA flew three different 'optimum' profiles to obtain that end point. One profile was computer generated. A second was the more or less standard profile used by the military and the third was one Project pilot Einar Enevoldson developed to reach 50,000 feet altitude.

A second major experiment flown on N820NA obtained data for the development of the Center's aircraft agility techniques. These data permitted an evaluation of the effects of certain parameters (buffet, wing rock, high g forces and so forth, on the piloting precision of a closed-loop tracking task. These data were obtained by using a 'target' aircraft to fly a predetermined profile while being tracked by the test F-104 N820NA. Other experiments included validation of instrumentation and data sensors that would be flown on other test aircraft such as the YF-12 and the F-8 Supercritical Wing aircraft. During its initial career as both a research and support aircraft, N820NA devoted 57 per cent of 308 flights to obtaining data for research programmes.

N820NA provided support for such research programmes as the YF-12, the basic F-15 tests, the F-111 TACT and the lifting bodies. Like other NASA F-104s, it served as an airborne simulator of landing patterns and approaches for

the wingless-body vehicles. Ten different pilots (nine from NASA and one from the Air Force) flew this Starfighter. These included a Center director and Apollo astronaut, Dave Scott; an X-l 5 pilot, Bill Danda, who made the last X-15 flight over 300,000 feet, as well as the last flight in the X-15 programme; three lifting-body pilots, John Manke, Bruce Peterson and Bill Dane; and two YF-12 pilots, Fitz Fulton and Don Mallick. N820NA was finally retired in April 1975 and put on permanent display at Edwards as a symbol of the Flight Research.

Less than a year later, on 21 April 1978 research pilot John Manke and flight test engineer Ray Young took F-104 N819NA (57-1303) on its final mission, a one-hour crew training flight. During its eighteen-year-long career N819NA had made 1,730 previous flights. Under the skilful direction of Dr William 'Bill' Winter this Starfighter had provided data that made a significant impact in the field of biomedical research. Many of the research flights with this F-104 were to acquire flight data on a number of biomedical experiments. Data attained by this aircraft also played a vital role in establishing the Ground Command Guidance system as a valuable flight test tool to be used by the Center.

Two other areas in which the aircraft made important contributions were the development of the low-lift/drag approach and landing patterns

used by the X-15 and lifting-body vehicles, as well as the testing of a ballute (cross between a balloon and a parachute) system. This aircraft was a major player in the early work, including night flights, flown to develop and 'standardize' the low-lift/drag approach and landing technique used so successfully in numerous programmes flown at Dryden. The prime ballute experiment involved obtaining data to evaluate a towed high speed decelerator through a Mach number range from 0.7 to approximately 2.0 and a system that could be used to increase the drag of an asymmetrical vehicle.

The ballute was a semi-spherical shaped device, 4 feet in diameter, similar to a small balloon that self-inflated with the air picked up by the small air scoops located around its circumference when deployed. It was installed in the drag-chute compartment of the Starfighter and deployed in a manner similar to that of a standard drag chute. Up until these tests, the state-of-the-art research on ballutes was limited to wind-tunnel studies and rocket-flight tests of ballutes behind symmetrical bodies. The F-104 presented a test platform by which the study of the ballute system could be expanded. During its career of more than eighteen years, N819NA flew 1,731 flights and was flown by at least nineteen different pilots (sixteen from Dryden, two from Ames and one from the Air Force). These included Apollo astronauts and

X-15, lifting-body, XB-70A and YF-12 pilots. In June 1983 N819NA was put on display at McClellan AFB, Sacramento, California.

In 1986 the remaining F-104s were still being used as chase and research aircraft, notably as part of the NASA High Alpha Flight Research Program, together with the McDonnell Douglas F-18s which subsequently replaced the Starfighter at Edwards. The last two F-104s, N812NA and N826NA, were retired by NASA on 3 February 1994. (The following day F-104G/N N812NA arrived at Lockheed Palmdale for static display). Research pilot Tom McMurtry flew the last NASA flight, in F-104G N826NA, making a low-speed and a high-speed fly-by prior to landing in a salute to Dryden employees. The flight, which lasted 29 minutes 45 seconds, brought to an end more than thirty-seven years and more than 18,200 F-104 Starfighter flights.

As Dave Bashow says: *Thanks for the memories, Kelly Johnson.*

NASA F-104 Inventory

Serial	USAF Tail No.	NASA Tail No.	Acquired / Other
YF-104A-183-1007	55-2961	N818NA	acquired 8.56 (op by NASA until 18.11.75)
F-104G-183-1022	56-0734	-	acquired 7.10.57
F-104G-183-1037	56-0749	N824NA	acquired 13.4.59. Lost 20.12.62
F-104G-183-1037	56-0749	N824NA	acquired 13.4.59. Lost 20.12.62
F-104N 683C-4045	(011)	N811NA	acquired 8.8.63
NF-104A(F-104A)	56-756	-	del. 1.10.63. Ret. 20.12.71
F-104N 683C-4053	(012)	N812NA	acquired 1.10.63. Ret. 3.2.94
F-104N 683C-4058	(013)	N813NA	acquired 22.10.63. Lost 8.6.66 in mid-air collision with XB-70A Valkyrie)
NF-104A(F-104A)	56-760	-	del. 26.10.63. Lost, 10.12.63
NF-104A (F-104A)	56-762	-	del. 1.11.63. w/o June 1971
F-104G-183-1078	56-790	N820NA	acquired 27.12.66. Began operating in 1968. Ret. 1.6.77
TF-104G-583D-5735	-	N824NA	(ex-27+33) arrived July 1975
TF-104G-583F-5939	-	N825NA	(ex-28+9) arrived July 1975
RF-104G-8213	-	N826NA	Fokker-built (ex Luftwaffe 24+64 KG313) arrived July 1975. Last NASA flight 3.2.94

STARFIGHTERS

Starfighters Inc, based in Clearwater, Florida began as a private venture to restore and fly three former Canadair CF-104 Starfighters at air shows across the United States and Canada. Initially their CF-104s consisted of a two-seat CF-104D and two single-seat CF-104s. The aircraft were originally operated with the RCAF and all later served with the Royal Norwegian Air Force before being imported into the US in the early 1990s. In summer 2011 the company acquired five additional aircraft. All are F-104S versions built by Fiat for the Italian Air Force in the late 1970s.

Index